Commodity Derivatives

For other titles in the Wiley Finance Series
please see www.wiley.com/finance

Commodity Derivatives

Markets and Applications

Neil C. Schofield

John Wiley & Sons, Ltd

Other Wiley Editorial Offices

John Wiley & Sons Inc., 111 River Street, Hoboken, NJ 07030, USA

Jossey-Bass, 989 Market Street, San Francisco, CA 94103-1741, USA

Wiley-VCH Verlag GmbH, Boschstr. 12, D-69469 Weinheim, Germany

John Wiley & Sons Australia Ltd, 42 McDougall Street, Milton, Queensland 4064, Australia

John Wiley & Sons (Asia) Pte Ltd, 2 Clementi Loop #02-01, Jin Xing Distripark, Singapore 129809

John Wiley & Sons Canada Ltd, 6045 Freemont Blvd, Mississauga, Ontario, L5R 4J3, Canada

Anniversary Logo Design: Richard J. Pacifico

British Library Cataloguing in Publication Data

A catalogue record for this book is available from the British Library

ISBN 978-0-470-01910-8 (H/B)

Typeset in 10/12pt Times by Laserwords Private Limited, Chennai, India
Printed and bound in Great Britain by Antony Rowe Ltd, Chippenham, Wiltshire

Dedicated to Paul Roth
To Reggie, Brennie, Robert and Gillian
To Nicki

Contents

Preface   xv

Acknowledgements   xvii

About the Author   xix

1 An Introduction to Derivative Products   1

   1.1   Forwards and futures   2
   1.2   Swaps   3
   1.3   Options   4
   1.4   Derivative pricing   7
      1.4.1   Relative Value   8
   1.5   The spot–forward relationship   8
      1.5.1   Deriving forward prices: market in contango   8
      1.5.2   Deriving forward prices: market in backwardation   10
   1.6   The spot–forward–swap relationship   11
   1.7   The spot–forward–option relationship   16
   1.8   Put–call parity: a key relationship   18
   1.9   Sources of value in a hedge   18
   1.10   Measures of option risk management   19
      1.10.1   Delta   19
      1.10.2   Gamma   21
      1.10.3   Theta   22
      1.10.4   Vega   23

2 Risk Management   27

   2.1   Categories of risk   27
      2.1.1   Defining risk   28
      2.1.2   Credit risk   29
   2.2   Commodity market participants: the time dimension   29

	2.2.1	Short-dated maturities	29
	2.2.2	Medium-dated maturities	30
	2.2.3	Longer-dated exposures	30
2.3	Hedging corporate risk exposures		30
2.4	A framework for analysing corporate risk		31
	2.4.1	Strategic considerations	31
	2.4.2	Tactical considerations	31
2.5	Bank risk management		32
2.6	Hedging customer exposures		32
	2.6.1	Forward risk management	33
	2.6.2	Swap risk management	33
	2.6.3	Option risk management	33
	2.6.4	Correlation risk management	33
2.7	View-driven exposures		34
	2.7.1	Spot-trading strategies	34
	2.7.2	Forward trading strategies	35
	2.7.3	Single period physically settled "swaps"	35
	2.7.4	Single or multi-period financially settled swaps	35
	2.7.5	Option-based trades: trading volatility	36

3	**Gold**		**41**
3.1	The market for gold		41
	3.1.1	Physical Supply Chain	41
	3.1.2	Financial Institutions	42
	3.1.3	The London gold market	42
	3.1.4	The price of gold	44
	3.1.5	Fixing the price of gold	44
3.2	Gold price drivers		45
	3.2.1	The supply of gold	45
	3.2.2	Demand for gold	48
	3.2.3	The Chinese effect	51
3.3	The gold leasing market		51
3.4	Applications of derivatives		54
	3.4.1	Producer strategies	55
	3.4.2	Central Bank strategies	60

4	**Base Metals**		**69**
4.1	Base metal production		69
4.2	Aluminium		70
4.3	Copper		73
4.4	London metal exchange		75
	4.4.1	Exchange-traded metal futures	76
	4.4.2	Exchange-traded metal options	76
	4.4.3	Contract specification	77
	4.4.4	Trading	77

		4.4.5	Clearing	78
		4.4.6	Delivery	80
	4.5	Price drivers		81
	4.6	Structure of market prices		83
		4.6.1	Description of the forward curve	83
		4.6.2	Are forward prices predictors of future spot prices?	85
	4.7	Applications of derivatives		86
		4.7.1	Hedges for aluminium consumers in the automotive sector	86
	4.8	Forward purchase		87
		4.8.1	Borrowing and lending in the base metal market	88
	4.9	Vanilla option strategies		89
		4.9.1	Synthetic long put	89
		4.9.2	Selling options to enhance the forward purchase price	90
		4.9.3	"Three way"	92
		4.9.4	Min–max	93
		4.9.5	Ratio min–max	94
		4.9.6	Enhanced risk reversal	95
	4.10	Structured option solutions		95
		4.10.1	Knock-out forwards	95
		4.10.2	Forward plus	96
		4.10.3	Bonus forward	96
		4.10.4	Basket options	97
5	**Crude Oil**			**101**
	5.1	The value of crude oil		101
		5.1.1	Basic chemistry of oil	101
		5.1.2	Density	102
		5.1.3	Sulphur content	102
		5.1.4	Flow properties	102
		5.1.5	Other chemical properties	103
		5.1.6	Examples of crude oil	103
	5.2	An overview of the physical supply chain		103
	5.3	Refining crude oil		104
		5.3.1	Applications of refined products	105
	5.4	The demand and supply for crude oil		106
		5.4.1	Proved oil reserves	106
		5.4.2	R/P ratio	106
		5.4.3	Production of crude oil	108
		5.4.4	Consumption of crude oil	108
		5.4.5	Demand for refined products	109
		5.4.6	Oil refining capacity	109
		5.4.7	Crude oil imports and exports	111
		5.4.8	Security of supply	112
	5.5	Price drivers		114
		5.5.1	Macroeconomic issues	114
		5.5.2	Supply chain considerations	117

      5.5.3   Geopolitics   120

      5.5.4   Analysing the forward curves   121

  5.6 The price of crude oil   121

      5.6.1   Defining price   121

      5.6.2   The evolution of crude oil prices   122

      5.6.3   Delivered price   122

      5.6.4   Marker crudes   123

      5.6.5   Pricing sources   124

      5.6.6   Pricing methods   124

      5.6.7   The term structure of oil prices   125

  5.7 Trading crude oil and refined products   126

      5.7.1   Overview   126

      5.7.2   North Sea oil   128

      5.7.3   US crude oil markets   135

  5.8 Managing price risk along the supply chain   137

      5.8.1   Producer hedges   137

      5.8.2   Refiner hedges   142

      5.8.3   Consumer hedges   144

6 Natural Gas   **149**

  6.1 How natural gas is formed   149

  6.2 Measuring natural gas   150

  6.3 The physical supply chain   150

      6.3.1   Production   150

      6.3.2   Shippers   150

      6.3.3   Transmission   151

      6.3.4   Interconnectors   152

      6.3.5   Storage   152

      6.3.6   Supply   153

      6.3.7   Customers   153

      6.3.8   Financial institutions   153

  6.4 Deregulation and re-regulation   154

      6.4.1   The US experience   154

      6.4.2   The UK experience   155

      6.4.3   Continental European deregulation   155

  6.5 The demand and supply for gas   156

      6.5.1   Relative importance of natural gas   156

      6.5.2   Consumption of natural gas   157

      6.5.3   Reserves of natural gas   158

      6.5.4   Production of natural gas   158

      6.5.5   Reserve to production ratio   159

      6.5.6   Exporting natural gas   160

      6.5.7   Liquefied natural gas   160

  6.6 Gas price drivers   161

      6.6.1   Definitions of price   161

      6.6.2   Supply side price drivers   162

      6.6.3   Demand side price drivers   164

		6.6.4	The price of oil	164
	6.7	Trading physical natural gas		166
		6.7.1	Motivations for trading natural gas	166
		6.7.2	Trading locations	167
		6.7.3	Delivery points	167
	6.8	Natural gas derivatives		168
		6.8.1	Trading natural gas in the UK	168
		6.8.2	On-the-day commodity market	168
		6.8.3	Exchange-traded futures contracts	169
		6.8.4	Applications of exchange-traded futures	171
		6.8.5	Over-the-counter natural gas transactions	173
		6.8.6	Financial/Cash-settled transactions	176

7 Electricity   **181**

	7.1	What is electricity?		181
		7.1.1	Conversion of energy sources to electricity	182
		7.1.2	Primary sources of energy	183
		7.1.3	Commercial production of electricity	184
		7.1.4	Measuring electricity	184
	7.2	The physical supply chain		185
	7.3	Price drivers of electricity		186
		7.3.1	Regulation	188
		7.3.2	Demand for electricity	190
		7.3.3	Supply of electricity	191
		7.3.4	Factors influencing spot and forward prices	193
		7.3.5	Spark and dark spreads	193
	7.4	Trading electricity		196
		7.4.1	Overview	196
		7.4.2	Markets for trading	196
		7.4.3	Motivations for trading	196
		7.4.4	Traded volumes: spot markets	197
		7.4.5	Traded volumes: forward markets	197
	7.5	Nord pool		197
		7.5.1	The spot market: Elspot	198
		7.5.2	Post spot: the balancing market	199
		7.5.3	The financial market	199
		7.5.4	Real-time operations	199
	7.6	United states of america		200
		7.6.1	Independent System Operators	200
		7.6.2	Wholesale markets in the USA	201
	7.7	United kingdom		203
		7.7.1	Neta	203
		7.7.2	UK trading conventions	204
		7.7.3	Load shapes	205
		7.7.4	Examples of traded products	206
		7.7.5	Contract volumes	206
		7.7.6	Contract prices and valuations	207

    7.8   Electricity derivatives   207
          7.8.1   Electricity forwards   207
          7.8.2   Electricity Swaps   209

 8 Plastics   213

    8.1   The chemistry of plastic   213
    8.2   The production of plastic   214
    8.3   Monomer production   215
          8.3.1   Crude oil   215
          8.3.2   Natural gas   215
    8.4   Polymerisation   215
    8.5   Applications of plastics   216
    8.6   Summary of the plastics supply chain   217
    8.7   Plastic price drivers   217
    8.8   Applications of derivatives   218
    8.9   Roles of the futures exchange   219
          8.9.1   Pricing commercial contracts   219
          8.9.2   Hedging instruments   220
          8.9.3   Source of supply/disposal of inventory   222
    8.10 Option strategies   222

 9 Coal   225

    9.1   The basics of coal   225
    9.2   The demand for and supply of coal   226
    9.3   Physical supply chain   231
          9.3.1   Production   231
          9.3.2   Main participants   232
    9.4   The price of coal   232
    9.5   Factors affecting the price of coal   233
    9.6   Coal derivatives   235
          9.6.1   Exchange-traded futures   236
          9.6.2   Over-the-counter solutions   237

10 Emissions Trading   241

    10.1 The science of global warming   241
          10.1.1 Greenhouse gases   241
          10.1.2 The carbon cycle   242
          10.1.3 Feedback loops   243
    10.2 The consequences of global warming   243
          10.2.1 The Stern Report   244
          10.2.2 Fourth assessment report of the IPCC   244
    10.3 The argument against climate change   245
    10.4 History of human action against climate change   246
          10.4.1 Formation of the IPCC   246
          10.4.2 The Earth Summit   246
          10.4.3 The Kyoto Protocol   247

	10.4.4 From Kyoto to Marrakech and beyond	249
10.5	Price drivers for emissions markets	249
10.6	The EU emissions trading scheme	252
	10.6.1 Background	252
	10.6.2 How the scheme works	253
	10.6.3 Registries and logs	253
	10.6.4 National Allocation Plans (NAPs)	254
10.7	Emission derivatives	254
11	**Agricultural Commodities and Biofuels**	**261**
11.1	Agricultural markets	261
	11.1.1 Physical supply chain	261
	11.1.2 Sugar	262
	11.1.3 Wheat	262
	11.1.4 Corn	262
11.2	Ethanol	263
	11.2.1 What is ethanol?	263
	11.2.2 History of ethanol	263
11.3	Price drivers	264
	11.3.1 Weather	264
	11.3.2 Substitution	265
	11.3.3 Investor activity	265
	11.3.4 Current levels of inventory	265
	11.3.5 Protectionism	265
	11.3.6 Health	265
	11.3.7 Industrialising countries	266
	11.3.8 Elasticity of supply	266
	11.3.9 Genetic modification	266
11.4	Exchange-traded agricultural and ethanol derivatives	266
11.5	Over-the-counter agricultural derivatives	267
12	**Commodities Within an Investment Portfolio**	**269**
12.1	Investor profile	269
12.2	Benefits of commodities within a portfolio	270
	12.2.1 Return enhancement and diversification	270
	12.2.2 Asset allocation	270
	12.2.3 Inflation hedge	271
	12.2.4 Hedge against the US dollar	271
12.3	Methods of investing in commodities	271
	12.3.1 Advantages and disadvantages	271
12.4	Commodity indices	272
	12.4.1 Explaining the roll yield	273
12.5	Total return swaps	274
12.6	Structured investments	277
	12.6.1 Gold-linked notes	277
	12.6.2 Capital guaranteed structures	277

        12.6.3 Combination structures   278
        12.6.4 Non-combination structures   281
        12.6.5 Collateralised Commodity Obligations   282
    12.7 Analysing investment structures   285

Glossary   **287**

Notes   **299**

Bibliography   **303**

Index   **305**

Preface

Since the start of this century, the commodity markets have been the subject of much interest with reports in the media usually detailing that some commodity has reached a new all time price high. My motivation for writing the book, however, did not stem from this but rather the difficulty I had in finding people who could provide classroom training on the different products. Although many companies were able to provide training that described the physical market for each commodity, virtually no one provided training on over-the-counter (OTC) structures, which arguably comprise the greatest volumes in the market. As they say, if you want a job done properly. . . . While doing research for the courses I felt that much of the available documentation either had a very narrow focus, perhaps concentrating on just one product, or were general texts on trading commodity futures with little insight into the underlying markets. *As a result, I have tried to write a book that documents in one place the main commodity markets and their associated derivatives.*

Within each chapter, I have tried to keep the structure fairly uniform. Typically, there will be a short section explaining what the commodity is in non-technical terms. For those with a background in any one specific commodity, this may appear somewhat simplistic but is included to ensure that the financial reader has sufficient background to place the subsequent discussion within some context. Typical patterns of demand and supply are considered as well as the main factors that will influence the price of the commodity. The latter part of each chapter focuses on the physical market of the particular commodity before detailing the main exchange traded and OTC products.

One of the issues I was faced with when writing each chapter was to determine the products that should be covered in each chapter. As I was concerned that I might end up repeating ideas that had been covered in earlier chapters, I have tried to document structures that are unique to each market in each particular chapter, while the more generic structures have been spread throughout the text.

The other issue was to determine which products to include within the scope of the book. No doubt some readers will disagree with my choice of topics in the book, but I can assure you that this was still being discussed with the team at Wiley as the deadline for the final manuscript approached!

Chapter 1 outlines the main derivative building blocks and how they are priced. Readers familiar with these concepts could skip this chapter and go straight to any individual chapter without losing too much of the flow. However, it does include a section on the pricing of commodities within the context of the convenience yield. Chapter 2 sets the scene for a discussion on the concept of risk management. Two different perspectives are taken, that of a corporate with a desire to hedge some form of exposure and an investment bank that will take on the risk associated by offering any solution. Chapter 3 looks at the market for gold while Chapter 4 develops the theme to cover base metals. Some readers may complain that there is no coverage of other "precious" metals such as silver, platinum and palladium, but I felt that including sections on these metals would amount to overkill and that gold was sufficiently interesting in itself to warrant an extended discussion. The next three chapters cover the core energy markets, the first of which is crude oil. Chapter 6 covers natural gas markets while Chapter 7 discussed electricity. Chapter 8 describes the relatively new market for plastic, while Chapter 9 details one of the oldest markets, that of coal. Chapter 10 looks at another new market, the trading of carbon emissions. Chapter 11 covers agricultural products where the focus is on the relationship between some of the "soft" commodities and ethanol. The book concludes by considering the use of commodities within an investment portfolio.

Acknowledgements

As ever, it would be arrogant of me to assume that this was entirely my own work. The book is dedicated to the late Paul Roth, who was taken from us far too early in life. In the decade that I knew him, I was able to benefit considerably from his insight into the world of derivatives. It never ceased to amaze me how, after days of pondering on a problem, I could only half explain to him something that I only half understood, and he could explain it back to me perfectly in simple and clear terms.

Thanks also to the team at Wiley (Sam Whittaker, Emily Pears, Viv Wickham) who have helped a publishing "newbie" like me and tolerated the fact that I missed nearly every deadline they set.

General thanks go to my father, Reg Schofield, who offered to edit large chunks of the manuscript and tidy up "the English what I wrote". Rachel Gillingham deserves a special mention for helping me to express the underlying chemistry of a number of commodities within the book. Her input added considerable value to the overall manuscript.

At Barclays Capital I would like to thank Arfan Aziz, Natasha Cornish, Lutfey Siddiqui, Benoit de Vitry and Troy Bowler. They all have endured endless requests for help and have given generously of their time without complaint. In relation to specific chapters, thanks go to Matt Schwab and John Spaull (gold); Angus McHeath, Frank Ford and Ingrid Sternby (base metals); David Paul and Nick Smith (plastics); Thomas Wiktorowski-Schweitz, Orrin Middleton, Suzanne Taylor and Jonathon Taylor (crude oil); Simon Hastings, Rob Bailey and David Gillbe (electricity); Paul Dawson and Rishil Patel (emissions); Rachel Frear and Marco Sarcino (coal); and Maria Igweh (agriculture). Thanks also to Steve Hochfeld who made some valuable comments on the agricultural chapter. All of these "advisers" contributed fantastic insights into the different markets and often reviewed drafts of the manuscript, which enhanced it no end.

A very special thanks must go to Nicki, who never once complained about the project and has always been very interested and supportive of all that I do.

If I have missed anyone, then please accept my apologies, but rest assured I am grateful. Although I received a lot of help in compiling the materials, any mistakes that remain in the text are entirely my responsibility.

I am always interested in any comments or suggestions on the text and can be contacted at either neil.schofield3@ntlworld.com or www. commodity-derivatives.net

Neil C. Schofield

PS: *Hi to Alan Gamblin and Roger Jarvis, who dared me to include their names. The tea and toast are on you!*

About the Author

Neil C. Schofield is currently the head of Financial Markets Training at Barclays Capital, where he has global responsibility for all aspects of the bank's product-related training. As part of the job, he regularly delivers training on a wide range of subjects in commodities, fixed income, equity, foreign exchange and credit.

Prior to joining Barclays, he was a director at Chisholm Roth, a financial training company, where he delivered seminars to a blue-chip client base around the world. He has also worked in a training capacity for Chase Manhattan bank from 1988 to 1997. The author was appointed as a visiting fellow at ICMA Centre, Reading University, England in April 2007.

1
An Introduction to Derivative Products

SYNOPSIS **The purpose of this chapter is to outline the main features of derivatives and provide a description of the main ways in which they are priced and valued.**

This chapter is divided into two distinct sections that cover:

- The key features of the derivative "building block" products
- The principles of how each of the products is priced and valued.

The coverage is not particularly mathematical in style, although numerical examples are included where it helps to illustrate the key principles.

In the first section the fundamental concepts of the *main derivative products* are considered. The products covered include:

- Futures
- Forwards
- Swaps
- Options (mostly "vanilla" with some "exotic" coverage)

In the second section the focus is on the *pricing of derivatives*. The approach considers that all of the building block markets are linked through mathematical relationships and describes how the price of one product can be derived from another.

One of the unique elements of pricing commodity derivatives is the existence of the *convenience yield*, which is explained in conjunction with the concepts of *contango* and *backwardation*.

Two extra themes are developed in the pricing section that are relevant to other parts of the book. The first is a discussion on *put–call parity*, which will help the reader to understand how some structures are created. This idea is then developed to outline the potential *sources of value* in risk management solutions.

The chapter concludes with a description of the main measures of *option risk management* – the Greeks.

When analysing derivatives it is convenient to classify them into three main building blocks:

- Forwards and futures
- Swaps
- Options.

However, within the option category it is possible to make a distinction between two sub-categories, the so-called "plain vanilla" structures (that is, options that conform to a basic accepted profile) and those that are considered "exotic", such as binaries and barriers.

For ease of illustration we will use gold in the following examples.

1.1 FORWARDS AND FUTURES

A forward contract will fix the price today for delivery of an asset in the future. Gold sold for spot value will involve the exchange of cash for the metal in two days' time. However, if the transaction required the delivery in say 1 month's time it would be classified as a forward transaction. Forward contracts are negotiated bilaterally between the buyer and the seller and are often characterised as being "over the counter".

The forward transaction represents a contractual commitment; so if gold is bought forward at, say, USD 430.00 an ounce but the price of gold in the spot market is only USD 420.00 at the point of delivery, I cannot walk away from the forward contract and try to buy it in the underlying market. However, it is not impossible to terminate the contract early. This could be achieved by agreeing a "break" amount, which would reflect the current economic value of the contract.

A futures contract is traded on an organised exchange with the New York Mercantile Exchange being one example. Economically a future achieves the same result as a forward by offering price certainty for a period in the future. However, the key difference between the contracts is in how they are traded. The contracts are uniform in their trading size, which is set by the exchange. For example, the main features of the contract specification for the gold future are listed in Table 1.1.

There are some fundamental differences between commodity and financial products traded on an exchange basis. One of the key differences is that futures require collateral to be deposited when a trade is executed (known as initial margin). Although different exchanges will work in different ways, the remittance of profits and losses may take place on an ongoing basis (variation margin) rather than at the maturity of the contract. An example of this is detailed in the chapter on base metals.

Table 1.1 Gold futures contract specification

Trading unit	100 troy ounces
Price quotation	US dollars and cents per troy ounce
Trading hours	Open outcry from 8.20am until 1.30pm New York time (electronic trading is also available)
Trading months	Trading is conducted for delivery during the current calendar month; the next two calendar months; any February, April, August and October falling within a 23-month period; and any June and December falling within a 60-month period beginning with the current month.
Minimum price fluctuation	USD 0.10 (10c) per troy ounce (USD 10.00 per contract).
Last trading day	Trading terminates at the close of business on the third to last business day of the maturing delivery month.
Delivery period	The first delivery day is the first business day of the delivery month, the last delivery day is the last business day of the delivery month.
Margin requirements	Margins are required for open futures positions.

Source: NYMEX.

Settlement of financial futures is often for a single date specified by the exchange, such as the third Wednesday in March, June, September or December. For commodity futures settlement could be for any day within the ensuing three months (see "trading days" section in the above specification). By offering delivery on any day for the current and two successive months, this commodity future possess a feature of the forward market – the flexibility to settle for a variety of dates. Another difference is the concept of grade and quality specification. If one is delivering a currency, the underlying asset is homogeneous – a dollar is always a dollar. However, because metals have different shapes, grades and quality, there must be an element of standardisation to ensure that the buyer knows what he or she is receiving. Some of the criteria that NYMEX apply include:

- The seller must deliver 100 troy ounces (±5%) of refined gold.
- The gold must be of a fineness of no less than 0.995%.
- It must be cast either in one bar or in three 1-kilogram bars.
- The gold must bear a serial number and identifying stamp of a refiner approved and listed by the Exchange.

1.2   SWAPS

In a swap transaction two parties agree to exchange cashflows, the sizes of which are based on different price indices. Typically, this is represented as an agreed fixed rate against a variable or floating rate. Swaps are traded on an agreed notional amount, which is not exchanged but establishes the magnitude of the fixed and floating cashflows. Swap contracts are typically of longer-term maturity (i.e. greater than one year) but the exact terms of the contract will be open to negotiation. For example, in many base metal markets a swap transaction is often nothing more than a single period forward, which allows for the transaction to be cash settled, involving the payment of the agreed forward price against the spot price at expiry.

The exact form may vary between markets, with the following merely a sample of how they may be applied in a variety of different commodity markets.

- *Gold*:   Pay fixed lease rate vs receive variable lease rate.
- *Base metals*:   Pay fixed aluminium price vs receive average price of near dated aluminium future.
- *Oil*:   Pay fixed West Texas Intermediate (WTI) price vs receive average price of near dated WTI future.

Swaps will usually start as spot and so become effective two days after they are traded. However, it is also possible for the swap to become effective at some time in the future – a forward starting swap. The frequency with which the cashflows are settled is open to negotiation but they could vary in tenor between 1 month and 12 months. Where the payments coincide there is a net settlement between the two parties. One of the features of commodity swaps that is not shared by financial swaps is the use of an average rate for the floating leg. This is because many of the underlying exposures that commodity swaps are designed to hedge will be based on some form of average price.

The motivation for entering into a swap will differ between counterparties. For a corporate entity one of their main concerns is risk transference. Consider a company that has to purchase a particular commodity at the market price at regular periods in the future. To offset the risk that the underlying price may rise, the company would receive a cashflow under the swap based on movements in the market price of the commodity and pay a fixed rate. If the counterparty to the transaction were an investment bank, the latter would now have the original exposure faced by the corporate. The investment bank would be receiving a fixed rate and paying a variable rate, leaving it exposed to a rise in the price of the underlying commodity. In turn the investment bank will attempt to mitigate this exposure by entering into some form of offsetting transaction. The simplest form of this offsetting deal would be an equal and opposite swap transaction. In order to ensure that the bank makes some money from this second transaction, the amount it receives from the corporate should offset the amount paid to the offsetting swap counterparty.

Swaps are typically traded on a bid–offer spread basis. From a market maker's perspective (that is the institution actually giving the quote) the trades are quoted as follows:

Bid	*Offer*
Pay fixed	Receive fixed
Receive floating	Pay floating
Buy	Sell
Long	Short

Although the terms "buy" and "sell" are often used in swap quotes the actual meaning is often confusing to anyone looking at the market for a first time. The convention in all swap markets is that the buyer is receiving a stream of variable cashflows for which the price is a single fixed rate. Selling a swap requires the delivery of a stream of floating cashflows for which the compensation is a single fixed rate.

1.3   OPTIONS

A forward contract offers price certainty to both counterparties. However, the buyer of a forward is locked into paying a fixed price for a particular commodity. This transaction will be valuable if the price of the commodity subsequently rises, but will be unprofitable in the event of a fall in price. An option contract offers the best of both worlds. It will offer the buyer of the contract protection if the price of the underlying moves against him but allows him to walk away from the deal if the underlying price moves in his favour.

This leads to the definition of an option as the right but not the obligation to either buy or sell an underlying commodity at some time in the future at a price agreed today. An option that allows the holder to buy the underlying asset is referred to as a *call*. Having the right to sell something is referred to as a *put*. Options may be either physically settled (that is the commodity is actually delivered/received) or cash settled. The price at which the underlying is traded if the option is exercised is referred to as the *strike* price. The strike price is negotiated between the option buyer and seller. Cash settlement involves the seller paying the buyer the difference between the strike and the spot price at the point of exercise. Cash settlement is advantageous to the buyer as it may be more convenient to either source or deliver the commodity separately; the option would simply offer price protection.

Options come in a variety of styles relating to when the holder can actually exercise his right. A European style option allows the holder to exercise the option only on the final maturity date. An American style option allows the holder to exercise the option at any time prior to final maturity. A Bermudan option allows the holder to exercise the option on a pre-agreed set of dates prior to maturity.

An option that is "in-the-money" (ITM) describes a situation where it would be more advantageous to trade at the strike price rather than the underlying market price. Take for example an American style option to buy gold at USD 400 an ounce when the current spot price is, say, USD 425; the option to buy at the strike is more attractive than the current market price. Where the option is "out-of-the-money" (OTM) the strike is less attractive than the market price. If the same American style option had a strike rate of USD 430 the higher strike makes the option less attractive than being able to buy the underlying at a price of USD 420. Finally an option where the strike is equal to the current market price is referred to as being "at-the money" (ATM).

Since options confer rights to the holder a premium is payable by the buyer. Typically this is paid up front but certain option structures are constructed to be zero premium or may involve deferment of the premium to a later date. Premiums on options are quoted in the same units as the underlying asset. So since physical gold is quoted in dollars per troy ounce, the premium will be quoted in the same manner.

Many of the derivatives strategies based on options that are discussed and illustrated within the text are based on the value of the option at maturity. These are presented in Figure 1.1.

In the top left-hand part of Figure 1.1, the purchase of a call option is illustrated. If, at expiry of the option, the market price is lower than the strike, the option is not exercised

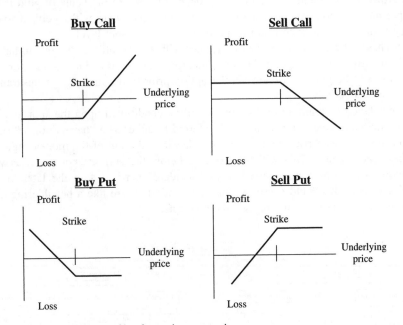

Figure 1.1 Profit and loss profiles for options at expiry

and the buyer loses the premium paid. If the underlying price is higher than the strike price the option is exercised and the buyer receives the underlying asset (or its cash equivalent), which is now worth more in the underlying market than the price paid (i.e. the strike price). This profit profile is shown to the right of the strike price. On the other side of the transaction there is the seller of a call option (top right-hand quadrant of Figure 1.1). The profit and loss profile of the seller must be the mirror of that of the buyer. So in the case of the call option the seller will keep the premium if the underlying price is less than the strike price but will face increasing losses as the underlying market price rises.

The purchase of a put option is illustrated in the bottom left-hand quadrant of Figure 1.1. Since this type of option allows the buyer to sell the underlying asset at a given strike price, this option will only be exercised if the underlying price falls. If the underlying price rises, the buyer loses the premium paid. Again the selling profile for the put is the mirror image of that faced by the buyer. That is, if the underlying price falls, the seller will be faced with increasing losses but will keep the premium if the market price rises.

Exotic options are a separate class of options where the profit and losses at exercise do not correspond to the plain vanilla American/European styles. Although there is a proliferation of different types of exotic options (many of which will be introduced in the main text), it is worth introducing two key building blocks, which feature prominently in derivative structures.

A binary option (sometimes referred to as a "digital") is very similar to a simple bet. The buyer pays a premium and agrees to receive a fixed return. Very often the strike rate on the digital is referred to (somewhat confusingly) as a "barrier". With a European style call option the holder will deliver the strike price to the seller and receive a fixed amount of gold. However, the value of the gold will depend on where the value of gold is trading in the spot market upon exercise. With a binary option the buyer will receive a fixed sum of money if the option is exercised irrespective of the final spot level.

The purchaser of a barrier option will: (1) start with a conventional "plain vanilla" option that could subsequently be cancelled prior to maturity (known as a "knock-out"), or (2) start with nothing and be granted a plain vanilla option prior to the maturity of the transaction (known as a "knock-in").

The cancellation or granting of the option will be conditional upon the spot level in the underlying market reaching a certain level, referred to either as a "barrier" or a "trigger".

The position of the barrier could either be placed in the out-of-the-money region or in the in-the-money region. This will be above or below the current spot price, as we will show below. The former are referred to as "standard" barriers with the later known as "reverse" barriers. This could result in what may initially seem like a bewildering array of possibilities, and Figure 1.2 summarises the concepts.

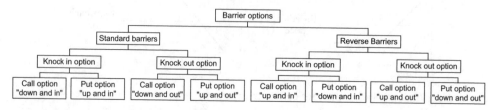

Figure 1.2   Summary of barrier options

To illustrate the concept further, let us return to the option example illustrated earlier and concentrate on analysing a call option. We will assume that the option is out-of-the-money and the current market conditions exist:

Spot   USD 425
Strike   USD 430
Maturity   3 months

The purchaser of a standard knock-in barrier option would be granted a European style option if spot hit a certain trigger. Since it is a standard barrier option, the trigger has to be placed in the out-of-the-money region so it would be set at, say, USD 420. Consequently, spot has to reach USD 420 or below before the option is activated ("knocked in"), hence the name "down and in". If the purchaser started with a standard barrier call option with the trigger at USD 420, it would be a "down and out". That is, if spot were to fall to USD 420 or lower, the option contract would be cancelled. A reverse knock-in call option would have the barrier placed in the money, say at USD 435. A purchaser of such an option would have a contract that would grant a call option with a strike of USD 430 if spot hits USD 435. The final example would be a reverse knock-out call option, with the trigger again set at USD 435. Here the purchaser starts the transaction with a regular call option which would be cancelled if spot reached USD 435 – an "up and out" contract.

Options arguably offer great flexibility to the end user. Depending on their motivation it could be argued that option usage could be categorised in four different ways. Firstly, options can be used to take a directional exposure to the underlying market. So, for example, if a user thought the underlying price of gold was to rise, he could buy physical gold, buy a future or buy a call option. Buying the gold requires the outlay of proceeds, which may need to be borrowed; buying a future reduces the initial outlay of the physical but will incur a loss if the future's price falls. Buying a call option involves some outlay in the form of premium but allows for full price participation above the strike and limited downside if the price falls. The second usage for options is an asset class in its own right. Options possess a unique feature in implied volatility and this can be isolated and traded in its own right. The focus of this type of strategy is how the option behaves prior to its maturity. The third motivation, which is particularly relevant to the corporate world, is as a hedging vehicle that allows a different profile than that of the forward. With a little imagination it is possible to structure solutions that will offer differing degrees of protection against the ability to profit from a favourable movement in the underlying price. The final motivation concerns options as a source of outperformance. For example, if an end user owns the underlying asset (e.g. central bank holdings of gold) he can use options to exceed some performance benchmark such as money market deposit rates. From a hedger's perspective, options could be used to outperform an ordinary forward rate.

1.4 DERIVATIVE PRICING

The purpose of this chapter is to arm the readers with sufficient knowledge to enable them to follow the main pricing issues referred to in the main text. It is not intended to be an exhaustive treatment of all aspects of derivative pricing. Readers interested in delving into more detail should refer to the bibliography for a list of suggested titles.

The principles of pricing commodity derivatives can often differ from financial products such as bonds or equities and these key differences will be highlighted as appropriate. Again, for the sake of simplicity, gold will be the main focus of the chapter.

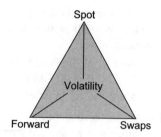

Figure 1.3   The relative value triangle

1.4.1   Relative Value

One of the key themes of trading all financial assets is the concept of relative value. This is defined as the optimum way to take exposure to a particular asset. If I wish to take exposure to the gold market, which instruments (or combination thereof) would give me the greatest return? This approach regards the spot, forward, swap and option markets as being interrelated through a series of mathematical relationships and therefore allows the trader to identify the particular market that offers an enhanced return/reduction in cost.

This approach can be encapsulated by the relative value triangle shown in Figure 1.3. A feature of the relative value triangle is not only the mathematical relationships that are implied between each of the instruments, but also the different trading strategies that exist by reading down each side of the triangle. For example, trading the spot market against the forward (or future) is referred to as a basis trade. The aim of the remaining part of this chapter is to illustrate the mathematical relationships between each of the components of the triangle.

1.5   THE SPOT–FORWARD RELATIONSHIP

1.5.1   Deriving forward prices: market in contango

Within the commodities world, there are two ways of describing the state of a forward market – contango or backwardation. Contango describes a situation where the price for forward delivery is higher than the price for spot delivery, while backwardation exists when the forward price is below the spot price. Although both of these states exist in the pricing of traditional financial products, the role of the underlying physical markets in commodities is much more important, particularly when demand exceeds supply.

We will use the example of a gold producer who approaches a bank asking for a price for delivery of gold in, say, 6 months. The price quoted by the bank is not a guess and neither is it a forecast of where it thinks the price of gold will be at the time of delivery. Rather the price quoted will be driven by the cost of hedging the bank's own exposure. This illustrates one of the key maxims of derivative pricing – the cost of the product is driven by the cost of the hedge.

If the bank does not hedge its price exposure then in 6 months' time it will take delivery of gold at the pre-agreed price and will then be holding an asset whose market value could be lower (or higher) than the price paid to the producer.

To avoid the risk of a fall in the gold price, the bank executes a series of transactions on the trade date to mitigate the risk. Since the bank is agreeing to receive a fixed amount of gold in the future, it sells the same amount in the spot market to another institution – say another investment bank. However, the bank has sold a quantity of metal now that it will not take delivery of until a future time. To fulfil this spot commitment it can borrow the gold until it receives the gold from the producer. The gold could be borrowed from a central bank that would receive interest at maturity. Having sold the gold spot and borrowed to cover the sale, the bank is now holding dollar proceeds. Since the bank would be seeking to manage its cash balances prudently, these dollars would now be invested until the producer delivers the gold.

As a result it is possible at the inception of the forward trade to identify all the associated cashflows, allowing the bank to quote a "fair value" or theoretical price that will ensure no loss at the point of delivery, irrespective of the prevailing price. In this example the maximum amount the bank will pay the producer cannot exceed:

- proceeds received from the spot sale *plus*
- the interest received from the dollar deposit *less*
- the interest paid to the lender of gold.

A simple example may help to illustrate the point. We will assume that the producer asks for a 6-month (182-day) forward price. For simplicity we will calculate the forward price for a single ounce. In the cash market gold is trading at USD 425.40 per ounce, so the dealer agrees to sells 1 ounce. In order to complete the spot delivery he borrows the same amount from the local central bank for 6 months at a lease rate of 0.11570% per annum. The dollars received from the spot sale are put on deposit for 6 months at a LIBOR to earn, say, 3.39% per annum. The interest cost of borrowing the metal is USD 0.2488 (spot × lease rate × 182/360) and that USD 7.29 is earned from the cash deposit (spot sale proceeds × 6-month LIBOR × 182/360). So the maximum amount he can afford to pay the producer is USD 432.4418. This is calculated as spot sale proceeds plus interest on LIBOR deposit minus the borrowing fee (USD 425.40 + USD7.29 − USD 0.2488). This fair value is a breakeven price for the trader and so may be adjusted to build in an element of profit.

The forward price is therefore the spot price plus the cost of carrying an underlying hedge. It is important to note that the shorter the time to maturity the smaller will be the differential between the spot and forward price since the hedge is carried for a shorter period. Indeed, if we were to recalculate the forward price applicable for a fixed date in the future on a regular basis, the differential would reduce every day (all other things being equal) until the final date when spot and forward become the same thing and the two prices will have converged.

The observed forward price of a commodity is kept in line with its fair value by the possibility of arbitrage. Take the previous example where the fair value of gold for 6-month delivery was USD 432.44. It is unlikely that the market price would be significantly different. Let us assume that a market price of USD 425.00 was observed. With the fair value of the instrument calculated at USD 432.44, the commodity would be described as being "cheap to fair value". In this situation an arbitrager could:

- buy the commodity forward, paying USD 425.00 upon delivery;
- short the underlying in the spot market to earn USD 425.40;
- invest the cash proceeds at LIBOR, earning 3.39% for 6 months to earn USD 7.29;
- borrow gold in the lease market in order to fulfil the short spot sale paying a 6-month lease rate, which equates to a cash amount of USD 0.2488;

- repay the gold borrowing upon receipt of the metal under the terms of the forward contract.

The arbitrager would end up with a net profit of USD 7.44, the difference between the theoretical value of the forward contract (USD 432.44) and the market value of the forward (USD 425.00).

1.5.2 Deriving forward prices: market in backwardation

Backwardation describes a situation where the prices for shorter-dated contracts are higher than those of longer-dated contracts. Forward pricing theory dictates that the market maker quotes a forward price such that all expenses are passed on to the customer as well as any income benefits he may have derived from carrying an underlying hedge. With gold storage on an unallocated basis is not consider to be a significant expense and so is traditionally not included in forward pricing considerations. However, with base metals warehousing and insurance costs included, this should give us the following relationship:

$$\text{Forward price} = \text{Spot price} + \text{LIBOR} + \text{Warehousing/Insurance costs}$$

This would also suggest that the fair value of a forward contract should always be greater than the spot value. However, many commodity markets move into backwardation (e.g. some base metals, crude oil), which suggests that the previous equation is incorrectly specified. Over time, to explain this apparent anomaly, the market has added an extra expression referred to as the "convenience yield". This is defined as the premium that a consumer is willing to pay to be able to consume the commodity now rather than at some time in the future, and the equation now reads:

$$\text{Forward price} = \text{Spot price} + \text{LIBOR} + \text{Warehousing/Insurance costs}$$
$$- \text{Convenience yield}$$

The magnitude of the convenience yield will vary according to the physical balance of demand for the underlying commodity. If the commodity is in very short supply, its value will rise, moving towards zero in "normal" supply conditions. If, however, the minimum value of the convenience yield is zero, there is no maximum as its value is driven by the consumer's need to obtain the physical commodity immediately. For example, as it is difficult and expensive to store oil, the cost of closing a refinery for, say, 3 months would be very high. As a result, the consumer is willing to pay a premium for spot delivery.

The concept of convenience yield will seem particularly strange to someone new to the commodities market. Market practitioners tend to view it as a financial mathematician's tool to try to describe a market behaviour they never witness in traditional financial products such as bonds and equities and so cannot explain it; in reality no one in the real world uses the convenience yield. An article in *Risk* (November 2006) described it as the

flow of services and benefits that accrues to an owner of a physical commodity, but not to an owner of a contract for future delivery of the commodity. This can come in the form of having a secure supply of raw materials and hence, eliminating the costs associated with stock outs.

Since, however, it is an intangible element that allows the equation to balance, it doesn't really explain backwardation to any degree of satisfaction.

In the case of a backwardated market the forward market price is lower than the spot price suggesting that the contract is mispriced or trading "cheap to fair value". If this is the case, a speculator should be able to buy the cheap forward contract, sell it for spot value and hold the combined position to maturity. This strategy, which is very common in the financial markets, would allow the arbitrager to earn the difference between the mispriced forward and its theoretical value. The reason this cannot happen, and why the market will remain in a prolonged state of backwardation, is that when selling the contract in the spot market, the participant will need to obtain the commodity to fulfil the selling commitment. Since the availability of the commodity in the spot market is very scarce, these supplies simply cannot be obtained. Hence, this apparent mispricing will persist for prolonged periods, as there is no mechanism to exploit the potential arbitrage.

If we were to plot the prices of the commodity for various times to delivery we would derive a forward curve, which in a backwardated market would be negatively sloped. That is, shorter-dated contracts would have a higher price than longer-dated contracts. Another way of explaining the slope of the curve is to consider the nature of the activities of the participants at certain maturities. Intuitively it is reasonable to suggest that the producer of a commodity would be more likely to sell his production forward, while a consumer is more likely to want to buy the commodity in the spot or near months. This combination of longer-dated forward sales and shorter-dated purchases combines to create a negatively sloped curve. This poses another question: Who are the shorter-dated sellers and who are the longer-dated buyers? This role is filled by entities that have no underlying economic commodity exposure but are willing to take views on the slope of the curve. For example, let us assume that the forward curve for a particular commodity is steeply inverted but a hedge fund believes that the slope between the 3-month and 12-month forward will gradually flatten. They could execute a trade that would involve the simultaneous sale of a short-dated forward (or future) and the purchase of the longer-dated contract. If the price differential between the two contracts does narrow as expected, a reversing transaction could be initiated to close out the original exposure at a profit.

1.6   THE SPOT–FORWARD–SWAP RELATIONSHIP

The price of any swap, irrespective of the underlying asset class, is the fixed element of the transaction. Since we are focusing on the gold market the fixed element would be a fixed lease rate with the opposing leg being a variable lease rate. (The mechanics of the transaction are explained in Chapter 3.)

To calculate the price of a gold swap the first starting point is to appreciate that all swaps should be considered an equitable exchange of cashflows on the day they are traded. That is, the present value of the expected payments must equal the present value of the expected receipts. To a reader new to the world of swaps, this seems a strange situation – a transaction that does not seem to have any initial profit. However, note that the fair price of the swap was described in terms of expected cashflows. Profits and losses will arise as actual payments are crystallised – these could be substantially different from those expected at the start of the transaction.

Since we are trying to solve for an unknown fixed rate, our analysis of swap prices starts with floating or variable cashflows. The aim on the floating side is to calculate the present value of the future cashflows, which are linked to a series of yet to be determined unknown lease rates. To solve this problem we can revert to the forward market and derive a series of lease rates that we expect to occur at different points in time in the future–forward lease rates.

At this point it is necessary to take two short diversions to see how forward rates are calculated. Let us assume that the 6-month lease rate is 0.11571% and the 12-month lease rate is 0.18589%. If a market participant were looking to deposit gold for 1 year, we have a choice between

- one 12-month deposit at 0.18589% or
- a 6-month deposit at 0.11571%, which would be rolled over at the end of 6 months, earning whatever the 6-month rate is at that time.

When posed with the question of which decision the lender should make, a common reaction is that the choice depends on the lender's view on what interest rates are likely to be for the final 6-month period. However, if a market participant is offered two choices that are identical in terms of maturity and credit risk, they must offer the same potential return. If the two strategies offered different returns, the investor would opt for that choice that offered the higher yield. As other market participants identify this, the excess returns will gradually diminish until the advantage disappears. It is therefore possible to calculate a lease rate for the 6- to 12-month period whose value will make the two choices equal to each other. This rate is referred to as the forward lease rate and can be calculated using the formula:

$$\text{Forward rate}_{b \times c} = \frac{(\text{Lease rate}_{a \times c} \times \text{Days}_{a \times c}) - (\text{Lease rate}_{a \times b} \times \text{Days}_{a \times b})}{\text{Days}_{b \times c} \times (1 + \text{Lease rate}_{a \times b} \times (\text{Days}_{a \times b}/\text{Day basis}))}$$

where: $\text{Lease rate}_{a \times c}$ = the lease rate from spot to final maturity

$\text{Days}_{a \times c}$ = number of days from spot to final maturity

$\text{Lease rate}_{a \times b}$ = lease rate from spot to start of forward period

$\text{Days}_{a \times b}$ = number of days from spot to start of forward period

$\text{Days}_{b \times c}$ = days from start of forward period to final maturity

Day basis = 360 days.

Applying the 6- and 12-month lease rates given above, and assuming 182 days for the first 6-month period and 183 days for the second 6-month period, the value for the forward rate is given as *6 months rates equal to 12 month rate.*

2

$$\text{Forward rate}_{6 \times 12} = \frac{(0.18589\%_{0 \times 12} \times 365_{0 \times 12}) - (0.11571\%_{0 \times 6} \times 182_{0 \times 6})}{183_{6 \times 12} \times [1 + 0.11571\%_{a \times b} \times (182_{0 \times 6}/360)]} = 0.255537\%$$

end 6 month forward rate

0.11521 to 0.255537% = 12 month rate.

no of days

is this formula correct?

made up

The interpretation of the forward rate depends on its usage. In the market for trading short-term interest rates, the forward rate is used as a mechanism for trading expectations of future expected movements in central bank rates. In that sense one interpretation is that the forward rate is simply the market's current "best guess" over future cash rates. For example, if we applied that logic to the previous calculation, we could say that although current 6-month rates are 0.11571%, the market expects them to be 0.2555375% in 6 months' time. However, it does not mean that actual lease rates at that time will take that value; the actual value will only be known at the start of the period. Also, forward rates are notoriously bad predictors of actual rates but despite this they are still very popular for the purpose of trading future views.

The second interpretation is that of a breakeven rate. In the previous example, the forward rate is clearly a rate that equates the two investment alternatives. This brings us back to the initial question: Where does the lender place the gold? Since the forward rate can be thought of as a breakeven rate, the two choices would appear to be equal. The correct decision for the lender is driven by where he thought the actual lease rate would be at the start of the 6×12 period. If he thought the lease rate was going to be greater than the implied forward rate, he would invest in the two 6-month strategies. If he thought the lease rate was going to be less than the implied forward, he would execute the single 12-month deposit. Note that it is not necessarily an issue of whether rates will rise or fall, it is more a case of where actual rates will be in relation to the implied forward rate.

The other piece of information necessary to price a swap is a series of discount factors. Discount factors have a value between 0 and 1 that can be used to give a present value to a future cashflow. The discount factor can be applied to a future cashflow using the following simple relationship:

$$\text{Present value} = \text{Future value} \times \text{Discount factor}$$

The source of these discount factors are yields on zero coupon instruments that have the same degree of credit risk as the cashflow to which they will be applied. A zero coupon instrument pays no cashflow until maturity with the buyer's return usually in the form of a capital gain. However, interest-bearing deposits may also be in zero coupon form if they only have two cashflows – the initial and final movement of funds.

The reason these instruments are used to present value cashflows is that the investor's exact return can be calculated. This return is different from that offered by an interest-bearing instrument that pays a series of cashflows prior to maturity. Although a yield to maturity could be calculated for such an instrument, it would not be a true measure of the overall return as this measure requires the interim interest payments to be reinvested at the yield that prevailed at the start of the transaction. This is referred to as reinvestment risk.

The only problem with zero coupon yields is the lack of available market observations. As a result, the analyst is often forced to use mathematics to transform the yield on an interest-bearing instrument into a zero coupon equivalent. A comprehensive treatment of this subject can be found in either Galitz (1996) or Flavell (2002).

If we were, for example, pricing interbank interest rate swap cashflows, then LIBOR (London InterBank Offered Rate) interest rates would be appropriate. LIBOR discount factors can be derived from three principal sources:

- Short-term LIBOR deposits, which are zero coupon in style as the transactions only have two cashflows, one at the start and one upon maturity.
- Short-term interest rate futures, also zero coupon as they are priced off expectations of future LIBOR.
- Interest rate swaps, which require some mathematical manipulation since they suffer from the reinvestment issue noted earlier. Readers new to the pricing of swaps may be suspicious of pricing swaps from existing swaps, as they cannot reconcile the circularity. However, the fact is that a liquid market exists for the instruments with banks willing to quote for a variety of maturities, which therefore allows new swaps to be priced.

Table 1.2   Swap pricing inputs

Time period	LIBOR/swap rates	Cash lease rates	Lease rate discount factor	Forward lease rate
0.25	3.13%	0.09%	0.999775	
0.50	3.39%	0.12%	0.999400	0.1500%
0.75	3.60%	0.16%	0.998839	0.2249%
1.00	3.79%	0.19%	0.998104	0.2947%
1.25	3.89%	0.21%	0.997441	0.2658%
1.50	3.98%	0.22%	0.996705	0.2952%
1.75	4.07%	0.24%	0.995896	0.3252%
2.00	4.09%	0.25%	0.995012	0.3553%

Source: Barclays Capital; intermediate rates interpolated.

However, for gold lease swaps the situation is somewhat easier as it is possible to obtain lease rates as long as 10 years, which by convention are zero coupon in style. These lease rates can then be easily manipulated into discount factors.

To calculate the discount factors from zero coupon instruments of a maturity of up to one year, the necessary formula is:

$$\text{Discount factor}_t = \frac{1}{1 + (\text{Zero coupon rate}_t \times \text{Fraction of year})}$$

So, the calculation for the 9-month discount factor becomes:

$$\text{Discount factor}_{0.75} = \frac{1}{1 + (0.16\% \text{x } 0.75)} = 0.998801$$

(There is a small rounding difference between this result and the figure used in Table 1.2, which was derived using a spreadsheet.)

To calculate the swap rates beyond one year the formula is:

$$\text{Discount factor}_t = \frac{1}{(1 + \text{Zero coupon rate}_t)^n}$$

In this case n is defined as the number of years (or fraction thereof) from the effective date of the swap until the time of the cashflow. Therefore, for the 2-year discount factor the calculation is (again with a small rounding difference):

$$\text{Discount factor}_2 = \frac{1}{(1.0025)^2} = 0.995019$$

Table 1.2 provides an overview of a typical lease rate swap. The rates were observed in the market for value 11 April 2005. The terms of the swap are:

Underlying asset   Gold
Notional amount   50,000 ounces
Maturity   2 years
Settlement   Quarterly for both fixed and floating

Floating payments	Based on the 3-month lease rate at the start of each period
Fixed payments	Based on a single fixed rate of 0.2497%
Payment timing	Payments to be made in arrears
Base price	USD 425.40 (current spot rate)

In Table 1.2:

- The second column comprises LIBOR deposit rates up to 9 months and swap rates there-after.
- The third column contains lease rates of different maturities observed from the market.
- The lease rate discount factor column represents discount factors of different maturities, which have been derived from the lease rates in the third column.
- The final column represents 3-month forward lease rates. For example, the rate of 0.15% represents the 3-month rate in 3 months' time. The lease rate discount factors in column 4 are used in the following mathematical relationship:

$$\text{Forward rate}_{a \times b} = \frac{\text{Short dated discount factor}}{\text{Long dated discount factor}} - 1 \times 4$$

$$\text{Forward rate}_{0.25 \times 0.50} = \frac{0.999775}{0.999400} - 1 \times 4 = 0.15\%$$

Table 1.3 details the swap cashflows required to determine the fixed rate on the swap. The floating cashflows in the fourth column of Table 1.3 are calculated as:

Notional amount × Spot value of gold × Forward lease rate × Fraction of a year

The first floating cashflows payable at the end of the first quarter used the current 3-month lease rate of 0.09%. Hence, as a worked example, the floating payment due at the end of the first year would be:

$$50,000 \times \text{USD } 425.40 \times 0.2947\% \times 0.25 = \text{USD } 15,670 \text{ (small rounding difference)}$$

Table 1.3 Swap cashflows

Time period	Fixed cashflows		Floating cashflows	
	Gross	PV	Gross	PV
0.25	USD 13,275	USD 13,272	USD 4,786	USD 4,785
0.50	USD 13,275	USD 13,267	USD 7,974	USD 7,970
0.75	USD 13,275	USD 13,260	USD 11,957	USD 11,943
1.00	USD 13,275	USD 13,250	USD 15,668	USD 15,639
1.25	USD 13,275	USD 13,241	USD 14,079	USD 14,043
1.50	USD 13,275	USD 13,232	USD 15,671	USD 15,620
1.75	USD 13,275	USD 13,221	USD 17,263	USD 17,193
2.00	USD 13,275	USD 13,209	USD 18,855	USD 18,761
TOTALS		**USD 105,953**		**USD 105,953**
	NET PRESENT VALUE		0	

Note that the magnitude of the spot price is irrelevant and will not alter the fixed rate, which is eventually derived. Its main purpose is to convert the cashflows into a USD value. The third and fifth columns of Table 1.3 simply gives the present values of the cashflows by multiplying the gross cashflows by the discount factor of the appropriate maturity. Using the 1-year floating values in Table 1.3, this yields:

$$\text{USD } 15{,}668 \times 0.998104 = \text{USD } 15{,}638 \text{ (small rounding difference)}$$

The remaining floating cashflows are calculated in a similar fashion. The present values of the floating cashflows are then summed to give a value of USD 105,953. Since the swap has to be considered as an equitable exchange of cashflows at its inception – implying a net present value (NPV) of zero – we know that the present value of the fixed side must also be USD 105,953. The calculation of the present value of each fixed cashflow is:

$$\text{Notional amount} \times \text{Spot rate} \times \text{Fixed rate} \times \text{Fraction of year} \times \text{Discount factor}$$

This means that we have to solve for the unknown fixed rate by iteration. The single fixed rate that returns a present value of USD 105,953 for the fixed cashflows is found to be 0.2497%.

By looking at the fixed rate in relation to the forward lease rates in the final column of Table 1.2, it can be seen that the former is a weighted average of the latter. By looking at the fixed rate in this manner we receive an insight into the essence of swaps. Ignoring any underlying economic exposure, an entity paying a fixed rate must believe that over the life of the swap he will receive more from the floating cashflows. In other words the fixed rate payer must believe that actual lease rates will rise faster than those currently implied by the forward market. The opposite would be true of a fixed rate receiver; that is, he expects actual future lease rates to be below those currently implied by the forward market.

1.7   THE SPOT–FORWARD–OPTION RELATIONSHIP

Probably one of the most documented areas of finance is that of option pricing. Since the aim of this chapter is to give readers a basic understanding of where the value of a derivative instrument comes from, the analysis will avoid excessive discussions on the mathematics of options and concentrate on the intuition. Those interested in understanding the mathematics are recommended to refer to a variety of texts such as Galitz (1996), Tompkins (1994) and Natenberg (1994). A more recent and commodity specific text has been written by Geman (2005).

An option's premium is primarily dependent on:

• the expected payout at maturity
• the probability of the payout being made.

Although at an intuitive level these concepts are easy to understand, the mathematics behind the principles is often complex and discourages many readers. To determine the premium on an option, a variety of inputs are required, as is an appropriate model. Those inputs will include

Table 1.4 Option pricing parameters

Spot	USD 425.40
Strike	USD 425.40
Time to maturity	6 months
Six month LIBOR	3.39%
Six month lease rate	0.11571%
Six month forward price	USD 432.40
Implied volatility	15%

- The spot price
- The strike price
- Time to maturity
- The cost of carrying the underlying asset as a hedge (i.e. any income earned through holding the underlying asset less any expense incurred)
- The implied volatility of the underlying asset.

Table 1.4 shows the values that will be used for the following option pricing examples. We will assume that the option is European in style and, given the parameters set out in the table, a call option would be in-the-money since the strike price is less than the forward price. Using a Black–Scholes–Merton model, the premium is estimated at USD 21.50 per troy ounce (option premiums are quoted in the same format as the underlying asset).

An option premium can be decomposed into two elements: time value and intrinsic value. The intrinsic value can be thought of as the amount of profit the buyer would make if he were to exercise the option immediately. However, the term is defined in such a way that it does not take into account the initial premium paid. The intrinsic value for a call option can be expressed in the following manner:

$$\text{Intrinsic value of a call} = \text{MAX}(0, \text{Underlying price} - \text{Strike})$$

For put options it is expressed as

$$\text{Intrinsic value of a put} = \text{MAX}(0, \text{Strike} - \text{Underlying price})$$

In both expressions the underlying price is the forward price for European style options and spot for American style. In the original definition of intrinsic value prior to maturity, the difference between the underlying price and the strike price should be present valued since exercise of the European style option could only take place at expiry. However, when analysing options intuitively, traders would probably disregard this aspect.

Time value is the extra amount that the seller charges the buyer to cover him for the probability of future exercise – a sort of uncertainty charge. Time value is not paid or received at expiry of the option as, for buyers, it will fall to zero over the option's life. When an option is exercised the holder will only receive the intrinsic value. Time value is only paid or received upon the sale or purchase of an option prior to maturity. This explains why early exercise of an option is rarely optimal. If a purchased option is no longer required, it would usually be more efficient to neutralise the exposure by selling an opposite position in the market in order to receive the time value.

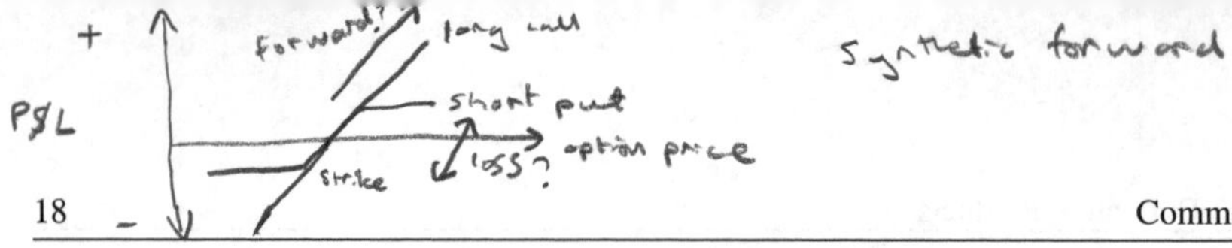

(handwritten annotations in top margin: "Forward", "long call", "short put", "Strike", "loss?", "option price", "Synthetic forward")

An understanding of the two option premium components is vital in order to understand the logic of interbank transactions. Tompkins (1994) shows clearly that movement in the underlying market will drive intrinsic value, while time value is influenced primarily by time and implied volatility.

1.8 PUT–CALL PARITY: A KEY RELATIONSHIP

Although pricing models provide one linkage between the underlying price, the forward rate and the option premium, the concept of put–call parity is an alternative representation. (Tompkins, 1994, provides a detailed analysis of the concept.)

Put–call parity is a concept that attempts to link options with their underlying assets such that arbitrage opportunities could be identified. The conditions of put–call parity will hold as long as the strike, maturity and amount are the same.

Although put–call parity varies according to the underlying asset, in its simplest form it can be represented by the expression:

$$C - P = F - E$$

where C = price of a call option
   P = price of a put option
   F = the forward price of the underlying asset
   E = the strike rate for the option.

For the purposes of this case study the formula will be truncated to

$$C - P = F$$

where F is redefined as a position in the underlying, in this case a forward position. Each of the symbols will be expressed either with a "plus" or a "minus" to indicate a buying or a selling position, respectively. By way of the previous expression, one could therefore link the underlying market and the option by rewriting the equation as:

$$+C - P = +F$$

That is, buying a call and selling a put is equivalent to a long position in the underlying. Although this may seem a very dry concept, the relationship is frequently used in financial engineering to create innovative structures.

An option's "Greeks" (see section 1.10) are measures of market risk that have been developed over time to help market participants to manage the risk associated with the instruments. Each of the option model inputs has a related Greek whose value can be calculated numerically (see Tompkins, 1994, or Haug, 1998) or derived by perturbing the appropriate option model. The majority of the Greeks look at how a change in the relevant market input affects the value of the option premium – that is, they are "first order" effects; measures such as gamma are second order in nature.

1.9 SOURCES OF VALUE IN A HEDGE

One way in which a put call could be applied is in the construction of hedges. Let us take an example of a client wishing to buy a commodity forward (e.g. an automotive hedger).

If the hedger wanted to buy the commodity at a strike rate equal to the current forward rate, then the price of a call and a put will be the same. Not unreasonably, he may wish to achieve a strike rate E that is less than the current forward rate F, which would suggest that, for the relationship to hold, the price of the call will increase relative to the put. The challenge therefore becomes to obtain a more favourable hedging rate by cheapening the value of the call option.

This can be achieved using three possible strategies:

• Buy a call on a notional amount of N and sell a put with a notional amount of $2N$ (sometimes referred to as a ratio forward).
• Buy a reverse knock-out call option with the barrier set at a level that is unlikely to trade.
• Buy a short-dated call option and finance this by selling a longer-dated put option at the same strike.

1.10   MEASURES OF OPTION RISK MANAGEMENT

1.10.1   Delta

The delta of an option looks at how a change in the underlying price will affect the option's premium. In one sense, delta can be thought of as the trader's directional exposure. There are a variety of different definitions of delta:

• The rate of change of the premium with respect to the underlying
• The slope of the price line
• The probability of exercise
• The hedge ratio.

The most traditional way of defining delta is the rate of change of the premium with respect to the underlying. Using this method, with a known delta value the analyst can see how a small change in the underlying price will cause the premium to change. In formula, delta is expressed as:

$$\text{Delta} = \frac{\text{Change in premium}}{\text{Change in underlying price}}$$

So, if an option has a delta value of 0.58, we can say that the premium should change by 58% of the change in the underlying. Using the option parameters presented in Table 1.4, if the underlying price rises by 50 cents from USD 425.40 to USD 425.90, the premium should rise by 29 cents to USD 21.79.

Delta will be either positive or negative depending on whether the option has been bought or sold or is a call or a put. If I have bought a call or sold a put the associated delta value will be positive because, in both instances, the value of the option will rise if the underlying price rises – a positive relationship. If I have bought a put or sold a call the delta value for these options will be negative because a rise in the underlying price will cause the options to fall in value – a negative relationship. Both of these statements can be verified by looking at the payoff diagrams that were introduced in Figure 1.1.

Table 1.5 Premium against underlying price;
illustrating delta

Underlying price (USD)	Premium (USD)	Delta value
325	0.11	0.01
350	0.77	0.05
375	3.27	0.16
400	9.60	0.35
425	21.27	0.57
450	38.23	0.77
475	59.16	0.89
500	82.40	0.96
525	106.74	0.99

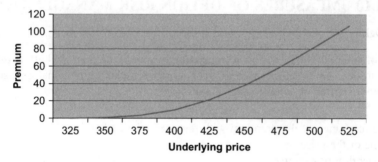

Figure 1.4 Premium against price (prior to maturity)

The second way of illustrating the concept of delta is to see how the value of the premium changes as the underlying spot price changes (all other things being equal). Table 1.5 shows the premium and delta values for an instantaneous change in the spot value.

The result of plotting these values is shown in Figure 1.4.

The second definition of delta is the slope of the price line prior to maturity (e.g. premium against price). Delta is the slope of a tangent drawn at any point on the curve. This also suggests that delta should only be used to measure small changes in the underlying price. As the premium – price relationship is convex in nature, using delta to determine the impact of significant price movements would give an incorrect estimate.

Although it is not strictly true, delta is often interpreted as the probability of exercise. The application of the term in this definition is not uniformly accepted but it certainly provides a useful rule of thumb.

Delta can be measured in a variety of ways:

- As a number whose value will range from 0 to 1.
- As a percentage.
- As a delta equivalent figure.

The most common way of expressing delta is a value ranging between 0 and 1, with an associated positive or negative sign. Out-of-the-money options will have a delta that ends towards 0 while in-the-money options will tend towards 1. It would be incorrect to say that all at-the money options have a delta of 0.50 but the value will certainly be close. An alternative method is to express it as a percentage number, which was also illustrated earlier. The third way is to express it as a delta equivalent value. This technique compares the market risk position of the option with that of an equivalent underlying asset. Thus, if for example we were to buy a call option on a notional amount of 50,000 ounces with a delta value of 0.58, the option has the same degree of market risk (for small changes in the underlying asset) as 29,000 ounces (50,000 × 0.58)

The concept of delta can be extended to option positions. If we were to add another bought call option to the above position with a notional of 60,000 ounces and a delta of 0.40, this individual position would have a delta equivalent value of 24,000. On a net basis, therefore, the entire option position has a delta exposure of 53,000 ounces (24,000 + 29,000) – the option trader's position that would have the same exposure to small movements in the underlying price as an actual physical holding of 53,000 ounces. This technique is referred to as delta hedging and demonstrates the use of delta as hedge ratio.

If the option trader chose to neutralise this exposure, he could take an offsetting position in other options or the underlying instrument. He may wish to do this if he is seeking to benefit from a change in another market factor, such as implied volatility. In the previous example the trader is delta positive, so his option position will rise in value if the underlying market price rises and vice versa. To neutralise the exposure he could therefore sell 53,000 ounces of gold in the underlying market or trade options in different combinations to achieve a net delta exposure with which he is comfortable. If the net delta position is reduced to zero, this is described as delta neutrality.

If the delta neutralising trades are executed in the underlying market, the trader is faced with making a choice between trading in either the spot or the forward market. If the option position is European then the forward market should be chosen, because the European option can only be exercised upon maturity and the appropriate equivalent market is therefore the forward market. However, some traders may choose to hedge in the spot market and then hedge the resultant interest rate risk (recall that the difference between the spot and forward markets is driven by interest rate considerations).

We have seen that delta changes as a function of the underlying price but will also evolve over time. For example, as the option approaches maturity the price line shown in Figure 1.4 above will become more linear in nature and at maturity will resemble the hockey stick shape that was introduced Figure 1.1. As a result, the delta of the option will tend towards 0 or 1.

1.10.2 Gamma

Gamma is correctly defined as the rate of change of delta with respect to the price. By looking at the rate of change, this makes it a second-order function.

$$\text{Gamma} = \frac{\text{Change in delta}}{\text{Change in underlying price}}$$

However, this definition is not really helpful in trying to grasp what gamma is actually doing. Gamma will be studied in detail in Chapter 2, so some of the definitions given here may not seem clear at this point. We will define gamma as:

- The speed with which a delta hedged position becomes unhedged
- The exposure to actual volatility in the market
- The rate of change of a trader's profit or loss
- The exposure to significant changes in the underlying price.

Gamma is positive for option buyers (irrespective of whether the option is a call or a put) and negative for sellers. Using the call option in Table 1.3, the option pricing model returned a value of 0.58 for delta and 0.009 for gamma. If we take an exposure of 50,000 ounces the delta exposure is equivalent to owning 29,000 ounces of the underlying of the asset. We will assume that the trader hedges this exposure by selling an equivalent amount in the underlying market. However, although the position is initially delta neutral a movement in the underlying will lead to a change in delta and the position will no longer be 100% hedged. The gamma measure can be used to predict the magnitude of any move in delta for a small move in the underlying price. So, in this instance we can say that for a small increase in the underlying market price, the delta will move to 0.589 and for a small downward move it would move to 0.571.

1.10.3 Theta

Theta reflects the impact of time on the value of the option and is defined as:

$$\text{Theta} = \frac{\text{Change in premium}}{\text{Change in time to expiry}}$$

Theta is positive for sellers and negative for buyers. This reflects the fact that, for buyers, options will experience time decay. In other words, the buyer will pay a premium and will acquire a contract that has time value and possibly intrinsic value. However, over time, the time value element will fall to zero. Using the original call option example, and holding all the other parameters constant, the effect of the passage of time on the option is reflected in Table 1.6.

Table 1.6   The effect of time on an option

Time to expiry (years)	Premium (USD per troy ounce)	Change in premium
1.0	32.74	–
0.9	30.74	2.00
0.8	28.66	2.08
0.7	26.49	2.17
0.6	24.21	2.28
0.5	21.79	2.41
0.4	19.19	2.60
0.3	16.33	2.86
0.2	13.06	3.27
0.1	9.02	4.04
0.01	2.88	6.14

Table 1.6 shows that, for the buyer of an option, its value will decrease as time passes and that the rate of decay will accelerate as the option approaches maturity. The opposite will hold true for sellers of options. Theta can be thought of as the slope of the price line (column 2 in Table 1.6) with respect to the time to expiry. Theta will be small initially and will increase with the passage of time (column 3 in Table 1.6).

1.10.4 Vega

Vega is defined as the change in the option premium for a 1% change in an options implied volatility. It is expressed as:

$$\text{Vega} = \frac{\text{Change in premium}}{\text{Change in implied volatility}}$$

Although most people are happy with the concept of volatility in general terms – change in the market with no direction suggested – the notion of implied volatility still remains difficult to grasp.

A related concept is historical volatility, which, as the term suggests, measures the magnitude of movement of the underlying asset over a historical period, measured in per cent per annum. The statisticians would describe this as a standard deviation. However, as is often cited in financial markets "that past performance is not a guide to future performance", there is a need for a more forward-looking measure of volatility.

One of the most popular ways of trying to explain the concept is to describe it as the volatility implied in an observed option price. The rationale for this is that if one looks at all of the option pricing model inputs, the only real unknown is the implied volatility. Terms such as the spot rate or strike are either easily observable or negotiated as part of the option contract. Since it is the only unknown factor, the traditional definition suggested taking an observed option premium, inserting the value into the option pricing model, running the model in reverse and backing out the volatility implied by this price. However, this argument traditionally ceases at this point and does not address the obvious circular argument: Where did the market maker quoting the observed option price obtain his volatility input? It also gives no real feel for what the measure is trying to achieve. Tompkins (1994, p. 139) describes it as "the risk perceived by the market today for the period up until the expiration of a particular option series". However, since no one can foretell the future with complete certainty, this is nothing more than a "best guess". As an anecdote, the author recalls teaching a class attended by an experienced option trader who described the interbank options as the "market for guesses". In the interbank market option prices are quoted in terms of a bid–offer implied volatility number. Since implied volatility is the only truly unknown variable, this is the factor that is traded on an interbank basis. Trading strategies that aim to exploit movements in implied volatility will be analysed in the chapter on interbank trading strategies.

The main confusion regarding implied volatility often surrounds the relationship with movements in the underlying asset price. The delta value of an option is sensitive to the magnitude of the implied volatility input, and as the size of the volatility number increases the delta on the option will tend towards 0.50. This is because the range of values that the underlying is expected to take at maturity is wider and the likelihood of exercise of

Table 1.7   The impact of implied volatility on a variety of options

Implied volatility	OTM option		ATM option		ITM option	
	Premium	Change in Premium	Premium	Change in premium	Premium	Change in Premium
0%	0.00		0.00		17.60	
5%	1.00	1.00	6.01	6.01	18.02	0.42
10%	5.48	4.48	12.00	5.99	22.25	4.23
15%	10.98	5.50	17.99	5.99	27.49	5.24
20%	16.77	5.79	23.98	5.99	33.03	5.54
25%	22.68	5.91	29.95	5.97	38.69	5.66
30%	28.64	5.96	35.92	5.97	44.41	5.72

an out-of-the-money option will therefore increase and for an in-the-money option it will decrease. However, it does not follow that as the underlying price starts to move, the implied volatility must also move. In an option model the implied volatility and the spot price are two independent variables and, as such, a movement in one factor can be independent of the other. Although it may be reasonable to assert that current observed movements in the spot price may alter a trader's expectations on the distribution of spot values at maturity, there is no inbuilt dependency. There is no "ruling" that says if spot were to change by $X\%$ that implied volatility must change by $Y\%$.

The confusion over the relationship between spot and volatility is similar to that seen between vega and gamma. Gamma was earlier introduced as a trader's exposure to actual volatility. If we saw a large value for gamma then the difference between two delta values will be substantial for a given change in the underlying market. If the difference between two delta values is significant, this means that the movement of the spot prices was quite large, and one could reasonably describe such a market as being currently volatile.

Table 1.7 shows the effect of implied volatility on the premium for three variants of the call option introduced in Table 1.4:

- An out-of-the-money (OTM) option with a strike rate of USD 450.
- An at-the-money (ATM) forward option with the strike rate equal to the forward rate of USD 432.40.
- An in-the-money (ITM) option with a strike rate of USD 415.

As before, all of the other pricing parameters are held constant.

From Table 1.7 we can draw a number of conclusions:

- The relationship between an ATM option premium and implied volatility is proportional. Doubling the implied volatility will double the premium.
- If the option has no implied volatility, an OTM or ATM option will have no premium, although the ITM option will have its intrinsic value. This also suggests that volatility is arguably the defining factor that distinguishes an option from its underlying asset.
- The relationship between an OTM option premium and the implied volatility is also non-linear. Notice how a doubling of the implied volatility at low levels causes the premium to rise by a much greater magnitude.

Option buyers are said to be long vega (i.e. they will benefit if implied volatility rises), while sellers are short vega – they will suffer if implied volatility rises, but will benefit if it falls. The logic behind this lies in the pricing formula for options. Recall that the premium of an option is composed of the intrinsic and time value. The intrinsic value of the option is driven by the difference between the price of the underlying and the strike price. The main drivers of the time value are time and implied volatility. The buyer of an option acquires both elements and, all other things being equal, an increase in implied volatility will increase the value of the option – a positive relationship.

2
Risk Management

SYNOPSIS **The purpose of this chapter is to define the concept of risk, within a corporate and investment banking context**.

The word "risk" used without any context is meaningless. It is like saying that some is physically "fit" – fit for what? Just because someone can run a marathon doesn't guarantee that he or she will be able to swim 26.2 miles. I doubt if many accomplished marathoners would be able to swim even one mile continuously, let alone 26.2!

For much of this book we will define the concept of risk as uncertainty, but even this is a contentious definition. Among many of my classroom participants there is a belief that fixing the price of a contract somehow results in a risk-free situation. Although it may give certainty of cashflow, it does not allow a participant to benefit from a favourable move in market prices. Hence there is an opportunity cost.

The first part of the chapter attempts to *categorise risk* into terms that will allow for a clearer analysis of exposures faced by market participants. As one key theme within commodity risk management is the concept of time, *the structure of market prices* will be analysed according to the activities of market participants.

The chapter focuses on some of the risk management issues faced by corporates and investment banks [1]*. From the *corporate perspective* the question of whether to hedge or not is discussed and a framework for analysing risk is presented. The presented framework is a "top down" approach to identifying risk.

From the *investment bank's perspective* risk is looked at from two different angles. An investment bank will inevitably take on exposure as a result of some asset or liability risk management solution, and the associated risks will need to be managed.

2.1 CATEGORIES OF RISK

The use of the phrase "risk management" needs to be clarified. For our purposes, risk within a financial context can be broken down into five major sub-categories:

- *Market risk* – the risk that something that is owned or owed will change in value as market prices change.
- *Credit risk* – the risk that monies owed will never be repaid.
- *Business risk* – the risk that an entity enters into a business, that is not fully understood.
- *Operational risk* – the risk that an entity loses money as a result of an operational control weakness.
- *Legal and documentary risk* – the risk that a contract is deemed to be null and void (e.g. *ultra vires*) or that a loss is incurred as a result of a contractual commitment.

---

*Figures in square brackets relate to the entries in the Notes section at the end of the book.

Although most institutions would be concerned about market and credit risk, in reality most catastrophic losses have probably been caused either by a lack of understanding of the business in which the entity has been involved (business risk) or by very poor internal controls (operational risk). In certain respects there is an irony in that the risks that are commonly at the root of most institutions losses cannot be easily hedged. For example, poor internal control issues are usually the result of cultural issues and a lack of discipline. For market risks a host of products exist that allow an institution to protect themselves against an adverse move in prices. The next time there is an announcement by an institution of losses incurred that are initially blamed on price movements, consider how it was that the perpetrator was allowed to engage in such activities for so long without any independent control highlighting the problem.

2.1.1 Defining risk

Within each of the individual risk headings it is possible to break down the risk into a series of subheadings. For example, within market risk one could consider:

- *Interest rate risk*: The risk that entity loses money from an adverse movement in interest rates. For example, a company may borrow money on a variable rate basis and then be faced with higher costs if interest rates subsequently rise. This exposure equally applies to interest earned on cash surpluses, which is often ignored.
- *Inflation risk*: Although not always obvious, this may be an exposure for a corporate whose revenues or expenses are linked to inflation. Indeed, a corporate may be faced with a hidden inflation cost if it were to offer its employees a pension scheme that is linked to a change in inflation.
- *Foreign exchange rate risk*: Typically, foreign exchange rate risk arises from two sources. Transactional FX risk arises as a result of a company's day-to-day business. For example, a US importer of goods and services from abroad will have a foreign currency payable. Translational FX risk arises from expressing a foreign currency asset or liability in the company's domestic accounting currency. With respect to commodities, since they are mostly traded and quoted in US dollars, foreign producers or consumers will also be exposed to FX risk.
- *Equity risk*: This can arise in a number of different forms from a corporate perspective. Again one source of equity risk could be hidden in a company's defined benefit pension scheme. Proposed share buybacks and employee share option schemes may require the company to buy equity at an unfavourable price. Investments in other publicly quoted companies gives rise to a form of equity investment risk.
- *Liquidity risk*: Liquidity risk can be thought of as the potential inability of a company to meet its short-term cash requirements. This may arise from the inability to borrow money from its bankers or the inability to be able to liquidate assets to cover any shortfall.
- *Commodity risk*: Simply, this is the exposure that a company will face as a result of a change in commodity prices. This may be either explicit or as a side product of a company's business. For example, a gold producer will be exposed to a fall in the price of the commodity, which is a direct function of his production. A haulage company's exposure to diesel prices is arguably a secondary exposure to their main line of business. Companies that are fully integrated along a particular supply chain will arguably face offsetting price risks.

2.1.2   Credit risk

The other main risk from the "big five" noted previously that can be hedged is credit risk – although the use of credit derivatives is beyond the scope of this book.

To illustrate the principles let us consider the issues faced by a consumer of base metals within the automotive sector. It would be possible for that person to enter into direct physical hedging contracts with the producers of the metal, but this is not without difficulty. There would be three main risks that the producers would face. Firstly, there is the issue of product specification. Hedging directly with, say, a mine is not necessarily a good idea, as the metal will not be produced in its primary form. It is more likely to be in an intermediate form that needs further work to make it usable by the consumer. Although a physical hedge may be possible with a smelting company, there is still no guarantee that they will be able to produce the metal in the exact specification required. The second issue relates to the counterparty credit risk. If either the mine or the smelter suffers any operational problems, they may not be able to meet their future physical obligations. Finally, there is the issue of price expectations. Consumers of the metal will be looking to hedge at times when the commodity price is at the bottom of the price cycle, while producers will be looking to hedge towards the peak of prices.

One of ways that the metal consumers have sought to get around this is through fixed price component supply. However, this raises the issue of credit risk once again. If the metal consumer enters into an agreement with a component manufacturer, the latter will have to make a decision whether to hedge to avoid a price mismatch. If the component suppliers choose to hedge directly and are of a poor credit standing, the terms of their hedge may not be favourable and this may result in poor terms being passed on to the automotive producer. Alternatively, if the component supplier chooses not to hedge their raw material costs, they will be impacted if the price of the underlying metal subsequently rises.

2.2   COMMODITY MARKET PARTICIPANTS: THE TIME DIMENSION

When analysing commodities it is useful to try to develop an understanding of the likely activity of market participants for different times to delivery. This is done by analysing the forward curve, which indicates the clearing price where demand equals supply for different delivery points in time. In each of the subsequent chapters the price drivers for each specific commodity are considered, but here we will try to provide a generalised approach to the issue of participant's activity.

2.2.1   Short-dated maturities

Typical participants and their related activities in these markets are:

- Companies (e.g. banks and commodity trading companies) managing short-term trading risk.
- Investors tracking commodity indices.
- Hedge funds and Commodity Trading Advisers using futures to express short-term views on the market.

2.2.2 Medium-dated maturities

These maturities are dominated by the strategic risk management activities of producers and consumers. Examples of this include oil refinery margin hedging and consumer hedging, such as airlines seeking to hedge their Jet Fuel exposures.

2.2.3 Longer-dated exposures

These maturities will involve producers who are selling their production forward, perhaps as part of the terms of a loan facility where the lending institution is seeking to minimise the volatility of the borrower's cashflow. If the curve is steeply backwardated, consumers may be tempted to take the opportunity to buy forward at what could be an attractive level. The other main participants in these maturities are investors buying OTC structured notes issued by investment banks. As a generalisation, these notes may be constructed as a zero coupon bond plus a call option.

2.3 HEDGING CORPORATE RISK EXPOSURES

When deciding whether to hedge, a corporate is faced with a number of possible strategies. These will be considered from the perspective of an automotive metal consumer to give the examples a context.

- *Do not hedge*: Here the decision not to hedge may be driven by the fact that the metal may only make up a small proportion of the finished product, and price fluctuations will only have a limited impact on margins. It may also be that the producer can pass on any increase in the price of the underlying metal to the consumers without impacting its own margins. If the underlying price were to fall the producer can of course cut the final price but the price reduction may be as large as the underlying price falls.
- *Hedge to guarantee future unit costs*: In this instance the manufacturer tries to lock in much of the future cost of a production run by hedging a significant proportion of the commodity price exposures. This allows the price of the final product to be fixed and ensures that there is an adequate margin. It also benefits the end customers, as they are immune to excessive price volatility.
- *Timing mismatch between raw material cost and final product income*: This situation arises if the manufacturing process is relatively long and the price of the final product is linked in part to a commodity price. Having paid for the raw material, the manufacturer will be exposed to a fall in the price of the commodity prior to its sale. If the company could receive the raw material on a constant basis and match this with sales of the final production, the timing mismatch may not be a significant issue. However, in reality companies may receive irregular shipments of the raw material and may also choose to carry large levels of stocks. Thus the timing mismatch issue becomes more acute.
- *Active hedging based on directional views of the market*: Many non-financial companies are uneasy about developing views on potential commodity price movements. The result would be that the hedges would only be implemented on the basis of planned production levels. However, a number of firms have been willing to take advantage of favourable market conditions to implement hedges in anticipation of future needs as the companies realise that they will always have a certain need for a particular commodity.

Another difficult problem is deciding the size of the hedge. Hedges may be put in place of a forecasted purchase of the raw material. If the actual raw materials are not purchased, then the manufacturer may be faced with a hedge for which there is no underlying exposure. For this reason a number of companies choose to hedge a proportion of their exposure. Many of the hedges put in place by companies are financially settled, and this allows the hedger to source the metal from a particular supplier who can provide a specific grade or shape.

2.4 A FRAMEWORK FOR ANALYSING CORPORATE RISK

Very often when risk management solutions are considered, solutions to a potential market risk are considered at a micro level, without including the "big picture" implications for the corporate. This approach ignores the fact that a corporate will be ultimately focused on some high-performance metric such as the share price, profit or cashflow. As a result it would be more appropriate to consider a two-stage approach to the issue – strategic and tactical. The following framework considers risk management, which develop ideas presented by Banks and Dunn (2003).

2.4.1 Strategic considerations

At the strategic level a risk management strategy should consider the following issues to enable the hedging solution to be placed within a particular context:

- What are the company's strategic corporate goals?
- What issues do the internal and external stakeholders consider to be important?
- What is the universe of financial risks to which the company is exposed? Which of the financial risks can be hedged?
- What is the appropriate strategic performance metric against which the success of the hedging programme can be assessed (e.g. share price, cashflow)?
- What is the company's existing risk management strategy?
- What is known about the competitors' activities?

2.4.2 Tactical considerations

Only after the strategic issues have been addressed should the tactical side of hedging be considered. Some of the key issues to be addressed include:

- What is the nature of the specific exposures to which the company is faced?
  - How certain is the company?
  - When should the hedge start? Now? In the future?
  - What percentage of the underlying exposure should be covered (i.e. how much risk is the company willing to take)?
  - Is there a specific target rate or price that the company is trying to achieve (e.g. some form of budget rate)?
- What is the company's current view on the market? This could be with respect to:
  - the direction of the market
  - timing
  - magnitude.

- What hedging instrument is the company allowed to use?
- Is the company willing to pay a premium fee for protection?

Corporate hedgers may be reluctant to express a view on the future movement of the market, sometimes claiming that they are not qualified to express a view on the market. However, it would be fair to say that any view expressed by an investment is just that – an opinion rather than a guarantee. A more efficient hedge could be constructed by a bank if the customer was able to express a view on these elements as option-based strategies are normally three dimensional – that is, they extract value from (1) directional movements in the underlying price, (2) the time to maturity and (3) the implied volatility (i.e. the magnitude of expected price movements).

Reasonably, many hedgers may be concerned about the potential outcome of the hedging strategy. This can be addressed in a very simple manner by the use of scenario analysis. By constructing a few simple "what if?" scenarios the potential outcome of the hedged position could be shown. Indeed the use of scenarios should ideally feed back into the strategic questions that are addressed at the start of the process. We argued that all hedging strategies should be placed within a "bigger picture" context, as most firms hedge to solve a particular problem, such as a share price decline or an adverse movement in cashflow. The scenario analysis should feed back into how the hedged position will influence this key metric. Readers interested in this approach are referred to Charles Smithson (1998).

2.5   BANK RISK MANAGEMENT

At the heart of all investment banks sits the trading function whose main responsibility is to make decisions on how to manage the bank's market and credit risk. These risks arise either from client business or from transactions designed to profit from a trader's view of how market prices are expected to evolve. The way in which these risks are managed will have an influence on market activity and, consequently, market price.

The essence of derivative solutions is that they offer to market participants – corporates, institutional investors and other financial institutions – the ability to transform some form of market or credit risk. As a result the institution offering a particular solution will be taking on some form of risk and will therefore look to offset this in the market participant. This will also apply to both asset and liability structures.

It would also be reasonable to suggest that, in addition to managing exposures generated by client business, some traders will have discretion to execute trades that take advantage of an anticipated movement in market rates. Looking at all of these perspectives, a trader's "book" would therefore comprise a portfolio of different exposures that will be managed on an ongoing basis.

2.6   HEDGING CUSTOMER EXPOSURES

Throughout the book we will analyse how commodity exposures are created and hedged using a suite of derivative products:

- Futures and forwards
- Swaps
- Options (vanilla and exotic).

2.6.1 Forward risk management

If a client were to enter into an exchange-traded futures contract, this does not result in any market risk for the bank, as the client's counterparty is the exchange's clearing house. Any change in the value of the future is managed by the clearing house by the collection of collateral – margin calls – from the customer.

If a client executes a forward deal, the bank is now acting as a principal to the trade and, as such, this generates both credit and market risk. Given the way in which a forward price is calculated (i.e. spot price plus net carry) the bank has an exposure to a movement in these components. By taking an equal and offsetting position, the bank can manage these risks. This concept is illustrated in Chapter 3, where the pricing and risk of a forward deal is considered in detail.

2.6.2 Swap risk management

Hedging of swap risks can be more complex, but it is possible to make some general observations. Again the simplest hedge for the bank is an equal and opposite transaction with another market participant. However, if even the particular swap market is exceptionally liquid this may be difficult to achieve, and consequently many banks will select instruments that are a close proxy for the exposure and run an element of market risk, usually within defined parameters. This type of market risk is referred to as basis risk and describes a situation where the value of the exposure does not change by the same amount as the hedging instrument. For example, in certain types of energy swap based on one or more of the refined products (e.g. Jet Fuel), the traders may convert the exposure to a crude oil equivalent and manage the risk using exchange-traded futures.

2.6.3 Option risk management

When a bank executes an option transaction it is faced with a number of different market risks. The market risks it wishes to manage relate to changes in:

- The underlying price
- The strike price
- Time to maturity
- The cost of carrying an underlying hedge
- The implied volatility of the underlying asset.

Each of the listed market risks has an associated "Greek" measure that is used by the banks to measure and manage a particular exposure. These Greeks, and how they are used to manage market risk, were analysed in section 1.10 of Chapter 1.

2.6.4 Correlation risk management

One additional market risk worthy of mention is that of correlation risk. Correlation measures the tendency of variables to move in the same direction. Within the context of this book the focus will be on price correlation, although it is acknowledged that alternative correlation measures exist elsewhere within finance (e.g. default correlation within the credit world).

Correlation risk may arise in a number of ways:

- From options that require it as a pricing input (e.g. basket options).
- In the nature of the price relationships that commodities have with each other (e.g. platinum and palladium).
- In the price relationships that commodities have with financial assets such as bonds or equities.

Similar to volatility, correlation could be estimated from historical data or be implied from current market prices. However, correlation measures tend to be unstable in volatile markets.

2.7   VIEW-DRIVEN EXPOSURES

The second aspect of an investment banking trading function will be the willingness and ability to profit from an anticipated move in market prices. There are a whole series of strategies that fall within this category and as such the following highlights a few key themes.

2.7.1   Spot-trading strategies

A trader may decide to take an outright view on the movement of an asset. An outright deal is a single buy or sell strategy rather than some combination of deals. For example, let us assume that a trader is looking at an investment period of 6 months but is not sure whether he should buy or sell. The decision is not as simple as suggesting that if he expects the price to rise then he should buy and vice versa. The decision is a function of the investment horizon and how the trader thinks that spot prices will evolve relative to forward prices. Let us assume that gold is trading in the spot market at USD 425.40 per troy ounce while the 6-month forward is priced at USD 432.44 (these are the same values as those presented in Chapter 1, on pricing of derivatives). The forward price is not a predictor of the future spot prices but should be used as a breakeven value against which all investment decisions should be judged, because a spot purchase, which is held for a given period, will have a value equal to the forward price. This gives the trader one of three possibilities:

- If the trader believed that the actual spot price in 6 months' time was going to be greater than the current forward price, then he should buy the gold, borrow money to finance its purchase and lend out the gold to earn the lease rate. If that materialises, he will be able to sell the gold at the end of the period at a price that will be greater than the cost of carrying the metal for the period.
- If the trader believed that the actual spot price in 6 months was going to be less than the current forward rate, then a selling position would be appropriate. He should sell the gold and place the proceeds on deposit to earn interest for 6 months. In order to ensure that the short position is covered, the bank would borrow the gold and pay a leasing fee. At the end of the 6-month period, the gold is repurchased at the prevailing spot price and delivered to the lender of the metal. The net result is that the cashflows received exceed the cashflows paid.

- If the trader believed that the actual spot price in 6 months was going to be equal to the current forward rate, then he would be indifferent to buying or selling the gold.

Note that in the second scenario it would be possible for the trader to believe that the price of gold was going to rise – albeit to a level less than the current forward rate – and this would still indicate a selling strategy. The key, therefore, is not whether the spot price will rise or fall but where it will be in relation to the forward rate.

2.7.2 Forward trading strategies

One obvious motivation for executing a forward trade is the fact that the trader does not have to take physical delivery of the underlying asset. In this sense it may be considered to be a more cash efficient manner of expressing a view on the market. Similar to the spot market, forward starting deals could be used to express a view on a directional movement in the underlying price.

However, it may be more common to use forward transactions to exploit relative price movements. These would be executed as a pair of trades and may include:

- Taking a view that contracts trading with two different maturities may be mispriced relative to each other. Here the trader buys the contract considered to be underpriced and sells the contract that is overpriced.
- Taking a view that a historic relationship between two related prices may change. For example, a trader may identify a seasonal relationship between prices for delivery in say, winter and spring, that he believes will change.
- A trader may initiate a transaction that exploits a differential between two different commodities. For example, popular spread trades in the commodity markets include:
  - crack spreads (e.g. gasoline or heating oil vs crude oil)
  - spark spreads (e.g. natural gas vs power)
  - base metal spreads (e.g. copper vs aluminium)
  - precious metal spreads (e.g. gold vs silver or platinum vs palladium).

2.7.3 Single period physically settled "swaps"

These are constructed as a simultaneous combination of a spot and a forward transaction. It is a temporary exchange of an asset for cash, which can be used for

- borrowing money at an attractive rate, or
- obtaining temporary supplies of a commodity.

A fully worked example of this type of structure is documented in Chapter 3 (gold).

2.7.4 Single or multi-period financially settled swaps

A "financial" swap is either a single or multi-period exchange of cashflows that does not involve the physical movement of the commodity. A single period swap will be economically equivalent to a cash-settled forward. From a trading perspective swaps could be used in a similar manner to forwards.

2.7.5   Option-based trades: trading volatility

Recall from Chapter 1 that options are priced using a number of variables. The variables are agreed with the counterparty (e.g. maturity, strike) while other variables are easily discernible from market sources (e.g. the underlying price and interest rates). However, there is one variable – implied volatility – that, although it may be discernible from market sources, is the source of a number of trading opportunities.

Implied volatility is a measure of how volatile the market expects the asset to be until the expiry of the option. Since it attempts to quantify something in the future, it is nothing more than an educated guess – a perception of how risky the asset is expected to be. Market price screens do exist for implied volatilities but these simply represent a consensus or equilibrium. However, as it does need to be grounded in reality, it should bear some resemblance to how volatile the asset has been over a particular period (e.g. historical volatility). Expressed as an option "Greek", implied volatility is referred to as vega.

Accordingly, traders talk about buying and selling (implied) volatility as if it were a commodity in itself. Recall from Chapter 1 that an option buyer benefits from a rise in implied volatility, while sellers benefit from a fall. In some respects trading volatility is simple; if an option is bought, a premium is paid and a subsequent rise in implied volatility allows the buyer to take a reversing position in the market ("sell the option back to the market") to receive a higher premium. However, this strategy is not without risk as the option position leaves a trader with a number of other market risks (e.g. changes in the spot price, passage of time) that need to be managed. The following example illustrates how volatility could be traded, and the associated risks.

Trading of volatility is achieved by buying or selling options to achieve a particular vega exposure, while neutralising the position's exposure to movements in the underlying price. The typical strategies for achieving this are:

- *Selling volatility (trader believes that implied volatility will fall)*
  - Sell an at-the-money (ATM) call, sell an ATM put, same strike, same maturity (known as a short straddle).
  - Sell a call option and delta hedge.
  - Sell a put option and delta hedge.
- *Buying volatility (trader believes that implied volatility will rise)*
  - Buy an ATM call, buy an ATM put, same strike, same maturity (known as a long straddle).
  - Buy a call option and delta hedge.
  - Buy a put option and delta hedge.

Initially it can be confusing to grasp how volatility could be traded using the single option strategy but this is usually because the option's exposure is viewed along a single dimension. It would be more accurate to say that when executing option transactions a trader must think in two or three dimensions, namely volatility (actual and implied) and direction. The sale of either a call or a put will result in a negative vega exposure while the delta exposure is negative for the sold call and positive for the sold put. This directional exposure is neutralised by buying the underlying (for the call) and selling the underlying (for the put) – a technique referred to as delta hedging.

Let us assume that a bank has sold a 3-month out-of-the-money (OTM) option on gold on a notional amount of 10,000 troy ounces with a strike rate of USD 450 at a premium of USD 10.98 per troy ounce and priced with an implied volatility of 15%. To hedge the delta exposure the trader decides to use the spot market, which is currently trading at an price of USD 425.40 per troy ounce.

The delta of this OTM option is −0.373, which means that if the price of the underlying were to change by a small amount the premium on the option would change by 37.3% of this amount. Since a rise in the underlying price would cause the option to lose money, the trader decides to hedge this exposure by buying the underlying in the proportion dictated by the delta value. Since the option was written on a notional of 10,000 troy ounces the trader must buy 37.3% of this amount, namely 3,730 troy ounces. Therefore if there is a small increase in the price of gold, the losses on the option should approximately be offset by the profits on the delta hedge.

All other things being equal – mainly that the underlying price does not change – holding this position to expiry will yield a profit to the trader. The passage of time will reap a profit to the trader through the accretion of the option's value by the theta effect. If this assumption is relaxed, the main risk to the trader is to large changes in the underlying price. At first glance this may seem counter-intuitive as the delta hedge was designed to ensure that the trader's directional exposure was neutralised. However, although delta neutralises the trader against small changes in the underlying price, he is still exposed to large changes in the underlying price.

Let us say that the price of gold rises by USD 5 per troy ounce. The option position is now valued at USD 12.89 per troy ounce, a loss to the trader of USD 1.91 per troy ounce or USD 19,100 on the option position. However, the trader will gain USD 5 per troy ounce on the underlying hedge. Since the delta hedge was for 3,730 troy ounces, the profit would be USD 18,650, which is insufficient to cover the loss on the option position and results in an overall mark to market loss of USD 450. At this point the trader is faced with a difficult decision. If the price of the underlying continues to rise the losses on the option, which move in a non-linear manner, will increase more quickly than the profits on the future, which change in a linear manner. As a result, he decides to rehedge at the new higher level where the delta on the option is now – 41.4%. This means that to be delta neutral he needs to buy a total of 4,140 troy ounces of gold. Since he already owns 3,730 troy ounces he only needs to buy the difference (410 troy ounces), albeit at a new higher price of USD 430.25 per troy ounce.

After rehedging, the trader then sees that the market falls back to its opening price of USD 425.40. On a mark to market (MTM) basis, the option position gains in value by USD 1.91 or USD 19,100 for the position. However, the position in gold now loses USD 5.00 per troy ounce to give a hedge loss of USD 20,700. His net loss on the trade is therefore USD 1,600. His total losses as a result of these two price movements are therefore USD 2,050 (USD 450 + USD 1,600).

If there were no further price movements during the trading day:

- The trader will have broken even on the option position (note the analysis is done on an intra-day basis, so theta is not an issue).
- The trader will have broken even on the initial hedge position (3,730 troy ounces bought at USD 425.40).

- The trader will have lost money as a result of the rebalancing of the portfolio. (An extra 410 troy ounces bought at USD 430.40 and revalued at the close of business at USD 425.40 to give a total loss of USD 2,050).

What would have happened if the price had first fallen and then subsequently risen? If the price of the underlying had fallen, the delta on the option would also have fallen indicating to the trader that he had overhedged. He would then have to sell part of the hedge at a lower price. However, if the price were subsequently to rise, then the hedge would have to be repurchased at a higher price. The result is therefore the same; when rebalancing the trader will be buying the hedge at a higher price and selling it at a lower price.

This is the primary risk of selling options on a delta-hedged basis into a volatile market. The rate at which the option changes in value is different to that of the hedge. If the price of the underlying were to become more volatile, the delta of the option would change, indicating to the option trader that the delta hedge needs to be adjusted. The magnitude of the change in delta as a result of a move in the underlying price will dictate the size of the rebalancing. With a short option position in a volatile market this will result in a mark to market loss. The rate of change of delta with respect to the underlying price is called gamma. Gamma is always expressed in relation to a range of price movements. So in the above example the gamma for a USD 5 movement in the price of gold is 4.1% (41.4% − 37.3%). Intuitively, gamma can be thought of as:

- the trader's exposure to significant changes in the underlying (since delta only covers him for small changes);
- the a trader's exposure to movements in actual as opposed to implied volatility.

Additionally, some traders think of gamma as the speed with which their profit and loss changes with respect to a change in the underlying price. The larger the gamma, the greater the difference between two delta values for a given change in the underlying price and the larger the required adjustment to the delta hedge. Hence an option with a large gamma value will generate large changes to the trader's profit or loss.

If the trader had bought options and delta hedged under the conditions noted above, then he would have enjoyed a profit. However, there is a cost to this, as the options will decay in value over time. This is why option traders sometimes describe theta as "gamma rent"; it is the "price" one has to pay when buying volatility or the "reward" one receives from selling volatility.

An option trader who buys volatility is hoping that:

- implied volatility will increase, leading to an increase in the value of their option position;
- the market will experience more (actual) volatility;
- some combination of the two occurs.

If he decides to take a view on the actual volatility of the market, he hopes to make more in delta hedging profits than he loses in time decay.

An option trader who sells volatility is hoping that:

- implied volatility will decrease, leading to an decrease in the value of his option position;
- the market will experience less (actual) volatility;
- some combination of the two occurs.

If he decides to take a view on the actual volatility of the market, he hopes to make more from time decay than he loses in delta hedging activities.

As the underlying price evolves, traders may adjust their implied volatility quotations accordingly. One simple process to do this is as follows. By convention, implied volatility numbers tend to be quoted as percentage per annum. It is possible to convert this to a daily value by dividing by the square root of the number of business days in the year (e.g. 250). An annual volatility of 15% is therefore equivalent to a daily figure of 0.95%. Very approximately the trader would expect the underlying price to trade within plus or minus of this range, so using our previous opening futures price of USD 425.40, this would imply a range of values from USD 421.40 to USD 429.44. Since it traded outside of this range during the day, the underlying was actually more volatile than the market predicted and, as a result, the option trader may decide to increase his implied volatility quote accordingly.

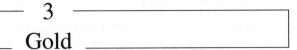

3
Gold

Boys, by God, I believe I've found a gold mine.

James Marshall*

SYNOPSIS **The purpose of this chapter is to describe the physical and derivative markets for gold.**

The first section of the chapter outlines the main components of *the physical gold market*. This includes a description of the *physical supply* chain with special reference to the role of financial institutions. London is the home to the largest physical market and the main conventions such as fixing the price for gold are highlighted.

The second section considers the *demand and supply of gold* and the impact each component has on the market price. Given that there are substantial amounts of gold above ground and that it is virtually indestructible, the dynamics of the demand and supply equation for gold are different to other metals such as those considered to be "base" or industrial (e.g. copper and aluminium).

The third section outlines the features of the *gold leasing market*, which lays the foundation for a description of *gold derivatives*. The main emphasis is to describe those products that are, to an extent, unique to the gold market (e.g. a floating rate forward). In addition, since central banks hold a significant amount of the commodity within their reserves, the use of derivatives to help gold to "earn its keep" is considered.

The chapter does not include coverage of other precious metals such as silver, platinum and palladium but many of the principles within the text would also apply in these markets.

3.1 THE MARKET FOR GOLD

3.1.1 Physical Supply Chain

Gold is extracted from open pits or underground mines by blasting or digging. The economics of mining are such that deep level mines extract gold at purities of less than 10 grammes of gold per tonne of dirt (or ore), while for open pit operations the figure can be below 1 gramme per tonne. However, at this stage in its production it will contain a number of impurities and will certainly not be in any usable form. It is first milled to release the metal before being refined and partly purified on site to produce dore gold bars. These bars will then be sent to dedicated refining operations to produce metal in a form that can be used by a variety of industries. The resulting output from the refiners may be in the form of bullion bars or "blank" jewellery. Fabricators will then take the refined product to make jewellery or will build it into other products such as electronics, which benefit from gold's physical properties–resistance to corrosion, thermal and electrical conductivity.

---

*Along California's Highway 49, tucked away in a beautiful valley in the Sierra Nevada foothills, is the tiny town of Coloma. Running through the centre of the village is a fork of the American River where, on 24 January 1848, James Marshall found some gold flakes in the streambed, sparking one of history's largest human migrations.

3.1.2   Financial Institutions

Outside of the physical supply chain sits two important entities: investment banks and central banks. Traditionally central bankers have been thought of as buyers of gold for reserve asset purposes. However, increasing pressures on central banks to make more effective use of their reserves has led this sector to become net sellers.

Investment banks will offer a variety of services that include:

- Helping mining companies ("producers") to manage their exposure to a change in market prices.
- Lending metal to refiners or fabricators to finance "in process" inventories.
- Borrowing gold from central banks.
- Helping central banks to manage their gold holdings.
- Acting as an intermediary between the main players in the production lifecycle.
- Trading with other banks.

From this brief description of the various entities within the supply chain, it is possible to envisage a simple supply and demand model. Without considering the relative size of each component, the main supply of gold comes from three main sources:

- New mine production
- Existing central bank holdings
- Recycling of scrap metal.

The demand for the metal is driven by:

- Jewellery
- Investment
- Industrial requirements.

3.1.3   The London gold market

Although gold is traded in a variety of different locations, London is the largest bullion market in the world. Although this may be true for over the counter (OTC) gold transactions, the main exchange-traded futures market is based in New York. The pre-eminence of London as the centre of OTC gold trading has led to the development of certain market conventions that are now accepted globally.

In terms of market size, statistics produced by the London Bullion Market Association (LBMA) for 2006 show a total of 258.3 million ounces transferred with a corresponding total monetary value of USD 156.60 billion [1]. Although this does not encompass the entire gold market, it perhaps shows that the market is not as large as other mature sectors such as foreign exchange. Daily turnover in the London bullion market is believed to be about 0.5% of the foreign exchange market.

To ensure that a common set of dealing standards exists, professional market associations often emerge to manage the interest of their members. For gold, the London Bullion Market Association (LBMA) fulfils this function for precious metals. In order to promote liquidity in the market the LBMA has established a category of membership known as market maker.

Market makers are required to offer ongoing quotes in spot, forward and option-based products throughout the trading day.

Another key feature is the existence of a leasing market. Since there is an abundant supply of gold above ground, many entities (particularly central banks) are willing to lend out their gold reserves for those who have a temporary need for the metal. The lender of the metal will be paid interest in the form of either gold or cash, similar to a cash deposit. This rate of interest is referred to as the lease rate. Although the main purpose of the leasing market is to borrow and lend metal, care must be taken when using these terms within other metal markets. For example, within the base metals market a borrow is a simultaneous purchase and sale for different value dates. This type of transaction will be analysed in greater detail in Chapter 4. Therefore the terms "leasing" and "deposits" should be used with respect to the gold market in order to avoid confusion.

Since metals may be of different purities, an element of standardisation is still vital even in OTC markets. Therefore, counterparties trading on a "loco London" basis (literally location London) will have an assurance that the metal traded will meet the criteria necessary for "London Good Delivery". This ensures that the different bars are fungible within the market and will be delivered to a London-based vault nominated by the seller. London Good Delivery means that a bar must conform to the following standards [2]:

- *Weight*
  Minimum gold content: 350 fine ounces (approximately 10.9 kilograms)
  Maximum gold content: 430 fine ounces (approximately 13.4 kilograms)
  The gross weight of a bar should be expressed in ounces troy, in multiples of 0.025, rounded down to the nearest 0.025 of an ounce troy.
- *Fineness*
  The minimum acceptable fineness is 995 parts per thousand fine gold.
- *Marks*
  Serial number
  Assay stamp of acceptable refiner
  Year of manufacture (expressed in four digits)
  Marks should be stamped on the larger of the two main surfaces of the bar.
- *Appearance*
  Bars should be of good appearance, free from surface cavities and other irregularities, layering and excessive shrinkage. They must be easy to handle and convenient to stack.

As an extension of these market standards there is also a "loco London" price. Settlement for the gold will take place two good London business days after trade date. Loco London is the normal basis for settlement for gold in the same way that New York is for the purchase or sale of US dollars. If an entity wishes to settle a transaction at another location or for a different level of purity, an adjustment to this benchmark price is normally made.

Reference is often made to the purity of gold, which can be expressed in different ways. When using carats, the purity of gold is measured on a scale of 1 to 24. For example, gold described as being 18 carats is equal to 18/24 of 1,000 parts – i.e. 750 fineness. However, the financial markets very rarely make reference to carats. London Good Delivery Bars are a minimum 995/1,000 fineness (or "two nines five" in the market parlance).

London Good Delivery Bars represent bars that have a gold content of between 350 and 430 fine ounces, although most bars are generally close to 400 ounces (12.5 kg/27 pounds).

Delivery will usually take place at the vault of a clearing member of the LBMA either on an allocated or an unallocated basis. Holding gold on an unallocated basis means that the metal is held in a vault in common with other holdings and the customer has a general entitlement. Holding gold on an unallocated basis incurs only minimal storage costs but reduces the holder to being an unsecured creditor – that is, the owner has a claim on the bank where the gold is held, but does not have title to specific bars. If gold is held on an allocated basis the metal is physically segregated from other customer holdings with detailed records being kept. Segregating the holding in an allocated account increases the degree of security as the holder is now secured but will incur substantially higher charges. The vast majority of market trading is done on an unallocated basis.

3.1.4   The price of gold

Like most metals, gold is denominated in US dollars (USD) and in terms of volume it is traded in troy ounces. A troy ounce is slightly less than a conventional avoirdupois ounce. Figure 3.1 illustrates the monthly nominal movement of the price of gold in USD over the period January 1977 to March 2007. The maximum price of gold (although not shown in this figure) occurred in 1980 when it reached a level of USD 850. It is often said of gold that it is a good hedge against inflation, but if we "eyeball" Figure 3.1 unscientifically, it is clear that the nominal price has not matched the movement of inflation over the period. The relationship between commodities and inflation is addressed in greater detail in Chapter 12 – on the role of commodities within an investment portfolio.

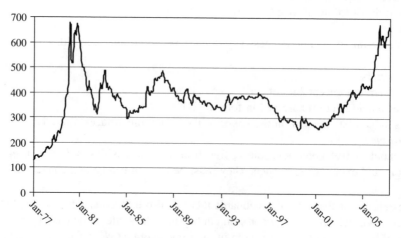

Figure 3.1   Monthly price of gold: January 1977–March 2007
Source: Barclays Capital.

3.1.5   Fixing the price of gold

Although the price of gold is market determined, its value has been fixed twice daily (at 10.30 am and 3.00 pm) since 1919, apart from a 15-year period between 1939 and 1954. The fixing process provides a benchmark value for the metal that facilitates the settlement of a variety of over-the-counter transactions. Clients who wish to execute deals at the market fix (rather than the price at any other time) will communicate their demands to one of the fixing institutions. The price will then be declared "fixed" when demand and supply within the fixing ring are deemed to be matched.

At the time of writing, the five members of the LBMA who participate in fixing the price of gold are:

- Bank of Nova Scotia
- Barclays Bank plc
- Deutsche Bank AG
- HSBC Bank USA NA (London branch)
- Societé Generale.

Although these five names are market-making members of the LBMA, the fixing is actually managed by the London Gold Fixing Company Limited.

In addition to the two daily fixes of the spot price, the market-making members of the LBMA operate a second fixing at 11 am London time. The purpose of this fixing is set the leasing rates for the market. At this second fixing the "GOFO" (gold forward offered) rate is set. However, instead of fixing the outright forward price, the market makers quote the GOFO rate as the difference between the spot and forward rate expressed as a percentage per annum. Since outright gold forward prices are normally higher than spot, this is also sometimes referred to as either the "contango bid" or the "gold swap rate". The GOFO rates are input to the Reuters page and sent to the LBMA, who ranks them, discards the highest and lowest, and takes the average of the remaining values. To derive the lease rates, the GOFO rates are simply subtracted from the prevailing USD LIBOR rates set by the financial markets (see Table 3.1).

3.2   GOLD PRICE DRIVERS

It is generally accepted that there is no direct link between the price of gold and the balance of supply and demand for the physical commodity. This is because gold is almost indestructible and there is a large inventory of the metal held above ground. This means that a sudden increase in demand could easily be met out of existing supplies. For example, in 2003 there was a net increase in supply over demand but the market still experienced a rise in price. In this instance the price rise was attributable to an increase in speculative investment demand as well a weakening in the dollar, which made the metal relatively cheaper for non-USD investors.

Arguably, the key exchange rate relationship for gold is EUR/USD with the correlation coefficient in the early twenty-first century measured as over +0.90. Although this statistic does not imply any causality, its importance can be explained by the fact that the cost of the metal for non-USD entities decreases as the USD weakens. This relationship with the exchange rate is often cited as the rational for viewing gold as a currency rather than as a commodity.

3.2.1   The supply of gold

Production of gold over the past 6,000 years has totalled between 125,000 and 150,000 tonnes, of which approximately 80% is still in existence with the remaining balance probably lost at sea. However, the majority of gold has been produced in relatively recent times with 90% of all gold having being mined since the Californian gold rush of the mid nineteenth century. After central bank attempts to control the market value of the metal proved to be futile, true liberalisation of the gold price really started to be seen in the 1960s and 1970s. This prompted a massive boom in production of the metal and is evidenced by the fact that 60% of all gold has been mined since the 1950s. At this time the metal was trading at about USD 35 per troy ounce, and by 1980 it had reached its all time peak of USD 850. The rise in price made production of the metal more attractive, which led to a rise in volume to the current level of about 2,500 tonnes per annum.

Although estimates vary considerably, as a rule of thumb it costs about USD 300 to produce an ounce of gold [3] and so production can be sensitive to price. However, it would be fair to say that this is true only over longer periods of time. Because of the significant costs of mothballing a mine, the operation is unlikely ever to close down. In times of high prices the producers will mine low-grade ore, and in low price environments they will try to mine higher grade ores. In the late 1990s, as the price of the metal fell back, many producers reduced the amount of expenditure on exploration, and production in subsequent years was relatively flat. It is also noticeable that the production of gold has experienced a certain geographical drift away from the mature markets of South Africa and North America to new areas of production such as Latin American and Russia. It is also worth noting that reserves of the metal are becoming more difficult and expensive to extract. For example, in South Africa, the producers are already operating at depths of 4 kilometres.

Figure 3.2 shows the way in which supply has evolved over the period from 1980 to 2007. The key features are:

- Overall production from mines has risen but still accounts for roughly the same proportion of output (about 70%).
- Official sales by central banks have become a key component of the available supply.
- As the price of the metal has risen there has been more incentive to recycle gold and hence the relative importance of scrap has increased. This aspect is also subject to regional

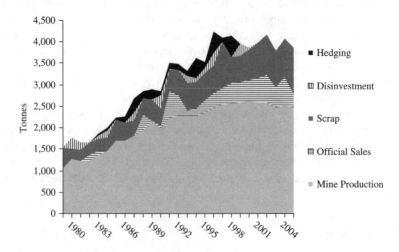

Figure 3.2 Components of gold supply, 1980–2007
Source: Barclays Capital, World Gold Council and GFMS.

differences. For example, in Asia it is quite common to trade old or unfashionable pieces for new items, unlike the West, where bid–offer spreads for this activity are not as attractive.

- Producer-hedging activities form an important component of supply.

The producers act of selling their production forward contributes to an increase in supply. This is because, on the other side of the transaction, there will be an investment bank, which then has an exposure to falling gold prices. To hedge this exposure the investment bank will sell gold in the spot market and borrow, probably from a central bank, to cover this sale. When the forward matures the producer delivers the gold at a fixed price and the bank uses this to repay the borrowing. It is this borrowing by the investment bank from the central bank that introduces more gold onto the spot market, therefore increasing the supply. This could, of course, work in the opposite direction. As the price of gold started to rise in the late 1990s and early twenty-first century, mining companies that had fixed the price of the metal for forward delivery came under pressure from shareholders to unwind the transactions to allow the companies to benefit from the rising price. As the positions were bought back the opposite effect occurred, the investment banks bought the metal for spot value and lent the gold, effectively reducing the available supply. In some respects this method of managing price risk from the investment bank's perspective is somewhat idealised; in reality the bank will have a significant number of positions on its books and so will manage their risk on a macro basis rather than hedging each individual deal.

South Africa has traditionally been the largest producer of the metal in recent times. However, over the last 20 years they have seen production fall in both absolute and percentage terms. In the early 1970s the country was producing about 1,000 tonnes per annum, which accounted for about 70% of total world production. Although it is still the largest producer by volume, by 2004 production had fallen to 345 tonnes (14% of global production) mainly due to ageing mines. Figure 3.3 illustrates the shift in production that has seen the growth in importance of emerging regions such as Latin America and Indonesia.

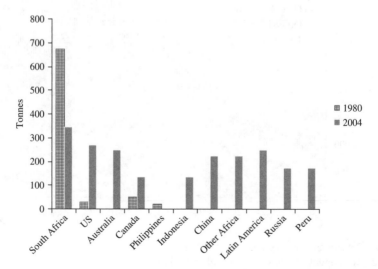

Figure 3.3   Production of gold by geographic location
Source: Barclays Capital.

In 2002, it was estimated that there were 1,227 million ounces or just over 38,000 tonnes of the metal remaining in the ground [4]. This represents about 15 years of production at current rates. However, as a result of exploration, new sources of the metal have been located so the estimate has remained fairly constant.

3.2.2 Demand for gold

The factors that influence the demand for gold include

- Investment
- Industrial uses
- Official Central Bank purchases
- Jewellery
- Producer hedging activities.

Since 1980, there has been a steady decline in the investment demand for gold. The poor returns on equities in the four years that followed 1999 forced many investment managers to seek out alternative investments, and commodities in general benefited from this trend. The largest component of demand is traditionally jewellery but it is very sensitive to increases in the price of gold. Figure 3.4 demonstrates the decline in demand for jewellery since the mid-1990s.

One of the points shown on Figure 3.5 is the changing role of central banks in the demand and supply equation. Like most financial institutions central banks hold assets,

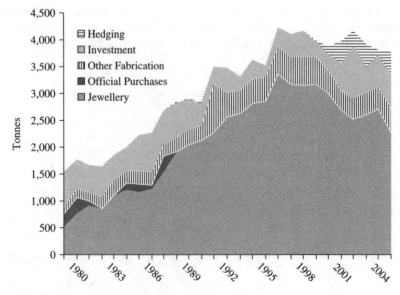

Figure 3.4 Components of gold demand, 1980–2007
Source: Barclays Capital, World Gold Council and GFMS.

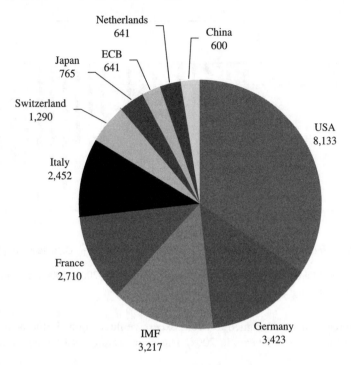

Figure 3.5   Central bank gold holdings (tonnes; figures as of March 2007)
Source: World Gold Council and GFMS.

which have traditionally included gold. The traditional argument for holding gold is that it is not affected by the economic policies of any one country; so holding the asset acts not only as a valuable diversifier but also gives an element of economic security. It has also been seen as an effective hedge against inflation and currency weakness. However, some governments have questioned the need to hold gold since it does not intrinsically earn any income. Although there is an active market for leasing gold the returns from this may be below alternative investments.

As of March 2007 the Federal Reserve in the USA still has the largest holding of reserves at some 8,133 tonnes, with Germany holding the second largest amount (3,423 tonnes). The United Kingdom has been one country that has been seeking to manage its gold reserves more actively and now only ranks 17th in the overall rankings with a holding of about 310 tonnes [4].

During the 1980s governments purchased a net amount of over 600 tonnes, but in the following two decades they disposed of about 4,400 tonnes on a net basis. Figure 3.6 shows the reported central bank activity over the period from 1980 to 2005 (with estimates for the period 2006–2008), showing the annual purchase and sales and the cumulative activity.

With the central banks holding a significant proportion of metal above ground this selling action pushed the price of gold towards USD 250 per ounce. As a result, pressure from producers led to the first European central bank gold agreement ("The Washington Agreement") in 1999. The original agreement existed for 5 years and was signed by 15 central

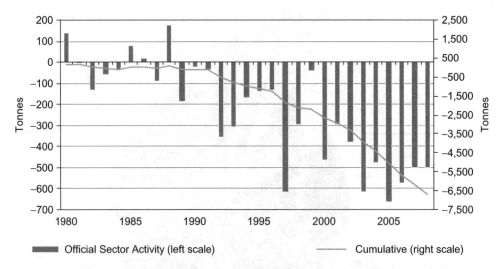

Figure 3.6   Central bank sales/purchases 1980–2008 (figures for 2006–2008 are estimates)
Source: Barclays Capital.

banks. The agreement was designed to avoid excessive fluctuations in the price of gold and was extended for a further 5 years in 2004. The main features of both agreements were:

- Gold will still be used as part of the signatories' monetary reserves.
- The signatories to the agreement will not enter as sellers, apart from already decided sales.
- The initial 1999 agreement stated that sales would not exceed 400 tonnes annually or 2,000 tonnes cumulatively until 2004.
- The revised agreement in 2004 stated that annual sales would not exceed 500 tonnes with total sales until 2009 (date of next revision of the deal) not exceeding 2,500 tonnes.
- There will be no expansion in the use of gold leases, futures and options.

The 2004 agreement was also signed by 15 central banks although the make-up of signatories was slightly different. The UK government chose not to sign the agreement and was replaced by the Bank of Greece. The UK government stated that it did not have plans to sell its gold holdings and was still committed to holding the metal as a reserve asset.

Jewellery demand has risen by over 440% since 1980 and reached 2,267 tonnes by the end of 2006. This now accounts for about 67% of all demand. Looking at the difference between the size of this component in 1980 and in 2006, the increase has been largely attributable to the long-term decline in the gold price from its peak in 1980. However, taking a much shorter time horizon, demand for jewellery has declined as the price of gold has risen from the relatively low values seen in the early to mid-1990s. Jewellery has absorbed not only the increase in supply from new mine production but also the switch by central banks from being buyers to sellers.

In 1980, the year that gold witnessed its highest ever nominal price, investment accounted for over 360 tonnes, which was about 70% of total demand. During the 1980s it averaged 30% but during the 1990s it only accounted for only about 8% of the total. By 2001, the figure had fallen to 6% but with the rise in the price of gold during the next few years it rose briefly, fell quite sharply in 2004 to 306 tonnes, before recovering in 2006 to 637 tonnes. Part of the reason for the increase in investment demand has been the introduction of Exchange Traded Funds (ETFs). These are securities that can be traded on a stock exchange that tracks the price of gold. The securities are backed 100% by physical gold holdings and do not offer leverage in the same way as derivatives. Leverage is the ability to use a relatively small amount of capital to control a much larger exposure; thus, if an investor were to use, say, a gold future to gain exposure to the metal, he would only be required to pay an initial deposit ("margin") to control an investment whose profit and loss would be calculated on a larger exposure.

When analysing the drivers of demand it was noted that producer hedging had an impact on the demand and supply balance. Although producers will have a natural tendency to hedge their production by selling it forward, the rise in the price of gold had an effect on this activity. Pressure from shareholders forced many companies to unwind their forward sales in order to benefit from the rising price of the metal. As the producers unwound their hedges, the banks on the other side of the transaction would offset their exposures by buying the metal in the spot market and leasing the metal for the duration of the transaction. The combination of this purchase and leasing activity was not only to increase demand, but also led to an increase in the price of the metal, creating something of a virtuous circle for producers and pushed lease rates to all time historic lows.

3.2.3   The Chinese effect

At the time of writing, the industrialisation of China was having a significant upward impact on the price of many commodities. However, the impact on gold was less clear. Although there may be a tendency to assume that the influence of China is purely on the demand side, it does not seem unreasonable to suggest that there will be an impact on supply. As was shown earlier, production of the metal is gradually moving away from traditional markets and potentially China may evolve to become a major supplier of the metal through new mine production.

3.3   THE GOLD LEASING MARKET

One of the factors that distinguish the gold market from that of, say, base metals, is the large amount of metal that already exists above ground. This excess of metal has led to the development of an active leasing market. In a leasing transaction the lender will temporarily transfer title of the gold to another entity for an agreed period of time in return for earning interest either in gold or in cash. From the lender's point of view this could be a useful way of earning income on an asset that otherwise has no intrinsic return. However, it should always be borne in mind that an opportunity cost exists, as gold interest rates are generally lower than those of currencies. The holder of gold can always sell the metal and invest the proceeds in a simple USD deposit; and with pressure coming to bear on central banks to make gold "earn its keep", many entities have been tempted to go down this path, particularly in a low lease rate environment. A typical series of quotes are shown on Table 3.1 (for value, 11 April 2005).

The GOFO rate is the difference between the spot and forward price of gold expressed as a percentage per annum. As indicated earlier, this is sometimes referred to as the gold swap rate as it relates to the most popular type of interbank transaction. The GOFO rate

Table 3.1 Market rates for gold

Maturity	GOFO	LIBOR	LIBOR minus GOFO
1 month	2.85000%	2.92000%	0.07000%
2 month	2.95714%	3.05000%	0.09286%
3 month	3.04286%	3.13000%	0.08714%
6 month	3.27429%	3.39000%	0.11571%
12 month	3.60286%	3.78875%	0.18589%

Source: LBMA.

indicates the rate at which the bank will sell gold for spot value (and receive US dollars in return) and sell the same amount of gold for forward value (and repay the US dollars with interest). Expressed in this manner, it is effectively the cost of borrowing dollars using gold as collateral. This GOFO rate is defined as an offer rate (the bank is selling the gold for spot value) but is also sometimes referred to as the contango bid. The use of the word "bid" in this context relates to the fact that the metal is being bought for forward delivery. This type of swap deal is very common as the US dollars can be borrowed at a more favourable rate than the prevailing LIBOR level. The favourable rate is achieved by the fact that gold is being exchanged at the same time. This mechanism could of course be used to lend money with the bank buying the gold spot (thereby delivering US dollars) with an agreement to resell the gold at an agreed time in the future (receiving US dollars in return). An example of this type of gold swap (not to be confused with a gold interest rate swap) is given later in the chapter, where central bank yield enhancement strategies are considered.

The LIBOR minus GOFO rate is the theoretical rate at which a bank would lend gold (ignoring issues such as credit considerations). This 11am mean fixing is used as a benchmark for the settlement of a number of transactions.

On the supply side of the lease market the main players include central banks and institutional investors, all of whom are seeking to enhance the return on their physical holdings. On the demand side a variety of factors could impact the level of lease rates. They include:

- The level of money market interest rates (e.g. LIBOR, although this relationship has experienced times of dislocation).
- Producer hedging programmes.
- Demand from jewellery manufacturers.
- Demand from speculative short selling.

Firstly, there is the absolute level of interest rates. It would seem reasonable to assume that a fall in interest rates will cause lease rates to fall. Secondly, one of the key reasons why gold is borrowed is to facilitate producer-hedging programmes. As producers reduce the hedging of their mined product this will lead to a fall in lease rates. This was covered in the section that analysed demand and supply price drivers. The lease market displays a term structure in which different rates are charged depending on the maturity of the transaction. As a rule of thumb, producer-hedging activity tends to drive the longer end of the curve towards the 12-month maturity and beyond, while central bank lending activity tends to be

Table 3.2   Long-dated lease rates

Maturity	Bid rate	Offer rate
2 years	0.16%	0.25%
3 years	0.26%	0.37%
4 years	0.37%	0.47%
5 years	0.47%	0.57%
7 years	0.59%	0.72%
10 years	0.70%	0.84%

Source: Barclays Capital.

focused on shorter maturities. A change in the level of activity of either of these entities can cause the shape of the curve to change.

The curve can extend out to about 10 years and indicative rates beyond 12 months quoted for value on 11 April 2005 are shown in Table 3.2. The rates are zero coupon annualised, quoted on an actual/360 day basis.

However, there are exceptions to this generalised explanation of how the curve moves. For example, certain producer-hedging products (e.g. a floating rate forward or a spot deferred contract) derive their value from shorter-term rates and therefore drive that part of the curve.

Another factor influencing the level of lease rates is the utilisation of the market by refiners or fabricators. For example, in normal circumstances one would expect a jewellery fabricator to have to buy the gold and then transform it into jewellery. However, he may have to pay for the raw materials before actually selling the gold, and this may involve having to borrow US dollars, which leaves him open to an element of price risk (i.e. the difference between what he pays for the raw material and what he eventually raises from the final sale).

Another alternative is for the fabricator to borrow gold from a bank and use that to produce the final product. When the end product is sold, he can then use the proceeds of the sale to buy the physical gold from the spot market and repay the gold loan. In this way the price risk is eliminated and as the cost of leasing the gold is lower than the US dollar LIBOR rate, he will have paid to finance a purchase of metal from a producer.

If a speculator believed that the price of gold was going to fall then he could sell the metal for spot delivery, borrow it on the leasing market to fulfil the sale, and wait for the price of gold to fall before buying it back from the market, hopefully at a lower price. The purchase would be used to repay the loan of the metal. The profit to the short seller would be the difference between the buy and sell price less the lease rate paid. However, in a rising price scenario this strategy may be less popular, and so no demand for borrowing gold is created, thus putting further downward pressure on lease rates.

It is also possible for lease rates to turn negative. For example, in late April 2005 one short-term lease rate quote was – 0.07% (bid), 0.00% (offer). In other words, at the bid price the market maker was willing to borrow gold but charge the lender for the transaction! This was attributable to the fact that the costs for storing gold on an unallocated basis are included in the quoted rate. If the rate goes to zero, these costs will still have to be paid, so the rate will go negative.

The rates presented in Table 3.2 were applicable to leasing transactions where the interest payments were to be made in cash. However, it is possible for the payments to be made in gold, the so-called "gold in gold" contracts. The interest rates for these transactions differ from those charged for cash transactions. Assume that we have a 10-year lease rate (zero coupon, actual 360 day basis) of 0.75%, a gold swap rate of 3.75% (defined here as the annual percentage difference between the spot and the forward rate) and a spot gold price of USD 425.40. If we assume that a financial institution lends out 100,000 ounces for this 10-year period (3,650 days, ignoring leap years), then this would give the following payment in ounces:

$$100,000 \times 0.75\% \times 3,650/360 = 7,604$$

The monetary equivalent for forward value in 10 years can be determined by applying today's 10-year forward price to the number of ounces settled. The 10-year forward price is calculated as:

$$\text{Spot price} \times [1 + (\text{Swap rate} \times \text{Days in period}/360)]$$

$$= \text{USD } 425.40 \times [1 + (0.0375 \times 3,650/360)] = \text{USD } 587.14$$

which, when applied to the settlement amount in ounces, gives a forward value of USD 4,464,617 (7,604 ounces x USD 587.14).

If the same transaction were done for payment in cash, we would need to include the current spot rate to give:

$$100,000 \times \text{USD } 425.40 \times 0.75\% \times 3,650/360 = \text{USD } 3,234,741$$

To make both transactions equal in monetary terms 10 years forward, the lease rate for "gold in gold" transactions would have to be 0.54335%, which is calculated as:

$$[(\text{USD } 3,234,741/\text{USD } 587.14) \times (360/3,650)]/100,000$$

3.4   APPLICATIONS OF DERIVATIVES

Having analysed the physical market, we are now in a position to look at a variety of derivative applications. The analysis is not exhaustive, with certain structures emphasised to avoid repetition in subsequent chapters. Typical derivative deal sizes for the gold market are presented in Table 3.3.

Table 3.3   Typical market transaction sizes

Product	Standard Interbank transaction size (ozs)	Minimum size (ozs)	Large size (ozs)
Spot	5,000–10,000	100	>100,000
Deposit	32,000	5,000	>250,000
Gold swap	32,000	5,000	>250,000
Outright forward	5,000–10,000	100	>100,000
Lease rate swap	32,000	5,000	>250,000
FRA	32,000	5,000	>250,000

3.4.1   Producer strategies

Forwards

Arguably, one of the main risk management issues for producers is the amount of revenue generated from either current or future production. From a logistical perspective the producer needs to match the timing of hedging transactions with planned future mining activity. The interested reader is referred to the research document written by Jessica Cross (2001) for an outline of producer motivations and hedging philosophies.

Given the relatively large amount of supply of gold that exists above ground, the forward price of gold is usually in contango (that is, where the price for future delivery is greater than the current price - see Chapter 1 for more details). The relationship between the forward price and the current spot price can be derived using the time value of money principles. That is, the forward price of gold can be calculated as:

$$\text{Forward price} = \text{Spot price} + [(\text{Spot price} \times \text{Gold forward rate})/360 \times \text{Actual days}]$$

The gold forward rate part of the expression is sometimes also referred to as the contango, and accounts for the difference between the spot and the forward price. From a producer's perspective a sizeable contango may be attractive as it could encourage that company to sell its production forward.

An increase in the forward price could come about as a result of (all other things being equal):

- An increase in the spot price
- An increase in LIBOR
- A decrease in the lease rate
- Increasing the maturity of a forward deal.

There is also a currency related consideration. If the producer is not a USD-based company, a strengthening in the dollar with respect to their home currency will increase the domestic currency proceeds of any sale.

Producers have typically favoured hedging products that are easy to understand, cheap to purchase and do not present processing difficulties. It comes as no surprise to find that simple forward products are often the most preferred structures. However, there is evidence that producers are willing to use both vanilla and exotic options such as barriers [5].

It would be reasonable to assume that producers of gold will always be seeking to maximise their future revenues. Take, as an example, producer who wishes to achieve a degree of price certainty over future production. It is possible that the hedging of future revenues may also be associated with some form of bank financing – that is, the bank will only lend money to a producer if that producer takes steps to ensure the stability of future income in order to service the debt.

The producer approaches a bank asking for a price for delivery of gold in, say, 6 months' time. The price quoted will be driven by the cost of hedging the bank's own exposure. If the bank does not hedge itself, then in 6 months' time it will take delivery of gold at the pre-agreed price and will then be holding an asset whose current market value could be lower (or higher) than the price paid to the producer.

To avoid the risk that the price of gold will fall, the bank executes a series of transactions on the trade date that will mitigate this risk. Since the bank is agreeing to receive a fixed amount of gold in the future, it sells the same amount in the spot market. However, the bank has sold a quantity of metal now that it will not take delivery of until a future time period – 6 months in this case. In order to fulfil the spot commitment it leases the gold until maturity of the contract with the producer.

Having sold the gold spot and borrowed to cover the sale, the bank is now holding dollars. Since the bank would be wishing to manage its cash balances efficiently, these dollars would now be invested until the producer delivers the gold in 6 months' time. As a result, it is possible at the inception of the trade to identify all the associated hedging cashflows, allowing the bank to quote a price that will ensure no loss at the point of delivery. This is why the forward price is higher than the spot price. The bank is effectively charging the producer for borrowing gold and crediting him with the interest earned by putting the US dollars on deposit.

The maturing principal plus interest on the USD cash deposit is used to pay the producer on the maturity of the contract. The gold received from the producer is used to repay the gold leased from the central bank.

In this example the maximum amount the bank will pay the producer cannot exceed the proceeds received from the spot sale plus the interest received from the dollar deposit less the fee to the lender of the gold.

A simple example may help to illustrate the point. We will assume that the producer asks for a 6-month (182-day) forward price. For simplicity, we will base the calculations on a single ounce and use the quoted prices for value at 11 April 2005. The trader sells the metal for spot value at USD 425.40 and in order to complete the delivery he borrows from the local central bank for 6 months at a lease rate of 0.11570% per annum. The dollars received from the spot sale are put on deposit for 6 months at LIBOR to earn the prevailing rate of 3.39% per annum. Performing a quick calculation, the trader calculates that the borrowing fee equates to USD 0.2488 (spot price × lease rate × 182/360) and that he will earn USD 7.29 from the deposit (spot sale proceeds × LIBOR × 182/360). So the maximum amount the bank can afford to pay the producer is USD 432.4418. This is calculated as spot sale proceeds plus interest on the LIBOR deposit minus the leasing cost.

The forward price, therefore, is simply the spot price plus the cost of carrying an underlying hedge. It is important to note that the shorter the time to maturity the smaller will be the differential between the spot and forward price since the hedge is carried for a shorter period. Indeed, if we were to recalculate the forward price applicable for a single fixed date in the future, the differential would reduce every day (all other things being equal). On the final date the two prices will have converged, although not necessarily in a linear fashion; the rate of convergence is dependent on how the components of the forward price move.

When interpreting the interbank quotations and the GOFO rates, we have to rework the above example and express the figures in a different manner to match market convention. Instead of expressing the values for the spot and forward market as a price, the convention is to quote the GOFO/swap rate/contango bid, which is defined as the percentage per annum difference between the spot and forward price. It is in effect the net carry element of the transaction. So, for the above 6-month transaction, the GOFO rate is calculated as:

$$\frac{\text{Forward price}}{\text{Spot price}} - 1 \times \frac{360}{182}$$

$$\frac{432.44}{425.40} - 1 \times \frac{360}{182} = 3.27\%$$

This was also the 6-month GOFO rate quoted for that particular maturity – see Table 3.1.

From this basic structure, investment banks have developed a wide range of variations on this simple theme. A comprehensive analysis of the relative merits of each product is provided in the publication "Gold Derivatives: the market view" (Cross, 2001). The following is short description of some of the main products. With all of these structures the structuring bank simply alters the constituents of the forward price (LIBOR, lease rate, maturity), which allows the producer more flexibility to express views on the direction of certain market parameters.

- *Spot deferred*: In this transaction the two parties agree the spot price at the outset. However, there is no fixed maturity and the deal can be terminated with the appropriate amount of notice. The final forward price is based on the daily movement of the LIBOR and lease rates. This is in effect a rolling contract where gold is initially sold for spot value (trade date plus two business days); the following day, the position is rolled forward by buying back and then reselling for spot value, which effectively pushes the settlement date a further day forward. As part of the transaction, the dollar proceeds earned from the sale are invested on an overnight basis while lease costs are incurred to cover the short sale. The transaction settles daily with a debit/credit being made to the customer's account based on the movement of LIBOR and the lease rates. This structure allows the producer to earn the short-term contango.
- *Floating rate forwards*: Here the contract fixes the appropriate spot gold price and LIBOR components of the contango for the maturity of the contract. However, the final forward price is not calculated until maturity and is based on an average value of a short-term lease rate over the life of the deal (e.g. the 3-month lease rate). This is constructed by combining a "vanilla" forward with a gold interest rate swap.

  In the pricing of a forward contract we showed that the forward price was constructed as:

  Forward price = Spot price + [(Spot price × Gold forward rate)/360 × Actual days]

  Let us assume that the producer enters into a conventional forward transaction with a 12-month maturity. If, in addition to entering into this conventional forward transaction, the producer transacts an interest rate swap where he receives a single fixed lease rate at maturity and pays a 3-month variable lease rate. The two fixed lease rates should net out, leaving the producer with a forward contract that has a fixed LIBOR component and a floating 3-month lease rate (Figure 3.7).
- *The flat rate forward*: In this contract the producer sells its production forward in stages over an agreed time period. For example, the producer may agree a contract with a 12-month final maturity with the gold being delivered every 3 months. Under normal

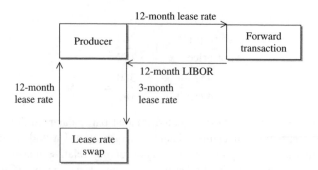

Figure 3.7 Floating rate forward

forward pricing theory this would involve a different price for each settlement. However, as the product name suggests, the contract is structured in such a way that each of the four deliveries takes place at a single forward price.

The single price is based on the weighted average of the forward prices at each settlement date. The calculation is the sum of the forward rates at each of the delivery dates weighted by a discount factor of the same maturity, all divided by the sum of the discount factors.

Although not strictly a forward deal an interesting variant is:

- *Convertible forward*: This can be constructed by combining the purchase of a vanilla put option and the sale of a reverse knock-in call option, both with the same strike. This transaction is structured to have zero cost by manipulating the barrier on the reverse knock-in call. The strategy is based on the principle of put–call parity to create a synthetic forward. The mathematical form of put–call parity varies according to the type of underlying asset (see, for example, Tompkins, 1994) but can be expressed in a convenient way as:

$$+C - P = +F$$

That is, the purchase of a call $(+C)$ and the sale of a put $(-P)$ with the same strike, notional and maturity will be equivalent to having purchased the underlying asset $(+F)$. For the convertible forward structure, the initial position is that the producer owns a given amount of the physical gold in addition to which it has bought protection against a price decline by buying a put. In addition, the producer sells a reverse knock-in call option. This barrier option has a trigger point placed above the spot rate, which will activate the option if the price of gold rises. This makes the barrier an "up and in" call option. If the trigger is hit activating the short call, combining this with a long put will give the producer a synthetic short position in gold (e.g. $-C + P = -F$), which, when combined with their long physical holding in the metal, will ensure them of a fixed delivery price.

Revaluation of forward positions

The value of any forward position will change as the underlying price drivers change. For example, a producer may be tempted to unwind a forward hedge if the spot price of gold has risen substantially, since it would now be better to sell the gold in the spot market.

Assume that the producer has fixed a 6-month forward price for the sale of gold at a price of USD 432.44. Four months later, we will assume that the spot price of gold has risen, moving the 2-month forward price to USD 445.00. The forward position is now unfavourable relative to the underlying market. The producer contacts an investment bank requesting a price to unwind the hedge. This "break cost" will simply be the "mark to market" (i.e. the current value) of the transaction. The producer has an agreement to deliver a fixed amount of gold for a fixed price. To neutralise this exposure the producer could do a reversing deal, where, for the same maturity date, he could agree to buy the same amount of gold and pay a fixed sum of money. The break cost is simply the difference in value between the original deal and the reversing position, which is settled in cash.

Using the figures quoted above, the producer would lose USD 12.56 (USD 445 - USD 432.44) at the maturity of the transaction. Since this maturity is still 2-months away this would need to be present valued using an appropriate 2-month zero coupon rate. If we assume that the 2-month zero rate is 5% and there are 62 days to maturity, the calculation is:

$$\frac{\$12.56}{(1 + 0.05 \times 62/360)} = \$12.45$$

This represents the mark to market loss. If the producer were a non-USD entity this would then have to be translated back to the producer's domestic currency, using the 2-month forward currency rate.

Options

In addition to using forward-based strategies, gold producers can hedge their production using options. Evidence [5] suggests that the most favoured products tend to be relatively simple strategies.

The simplest structure for a producer is to buy a put option. This gives them the right but not the obligation to sell a pre-agreed amount of gold to the bank at some future date at a price agreed today. Let us assume that the producer decides to buy the put at a strike price of USD 400 per ounce with the current forward market at USD 432.44. This option is out-of-the-money as the strike price (USD 400) is less favourable than the underlying forward market (USD 432.44). Since the producer has bought a European style option that can only be exercised on maturity, the underlying is the forward market rather than the spot market.

The put option will give the producer protection if the market falls below this strike level but will allow him to walk away from the contract if the price of gold rises. A common misconception concerning this strategy is that it would be appropriate if the producer expected the price of gold to fall. If the producer held this view, it would be cheaper for him to sell the gold forward, particularly if the market were in contango. The purchase of a put would be appropriate if the producer felt that the price of gold would rise but wanted insurance in case his view of the market was wrong.

Although the purchase of a put option is a simple strategy, it is often unpopular due to the premium cost. With implied volatilities for gold often close to 20% (for short-term options) the premium on a substantial production target could be very high. For example, pricing a 6-month option with a strike of USD 400, a forward price of USD 432.44 and an implied volatility of 20% would return a theoretical premium of USD 10.54 per ounce. This represents about 2% of the current spot price, which on a position of, say, 50,000 ounces would represent a substantial up-front cashflow (USD 527,000).

To make the option strategies more popular, banks often recommended premium reduction strategies such as the "min-max". When buying a put option the producer can walk away if the price of gold rises sharply. The ability to benefit from the appreciation of the price is unlimited. However, if the producer believes that gold may rise in price but that the rise will not be substantial, he can take on risk in areas where the metal is not expected to trade. The producer sells options (calls in this case) with the strike set at such a level as to return an overall zero premium. Using the same pricing inputs as before, buying a put with a strike of USD 400 and selling a call option with a strike of USD 470.82 will return a zero net premium. The effect of this structure is suggested in its name: it fixes the maximum and minimum price for the sale of the production. If the price of gold is less than USD 400, the producer exercises the put option and buys the gold at the strike price USD 400. If the price of gold appreciates sharply to, say, USD 480, the call options will be exercised against the producer, who will have to deliver the gold at a price equal to the strike (USD 470.82). Between the two strikes, neither option is exercised and the producer simply sells the gold in the open market.

Another strategy that is sometimes used is the sale of out-of-the-money call options while holding an equal amount of gold – a strategy sometimes referred to as a "covered call". This technique that can be used for enhancing returns and is analysed below in relation to the strategies employed by central banks.

3.4.2   Central Bank strategies

Yield enhancement

In recent years some governments have decided to sell off part of their gold holdings as the yield that can be earned by lending it out is less than that for simple US dollar deposits. Despite this, central banks still have considerable holdings of the metal and on a day-to-day basis may seek to earn a return on the holdings by either leasing a portion of them to the market or executing a variety of strategies to enhance the yield. For those central banks actively involved in the lending market, it is not uncommon for them to benchmark, their lending performance. As with any benchmark the policy could be aimed at either matching or exceeding a given target.

In addition to managing a country's gold reserves, the central bank may play a variety of other roles. For example, the Bank of England acts as a custodian of physical gold for either other central banks or a number of commercial banks that are active in the market. The bank is also prepared to accept gold deposits from other central banks and lend them on in the Bank of England's own name. However, it makes a charge for this service due to the credit risk it is absorbing. The amount of gold lent in the market by the Bank of England has varied between 45 tonnes to well in excess of 100 tonnes (Young, 2003).

Cash markets

One of the simplest ways in which a central bank can earn income from its gold holdings is through a straightforward gold deposit. This would simply involve the transfer of ownership of the gold to the leasing institution. The central bank will then earn interest at the current market rate. For example, a 1-month (31-day) deposit of 30,000 ounces based on a lease rate of 0.07% and a spot price of USD 425.40 would earn the central bank USD 769.27

$(30,000 \times 0.07\% \times 31/360 \times \text{USD } 425.40 = \text{USD } 769.27)$. This interest can be paid in either gold ounces or cash.

An alternative mechanism is the gold swap. As the name suggests, the central bank temporarily exchanges its physical holdings of gold for cash (typically US dollars). This deal would involve the sale of gold for spot value with a simultaneous agreement to repurchase it at a forward date. The amount of gold that is traded is the same for both legs of the transaction, but with different spot and forward prices. Although this may seem like a loan it is actually a sale and repurchase, with title to the gold passing from the selling institution. The deal maturities do not need to conform to the spot/forward example made here. It would also be possible to negotiate a deal where the first leg starts at a forward date and the second leg is completed at a date further forward in time (a forward/forward deal).

The motivation for the central bank is that it has obtained USD cash, which it is now free to invest for the duration of the transaction. If the forward price of the gold is above the spot price (i.e. the market is in contango) the central bank will have to repay a higher dollar amount than was originally borrowed. However, since the difference between the spot and forward price is driven by USD LIBOR less the lease rate, the bank has effectively borrowed the dollars at a rate lower than an unsecured money market deposit.

The following example illustrates the concept in greater detail. Let us assume that the following conditions exist:

Spot price	USD 425.40
Deal size	200,000 ounces
3-month contango	3.04286% (also referred to as the "swap rate" in this instance)
3-month LIBOR	3.13%
Days in period	92

As part of the first leg the bank sells 200,000 ounces to an investment bank and receives back the USD equivalent at the spot price (USD $425.40 \times 200,000 = \text{USD } 85,080,000$). Title of the gold passes to the investment bank but the terms of the deal require that bank to repurchase the metal in 3 months' time. During this time period the central bank may invest the USD proceeds and earn LIBOR. At the maturity of the deal the same amount of gold is returned to the central bank, which must repay the USD at the forward rate that prevailed at the outset of the transaction. This forward rate is calculated in the same manner as illustrated earlier, but an alternative formula is:

$$\text{Spot price} \times \left[1 + \left(\text{Swap rate} \times \frac{\text{Days in swap period}}{360} \right) \right]$$

Using the market data presented, this formula returns a value of USD 428.71, and from this we can see that the central bank borrows USD 425.40 for 92 days and repays USD 428.71, representing a cost of 3.04286%. This cost is below the current 3-month LIBOR rate of 3.13%.

Forwards

If a central bank is running a large lending book, it will be exposed to downward movements in the lease rate. It may be possible to hedge this exposure using forward rate agreements or lease rate swaps.

Forward Rate Agreements

A forward rate agreement (FRA) is a contract for difference where two entities agree to exchange cashflows based on a fixed lease rate that was agreed at the outset and an actual lease rate that occurs at a pre-agreed date in the future. The fixed lease rate that is set at the start of the transaction is a forward lease rate, while the rate against which the transaction is settled is a floating rate benchmark lease rate (i.e. the LIBOR minus GOFO rate on a particular date).

A forward lease rate is a rate of interest that applies to a period that starts and ends in the future but whose value is known today. Assume that a lender wishes to deposit gold for 12 months. He could:

- deposit the gold for a 12-month period at, say, 1.50% p.a.;
- deposit the gold for 6 months at, say, 1.00% p.a. and then rollover the loan for another 6 months at the 6-month rate that prevails at the time.

Most people's reaction is that the decision depends on the lender's view of where 6-month rates will be in 6 months' time. However, at the initial trade date the value of the two investment choices must be identical. If one investment were superior, demand and supply would erode the advantage over time. For the two choices to be identical, the 6-month rate in 6 months' time must be approximately 2% p.a. (ignoring compounding). But what exactly is this rate that we have just derived? It is certainly not the actual 6-month rate that will apply for the period; that will only be known in 6 months' time. It is perhaps most accurate to think of it as a breakeven rate – the rate that equalises the return on both strategies. It is also the forward rate – a rate of interest whose value is known today but applies to a future time period. In some financial markets (e.g. interest rates) traders use it as the "best guess" as to where actual spot rates will be in the future. To illustrate this anecdotally, the author recalls a discussion with an interest rate derivatives trader concerning the methodology he applied to quoting forward interest rates. The trader simply took a view as to where the central bank base rate would be at a particular time in the future, and added a few basis points to reflect credit risk. Very clearly this was an example of using FRAs to speculate on the future spot level.

To derive the implied forward rate (more commonly referred to as the "forward rate") from a pair of spot starting lease rates, the required formula is:

$$\frac{\left[1 + \text{Lease rate}_{long} \times (\text{Days}_{long}/360)\right]}{\left[1 + \text{Lease rate}_{short} \times (\text{Days}_{short}/360)\right]} - 1 \times \frac{360}{\text{Days}_{long} - \text{Days}_{short}}$$

where Lease rate$_{long}$ = lease rate to longest maturity date
       Lease rate$_{short}$ = lease rate to shortest maturity date
       Days$_{long}$ = number of days to longest maturity date
       Days$_{short}$ = number of days to shortest maturity date.

Returning to the FRA example, if the observed 3-month lease rate is 0.08714% and the 6-month lease rate is 0.11571%, the theoretical value for the implied forward lease rate for the period 3 to 6 months is 0.144456% (assuming 92 days for the 3-month period and 183 days for the 6-month period). However, it should be noted that this is not a market observed forward lease rate but is simply derived using the formula presented above. The actual market price of the FRA is what someone is willing to pay for the deal. It will, however, be fairly close to this theoretical or "fair" value.

FRAs are quoted on a bid–offer basis:

Bid	*Offer*
0.12%	0.16%
Buy FRA	Sell FRA
Pay fixed rate	Receive fixed rate
Receive floating	Pay floating

The floating rate is defined as the actual lease rate that prevails at the settlement of the contract (i.e. the LIBOR minus GOFO rate).

If a central bank is a net lender of gold to the market, it will have an exposure to a fall in lease rates. In this case it will choose to become a seller of an FRA. By selling the FRA it will receive the pre-agreed fixed lease rate and pay the actual lease rate that occurs when the forward period is reached. Let us assume that the central bank wishes to lock in the 3-month lease rate in 3 months' time. It sells a "3 × 6" FRA at a fixed rate of 0.144456% on a notional of 100,000 ounces and a spot gold price of USD 425.40. When describing the type of FRA ("3 × 6"), the first number relates to the start of the forward period, and the second to the final maturity date, with the difference between the two dates representing the tenor of the transaction.

As the FRA is traded with spot value, it will become effective 2 days after the transaction date. The next important date is 2 days before the start of the period to which the forward rate applies. This is referred to as the "fixing date" and is the date when the cashflows to be exchanged are actually quantified. At this point the actual lease rate that will apply for the next 3 months is agreed between the two entities. The central bank will also arrange for its deposit to become effective from the same date. Two days ("settlement date") later both counterparties will actually settle the cashflows due under the FRA. This seems strange since the cashflows relating to the underlying lease transaction will not materialise until the end of the 3-month period. This would suggest that one of the parties is receiving an advantage by receiving cashflows 3 months before they are due. To take account of the time value of money, the FRA settlement amount is present valued. The discount rate is LIBOR minus the GOFO rate of the same maturity against which the contract is settled. The final maturity date in 3-months' time does not involve any movement of cash under the FRA, which effectively terminated on the settlement date. At this date only the underlying leasing transaction matures. Like the majority of derivatives, FRAs are transacted on a notional basis, so there is no initial exchange of physical gold.

To illustrate the example let us assume that 3 months after the trade date interest rates have drifted down and the 3-month LIBOR minus GOFO rate fixes at 0.05%. The settlement amount on the FRA is calculated as:

$$\frac{(+0.144456\% - 0.05\%) \times 100,000 \times (91/360)}{(1 + 0.05\% \times (91/360))} = 23.87 \text{ ounces}$$

If the base price for the transaction was USD 425.40, then the amount due to the central bank is USD 10,155.69. Payment is made to the central bank, as the rate it had agreed to receive (0.144456%) was greater than the rate it had agreed to pay (0.05%).

What is the net impact of the FRA? Underlying this transaction is a regular 3-month gold deposit, so if the gold had been lent out for 3 months at 0.05%, the income on this would be 12.63 ounces, which at a rate of USD 425.40 would give interest of USD 5,376.58. If one combines this with the undiscounted proceeds of the FRA (USD 10,157.01) and expresses this as a percentage per annum of the amount lent (100,000 ounces at USD 425.40 per ounce) we would have a return of:

$$\text{USD } 15,533.68/\text{USD } 42,540,000 \times (360/91) = 0.144456\%$$

which, of course, is equal to the original fixed lease rate agreed on the FRA.

Lease rate swaps

A similar alternative to the forward rate agreement is a lease rate swap. The swap is an exchange of cashflows, fixed for floating, based on an agreed notional amount (expressed in ounces) and with a maturity of greater than one year. Cashflows are exchanged on a regular basis with the exact payment frequency being negotiated between the two entities. Typically the cashflows would be exchanged every 3 months and where the payment dates coincide, there would be a net settlement. The floating rate is again based on the LIBOR minus GOFO rate (e.g. the lease rate) that prevails at the start of each period. The single fixed rate can be thought of as a form of weighted average of the expected lease rates that will apply over the course of the transaction.

Swaps are quoted on a bid–offer spread basis, in the same fashion as the FRA. However, participants may say they are either paying fixed/buying the swap or receiving fixed/selling the swap. The use of the terms buy and sell are somewhat unclear but should be applied in relation to the floating side. That is, if I buy a swap I am buying a stream of floating lease rates for which the cost is a single fixed lease rate.

How, therefore, could a lease rate swap be used by a central bank to manage its gold lending programme? We will use the same rates quoted earlier for value 11 April 2005. These rates are used in the swap-pricing example developed in Chapter 1 but are also reproduced in Table 3.4. The LIBOR/swap rates represent zero coupon interbank deposit rates with maturities to one year and par swap rates thereafter. The cash lease rates are all zero coupon in style.

Table 3.4   Market rates for value 11 April 2005

Time period	LIBOR/swap rates	Cash lease rates
0.25	3.13%	0.09%
0.50	3.39%	0.12%
0.75	3.60%	0.16%
1.00	3.79%	0.19%
1.25	3.89%	0.21%
1.50	3.98%	0.22%
1.75	4.07%	0.24%
2.00	4.09%	0.25%

Source: Barclays Capital.

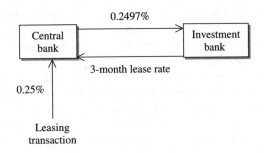

Figure 3.8 Lease rate swap

In Chapter 1, the fair value of a 2-year gold lease rate swap was calculated to be 0.2497%. Let us say that the central bank is seeking to enhance yield and has a 2-year time frame in mind. We will consider three options:

- Lend gold for 2 years at a zero coupon lease rate of 0.25%.
- Lease the metal on a rolling 3-month basis.
- Lend gold for 2 years at the same zero coupon rate as above and simultaneously enter into a gold lease rate swap, paying 0.2497% fixed, on a quarterly basis to receive the 3-month lease rate with the same frequency.

If the central bank felt that lease rates were going stay low for the maturity of the transaction, the simple zero coupon lease deposit may be appropriate. With the swap, the net cashflows in each period would involve a receipt of the 3-month lease rate plus the difference between the fixed rate the central banks receive on the cash lease (0.25%) and what they must pay on the swap (0.2497%). These cashflows are illustrated in Figure 3.8.

The net income received is therefore the 3-month lease rate plus 0.0003%. Although this return is only slightly greater than the 3-month lease rate, the swap may be more advantageous depending on the chosen maturity and the shape of the forward curve. We showed in Chapter 1 that the fixed rate on the swap could be thought of as the weighted average of the future expected lease rates; so if the central bank felt that, on average, the 3-month lease rates were going to rise higher than the implied forward curve used to derive the fixed rate, then paying fixed on the swap would be a more appropriate strategy.

Option strategies

Although the Central Bank Agreements indicated that the use of options would not be expanded, it does not necessarily follow that this implies no usage of the product. It should be remembered that some of the signatories were holding positions in options and the agreement does not cover all of the world's central banks. Two common methods of using options involve either the sale of calls or the purchase of puts. The use of put options to provide downside price protection was analysed in section 3.4.1, which focused on the applications of options for producers.

The sale of a call option while holding a position in the underlying asset is commonly referred to as a covered call strategy. The sale of the call option will require the seller to deliver the underlying metal if exercised. If the call is not exercised the central bank will simply collect the premium and enjoy an enhanced return. A common misconception is that selling options while holding the underlying asset is risk free. A simple example will demonstrate that this is not the case.

Assume that the central bank decides to sell a 12-month call option based on a portion of its physical holdings. We will assume that the current spot price is USD 424.40 per ounce, the 12-month forward price is USD 440.68 and the implied volatility is 20%. Using a simple option-pricing model, the premium on an OTM European style option with a strike at USD 450 is USD 30 per ounce. Figure 3.9 illustrates the concept with the analysis on a per ounce basis. The vertical axis is defined as the value of the overall position in USD, while the horizontal axis represents the current spot price of gold. The physical holding of gold is shown as a 45-degree line bisecting the horizontal axis at the current spot rate. This position suggests that as the spot price of gold rises, so does the value of the underlying holding. The sale of the call option is shown with an "at expiry" payoff, with the net position of the two transactions highlighted in bold. As the price of gold falls in the spot market, the value of the position declines but the loss is offset by the income received on the option. Although the premium provides a cushion for losses on the underlying holding, the overall position will show a loss.

If the price of gold were to fall, the overall position starts to lose money beyond a spot price of USD 394.40, so it is clearly not risk free. This is the point where the cushion of the USD 30 received as a premium is eroded. However, the central bank is still in a relatively better position than simply holding the metal.

The maximum value of the position is realised at a spot price equal to or greater than the strike of the sold call option. Beyond this position the central bank loses on the call but profits from the increased value of the underlying position. The net effect is that the profits are maximised beyond this point. If the call is exercised against the central bank, the bank does not need to deliver the metal and can choose to settle its obligations in cash.

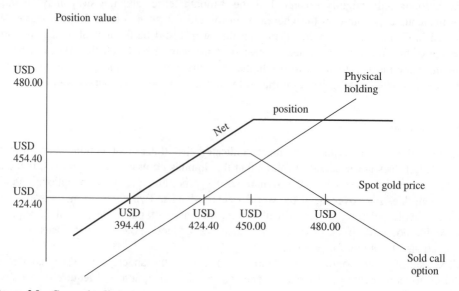

Figure 3.9   Covered call strategy

Figure 3.9 shows that beyond USD 480 the returns from holding the physical gold would exceed that of the combined strategy. So when considering the appropriateness of the strategy the central bank must believe that the price of gold will only rise by a relatively small amount. However, for central banks it could be argued that they would be happier to see the price go down – they have no intention of selling the gold and would be very happy to extract some value from their holdings.

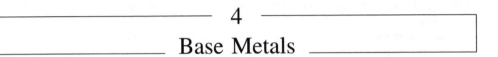

4

Base Metals

The American penny consists mainly of zinc and copper and at one stage in 2006 the rise in the price of base metals was such that the value of the constituent metal nearly exceeded its face value. This prompted the US government to issue a public warning that it was an offence to melt down coins.

SYNOPSIS   The purpose of this chapter is to describe the market for base metals, how they are traded and some common derivative structures.

This chapter covers the metals classified as either "base" or "industrial". This family of metals includes aluminium, copper, nickel, lead, zinc and tin. Although there are other metals that may fall into this category – such as steel – the selection has been based on those metals where an active traded market exists.

The chapter focuses on two of the most liquid traded base metals, *aluminium and copper*. The role of the *London Metal Exchange* (LME) is outlined and the main features of the instruments traded there are detailed.

One of the features of the base metals market is that physical metal contracts are often referenced to the LME price. *The factors that affect market prices* and *their term structure* are analysed.

The final section of the chapter covers the main *applications of derivatives* within the automotive industry. A wide range of structures is considered from simple forwards to structured option solutions.

4.1   BASE METAL PRODUCTION

Typically the *mining* process will begin with a geological survey of an area with test drilling being performed to determine the size of the deposit, its depth and quality. From this a decision will be made as to whether or not the value of the deposit will be greater than the cost to develop and operate the mine. This decision will take into account a number of factors, some of which may not be purely geological. These other considerations will include mining infrastructure issues, such as where to put the buildings or roads or related environmental issues. Lead times between the actual discovery and production can take many years and may often involve a substantial initial outlay. Many banks wishing to lend to mining operations may often link the repayments to the revenues generated by requiring the mine operators to take out some form of hedge.

About 80% of all elements found in the earth are metal. However, they rarely occur in a form that is commonly recognisable as a metal as they react to combine with other elements to create compounds. As a result, the production process will involve separating the metal from the individual components with which it has bonded. Different metals will react with other elements to varying extents so it is possible to say that metals have a *reactivity*. As silver and gold are very unreactive and do not readily combine with any other element, they are found in their pure state. At the other extreme it is impossible to find francium in its pure form, as it will immediately react with oxygen or water when exposed to the atmosphere.

Metals commonly occur in the form of compounds or ores where they are chemically bounded to one or more elements. For example the metal sodium is commonly found as sodium chloride; sodium has bonded to chlorine. To produce and transform the metals into a usable form the ore has to be separated from the host rock. The process of removing the host rock is similar regardless of the type of metal concerned; the rock and ore are ground down to a powder and separated mechanically.

The next stage in the production process involves the separation of the metal from the compound. Breaking down the ore to form pure metal can be carried out by a number of different processes. The more reactive a metal is, the harder it is to remove from its ore and the more expensive the process. Several metal ores are broken down using the addition of carbon and/or oxygen. Ores of very reactive metals have to be melted down (smelted) and the metal removed by electrolysis.

Refining is the final stage of the production process where impurities are removed and the metal is transformed into a state that would allow fabrication of an end product.

4.2 ALUMINIUM

More aluminium is produced today than any other non-ferrous metal, with more than 30 million tonnes produced each year (see Figure 4.1). The prospects for the metal are generally regarded as favourable as the demand for lighter, more durable, energy efficient and recyclable goods increases.

The starting point for the production of aluminium is bauxite. Once mined it is crushed and dissolved in caustic soda at high temperatures and pressures. The solution will contain

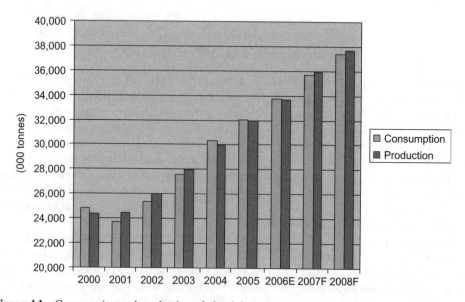

Figure 4.1   Consumption and production of aluminium
Data sourced from Barclays Capital. Figures for 2006 are estimates; figures for 2007 and 2008 are forecasted.

dissolved aluminium ore, which can be separated from any undissolved impurities, as they will have sunk to the bottom of the collection tank. Aluminium ore is chemically referred as aluminium oxide (Al_2O_3) but is also sometimes referred to as alumina. The alumina, which is in the form of a white powder, is dissolved into a molten solution capable of conducting electricity. Two electrodes are then attached, one positive and one negative, and the aluminium is extracted by electrolysis. Electrolysis uses electricity to separate the metal from its ore. As the electricity passes through the molten solution the aluminium is attracted to the negative electrode and can be siphoned off to yield very pure aluminium. This entire extraction process is energy intensive and, as a result, the cost of electricity will have a substantial impact on production costs.

Four tonnes of bauxite yield about 2 tonnes of alumina, which yield 1 tonne of aluminium. Figure 4.1 illustrates the evolution of demand and supply since the year 2000.

Another important component of this supply is the amount that is recycled. It has been estimated that about 7 million tonnes of aluminium is recycled annually. Much of this is produced as varying grades of aluminium alloy for specialist use in areas such as the automotive industry. (An alloy is a mixture of two or more metals which result in different physical characteristics such as a change in colour or extra hardness.) One of big advantages of producing aluminium via recycling is that the process consumes considerably less electricity than making it from the ore. The refining of aluminium is renowned for consuming considerable amounts of electricity. The largest producer (measured as smelting output) of aluminium is China, followed by North America and western Europe (Figure 4.2). One of the key issues faced by a producer of aluminium is the significant energy required during the production process, in an environment of rising power prices this could potentially act

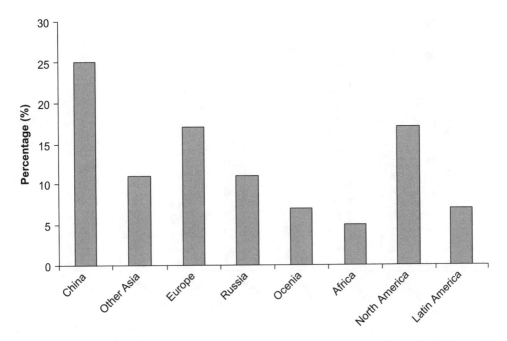

Figure 4.2 World smelting output by region
Data sourced from Barclays Capital.

as a break on production. The regional demand for aluminium is shown in Figure 4.3, and
Figure 4.4 considers the different applications of the metal within the western world.

The largest user of the metal is the transport sector, which accounts for about 29% of
demand. A significant proportion of this is in the automotive industry for such things as

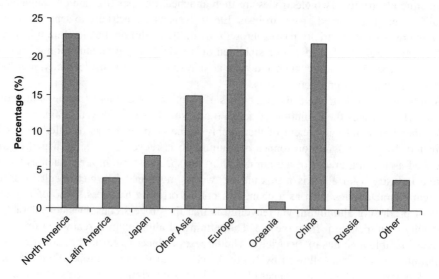

Figure 4.3 Regional demand for aluminium
Data sourced from Barclays Capital.

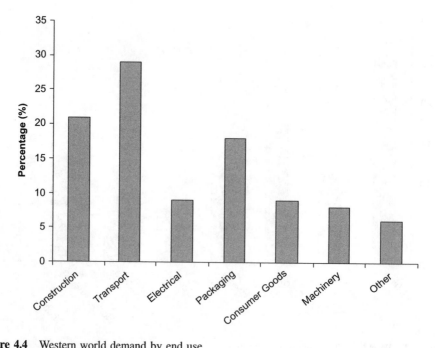

Figure 4.4 Western world demand by end use
Data sourced from Barclays Capital.

engine blocks and body panels. This would suggest that a downturn in demand in this sector would have a significant impact on the demand for the metal. Construction is the second largest user of the metal (20%) with packaging constituting a significant proportion (18%).

4.3 COPPER

Copper ore is ground down to a fine powder to which water and reagents are added to make the copper compound water repellent. Air is blown into the mixture and the copper compounds froth to the surface before being removed with some of the water. The resulting mixture of copper compound and water (called slurry) can then be smelted.

The process of smelting removes the copper from its compounds by a series of chemical reactions. The exact protocol depends on the copper compounds found in the ore but generally the slurry is heated and combined with oxygen-enriched air. The copper produced at this stage is about 99% pure but undergoes a further stage of electronic purification. The smelted copper is made into a number of electrodes and is placed in an electrolytic solution together with a negative electrode. An electric current is passed between them and over time 99.98% pure copper ions pass to the negative electrode.

Copper can be used (see Figure 4.5):

- to conduct electricity and heat
- within communication equipment
- to transport water and gas
- in roofing, gutters and down spouts
- as art.

It can also be combined with other metals to create alloys; for example, brass is a combination of copper and zinc.

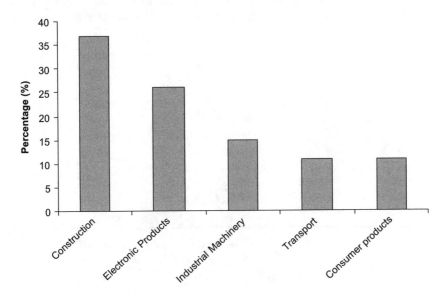

Figure 4.5 Demand by usage
Data sourced from Barclays Capital.

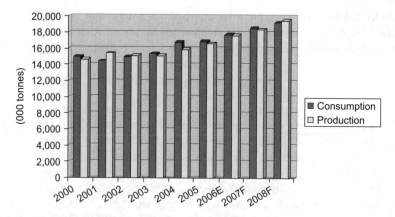

Figure 4.6 Consumption and production of copper 2000–2008. Figures for 2006 are estimated; figures for 2007 and 2008 are forecasted
Data sourced from Barclays Capital.

Figure 4.6 shows the trend of demand and supply from the year 2000 and also illustrates that in a number of years consumption exceeded production, resulting in a reduction in inventories and an upward movement in price.

No one has ever been able to determine how much copper is actually left as, similar to gold, new supplies are always being discovered. If there were a genuine belief that all finite supplies of copper had been discovered, then the price for "mega long dated" copper (i.e. prices for delivery in 10–15 years) would move very steeply into contango. This is because traders would lock into long-dated purchase contracts knowing that, given finite supplies, the price would rise steeply. As Figure 4.10 on page indicates, the market has spent many years in backwardation. Like other metals, scrap plays an important role and about 30% of the annual copper supply comes from this source. Figure 4.7 shows the origin of the global mine output.

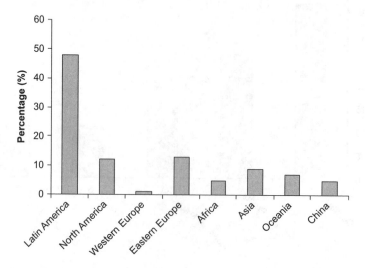

Figure 4.7 Global mine output
Data sourced from Barclays Capital.

The largest producer of copper is Latin America, with the majority of the supply coming from Chile and Peru. The second largest supplier of the metal is North America with significant production seen in the western part of the USA and western Canada.

Figure 4.8 shows the world demand by region. Although Latin America is a significant producer of the metal, the largest consumer is western Europe. The next most significant consumers are the USA and China, respectively.

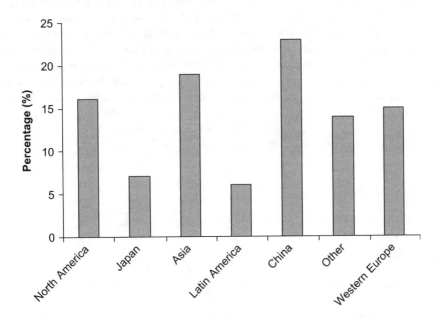

Figure 4.8 Demand by region
Data sourced from Barclays Capital.

4.4 LONDON METAL EXCHANGE

The prices set on the London Metal Exchange (LME) provide the basis for the majority of commercial transactions in non-ferrous metals and plastics. One common aspect of many commodity markets is the struggle to establish a single common and transparent basis for pricing a commodity. If the majority of commercial transactions were to be privately negotiated contracts, it would be difficult for any market participant to determine if they are paying a "fair price" for the particular commodity. In addition, the settlement of derivative transactions requires agreement on a single common price for the underlying asset.

The LME offers futures and options that will allow participants in these markets to manage their price risk effectively. Although the LME has many features in common with other financial exchanges (e.g. standardised contracts) the design of its forward price based contracts often have more in common with over-the-counter (OTC) style instruments.

However, it should be noted that a significant proportion of base metal transactions are executed on an OTC basis. If a corporate customer wished to execute a transaction that is exactly tailored to their needs, the OTC market offers greater flexibility and a wider range of products. However, the LME does offer an efficient mechanism where the risk accepted in an OTC contract can be offset or transferred to another trading entity.

4.4.1 Exchange-traded metal futures

Futures contracts represent the commitment to either buy or sell a particular metal at a pre-agreed price at a specified date in the future. LME transaction will require both parties to the trade to physically delivery the metal if the contract is held to maturity. Although it is possible to use the futures contract as a source of supply, it is more likely that the contract will be used as a financial hedge. Using the future in this fashion permits the user to separate the supply of the metal from the associated price risk. Physical settlement can be avoided by taking out an equal and opposite trade for the same delivery date (termed the "prompt" date). The two transactions will offset each other and the counterparty will cash settle the trade, paying or receiving the difference between the two prices.

The exchange currently offers futures contracts on the following metals:

- Copper A grade
- Primary aluminium
- Aluminium alloy
- North American Special Aluminium Alloy Contract (NASAAC)
- Standard lead
- Primary nickel
- Tin
- Special high-grade zinc.

The plastics futures contracts are:

- Polypropylene (PP)
- Linear low density polyethylene (LL).

The exchange also offers an index contract (LMEX) on the six primary base metals. This contract allows the user to take exposure to the market rather than a single metal.

4.4.2 Exchange-traded metal options

The exchange offers options on the underlying futures contracts, so the buyer has the right but not the obligation to buy or sell an LME futures contract at a predetermined price at a pre-agreed time in the future. The exchange also offers Traded Average Price Options (or TAPOs). Average price options (sometimes referred to as "Asians") are options where the settlement of the contract is not made against a single market price but against an average for a predetermined period. They are attractive from a buyer's point of view as they will be cheaper than an equivalent non-averaging option. TAPOs are settled against the LME Monthly Average Settlement Price (MASP), which is a figure published by the exchange and represents the average of all the daily settlement prices for a particular month.

4.4.3 Contract specification

One of the issues central to the metals markets is the exact form of the metal to be physically delivered at maturity. To ensure that the contracts are standardised and are useful to market participants, the exchange sets specifications for form, quality and shape, which are most widely accepted by the different market users. The LME contracts are usually for metals that can be easily be transformed into an end product by a commercial user. As a result the LME price can be used as the basis for pricing a wide variety of commercial metal contracts where the actual metal content may vary. For commercial contracts based on metal in a state different to that specified in the LME contract, a mutually agreeable adjustment to the LME price could be applied.

The exchange also stipulates common standards for weights and strapping. Participants trade in lots rather than tonnes, with aluminium, copper, lead and zinc being sized at 25 tonnes. The NASAAC is for 20 tonnes, with Nickel at 6 tonnes and tin at 5 tonnes. The specification for the primary aluminium futures contracts is outlined in Table 4.1, and the contract specification for aluminium options is given in Table 4.2.

Table 4.1 Primary aluminium futures contract specification

Contract	Aluminium of 99.7% purity (minimum)
Lot size	25 tonnes (with a tolerance of ±2%)
Form	1. Ingots 2. T-bars 3. Sows
Weight	1. 12–26 kg each. Parcels of ingots on warrant shall not exceed 2 tonnes each 2. Shall not exceed 5% more than 750 kg 3. Shall not exceed 5% more than 750 kg
Delivery dates	Daily from cash to 3 months (first prompt date* two working days from cash). Then every Wednesday from 3 to 6 months. Then every third Wednesday from 7 months out to 63 months
Quotation	US dollars per tonne
Minimum price movement	50 cents per tonne
Clearable currencies	US dollar, Japanese yen, sterling, euro

Source: London Metals Exchange (www.lme.co.uk)
*Prompt date refers to the day that the physical metal is exchanged for cash.

4.4.4 Trading

Trading at the LME is by a mix of open outcry and electronic transactions. The main focus of trading is the "ring" sessions. There is a morning and an afternoon session, which follow the same general structure. Each metal is traded twice in designated 5-minute sessions and

Table 4.2   Primary aluminium options contract specification

Delivery dates	Monthly from the first month out to 63 months
Value date	The third Wednesday of the prompt month
Exercise date	The third Wednesday of the prompt month
Premium quotation	US dollars per tonne
Strike price	• USD 25 gradations for strikes from USD 25 to USD 3,975
	• USD 50 gradations for strikes from USD 4,000 to USD 7,950
	• USD 100 gradations for all strikes over USD 8000

Source: London Metals Exchange (www.lme.co.uk).

at the end of the second ring in the morning session, LME staff monitoring activity within the ring will determine the "official" closing prices for the cash, 3- and 15-month maturities. This official fixing allows the market to establish a transparent benchmark against which trades can be settled. For example, for aluminium the ring trading times are:

> *First session*
> 1st ring   11:55 to 12.00
> 2nd ring (official)   12.55 to 13.00
> Kerb trading   13.15 to 14.45
>
> *Second session*
> 3rd ring   15.15 to 15.20
> 4th ring   15.55 to 16.00
> Kerb trading   16.15 to 17.00

Kerb sessions run after the main ring sessions and, during this time, all of the metals are traded with more than one trader per company allowed within the ring. In addition to the ring sessions it is possible to buy and sell metals around the clock on the exchange's electronic trading application.

There are five different types of membership to the LME. *Ring trading* companies are entitled to trade in the ring during designated sessions, issue client contracts and trade electronically around the clock. *Associate broker* clearing members are not allowed to trade in the ring but are allowed to trade electronically. Members designated as *associate trade clearing* may not issue client contracts and cannot trade in the ring; however, they are allowed to clear their own business. *Associate broker* members may issue LME contracts but they are not members of the clearing house and may not trade in the ring; they will, however, be able to trade electronically. *Associate trade* members have no trading rights except as clients.

4.4.5   Clearing

One of the features common to all exchanges is the existence of a central clearing house. In London, LCH.Clearnet performs this function. Its primary role is to ensure that all purchases and sales executed on the exchange are settled in a timely manner. Once a trade is executed, both sides to the deal input the transactions to a common computer system, and as long as the details agree, the trade is considered matched.

As a result the clearing house then becomes the legal counterparty to both sides of the transaction – that is, it becomes the seller to the buyer and the buyer to the seller. Neither of the original counterparties will have any further contractual commitments to each other, as the clearing house is now their counterparty. With the clearing house acting as the counterparty to both sides, the risk of the original counterparty defaulting is transferred to the clearing house. However, the probability of the clearing house defaulting is very slim as these entities are usually very well capitalised. Although the clearing process mitigates the counterparty credit risk for the transaction executed on the exchange, if the trade was done on behalf of a client, that particular risk of default still remains. However, it should be noted that this mitigation of credit risk only extends to those executed on the exchange directly. A corporate client who asks a broker to act on its behalf is not covered and is exposed to the full credit risk of its counterparty.

Even though the likelihood of the clearing house defaulting is slim, one of the techniques used to further mitigate the risk is the margining system. Margin is collateral that is collected at the start of the transaction ("initial margin") or as the value of the contract changes ("variation margin"). Although cash is the most popular form of collateral, it may also be possible to deposit risk-free securities (e.g. government bonds) or documentary guarantees. In addition to the formal margining system covering transactions executed in the ring (or electronically), institutions trading on behalf of clients will also margin customers in the same manner.

The margining system on the LME works in a different manner from that seen on the various financial exchanges. On financial exchanges, variation margin is calculated on the basis of the change from the previous day's closing price. The margins are paid or received daily over the life of the deal, with the final settlement price occurring on the last trading day – the exchange delivery settlement price (EDSP). The impact of this margining system is to effectively make the future a series of daily contracts, which are instantaneously closed out and reopened at the closing daily futures price.

Contracts executed on the LME will still involve the collection of initial margin and variation margin on the basis of daily price movements, but settlement of the contract price will take place on the designated prompt date at the original agreed forward price.

The following examples will illustrate the concept. We will assume that a ring member has executed a trade where it buys one lot of aluminium at USD 1,900 per tonne for delivery in 3 months' time. The member will have to pay an initial margin, which we will assume to be USD 500. Let us assume that one day later the price for delivery on the original prompt date is now USD 1,950.

In the first scenario we will assume that the member closes out the trade at this point. He has bought at USD 1,900 and sold one day later at USD 1,950. Assuming no further trades, the initial margin is returned on the close out of the trade but the USD 50 profit is not collected until the original prompt date, some 3 months in the future.

In the second scenario we will again assume that the price has risen but that the trader decides to keep the position. Even though his position has increased in value, he receives no cash benefit and assuming he goes to final delivery he will pay the original forward price of USD 1,900. However, if the price of the metal were to fall after one day to USD 1,850, the trader would be required to make immediate cash payment to the clearing house to support this loss.

As we saw earlier, an entity not authorised to deal on the exchange will not be covered by the margining provisions. For transactions between a trader and an end client, the credit risk could be managed in a variety of ways. Some institutions may allow profits and losses on contracts to be handled as part of some agreed credit facility. Other institutions may operate a system where all losses and profits are remitted as and when they occur or they may simply mirror the LME process. However, a very common method of managing the credit risk is through the taking of collateral. This is often governed by the terms of ISDA (International Swaps and Derivatives Association) documentation. The part of the documentation that refers to collateral is referred to the Credit Support Annex (CSA). This covers:

• How often collateral can be taken
• The point at which collateral will be taken (similar in some respects to an overdraft limit)
• The minimum amount that can be transferred between the two counterparties (for example £100,000)
• The type of acceptable collateral (e.g. cash and certain government securities).

4.4.6 Delivery

Settlement of futures contracts on the LME takes place in a unique fashion in comparison to a financial exchange. On financial exchanges instruments can be bought and sold at any time, although they will typically have fixed maturity dates set at 3-month intervals. LME contracts can be traded for settlement on any chosen day (the "prompt date") for up to 3 months from the trade date, then weekly for maturities between 3 and 6 months followed by monthly settlement and then monthly settlement out to 15, 27 or 63 months forward. This makes the LME future more like a centrally cleared OTC forward.

All LME contracts require physical settlement if they are held to maturity. To facilitate the potential delivery of the metal, the LME has approved over 400 warehouses in 32 different countries. The exchange does not own or operate the warehouses and neither does it own the metal that is held therein. However, market analysts watch the volume of metal held within the warehouses as a gauge of currently available inventories.

When an institution agrees to sell metal on the LME, it may choose the warehouse destination where delivery will take place. If the seller delivers metal to the warehouse it will receive a warrant, which acts as evidence of ownership. The deposit of metal into the warehouse need not be in support of an LME contract, and the issue of a LME warrant will only take place if the metal conforms to the contract standards outlined by the exchange. The right of a buyer to take delivery of the metal is conferred by the transfer of a warrant from the seller. The issue of warrants is done by the warehouse in the location chosen by the seller for delivery and is affected by the warehouse's agents in London.

In certain futures markets (e.g. bond futures) the contract seller has a variety of options upon delivery. In the metals market the seller can choose the location of delivery and the brand. If a seller is in possession of a number of warrants and is faced with having to deliver the metal, then logically he will choose the location that is least favourable to him and the brand that is of least use. This means that although there is a single futures price for all deliveries, the quoted price will track these considerations. As a result there is a market to "swap" warrants, which takes place off the exchange. So if the terms of the warrant are not suitable for the buyer, he may seek to swap the warrant for a more favourable type. This has led to the development of premiums for warrants that confer delivery in a popular location or for a popular brand of metal.

The LME have overcome the administrative difficulties of managing a physical warrant system by introducing an electronic transfer system (SWORD). This acts as a central depository for all LME warrants, which are issued in a standardised format and can now be transferred rapidly between buyer and seller.

On settlement date, the exchange will analyse the position of each individual entity netting off as many of their remaining purchases and sales, with any price differences settled in cash. The remaining net position will then go to settlement. Since the position on the exchange is always in balance – that is, the total number of purchases or "longs" equals the total number of sales or "shorts" – at expiry the exchange will take up the warrants from the market longs and will randomly assign them to the market shorts. The actual cash settlement amount may differ from the forward price agreed under the terms of the original deal because each contract allows the actual weight of the metal to differ by ±2% of the contract standard. The final price paid by the buyer will need to be adjusted to reflect the actual amount delivered and will need to take into account any warehouse-related costs (such as rent or insurance) for the period of the contract.

4.5 PRICE DRIVERS

The main factors that drive the price of base metals markets include:

Government fiscal and monetary policy

At a simple level, if the government were to implement an expansionary economic policy, this should stimulate economic activity and increase the demand for resources such as base metals. For example, in the copper market such factors as the level of car output, semiconductor demand and new housing activity all influence the price of the metal.

Exchange rates

As base metals are denominated in US dollars, movements in the exchange rate will have an impact on the demand and supply balance. If the dollar weakens relative to other currencies, the domestic currency cost of buying the metal will decrease, leading to an increase in demand.

Chinese and Indian demand

The industrialisation of the Chinese economy and the rapid development of India have made the two countries substantial importers of many metals due to the lack of their own natural resources. This has contributed substantial upward pressure to the price of many commodities, including base metals.

Capital spending and exploration

During periods of sustained low metals prices, mining companies are reluctant to invest in their own infrastructure or instigate new exploration projects. However, as the prices of metals rise, it will then prove difficult to bring new production on stream to benefit from rising prices. In the late 1990s, as a result of the "dot com" boom, investment capital was diverted towards information technology related products away from traditional investment areas such as mining. When this investment bubble burst, there was a general fall in the level of capital expenditure in the mining sector, which slowed investment. At the same time the prices of a substantial number of base metals were at very low levels, further discouraging investment.

With many commodity markets there may be a substantial delay until new supplies of metal can be brought to market, during which time the excess demand will cause the price of the metal to rise further. For example, it could take up to 10 years to produce metal from the point of its discovery. Over the years this production lag has increased owing to such factors as increased construction costs due to rises in the price of metals (such as steel), greater labour and environmental regulations and a weaker US dollar. Although the argument has been made from a mining perspective, similar arguments could be made with respect to smelting and refining capacity.

Substitution

As commodity prices rise, the possibility of product substitution increases. With respect to base metals this may not be possible in the short term but over the course of, say, two or three years this may well become feasible as manufacturers develop products with a smaller metal content.

Production disruption

This usually manifests itself in two ways. The first would be the cessation of production due to labour disputes. Although rising prices may boost a producer's profitability, it may lead to an increase in wage demands from the work force and possible industrial action. The second reason relates to industrial accidents such as landslides, which may halt production for a period of time.

Production costs

One of the features of the general rise of commodity prices is the impact it then has on the costs of subsequent production. Operating costs could rise due to factors such as higher steel prices and energy costs. For example, the impact of higher energy prices is perhaps most apparent in the aluminium market where 50% of the production costs arise from these charges.

Investment demand

The equity bear markets of the late twentieth and early twenty-first centuries led many institutional investors to seek out alternative asset classes to enhance their return. Evidence suggests that returns on commodities tend to be negatively correlated with those on financial assets, offering a powerful incentive for investors to diversify. Other investment motivations include the wish to find a hedge against inflation and the desire to benefit from the rise in prices in a bull market.

One of the most common indicators of this activity is the *Commitments of Traders* report produced by the Commodity Futures Trading Commission in the USA. This report shows the positions (in the US markets) for "commercial" and "non-commercial" users. Commercial

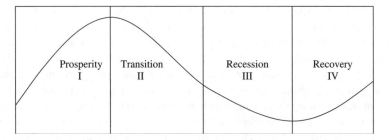

Figure 4.9   The impact of the business cycle on base metals

users are defined as those entities that would use futures for hedging some form of underlying exposure. Investment demand would therefore be captured within the non-commercial users category.

The balance between the industrial demand and supply

Here the focus is essentially on the level of metal inventories. Figure 4.9 illustrates in a generalised fashion the impact of the business cycle on the base metals market. In this very simple model the business cycle is represented as having four stages. Every economy will progress through each of these four stages in order, but the duration of each stage and the depth (how severe it will be) will be both different and unpredictable.

In phase I ("prosperity") of Figure 4.9 the economy is expanding and prices in general are rising. As economic activity increases there is an incentive to produce more and metal inventories tend to be relatively full. Available production capacity is able to catch up with the increase in demand. In phase II ("transition") asset prices overshoot their "fair value" and demand starts to fall. As a result of the general decline in demand, inventories are wound down. This is because consumers are reluctant to buy new metal at high prices and so meet their requirements by running down existing inventories. There will also be an incentive to recycle the metal from scrap products as it increases in value. At this point, financial investors will start to withdraw their funds. Phase III ("Recession") represents a bear market, as demand is very low. Here there is very little incentive to produce the metals given the combination of lower prices and lower demand. In phase IV ("Recovery"), growth accelerates as businesses restock metal inventories due to rising prices and demand. At this point inventories may tend to fall and metal prices rise, as the increasing demand cannot easily be met from the available productive capacity.

4.6   STRUCTURE OF MARKET PRICES

4.6.1   Description of the forward curve

A key feature of the base metal markets is the forward curve, which is a graphical representation of prices for different delivery dates in the future. Arguably there are three important aspects to consider when analysing the curve:

1. Whether the market is in backwardation or contango
2. Its absolute level
3. The degree of curvature.

If the prices for spot delivery are higher than for forward delivery, the market is said to be in backwardation. If the opposite applies (i.e. forward prices greater than spot prices) the market is said to be in contango. Applying time value of money principles to commodities (see Chapter 1) backwardation should never happen, and this apparent anomaly is often explained away by using the concept of convenience yield. However, market participants do not take into consideration convenience yield when creating structures, and explain a backwardated market in terms of simple demand and supply. If supplies of the metal are in short supply, consumers will be prepared to pay a premium to obtain the metal now, if the alternative – e.g. cessation of a production line – proves to be more costly. Thus, consumer buying activity will drive near-term prices higher than longer-term prices. As supplies of the metal return to "normal" levels, the price of shorter-term contracts fall relative to those of a longer maturity and the market moves into contango.

For example, on 11 April 2005, the LME settlement prices for primary aluminium were in backwardation (USD per tonne):

Cash	USD 1,968
3 month	USD 1,961
15 month	USD 1,838
27 month	USD 1,765

However, for the zinc market the prices were in both contango and backwardation (USD per tonne):

Cash	USD 1,362
3 month	USD 1,383
15 month	USD 1,392
27 month	USD 1,352

The buying and selling of metals is ultimately driven by one factor – the absolute sale price. For example, it might be logical to believe that a producer would never sell his production forward in a backwardated market, but this misses the point that, in these conditions, the absolute level of prices will tend to be high. This can be shown using a simple scatter graph (Figure 4.10), which plots the spread between prices in different time horizons against the price of the metal. The price of the metal against which this spread is measured is usually the 3-month forward price as this represents the most liquid contract traded on the London Metals Exchange.

Figure 4.10 illustrates that as the price of the metal rises the market is more likely to move into backwardation. Indeed, as the price rises the slope of the forward curve becomes more steeply backwardated. In these conditions (high prices and steep backwardation), producers will be less tempted to sell their production forward. Anecdotally, at very high price levels, producers are often less keen to lock into attractive prices. This is often a result of shareholder pressure that wants the company to benefit from rising prices. It may also be simple overoptimism. Somewhat paradoxically, producers tend to be more active hedgers in low price environments. In addition consumers may decide to take some advantage of the cheaper forward purchase price for the metal. In addition, investors may wish to take advantage of the rising price environment and take exposure to the market using exchange-traded futures, further adding to the longer-dated buying pressure. These actions will, to an extent, act as a brake on the degree of backwardation experienced by the market.

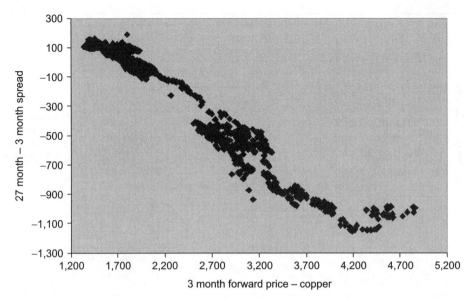

Figure 4.10 Price difference between 3 month forward and 27 month forward against 3 month forward price for copper (*Note*: The vertical axis is measured as the spread is calculated as the 27-month forward price less 3-month forward price. All prices are expressed on a per tonne basis). Dates: January 1999 – February 2006
Source: (Bloomberg.)

4.6.2 Are forward prices predictors of future spot prices?

Another often discussed issue is whether the forward rate is some form of predictor of future spot rates. There are two schools of thought on this subject. The first argument (Galitz, 1996) argues that although forward prices are derived objectively using fairly straightforward calculations, they must match the subjective estimates of where prices will be in the future. Take the 3-month copper price presented earlier of USD 1,961 per tonne. If the market believed that in 3 months' time the spot price of copper was going to be USD 2,000 per tonne, a trader could simply buy the metal forward at the current 3-month quoted price and then wait. If the trader was right in his belief, upon maturity of the contract he could take delivery of the metal and sell it in the spot market at a profit of USD 39 per tonne. If the market consensus were similar, then buying pressure in the forward market would drive the price higher until it reached USD 2,000.

The counter argument says that, as a forecasting tool, the forward rate is a notoriously bad predictor and therefore should only be treated as a value that allows a producer or consumer to lock into for future delivery or receipt. As such it is more appropriately viewed as a breakeven rate around which all hedging decisions should be made. Let us consider a consumer who believed that the spot price of copper in 3 months' time would be to be greater than the current 3-month forward rate. In this case he should buy the metal now for forward delivery. If he felt that the spot price was going to be below the forward price, he should do nothing, as locking into the forward rate would be unattractive relative to his view. If he believed that the spot price would be equal to the forward rate, then he would be indifferent as to whether to hedge or not.

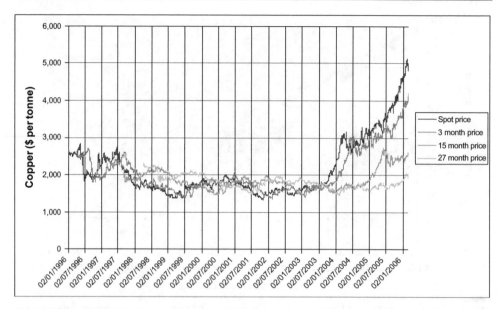

Figure 4.11   Forward rates as predictors of future spot rates. Spot, 3-, 15- and 27-month forward rates 1996–2006
Data sourced from Bloomberg.

Figure 4.11 shows the spot, 3-, 15- and 27-month prices for copper covering the period 1996–2006. The chart illustrates the accuracy of the forward price as a forecast of future spot rates. The forward rates are charted against the spot rate with a lag equal to the forward's maturity. So the 3-month forward rate as of 2 January 1996 (USD 2,632) is plotted against the spot price of 2 April 1996 (USD 2,512) to see if it accurately predicted the rate.

The figure illustrates that although the forward rate does sometimes "predict" the spot rate, its consistency is indeed highly questionable. Indeed over the entire 10-year period the 3-month rate, lagged by 3 months, only matches the spot price on one occasion.

4.7   APPLICATIONS OF DERIVATIVES

4.7.1   Hedges for aluminium consumers in the automotive sector

The commodities primarily hedged by the automotive sector are:

- aluminium (body panels, engine blocks)
- copper (wiring)
- zinc (stainless steel coating)
- lead (batteries)
- platinum and palladium (catalytic converters)
- plastics (cabin interiors).

Of these commodities, aluminium is the most significant in terms of volume because the physical characteristics of the metal are attractive. It offers a good strength/weight ratio and

Table 4.3 Aluminium prices
for settlement 11 April 2005

Spot	USD 1,968
3 month	USD 1,961
15 month	USD 1,838
27 month	USD 1,765

Source: LME.

since this reduces the weight of the vehicle, there is an added environmental benefit in that the level of emissions are lower.

One of the ways in which the aluminium content could be hedged is by using the NASAAC (North American Special Aluminium Alloy Contract) future on the LME. This futures contract was set up by the exchange to meet the specific hedge requirements of the US automotive sector. The contract specification is "engine block alloy" and delivery locations are in close proximity to the end users. It was introduced due to concerns that the price movements of the primary aluminium alloy contract was not sufficiently correlated with the actual metal used by the industry. However, the contract has, to date, experienced mixed success mainly due to poor liquidity. Although the car producers would be natural buyers of the contract, there are limited natural sellers. The sellers tend to be scrap merchants who are of poor credit quality and are therefore constrained as to the tenor to which they can sell forward.

For purposes of illustration we will assume that the following prices prevail for aluminium (for settlement 11 April 2005). We will also assume that all of the purchases of the physical metal are based on the monthly average LME cash price and are expressed on a per tonne basis. This averaging process is very common in all commodity markets and has a number of benefits. Take, for example, a consumer of metal who decides to link the contract to the average price of the metal. By using the average price the cost of the metal will not be based on an extreme level, as a sharp movement up prior to the month end will be averaged out. However, by the same token the consumer cannot take advantage of a sharp movement downwards, which would reduce his costs. The other main benefit is that options settled on the basis of an average price series are cheaper than an equivalent non-averaged European (Table 4.3).

4.8 FORWARD PURCHASE

The simplest (and often the most popular) method of hedging the purchase cost is to buy the metal for forward delivery. In this example we will separate the delivery of the metal from the hedge – that is, the consumer will buy the required tonnage of the metal from his normal supplier and enter into a cash settled hedge transaction with a bank. Since the manufacturer will take delivery of the metal from his regular supplier in the future he is said to be "short the metal for forward delivery" – that is, a rise in the price of the metal will incur extra costs while a fall in the price will save money.

Let us take an example of buying a cash-settled 3-month forward at a price of USD 1,961 on 1 tonne of aluminium. At the end of the 3-month period we will assume that the monthly average cash settlement price is USD 1,731.50. The manufacturer buys the required amount of metal at this price from his supplier and settles the forward contract in cash with the bank.

The forward is cash settled, as the hedge was not intended as a mechanism for obtaining physical supplies of the metal. The cash settlement amount on the forward is simply the difference between the monthly average cash price in the month prior to maturity and the forward price agreed at the outset of the hedging transaction. Somewhat confusingly, the market will refer to this type of deal as a "swap" transaction as it is in effect a single period contract for difference. However, it should not be confused with a multiperiod swap or a swap transaction where two entities execute a simultaneous purchase and sale for different maturities against cash (see Chapter 2, gold, for examples of both transactions).

Since the company has bought the contract forward it will receive cash if the monthly average settlement price at maturity is higher than the pre-agreed forward price. However, in this case the settlement price is below the forward price and so the manufacturer must pay USD 229.50 (USD 1,731.50 − USD 1,961) per tonne to the bank. However, from the manufacturer's perspective, his net cost is the cost of buying the underlying metal from his normal supplier (USD 1,731.50) plus the cash payment to settle the forward contract with the bank (USD 229.50) – a total cost of USD 1,961, which was equal to the price under the forward contract.

4.8.1 Borrowing and lending in the base metal market

One of the issues faced by end users of derivatives relates to the timing of the hedge. Let us assume that the consumer's supplier tells him that there will be a delay in the shipment of the metal. This means that the hedging transaction also needs to be delayed to avoid a mismatch in timing. The hedge can be restructured by closing out the original trade with an equal and opposite transaction and, simultaneously, executing a second transaction that re-establishes the original exposure but at a different time in the future.

Recall that the original hedge required the consumer to buy the metal for 3-month forward delivery at USD 1,961. After 1 month the consumer decides that he wants the forward delivery date to be moved back by a month. The original 3-month exposure now has a residual exposure of 2 months and so the consumer sells a 2-month forward and simultaneously buys the metal for 3-month delivery. This simultaneous sale and purchase of futures for different maturities is referred to as a "lend". This is because when the sell/buy transaction is analysed in isolation, the metal is being delivered out for one settlement date but being repurchased for delivery at another time.

Let us assume that after one month the market is still in backwardation and the prevailing 2- and 3-month forward prices are USD 1,980 and USD 1,970, respectively. From the consumer's perspective the original purchase at USD 1,961 is closed out at USD 1,980 to yield a profit at the prompt date of USD 29. The new forward purchase price in 3 months' time will be USD 1,970, which although higher than the original forward price of USD 1,961, can be reduced by the profit received on close-out of the original exposure. This would give a cost of purchase of USD 1,941 (USD 1,970 − USD 29) if one ignores the time value of money. If the close-out profit of USD 29 could be put on deposit to earn interest between months 2 and 3, the final purchase cost would be further reduced. The opposite of a lend is a borrow – a combination strategy where the metal is bought for near-dated future delivery and sold for a far-dated future delivery.

4.9 VANILLA OPTION STRATEGIES

4.9.1 Synthetic long put

One of the drawbacks for the consumer of buying the metal forward is that if the price of the underlying metal declines, the manufacturer is locked into paying a settlement price above the current market price. The alternative is some form of option-based strategy. The following strategies are priced using the market information in Table 4.3 and by assuming that implied volatility is trading at 20%. Each of the options is assumed to have a maturity of 3 months (92 days). All of the options are Asian in style and will be settled against the LME monthly average settlement price. All option prices are rounded to the nearest whole figure for ease of illustration.

With an average price option (sometimes referred to as an "Asian") the strike is fixed at inception with final settlement being based on an average of prices over a pre-agreed period. The averaging process will reduce the premium, due to the fact that the implied volatility used to price the instrument is based on an averaged price series. This volatility will always be lower than that of a non-averaged series. Although the averaging process cheapens the option, it should not be forgotten that this also means that the payout to the buyer will be lower than that of a non-averaging equivalent. However, although the above statements may hold in theory, the same may not hold in practice. In reality, the observed prices for Asians are very close to those of an equivalent European. This is because the averaging process imposes an extra administrative burden on the selling institution, which must be paid for. So although the contract will contain an averaging clause, the market maker will tend to price the option as if it were European in style. If the option covers a month, then, as a rule of thumb, the market maker will price the option as a European style option to the middle of that period.

In the previous example the manufacturer is short the metal for forward delivery by virtue of his physical contract with the supplier. To hedge this exposure the manufacturer buys a call option with the strike set a level with which the manufacturer is comfortable. In many cases an out-of-the-money strike is selected in order to reduce the cost. We will assume that the manufacturer decides to execute the call with a strike of USD 1,980, which makes the option out-of-the-money with respect to the 3-month forward price of USD 1,961. The premium for this option is USD 41. Figure 4.12 shows the "at expiry" position for the manufacturer. The vertical axis is defined as the cost of buying the metal, while the horizontal axis shows the current price of the metal. The intersection of the two is the current 3-month forward price of USD 1,961 per tonne. Notice how the net position resembles a long put option. Recall the short-hand version of put – call parity (see Chapter 1)

$$+C - P = +F$$

where $+C$ = long call option
    $-P$ = short put option
    $+F$ = long position in the underlying asset.

Although strictly speaking this condition only holds if the strike, maturities and notional amounts are the same, by applying the principles intuitively we can rearrange the formula to arrive at:

$$+C - F = +P$$

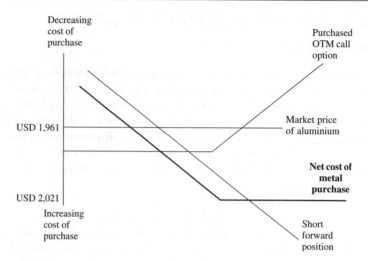

Figure 4.12   Short forward exposure combined with purchased option

That is, the combination of buying a call option and a short forward position will be equivalent to a long put.

The maximum cost to the manufacturer occurs when the market price rallies. Assume that the average price of the metal at expiry of the option is USD 2,000. The manufacturer

- buys the metal from his normal source and pays the average price of USD 2,000;
- exercises its call option and cash settles the contract,
- receives USD 20 per tonne (USD 2,000 minus the strike of USD 1,980).

This gives a net cost of USD 1,980, a sum equal to the strike of the option, but to this we must add the premium paid on the option. Ignoring the time value of money considerations (the premium was paid at the start of the contract and the net cost is calculated at the expiry of the option), the maximum cost of the metal is USD 2,021 (USD 1,980 + USD 41).

A common misconception about this strategy is that it would be appropriate for the manufacturer if the underlying price was about to rise. If this were the case a more effective strategy would be to buy the metal forward, as it does not incur any premium charge. In this particular instance, when the market is in backwardation the forward price locked into would be below the current price, further increasing the attractiveness of the forward to the consumer.

The purchase of the call option would be appropriate if the manufacturer believed the price was going to fall but couldn't afford for his view to be wrong. If the price of the metal falls, he forgoes the option and buys the metal in the underlying market at a price lower than the strike, although the premium will represent a sunk cost. If the metal rises in value against his expectations, the call option offers protection by providing a maximum purchase price.

4.9.2   Selling options to enhance the forward purchase price

In this example the consumer sells options (in a variety of permutations) in addition to entering a cash-settled hedge to buy the metal forward. However, instead of receiving premium as a cashflow, the bank adjusts the forward purchase price downwards. As in the previous examples we will assume that the consumer is short the metal for forward delivery.

Selling out-of-the-money puts

The first possible strategy is to buy the metal forward and sell out-of-the-money put options (both contracts being cash settled). Using the figures in Table 4.3, the manufacturer could buy the metal for 3-month forward delivery (at USD 1,961) and sell an out-of-the-money put option with the same maturity. At a strike of USD 1,950 the put option would generate a premium of USD 35 per tonne. The forward purchase hedges price risk if the underlying short position and the premium on the put are used to reduce the eventual purchase price. If the price of the metal falls through the strike price the company would have to compensate the bank for the difference. This would end up increasing the cost of the forward purchase. By way of illustration, let us assume that the average price of the metal falls to USD 1,900 per tonne. The manufacturer:

- buys one tonne of the metal for USD 1,900 from his usual supplier;
- cash settles the 3-month forward, which had a price of USD 1,961, and pays USD 61 to the bank;
- cash settles the put option, paying the difference between the strike (USD 1,950) and the spot price (USD 1,900) to the bank (i.e. USD 50);
- retains the premium on the option (USD 35).

Ignoring the timing of the premium payment, the total cost of buying 1 tonne of the metal is USD 1,976 (USD 1,900 + USD 61 + USD 50 − USD 35). However, if the price of the metal were to rise to an average price of USD 2,000 per tonne, the cost of buying the metal would be:

- the cost of purchasing the metal in the market at USD 2,000;
- less USD 39 compensation from the forward contract (USD 2,000 minus USD 1,961)
- less the USD 35 premium received on the option, which is not exercised.

This results in a cost of USD 1,926 per tonne, so the result is that as the underlying price rises the net cost of buying the metal decreases. This strategy will reduce the forward cost of the metal if the manufacturer expects the price of the metal to rise.

Selling OTM calls

In this strategy the manufacturer would buy the metal forward and sell call options, again both being cash settled. The strike of the call options would be set at a price level at which the manufacturer does not expect to trade. If the price of the metal falls, the options are not exercised and the premium income reduces the purchase cost. A similar situation arises if the underlying market rises but does not hit the strike. If the market trades beyond the strike, the calls are cash settled incurring a cost.

Combination option strategies

One possible example would be to:

- hedge the purchase of the metal with a forward purchase at USD 1,961;
- sell out-of-the-money calls at a strike of USD 2,050;
- sell out-of-the-money puts at a strike of USD 1,850;
- and the net option premium earned by the hedger would be USD 25.

Again these transactions would all be cash settled with the strikes set at levels that the manufacturer does not think will trade. This strategy will work if the manufacturer expected a stable underlying market as it would allow him to reduce the forward cost of the metal by the net premium received. If the average price of the metal settles anywhere between the two option strikes, neither will be exercised against the hedger and the cost of the metal will be USD 1,936 (the forward price less the net premium received). If the market were volatile in either direction there is a real risk that one of the options would be exercised against him. The hedger would then be faced with increased costs as a result of the option settlement. It should be pointed out that this particular strategy is much more speculative in nature and is more commonly executed by those institutions that are comfortable with such exposures.

4.9.3 "Three way"

In the "three way" structure the trade consists of a bull spread (constructed by calls), financed by the sale of a put.

A bull spread is created by the purchase of a low strike call and the sale of a high strike call. Since the purchased call is in-the-money and the sold call out-of-the-money, the combined position has an associated cost. This is financed by the sale of a put option with the strike set at a level that results in a zero premium. Using the previous data, one possible permutation is:

- Long a call option at USD 1,950
- Short a call option at USD 2,025
- Short a put option at USD 1,944.

In this strategy the minimum price of the metal is USD 1,944. If the market price is between the strike of the short put (USD 1,944) and the purchased call (USD 1,950) the consumer pays the prevailing market price. For market prices between USD 1,950 and USD 2,025, the consumer will pay a strike equal to the purchased call as neither of the sold options is exercised. Above the strike of the sold call (USD 2,025), the consumer will pay the prevailing price less USD 75. This USD 75 cost reduction is attributable to the bull spread element of the strategy and is simply a reflection that if I buy a call at USD 1,950 and sell a call at USD 2,025, the exercise of both options results in a maximum profit of USD 75, which is the difference between the two strikes. If the price of the underlying rises steeply and both options are exercised, then the underlying asset has effectively been bought at USD 1,950 and sold at USD 2,025 to generate a profit of USD 75.

If the underlying price is USD 1,800, the hedger buys the metal at this price and settles the obligation on the short put (USD 144). Since neither of the calls is exercised, the cost to the hedger is USD 1,944.

4.9.4 Min–max

Arguably the most popular trade used for hedging price risk by corporates is the "min–max" structure. This transaction is sometimes referred to as a risk reversal or zero premium collar. Recall that the purchase of the call option under the "synthetic long put" example incurred a cost of USD 41 per tonne, almost 2.0% of the current spot price. Many hedgers would be put off by this cost and so an effective way of offsetting the cost is for the company to take on risk in areas where it does not think will trade.

Combining options with the underlying exposure in the following manner would generate a "min–max" structure:

- The hedger is short the metal for forward delivery.
- Buy an out-of-the-money call with the strike set at a level with which the corporate is comfortable (assume USD 2,050 in this case).
- Sell an out-of-the-money put option, with the strike set at such a level that the premium generated is equal to that of the purchased call.

For this to be a zero premium structure the strike on the sold put would have to be set at USD 1,899. The net payoff of the structure is shown in Figure 4.13, which shows that the strategy fixes the maximum and minimum cost of the metal. These price boundaries are determined by the strikes of the two options, USD 2,050 and USD 1,899 in this instance. In between the two strikes, neither of the options is exercised and the manufacturer buys the metal in the open market.

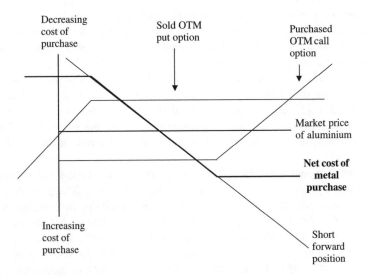

Figure 4.13   Min–max structure

To illustrate the effect of this strategy, consider three different scenarios: a steep rise in the average price of the metal; a steep fall in the average price of the metal; and no movement in the average price. If the average price of the metal were to fall to USD 1,800, the cost of buying the metal would be the cost of buying the metal in the underlying market at USD 1,800 plus the USD 99 cost of settling the sold put option. The call option is not exercised and there is no premium to be taken into account as it is a zero cost structure. The net cost to the manufacturer is therefore USD 1,899.

If the price of the metal rises to USD 2,100, the manufacturer pays this price to obtain his physical supplies of the metal but receives USD 50 from the purchased call option. The net cost to the corporate in this scenario is therefore USD 2,050. If the price of the metal does not move, neither option is exercised so the manufacturer simply buys the metal in the market at the prevailing price. Using the min–max structure, the manufacturer has the desired protection from a steep rise in the price of the metal but can participate in a fall in the price to a predetermined level. From this structure a number of permutations could be derived:

- The ratio min–max.
- Enhanced risk reversal.

4.9.5   Ratio min–max

In this structure, the strike on the purchased call is kept at USD 2,050. However, instead of selling options in equal proportions to the calls, the puts are executed with a transaction size of 50% of the underlying. This deal is structured to have a zero premium, which means that the strike on the put options has to be moved closer to the current forward price. In this instance it would result in a strike of USD 1,950 on the sold put.

As a result there is no longer a minimum price level at which the hedger will buy the metal. However, he will not get all of the benefit as the put option sold still represents a liability. Since the notional amount on the put is 50% of the call option, a 1 unit fall in the price below the strike of the put will result in the hedger benefiting by 50% of this change.

To illustrate the difference with the min–max structure, take a situation where the price of the metal falls to USD 1,800. Here the hedger buys the metal from his supplier at this price but must settle the put obligation, which is USD 75. This is the difference between the strike (USD 1,950) and the market price (USD 1,800) divided by 2 since the put is only 50% of the size of the underlying exposure. Thus, in this example, where the market at maturity is USD 150 lower than the strike on the put, the hedger benefits by 50% of the fall – a percentage equal to the transaction size of the put option. This gives a final hedge cost of USD 1,875 which is lower than that achieved on the simple min–max structure.

At first sight it would seem that this strategy is superior to the simple min–max as it does not impose a floor on the purchase of the metal in a falling market. However, like all option strategies it is not possible to obtain something for nothing and there is indeed a trade-off. With the simple min–max solution the hedger will benefit fully from any decline in price up to the strike of the put (USD 1,899). For the ratio min–max solution, the hedger may benefit in a falling price environment below a relatively high threshold level (USD 1,950), but he will only benefit from 50% of the decline, albeit with no floor.

4.9.6 Enhanced risk reversal

In the enhanced risk reversal, the call strike is kept at USD 2,050, while the strike on the short put is lowered to (say) USD 1,850. This makes the put more out-of-the-money, which lowers the consumer's minimum net purchase price but incurs a cost. To ensure that the structure remains zero premium in nature the consumer sells an additional out-of-the-money call to generate the required income. In this case the strike of the second call option would be set at USD 2,089.

The net result is that if the price of the metal falls below the strike of the sold put, the minimum cost to the consumer is USD 1,850. If the price is between the strike of the sold put (USD 1,850) and the long call (USD 2,050), none of the options is exercised and the consumer simply pays the current market price. If the price of the metal is above the purchased call (USD 2,050) but below the sold call (USD 2,089), the consumer pays USD 2,050. However, above USD 2,089, the consumer will pay an increasing amount (as a result of the short call) but still less than the prevailing market price (as a result of the long call).

Compared to the other two variants of this strategy, the enhanced risk reversal offers a lower minimum purchase price. In this case the trade-off is in a rising price environment. If the price rises steeply the consumer will be faced with an increasing purchase price.

4.10 STRUCTURED OPTION SOLUTIONS

The range of option-based strategies widens considerably if some were structure solutions that included some of the so-called "exotic" options such as barriers. Three possible strategies are highlighted here with an explanation of how they are structured.

4.10.1 Knock-out forwards

This is a standard forward contract that automatically terminates if the spot price trades at, or beyond, a predetermined outstrike before expiry. To compensate the investor for the potential early termination of the contract, the forward rate is set more favourably than the prevailing forward rate. The knock-out forward is generally structured for zero up-front cost.

Market rates	
Spot price	USD 1,968
3-month forward rate	USD 1,961

Contract rates	
Contract forward rate	USD 1,955
Knock-out rate	USD 2,277

In this transaction the consumer will buy aluminium at a rate of USD 1,955 at expiry of the contract as long as the knock-out rate of USD 2,277 does not trade during the life of the transaction. If the knock-out rate does trade, the forward contract is terminated and the consumer is left unhedged at what would now be a disadvantageous rate compared to the original 3-month forward.

The construction of this strategy is based on the principles of put–call parity using barrier options. The initial forward buying position is created by the purchase of a knock-out call and the sale of a knock-out put combining to give the synthetic forward position, but both of these barrier options will be terminated when a barrier of USD 2,277 is reached.

4.10.2 Forward plus

In a forward plus contract the client obtains protection against a steep rise in the underlying price by virtue of a zero premium call option that is struck slightly out-of-the-money. However, the contract contains a trigger level set below the current market rate, which, if activated, will alter the payoff of the structure. If the spot rate trades above this trigger rate during the life of the transaction, the client will retain the right to buy the underlying at the strike. However, if the spot rate trades below the trigger rate, this right becomes an obligation with the client being required to take delivery of the underlying at the strike rate.

To illustrate the concept, let us assume that the following values are observed in the market:

Market rates	
Spot price	USD 1,968
3-month forward price	USD 1,961
Contract rates	
Strike rate	USD 1,970
Trigger level	USD 1,850

If the spot rate rises during the life of the transaction and the trigger level does not trade, the consumer will buy aluminium at a rate of USD 1,970. This is slightly less advantageous than the initial forward rate, but this protection is obtained at zero premium. If spot falls below the strike, the consumer can walk away from the call and buy the metal at a cheaper price in the market. However, if the spot price falls to the trigger level of USD 1,850, the option to buy at the strike of USD 1,970 now becomes an obligation. This means that the consumer will never have to pay more than USD 1,970 for the metal but can only benefit from a fall in the price to USD 1,850.

This transaction is structured using the following components:

- Consumer buys a European style call option with a strike of USD 1,970 at a cost of USD 45 per tonne.
- Consumer sells a knock-in put option with a strike of USD 1,970 and a trigger level of USD 1,850 at a cost of USD 45 per tonne.

As long as spot does not trade at or below the trigger level, the consumer is left holding the European call. However, if the trigger level trades and the short put is activated, the combination of options creates a synthetic long buying position, again through the principles of put–call parity. The synthetic forward requires the consumer to buy the metal at the strike price of the two options.

4.10.3 Bonus forward

In a bonus forward contract the client is able to buy the underlying forward at a more advantageous rate than the initial forward rate provided that the spot price does not reach a certain trigger level before settlement. If the spot price reaches the trigger level, the forward rate is reset by a predetermined amount to the client's disadvantage.

Assume that the following terms and conditions apply:

Market rates	
Spot price	USD 1,968
3-month forward price	USD 1,961
Contract rates	
Bonus rate	USD 1,955
Protection rate	USD 1,975
Trigger level	USD 1,834

Under the terms of this contract the client will be able to buy aluminium at USD 1,955 (the bonus rate) as long as the trigger level of USD 1,834 does not trade. The bonus rate is more attractive than the initial forward rate. If the trigger level of USD 1,834 is hit then the customer will have an obligation to buy at USD 1,975 (the protection rate).

This structure can be thought of as a combination of two synthetic forwards:

- A synthetic long forward position struck at USD 1,955 that knocks out at USD 1,834 (i.e. long a knock-out call, short a knock-out put, which through put–call parity results in the synthetic long forward).
- Plus a synthetic long forward position struck at USD 1,975 that knocks in at USD 1,834 (i.e. long a knock-in call, short a knock-in put, which creates the second synthetic forward).

4.10.4   Basket options

Since an automotive producer may have a requirement to buy several different metals, a risk management strategy based on individual call options could prove to be very expensive.

An alternative structure that reduces the cost of protection is an option on a basket of metals. In the following example we will consider an equally weighted, two-metal basket option based on copper and aluminium. The payoff on this basket option at maturity is:

$$\text{Call option} : \max[0, (Q_1 S_1 + Q_2 S_2) - X)]$$

$$\text{Put option} : \max[0, X - (Q_1 S_1 + Q_2 S_2)]$$

where Q = weight of metal within the basket
  S = price of the metal at expiry
  X = strike price.

The strike price of the option, which is set at the start of the deal, is a weighted price. That is, the strike chosen for each individual metal is weighted by the proportion it contributes to the basket. Let us say that we select a strike that is at-the money forward for both metals and the respective values are USD 1,961 for aluminium and USD 4,856 for copper. The strike rate for an equally weighted basket would be USD 3,408.50 (50% × USD 1,961 + 50% × USD 4,856).

If a consumer were to buy a call option on this particular basket and the final prices at maturity were USD 2,000 and USD 5,000 for aluminium and copper respectively (ignoring premium costs), the value of the basket would be USD 3,500 (50% × USD 2,000 + 50% × USD 5,000). The payout on the option would be USD 91.50 (USD 3,500 − USD 3,408.50).

When pricing a basket option the key difference is the implied volatility input, as the price correlation between the constituent components needs to be taken into account. Price correlation describes the tendency of prices to move in the same direction and is expressed along a scale from +1 to −1. Positive correlation implies that both asset prices will tend to move in the same direction, while assets that have negative price correlation will have a tendency to move in opposite directions.

The form of the implied volatility input has been adapted from portfolio theory and is expressed as follows for a two-asset basket:

$$\sigma_{\frac{x_1}{x_2}} = \sqrt{(w_{x_1}^2 \sigma_{x_1}^2) + (w_{x_2}^2 \sigma_{x_2}^2) + 2 \times (w_{x_1} \ w_{x_2} \rho_{x_1 x_2} \sigma_{x_1} \sigma_{x_2})}$$

where $\sigma_{x_1}^2$ = variance of asset 1
$\sigma_{x_2}^2$ = variance of asset 2
$\rho_{x_1 x_2}$ = correlation between asset 1 and asset 2
σ_{x_1} = volatility of asset 1
σ_{x_2} = volatility of asset 2
w_{x_1} = proportion of asset 1
w_{x_2} = proportion of asset 2.

If we assume implied volatilities of 15% for aluminium and 20% for copper, Table 4.4 shows the composite basket volatility for a range of different correlation values and the associated premium for a 3-month option with a strike of USD 3,408.50.

If correlation increases, all other things being equal the volatility of the option will increase making the option more expensive. Intuitively, if the two assets are positively correlated then their prices are more likely to move in the same direction, increasing the magnitude of any expected payment to be made by the seller of a call option. Since the premium on an option can be thought of as the present value of the expected payout, this makes the option more expensive. The option will be cheaper where the asset prices are negatively correlated, as price movements will tend to be offsetting, reducing the expected payout.

Table 4.4   Composite basket volatility

Price correlation	Basket volatility	Option premium
−1.0	2.50%	USD 67.05
−0.5	9.01%	USD 85.08
0.0	12.50%	USD 100.08
+0.5	15.21%	USD 113.03
+1.0	17.50%	USD 124.64

The cost of the basket option can now be compared to the cost of two single 3-month call options purchased on the individual metals:

Aluminium
Strike   USD 1,961
Implied volatility   15%
Premium   USD 57.93

Copper
Strike   USD 4,856
Implied volatility   20%
Premium   USD 191.24

The total cost of purchasing two individual call options is therefore USD 249.17, compared to the maximum cost of the basket option of USD 124.64. Note that there is a relationship between the two individual call option assets and the basket option priced with a correlation of +1. At this level of correlation, the implied volatility of the basket option is 17.50%, equal to the weighted average of the two volatilities of the individual call options. Also the premium on the basket option is equal to the weighted average of the premia on the individual options. However, there is a small difference due to the fact that the individual call options were priced with a closed form model, whereas the basket option was priced with a binomial model, whose output is sensitive to the number of "steps" used.

However, note that the basket option is always cheaper than the individual options due to the effect of correlation. Even though, anecdotally, it may be perceived that prices of metals may move in the same direction, it is unlikely that they will be perfectly positively correlated. As a result of this the basket option will always be cheaper.

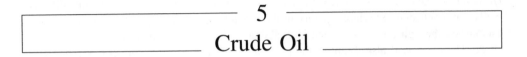

5
Crude Oil

I call petroleum the devil's excrement. It brings trouble...

Juan Pablo Perez Alfonso

SYNOPSIS **The purpose of this chapter is to describe the trading of crude oil and outline some of the derivative instruments that can be used to manage the associated price risk.**[*]

The first section details the *main chemical properties of crude oil*, which determine its value. An overview of the *physical supply chain* is presented, with a description of how crude oil is refined. Since crude oil is of little use in itself, the demand for crude oil is in effect refiner demand.

The main components of *demand and supply* are then analysed, which leads to a discussion of the main *price drivers*. Consideration is also given to *defining the price* of crude oil as well as detailing the term structure of prices.

The section on *trading of crude oil* outlines why trading takes place, the major participants, the key market risks and some of the associated strategies. This part of the chapter also highlights the main features of the Brent and West Texas Intermediate (WTI) markets.

The chapter concludes by considering a variety of *derivative risk management solutions* along the supply chain.

5.1 THE VALUE OF CRUDE OIL

The term "crude oil" does not really describe any specific type of oil, but rather the generic state of oils prior to their refinement. There are over 100 different types of crude oil, each with different chemical characteristics that are attractive for different reasons. Thus, when extracted from the ground crude oil may be a pale straw-coloured liquid or a thick tar-like substance. The value of crude oil therefore lies in what can be produced from the refining process; for example, crude oil that is classified as "light" (i.e. composed of short chain hydrocarbons) is sought for its relatively higher yield of gasoline.

5.1.1 Basic chemistry of oil

Crude oil is made up of hydrocarbons, which are molecules comprising of hydrogen and carbon atoms. The carbon atoms may be joined in a chain-like sequence or in a ring formation, with different numbers of hydrogen atoms attached. A certain crude oil may actually be made up of several different individual crudes, which are recovered from wells that are geographically close together and therefore share the same extraction facilities.

---

[*]Unless otherwise referenced, all data in this chapter was sourced from the annual *BP Statistical Review of World Energy 2006.*

However, as the quality of crude oil is not a constant and could change over time, different wells may contribute a variable quality in the overall supply. The quality of the crude oil is established through an assay, which is a laboratory-based assessment of the quality of the crude. The assay will also establish the percentage of each refined product that a particular crude can yield.

Since crude oil is of limited use in itself, its value lies in what can be produced from the refining process. As a result, it would seem that the demand for crude oil is effectively based on refinery demand. In addition, there may be a different set of factors that will influence the demand for refined products. Take, for example, one of the more popular refined products such as gasoline. The chemical specification may be influenced by factors such as government regulation (perhaps to reduce the lead content), current market prices, local demand and, possibly, seasonal influences.

When assessing the value of crude oil a number of important characteristics are considered.

5.1.2 Density

Density is a measure of the number of molecules within a defined volume. A simple analogy would be to compare a glass of water of a given volume with the same volume of mercury. Although they occupy the same space, the mercury will weigh considerably more than the water due to its greater density. From a crude oil perspective, density will help in quantifying the volume to weight ratio.

The density is usually expressed as an API gravity value. This is a measure of the weight of hydrocarbons according to a scale devised by the American Petroleum Institute. Crude oils that have a high API value are less dense ("lighter") and tend to produce greater volumes of higher value products (e.g. the so-called "distillates" as gasoline and kerosene) as part of the refining process. Heavy crude oils with a lower API are more difficult to refine and will produce lower yields of these higher value lighter products.

5.1.3 Sulphur content

Sulphur is an undesirable property when it appears in large quantities. Crude oil is classified as being "sweet" when the sulphur content is less than 0.5%; "sour" crude is where the sulphur content by weight is greater than 0.5%. Crudes with a high sulphur content require more processing and a greater energy input to complete the refining process.

5.1.4 Flow properties

Viscosity is a measure of the ability of the crude oil or refined product to flow or its resistance to pouring and can be measured on a number of different scales at a range of temperatures. At an intuitive level, it can be thought of as the "friction" of a liquid. For example, if a golf ball were dropped into a jar of water the resistance it would encounter would be less than that experienced if the ball were dropped into a jar of mayonnaise. Therefore, low-viscosity liquids flow more easily than high-viscosity liquids.

The *pour point* measures the lowest temperature at which either crude oil or a particular refined product flows as a liquid under a set of given conditions. A high pour point indicates that the product has to be heated for it to flow as a liquid. This will have an impact on how the oil is stored or transported.

5.1.5 Other chemical properties

- *Paraffinic* (literally "like paraffin"): This suggests that the crude has a low viscosity and high flammability. It would indicate that the crude could be used in the final production of lubricants. (In the UK, paraffin is the name given to kerosene.)
- *Naphthenic*: A crude oil with naphthenic properties is one that is has a high viscosity but is not highly flammable. This might make it suitable for the production of, for example, bitumen.
- *Intermediate*: This describes a crude oil whose properties sit between paraffinic and naphthenic.

5.1.6 Examples of crude oil

Some examples to illustrate the different chemical characteristics of crude oil are:

- *Light and sweet crude* (with an API of between 33° and 45°) are West Texas Intermediate (US crude oil) and Brent (North West European crude oil). These types of crude have a high gasoline yield.
- *Heavy and sour* (an API of between 10° and 45°) crude oils include Urals crude (eastern European crude oil), which is used as bitumen feedstock.

5.2 AN OVERVIEW OF THE PHYSICAL SUPPLY CHAIN

The main elements of the crude oil physical supply are:

- *Upstream activities*: This is the exploration and extraction of crude oil from either an off- or on-shore location.
- *Transportation and storage*: The crude oil has to be moved by pipeline or by tanker to a particular refining location. If the refinery is close to the extraction point, the oil can be stored locally prior to delivery or can be loaded onto ships for onward delivery.
- *Refining*: As crude oil by itself is of limited use, it must first be refined into a variety of products, such as gasoline.
- *Retail and wholesale distribution*: The refined products can then be delivered to the specific location for a wholesale purchaser (e.g. a particular airport for an airline buying Jet Fuel) or to a network of retail petrol/gas stations.

The main market participants will either be privately-owned companies such as BP or state-owned national oil companies (NOCs) such as Saudi Aramco. Although the privately-owned companies are among the largest corporates in the world (e.g. ExxonMobil), they are dwarfed in size by the NOCs.

Vertical integration is common along the supply chain but it is not necessarily the preserve of the private oil companies. For example, Saudi Aramco is vertically integrated with interests in exploration, production, refining, marketing and international shipping.

Although the analysis has so far concentrated on the larger participants, there are a number of independent companies who might specialise in one particular aspect of supply (e.g. production). Other relevant parties who trade in the market are financial institutions providing risk management solutions to supply chain participants, and private trading companies (e.g. Glencore). Private commodity trading companies sell to industrial consumers, obtaining their products either from third party sources or production assets they own.

5.3 REFINING CRUDE OIL

The process of refining takes the crude oil and separates it into various chemical components, which can be further treated to produce a series of new products. No two refineries are the same and their complexity will vary according to their ability to create a high-value end product.

Crude oil is pumped through a furnace to release different liquids and gases, which are then fed into a distillation tower. Inside the tower the liquids and gases separate into different components (referred to collectively as fractions) each with a different boiling point. The component with the lowest boiling point evaporates first and rises highest in the tower, while that with the highest boiling point evaporates last and is collected at the base of the tower.

From the top of the distillation tower downwards the components in Table 5.1 are collected. Once the crude has been separated into its fractions there is a second stage in which they are converted into intermediate products. Some of the fractions, such as liquefied petroleum gas, will not require much conversion. The conversion technique used is referred to as "cracking" as it takes the heavy hydrocarbon molecules and breaks them into lighter ones. Although there are a number of variants of the process (e.g. fluid catalytic cracking, hydro-cracking) the techniques use a combination of heat, pressure and a catalyst to achieve the required chemical reaction. The following products are usually produced:

- Gasoline
- Jet Fuel
- Diesel fuel
- Asphalt.

Depending on the configuration of the refinery, different fractions may be used to produce the various products. For example, there is usually a high demand for gasoline as it can be produced from either naphtha or gas oil, while diesel fuel could be made from either diesel distillate or gas oil.

Table 5.1 Refined products from crude oil

Temperature (°C)	Refined product
Less than − 45	Gas
−45 to 35	Liquid Petroleum Gas (LPG)
35 to 150	Gasolines and naphtha
150 to 230	Kerosene
230 to 340	Gas oil
340 to 400	Heavy gas oil
Above 400	Residue/fuel oil

The refined products have so far only been described in general terms. In reality, products such as gasoline will have very tight formulation guidelines that might be specified by law. The last stage of the refining process is therefore to modify the intermediate products into the form in which they will actually be consumed.

5.3.1 Applications of refined products

- *Gases*: The most significant products in this category are methane, ethane and propane. Methane is commonly referred to as "natural gas" and can be used for heating. Ethane is a feedstock for the petrochemical industry that can be used in the production of plastics. Propane may be used for cooking and heating purposes.
- *Gasoline and naphtha*: The main use of gasoline is to fuel motor vehicles. The gasoline will need to be of a certain specification, the most widely known being the octane number, which is frequently displayed on the forecourts of petrol stations. There are two ways of measuring this factor: the Research Octane Number (RON) or the Motor Octane Number (MON). Irrespective of which method is used, the higher the octane number the better the quality of the gasoline. Naphtha is most commonly used as a petrochemical feedstock.
- *Kerosene*: The principal use of kerosene is to produce Jet Fuel, which, similar to gasoline, will have different formulations. In some parts of the world kerosene is used for cooking and lighting.
- *Gas oils*: These are used to produce diesel engine fuels and for households that use oil as a source of heating.
- *Fuel oils*: These are often used as a source of fuel for the power requirements of refineries and power stations. They can also be used as fuel for ships, in which case it is termed "bunker fuel". (A bunker is simply a container in which the fuel for the ship is stored.)

Like any company making an end product, the refiners are concerned with maximising their revenue. In the jargon of the refiner, this is referred to as the "gross product worth" or "gross production value", which is a function of:

- *The yield from the particular type of crude*: This is the proportion of each refined product that can be made from a particular type of crude oil, which can be established by means of an assay.
- *The configuration of the refinery*: This is the way in which the refinery has been set up for the various products. For example, the refinery may choose different "cut points" (the different temperatures at which the refined products are collected).
- *Existing inventory levels*: In some respects these are rather like spare parts. The refiner may hold a stock of a particular refined product.

Gross production value can be used as another way of determining the value of crude oil. The refiner first calculates the total value of all the refined products produced, then subtracts all the associated costs incurred in their production (e.g. transport, insurance, operational costs and financing). The resultant figure is referred to as the "netback value" of crude oil. This value can be compared to the current market value of crude oil to determine whether it is more economical to buy or sell the oil.

5.4   THE DEMAND AND SUPPLY FOR CRUDE OIL

... as we know, there are known knowns; there are things we know we know. We also know there are known unknowns; that is to say, we know there some things we do not know. But there also unknown unknowns – the ones we don't know we don't know.

Donald Rumsfeld

5.4.1   Proved oil reserves

According to BP [1], proved oil reserves are

generally taken to be those quantities that geological and engineering information indicates with reasonable certainty can be recovered in the future from known reservoirs under existing economic and operating conditions.

Table 5.2 shows that the vast majority of proved reserves exist in the Middle East. However, the taste also indicates that despite anecdotal concerns over the scarcity of crude oil, the apparent level of reserves is increasing. At the end of 1985 the total recorded figure was 770.4 thousand million barrels (tmb). By the end of 2005 the figure had risen to 1,200.07 tmb, although this masked a steep decline in American reserves from 101.5 tmb to 59.5 tmb. However, it should be noted that it is difficult to derive a single figure on which the entire market will agree.

Table 5.2   Proved oil reserves (thousand million barrels)

	1985	1995	2005
Middle East	431.30	661.50	742.70
Europe and Eurasia	78.60	81.50	140.50
Africa	57.00	72.00	114.30
South and Central America	62.90	83.80	103.50
North America	101.50	89.00	59.50
Asia Pacific	39.10	39.20	40.20

5.4.2   R/P ratio

The Reserves to Production (R/P) ratio indicates the length of time (in years) that a country's remaining reserves would last if production were to continue at current levels. It is calculated by dividing the reserves remaining at the end of a year by the production in that year. On a global basis, the values would suggest that there are sufficient reserves for another 41 years of consumption at current levels. As we will see, however, this figure has to be treated with some caution and is only a snapshot at any point in time. It may change if new reserves are found or if demand for oil declines due to an increased use in alternative sources of energy. R/P figures for the main geographic regions are shown in Table 5.3, with additional values for certain individual countries.

Table 5.3 R/P values for different countries and regions

North America	11.9	*South and Central America*	40.7
USA	11.8	Ecuador	25.6
		Peru	27.1
Europe and Eurasia	22.0	Venezuela	72.6
Kazakhstan	79.6		
Azerbaijan	42.4	*Africa*	31.8
Russian Fed.	21.4	Libya	63.0
UK	6.1	Nigeria	38.1
		Sudan	46.3
Middle East	81.0		
Iran	93.0	*Asia Pacific*	13.8
Iraq	>100 years	Australia	20.0
Kuwait	>100 years	China	12.1
Saudi Arabia	65.6	India	20.7
Syria	17.5	Thailand	5.2
UAE	97.4	Vietnam	21.8
Global Total		40.6	

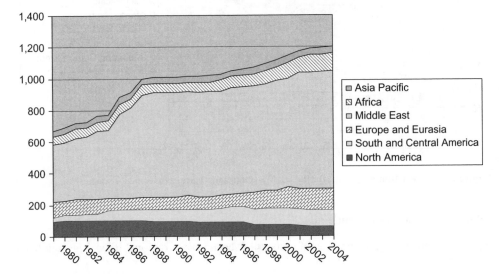

Figure 5.1 Evolution of proven oil reserves 1980–2005 (thousand million barrels)

Figure 5.1 shows that the level of proven reserves has not increased smoothly. For example, the following countries announced a sudden increase in proved reserves:

- *Kuwait* – from 67 to 92.7 tmb between 1983 and 1984 (38% increase);
- *United Arab Emirates* – from 33 to 97.2 tmb between 1985 and 1986 (195% increase);

- *Iran* – from 59 to 92.9 tmb between 1985 and 1986 (a 57% increase) and from 99.1 to 130.7 tmb (32% increase) from 2001 to 2002;
- *Saudi Arabia* – from 169.6 to 255 tmb between 1987 and 1988 (50% increase).

5.4.3   Production of crude oil

Figure 5.2 illustrates that between 1965 and 2005, production of crude oil rose from an annual figure of 31,803 thousand barrels daily (tbd) in 1965 to 81,088 tbd by 2005. During this period the share of production attributable to OPEC increased from 14,386 tbd (45%) to 33,836 tbd (42%). The other noticeable increase in production has been in the states that comprised the former Soviet Union.

For the UK, North Sea oil peak production was reached in 1999 with a total of 2,909 tbd, which made up about 2.5% of the total world production. The peak for US production came in 1972 at 11,185 tbd (21% of global production) but by the end of 2005, production had fallen to 6,830 tbd, accounting for 8.0% of global production.

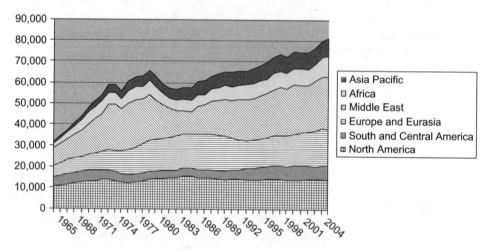

Figure 5.2   Production of crude oil 1965–2005 (thousands barrels daily)

5.4.4   Consumption of crude oil

Figure 5.3 shows the consumption of crude oil over time on a regional basis. The significant facts are:

- The consumption of crude oil has continued to rise globally.
- The USA is the largest single consuming country, accounting for 25% of the total world consumption.
- The influence of Asia Pacific countries, such as India and China, is growing; but this should be kept in perspective because China's consumption as a percentage of the global total is only 8.5%, while the figure for India is 3.0%.
- Although the Middle East produces over 31% of the world's crude oil it only consumes 7.1% of the total.

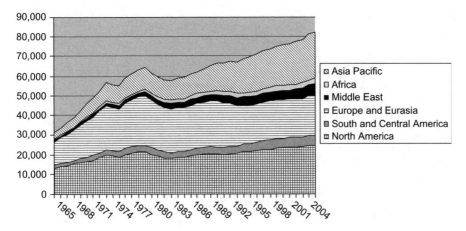

Figure 5.3 Consumption of crude oil 1965–2004 (thousand barrels daily)

5.4.5 Demand for refined products

The BP statistical review provides a regional breakdown of the demand for the refined products. It describes the products in four categories:

- *Light distillates*: Aviation and motor gasolines and light distillate feedstock.
- *Middle distillates*: Jet and heating kerosenes; gas and diesel oils.
- *Fuel oil*: Marine bunkers and crude oil used directly as fuel.
- *Others*: These consist of refinery gas, LPG, solvents, petroleum coke, lubricants, bitumen wax and refinery fuel.

The most significant regional consumer considering all refined products is North America while from an individual product perspective the demand for gasoline is the most significant (Table 5.4)

Table 5.4 Regional consumption of refined products – 2005 (thousand barrels daily)

	Light distillates	Middle distillates	Fuel oil	Others
North America	10,970	7,188	1,390	5,326
South and Central America	1,227	1,872	704	973
Europe and Eurasia	3,758	7,572	1,882	3,203
Middle East	1,210	1,816	1,473	1,240
Former Soviet Union	923	1,146	699	1,168
Africa	631	1,180	477	475
Asia Pacific	6,600	8,810	3,526	5,021

5.4.6 Oil refining capacity

Figure 5.4 illustrates the regional oil refining capacity from 1965 to 2005, and shows that, over the period, overall capacity has grown from 34,513 tbd to 85,702 tbd, an increase of

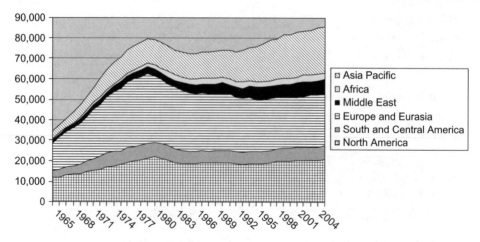

Figure 5.4   Regional oil refinery capacity: 1965–2005 (thousand barrels daily)

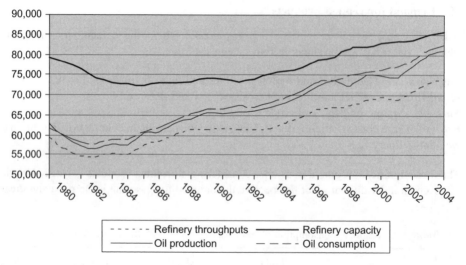

Figure 5.5   Global refinery throughput, refinery capacity, oil production, oil consumption: 1980–2005 (thousand barrels daily)

148%. This does mask, however, a decline in the 1980s due to the low price environment and poor returns on capital. As a result of relatively low investment in this period, refining capacity was unable to meet a sharp increase in demand in later years. In terms of refinery location, there has been a switch from Europe and North America towards the Middle East and Asia Pacific so that, although the Middle East produces 31% of the world's crude oil, it currently only has 8% of the world's refining capacity, although this is expected to increase over time.

Although Figure 5.4 illustrates the refinery capacity, Figure 5.5 shows the evolution of four related variables on a global basis:

• oil production (the supply of crude oil)

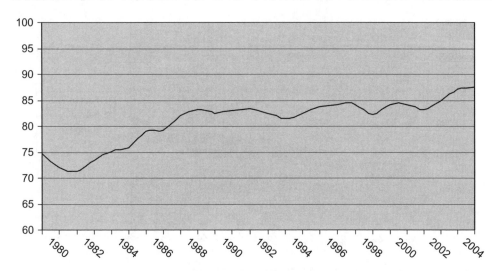

Figure 5.6 Global refinery capacity utilisation (expressed as a percentage) 1980–2005

- oil consumption (the demand)
- refinery capacity (how much the refineries can process)
- refinery throughput (how much crude oil was actually processed).

The data is presented on a global basis and so will not necessarily capture regional differences, but it does highlight how the increase in refinery capacity has lagged production and consumption due to lack of investment, in addition to the legal and environmental difficulties of building more facilities. Figure 5.5 also illustrates a very interesting issue in that consumption exceeds production on a consistent basis. Although this is feasible for short periods of time, with the short fall being made from inventories, it is not sustainable in the long run. However, the units of measurement–barrels as opposed to tonnes–are important in this respect and hence the diagram is correct. This is because 1 tonne of heavy crude oil will occupy a smaller space that 1 tonne of lighter crude. When the heavy crude is therefore refined into a series of "lighter" refined products, they will occupy a larger volume for the same weight. Hence it is possible for consumption of refined products on a per barrel basis to exceed production. However, if the values are expressed on a per tonne basis, 1 tonne of crude could never produce more than 1 tonne of refined products.

Figure 5.6 shows, on an ongoing basis, the percentages at which refineries (at a global level) have been operating over the period by expressing the throughputs as a percentage of the total capacity. Although there has been an increase in the demand for refined products, it is common for refiners to underutilise their capacity to keep upward pressure on the price of what they sell.

5.4.7 Crude oil imports and exports

Figure 5.7 illustrates the growth, in the amount of oil imported over the period 1980 to 2005 on a regional basis. This growth in imports is, of course, matched by a corresponding growth in exports, as is illustrated in Figure 5.8. Again, the Middle East dominates the

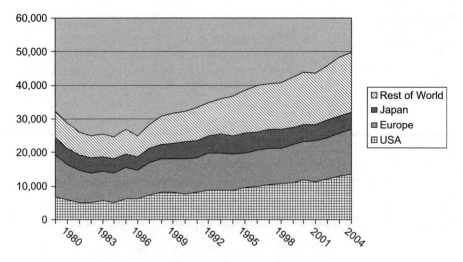

Figure 5.7   Imports of crude oil: 1980–2005 (thousand barrels daily)

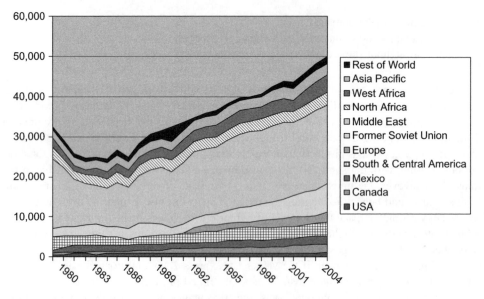

Figure 5.8   Exports of crude oil: 1980–2005 (thousand barrels daily)

figures. Note that the USA accounts for a very small proportion of the world's exports as, apart from Alaskan crudes, it is illegal to export the commodity.

The net trade position by country is illustrated in Figures 5.9 and 5.10.

5.4.8   Security of supply

One of the key themes in most energy markets is the issue of the security of supply. This can be interpreted in a number of ways but, at a simple level, it can be thought of as the

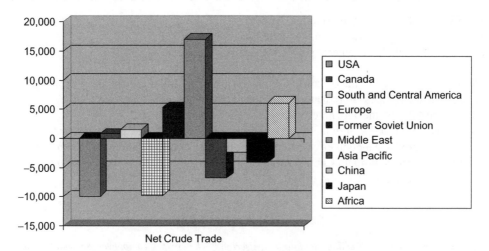

Figure 5.9   Net trade in crude oil: 2005 (thousand barrels daily; a negative figure indicates that the country is a net importer; a positive figure indicates that the country is a net exporter)

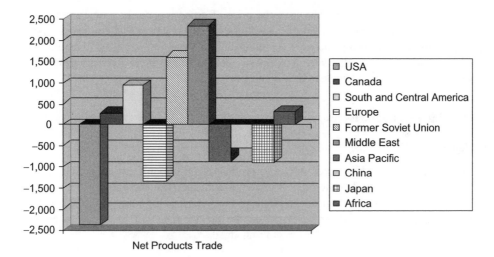

Figure 5.10   Net trade in petroleum products: 2005 (thousand barrels daily; a negative figure indicates that the country is a net importer; a positive figure indicates that the country is a net exporter)

ability of any country to ensure that there is a sufficient ongoing supply to meet expected demand. One of the ways in which this can be achieved is by diversifying the sources of supply. The largest individual importers as of 2005 are:

- USA 13,525 tbd
- Europe 13,261 tbd
- Japan 5,225 tbd.

For each of those countries the three main sources of supply are (in descending order of volume):

- *USA*:   South and Central America, Middle East, Canada
- *Europe*:   Former Soviet Union, Middle East, North Africa
- *Japan*:   Middle East, other Asia Pacific countries, Africa.

The Middle East is the major crude oil exporter, but it is notable that there are a number of regional differences. For example, Middle Eastern imports only make up 17% of US imports but 82% of the Japanese figures.

   Likewise, producers of crude oil are equally sensitive to changes in demand patterns and should therefore have a number of different supply destinations. Examples of a concentration of supply include South and Central America, which exports 81% of its output to the USA, while the Former Soviet Union exports 82% of its production to Europe.

5.5   PRICE DRIVERS

Oil is not ours, it's theirs. You don't find oil in Switzerland; when prices go up, everyone wants to share the bonanza.

Paolo Scaroni, Chief Executive of ENI [2]

There are a number of factors that drive the price of crude oil. For convenience, the issues have been collated under three generic headings: supply chain considerations, geopolitics (i.e. the study of relationships between nations) and macroeconomic issues. In addition there will be a series of factors that will influence the demand and supply for the various refined products, which may feed back to the price of crude oil.

5.5.1   Macroeconomic issues

Economic activity

If there is strong growth in gross domestic product (GDP), signifying increased economic activity, then it is likely that the price of crude oil will increase accordingly. This may also have another effect in that if consumers believe that prices will be higher in the future they may be tempted to buy forward. Sellers, on the other hand, will be happy to enjoy the benefits of a higher price and may remain unhedged.

Reserves

Arguably, the most contentious question that arises with respect to crude oil is how much is left? Undeniably, crude oil is a finite resource, which at some point will be exhausted.

   When discussing this issue, reference is often made to the concept of "Hubbert's peak". Hubbert, a US geologist, predicted in the 1950s that US crude oil production would peak in the early 1970s; according to BP's annual energy review, peak production was reached in 1972. On a global scale there is no consensus; a range of different estimates is available.

   Take a large publicly quoted oil company like BP whose accounts are prepared according to different regulatory guidelines in the UK and the USA. Although the adequacy and suitability of these guidelines is outside the scope of this book, the two different methods adopted have resulted in BP recording two slightly different figures for their remaining reserves.

Compare this to a national oil company such as Saudi Aramco, the largest oil company in the world. Since they are a private state-owned organisation, their accounts are not subject to the same degree of disclosure. This is not meant to imply that the figures for Saudi Arabia are inaccurate, but it becomes difficult to compare reserve figures between different countries and accounting regimes.

For existing wells the issue is more of how to extract what remains, as about only one-third of the oil within a known reservoir is likely to be extracted. At a very simple level it has to be economically viable for a producer to recover what is remaining. Although this will be a function of a number of variables it would seem reasonable to suggest that a producer has to earn an acceptable return on capital invested to make such extraction worth while.

This means that the effectiveness of technology to retrieve the oil, and the price they will receive for it, will play important roles. There will also be known reserves that are difficult to access, but with improved technology and an increasing price, it may become worth while to extract it. Then there is "unknown" technology where economic circumstances may act as a spur for further innovation that is at present inconceivable. It also may be that there are large reserves that are as yet undiscovered. Despite the often made remark that the world is getting smaller, there are large areas of many existing oil-producing countries that remain unsurveyed in terms of potential oil production. As a result, companies will continue to search for oil in the hope that they discover a major reservoir – sometimes referred to in the industry as an "elephant" field.

Availability of strategic reserves

The USA maintains a Strategic Petroleum Reserve, which was designed to provide the country with an emergency supply of crude oil. A system of 62 underground storage facilities, capable of holding some 700 million barrels, was set up in the 1970s on the Gulf of Mexico.

Possibility of substitution

One of the effects of the substantial rise in oil prices in the 1970s was that it ultimately encouraged oil users to switch to alternative sources, notably to natural gas. This movement away from crude oil was partly responsible for the low crude oil prices of the 1980s. With the prospect of many carbon fuels being eventually exhausted and 65% of each barrel of oil being consumed by the transport sector, many oil companies are now attempting to diversify into alternative sources of energy, which in some respects is leading to a redefinition of what is actually meant by crude oil. As the price of crude oil rises there is an incentive to switch to alternatives such as biofuels (ethanol), gas-to-liquids technology (a process that can be used to turn gas or coal into products normally produced from crude oil), hydrogen fuel and fuel cells, solar energy, nuclear power, and wind technology.

The use of hydrogen as a replacement for gasoline has been mooted as a substitute due to the lack of side effects. Hydrogen is added to a fuel cell and mixed with oxygen, which chemically reacts to produce electricity. This powers an electric motor, which propels the car. The resultant exhaust comprises nothing more than water or vapour. Even this technology is not without problems as one of the likeliest sources of hydrogen is expected to be natural gas. However, production of the cars in significant numbers has not transpired to date. A major obstacle to its development is the significant cost of the attendant global refuelling infrastructure.

A rising oil price may encourage users to seek out alternative products, but it may also encourage companies to look for oil in remote parts of the world and even in deep-water areas. One of the more unconventional areas of development is the Canadian oilsands of Alberta [3]. Oilsands is a general term for mixtures that have the consistency of molasses but may comprise several organic materials such as bitumen. Bitumen has naphthenic properties in that it has a high viscosity and is not particularly flammable. The API gravity of the bitumen found in the Canadian oilsands varies between about 7 and 13, while the sulphur content is 4–6%. Once recovered from the earth it is upgraded to heavy crude oil before being transported along pipelines to a refinery where it can be processed and refined. The attractiveness of the project is that it offers a source of crude oil supply many times greater than that of Saudi Arabia.

However attractive this may seem, there are some drawbacks. Two tonnes of oilsands yield about 1.25 barrels of bitumen and a single barrel of crude. Also the energy required for extraction is considerable and would consume a large proportion of the country's natural gas output. As the extraction process requires a significant amount of water, there are the related issues of origin, storage and transport. In addition, the environmental issues of restoring the countryside to its natural state can no longer be ignored.

Price of other crude oils

Since the majority of crude oils are priced as a differential from a series of core marker crudes such as WTI and Brent, movements in one of the marker crudes will have a knock-on effect to the remaining market.

Demand for refined products

Each refined product will have its own unique supply and demand dynamics and in some cases these may feed back into the crude oil market. For example, in winter crude oils that are favoured for the production of heating oils will gain in value, while a similar effect is seen in the summer for the crude oils that yield larger amounts of gasoline.

Taxation

In the late twentieth century, European governments gave drivers substantial tax incentives to buy diesel-powered cars partly because they emit fewer greenhouse gases. This led to an increase in the number of diesel cars sold in Europe, rising from 14% of all new car sales in 1990 to 50% by 2005 [4]. As a result, consumption of diesel increased accordingly. However, the increase in demand was not matched by a similar investment in refining technology that would allow the conversion of heavier fuel oils to the more attractive middle distillates such as diesel. As a result, diesel prices rose above those for gasoline.

Investor activity

As the price of oil increases, the market becomes more attractive to institutional investors. Given the volume of money flowing into the market, their activities are often cited as being responsible for creating a self-reinforcing circle.

Since most investors would be reluctant to take delivery of the physical commodity the most popular method to take exposure to the commodities market is by the futures market. However, some funds may be constrained in their ability to transact futures and so exposure is taken via a total return transaction. Here the investor enters into an agreement with an investment bank where the investor receives a cashflow that mimics the return on a commodity index such as the S&P GSCI. This index takes its value from the prices of a number of commodity futures and has a significant exposure to the price of oil. Although the nature of the index will be considered in more detail in a subsequent chapter, part of the return to an investor is generated by the rolling of futures contracts. The futures roll describes the process of selling the front month contract (the "prompt" contract) as it approaches maturity and buying the next delivery month to maintain exposure to the commodity. With significant investor inflows into the index, this activity can be significant and may drive the market into contango at the shorter end of the forward curve.

Investment in the S&P GSCI is essentially passive in nature as it is compiled according to a predetermined set of rules. As I have argued, it will influence the forward curve at shorter maturities and will generally be attractive to "real money" accounts such as pension funds and mutual funds as it is an unleveraged "long only" investment. However, active investors (such as hedge funds or commodity trading advisers) will operate along the forward curve and will be free to go long and short the commodity.

Movement of the USD

Like most commodities, crude oil is priced in US dollars and so a weakening of the currency should lead to an increase in the demand for the commodity from non-dollar users, as the cost is now lower in terms of domestic currency.

5.5.2 Supply chain considerations

Upstream production capacity and also spare production capacity

This is the capacity at the point of (on- or offshore) extraction. Some large producers have chosen to keep a certain amount of idle capacity in order to respond to any sharp increase in demand. Typically, Saudi Arabia has retained sufficient capacity to meet any temporary upswing in demand, but this should not suggest that it has an infinite capacity to be able to perform this function. Indeed its spare production capacity is in the heavier crudes with higher sulphur content. This will only be of use if there is sufficient refining capacity for this type of crude oil.

Refining capacity

If there is a sudden increase in demand there may not be sufficient physical refining capacity resulting, in an increase in the price of oil.

The construction of oil refineries has a very long lead time, is expensive and has to overcome many environmental considerations. For example, expansion of an existing facility could take at least two years while construction of a new refinery upwards of five years. In the USA in 1981 there were 325 refineries with a total capacity of 18.6 million barrels a day. By late 2005, there were 148 refineries with a slightly lower capacity of 17 million barrels a day, despite the fact that the country's demand for gasoline had increased by more than 20% [5]. Part of this capacity reduction was attributable to a low crude oil price in the 1980s, which reduced the return on investment in the refining industry to about 5.5%. Although it is likely that global refining capacity will increase, it will probably be driven by OPEC members in the Persian Gulf and Asia.

In some respects production and refinery capacity are interrelated, as refineries will be configured in different ways to process different types of crude oil. For example, in a rising price environment a complex refinery will be able to take the heavier and more sour crude oils and refine them into higher value products, giving them significant margins as these types of crude will tend to trade at a discount to the lighter, sweeter crudes. Therefore having spare production capacity in these types of crude is of little use if the refineries are working at full capacity. Equally, if spare simple refining capacity exists for the lighter sweeter crudes, but there is no spare production capacity, these types of crude will be priced at a premium.

Refinery margins

One of the key price relationships within the crude oil market, which measures the relative attractiveness of the refined products to crude oil, is the "crack spread". This measures the difference between the income generated by the refined products and the cost of the crude oil used in the refining process. After Hurricane Katrina in 2005, US petroleum prices rose to the equivalent of USD 122 a barrel. The cost of a single barrel of crude oil at the time was USD 70, pushing margins to about USD 50 a barrel. Traders did not believe that this level was sustainable and so drove the price of crude oil upwards as a result [6].

Storage capacity

US storage capacity has been estimated at about 360 million barrels [7] and given that it is finite by nature it will have an impact on price. Take a situation where there are concerns about the future security of crude oil supplies, encouraging participants to build their crude oil inventories. Storage should become more expensive, driving up the cost of oil for forward delivery. However, if there is nowhere to store the crude oil, producers may eventually be forced to cut production, increasing the cost of shorter-dated crude oil relative to longer-dated maturities.

Availability of supporting resources

Although much is made of the production – refining – demand triangle, an often overlooked feature of the supply chain is the availability and cost of such items as oil rigs, tankers and a skilled workforce. As commodity prices rise, the cost of raw materials such as steel will also increase, thus raising the cost of large projects such as oil rigs and refineries. This has a knock-on effect as it increases the cost of producing a barrel of oil, which has been estimated [8] at about USD 22 a barrel (2005 prices).

One interesting example relating to the cost of associated services is the cost of shipping oil. In mid-2006 BP announced the shutdown of crude oil production at Prudhoe Bay in Alaska due to maintenance issues. At the time the field was producing about 400,000 barrels of crude oil every day and was a major source of supply for refineries on the west coast of the USA. In order to meet its existing commitments BP were forced to look overseas for alternative sources of supply. Estimates [9] suggested that it would take 12 very large crude carriers (VLCCs) over a 60-day period to transport the deficit in production to the USA. In a market where the number of vessels capable of moving this amount of crude oil was estimated at 400 to 450, the extra demand for the freight would move charter prices significantly and have a knock-on effect on margins.

The cost of hiring ships to transport crude is reflected in the Baltic Freight Dirty Tanker index, while the Baltic Freight Clean Tanker index measures the cost of transporting refined products.

Infrastructure spending

In theory a rising oil price should encourage producers to spend more money on improving the existing infrastructure and to invest in new production opportunities. However, producers have very bad memories of crude oil priced at USD 10 a barrel and are often reluctant to invest in times of high oil prices in case of a subsequent fall.

Environmental considerations

As many governments increase the environmental regulations, the possibility of building large infrastructure projects decreases. Take the construction of a refinery in the USA; from the mid-1990s onwards refiners spent some USD 47 billion meeting the demands of a plethora of environmental laws. Further US Government regulations in 2006 required refiners to reduce the amount of sulphur in both gasoline and diesel at an estimated cost of USD 16 billion.

Oil field activity

Market participants closely monitor current production to identify any possible supply disruptions. For example, a monthly count of all rotary rigs is published, while the maintenance of existing fields is also closely scrutinised.

Natural disasters

In a similar vein, natural disasters that lead to shutdowns of rigs, entire fields or refining capacity, will have a substantial impact on the price of crude oil. For example, Hurricane Katrina that hit the US Gulf coast in the summer 2005 led to the closure of approximately 10% of the nation's refining capacity and 90% of the US Gulf of Mexico output. Shortly afterwards Hurricane Rita led to a temporary shutdown of 27% of refining capacity [6].

Quality of crude oil

The quality of oil from a particular field is not necessarily constant. Since oil extracted from different wells within a designated area may be collected into a single system, the quality of each constituent crude oil may be different.

5.5.3 Geopolitics

War and terrorism

Although the motives for the major Middle East conflicts are outside the scope of this book, the impact on the price of crude has been significant. A country with substantial reserves, such as Iraq, will have an effect on global production when physical capacity to produce and deliver is destroyed. Associated with the various conflicts have been acts of terrorism in Iraq and neighbouring countries such as Saudi Arabia. One concern relating to a potential terrorist attack is Saudi Arabia where two-thirds of its oil production is moved through two processing plants and a single terminal.

Internal unrest

Oil-rich countries such as Venezuela and Nigeria have suffered bouts of internal unrest that have threatened to reduce crude oil production in their respective countries

Political tensions and the security of supply

Reference is often made to the "fear factor" within commodity markets and usually in relation to concerns over the security of supply. In 2006, Iran revived its uranium enrichment activities generating fears that it would lead to the development of a nuclear weapon and, as a result, the price of crude rose by about USD 10 a barrel. As China continues to industrialise it has shown that it is prepared to secure supplies from countries with which the USA has refused to deal (e.g. Iran, Sudan, Angola). This has led some commentators to speculate on future tensions between the superpowers as they both wrestle for control of strategic oil supplies.

It is often assumed that the suppliers of crude oil exert more influence over the price than the buyers. However, this is not always the case, and it is valid to consider the notion of "security of demand" – that is, oil-producing companies have to be certain that they will be able to find a buyer for their output. Thus, while buyers are looking for diversification of supply, producers are looking for certainty of demand.

Resource nationalism

In some oil countries the substantial price rises of the early twenty-first century led to an increase in nationalism as newly elected governments threatened to nationalise oil production in their respective countries (e.g. Bolivia, Ecuador, Venezuela). Russia has also reasserted control over some aspects of energy production as prices have risen. However, resource nationalism may manifest itself in less obvious forms. For example, when concerns were being raised about nationalisation in South America, the UK increased taxes on revenues earned by oil companies operating in the North Sea.

Access to new reserves

A significant proportion (about 75%) of the world's oil is owned by national (i.e. government-owned) oil companies (NOCs), who may choose to allow international oil companies access to the oil when the NOCs do not possess a certain technical capability. This has made it difficult for private oil companies to replenish their reserves and has driven them into new areas of research (e.g. gas-to-liquids technology) or risky areas of exploration (e.g. Canadian oilsands or 10,000 foot waters)

Organisation of the petroleum exporting countries (OPEC)

According to the organisation's website [10] their mission statement is:

...to coordinate and unify the petroleum policies of Member Countries and ensure the stabilisation of oil prices in order to secure an efficient, economic and regular supply of petroleum to consumers, a steady income to producers and a fair return on capital to those investing in the petroleum industry.

The current list of OPEC members is:

Algeria	Indonesia	Islamic Republic of Iran
Iraq	Kuwait	Libya
Nigeria	Qatar	Saudi Arabia
United Arab Emirates	Venezuela.	

OPEC meets twice a year and the main technique used to achieve their objectives is to target output quotas for each of the member countries. Although the countries collectively do not produce the entire global output of oil (they are believed to control about only 40%) their output is significant and the market closely monitors their activities. In recent times their strategy has been to link their production quotas to the inventories of the OECD countries.

5.5.4 Analysing the forward curves

So far the analysis has concentrated on generic price factors without necessarily considering their term structure. Davis [11] argues that the term structure of oil can be broken into two segments: 0–18 months and beyond 18 months. He argues that the 0–18 month segment is closely linked to the physical market and reacts mostly to issues such as: demand and supply, the level of inventories, availability of storage and security of supply. Beyond those maturities market activities focus more on financial rather than physical concerns, which may include expectations over interest rates and inflation. It is also where market participants are likely to express their views on proposed capital expenditure and anticipated infrastructure projects.

He also notes that the term structure is more volatile than financial markets and may display seasonality, and that crude oil prices tend to display mean reversion over the longer term.

5.6 THE PRICE OF CRUDE OIL

5.6.1 Defining price

The price of crude oil is expressed in US dollars per barrel, sometimes shortened to USD per bbl. The origin of the abbreviation "bbl" is unclear, with two competing explanations. One story argues it derived from the practice of storing crude oil in blue coloured barrels, whereas some argue that the abbreviation arose from the fact that beer barrels were originally used for storage.

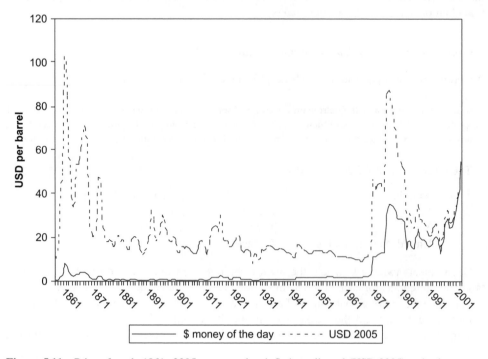

Figure 5.11 Price of crude 1861–2005, expressed as inflation adjusted (USD 2005) or in-the-money of the day

5.6.2 The evolution of crude oil prices

High crude oil prices are often seen as a modern-day problem. However, if one adjusts for the effect of inflation, a different picture emerges.

Figure 5.11 indicates that when adjusted for inflation there are two significant price peaks. The first was in 1864 (an early "boom and bust" period in the oil industry) when the price exceeded USD 100 a barrel, and in 1980 when the price nearly touched USD 88 (the first global oil crisis).

5.6.3 Delivered price

What will be delivered and the nature of the price to be paid has to be specified on the contract, which, typically will include:

- the price (usually expressed in USD per barrel)
- whether the contract is to be priced off an index or a "marker" crude
- any differential that should be applied to the price
- the quality (e.g. sulphur content)
- when it will be delivered

- where it will be delivered
- whether the price is CIF or FOB.

The price of crude oil is usually expressed in one of two ways: Free On Board (FOB) or Cost, Insurance and Freight (CIF). An FOB price is the most common pricing method as it represents the price of the commodity at the point of loading and therefore allows comparisons to be made between different crude oil prices around the world. However, a purchaser of crude is going to be more interested in the CIF price as it gives an indication of the total cost.

Typically the cost of delivering crude oil to a purchaser will include:

- the quoted FOB price;
- shipping costs;
- any associated "secondary" transportation expenses such as pipeline costs (if the refinery is not based on the coast);
- losses due to factors such as evaporation;
- insurance costs;
- cost of financing oil purchased while in transit and prior to product refinement (there will be a gap between when oil is paid for and when the refined products are sold to generate income).

5.6.4 Marker crudes

There is no single overarching price for crude oil. There are a number of so-called "marker" crudes, from which other grades will be priced. The key global marker crudes that are used as pricing benchmarks are:

- West Texas Intermediate (USA origin; global benchmark)
- Brent (North West Europe origin; global benchmark)
- Dubai (Middle East origin; Gulf benchmark)
- Tapis (Malaysian origin; Asia Pacific benchmark)
- Urals (Eastern Europe origin; Mediterranean benchmark).

The selection of a crude oil as a benchmark does not follow any predetermined formula. For example, Brent is a key global benchmark, even though it now only contributes less than 10% to total global output. However, an advantage is that it originates from a politically stable region and is supported by an actively traded derivatives market, similar to West Texas Intermediate (WTI) in the USA.

The price of crude oil referred to by OPEC is based on a basket of oils (ORB–OPEC Reference Basket) produced by the member countries. The ORB is made up of the following crudes:

- Saharan Blend (Algeria)
- Minas (Indonesia)
- Iran Heavy (Islamic Republic of Iran)
- Basra Light (Iraq)
- Kuwait Export (Kuwait)

- Es Sider (Libya)
- Bonny Light (Nigeria)
- Qatar Marine (Qatar)
- Arab Light (Saudi Arabia)
- Murban (UAE)
- BCF 17 (Venezuela).

However, members of OPEC are free to use different approaches in order to price their own physical contracts. For example, Saudi Arabia will price its oil depending on its final destination. If the crude is going to the USA, it is priced as a differential to WTI; while crude going to Europe is priced as a differential to Brent crude.

It may seem surprising, given that it holds a significant proportion of the proven reserves of crude oil and is also a key supplier, that Saudi Arabia's crude oils are not considered as global markers. The reason for this dates back to the 1980s when the crude oil producers introduced "net back pricing". Producing nations rationalised that the value of crude oil lay in the different products that could be produced from the refining process. At the time the refined products were trading at relatively high prices and so the producers set the price of crude on the basis these higher values, less a margin for refining and transportation. Under this system the refiners would earn a fixed margin irrespective of how much they produced and so were incentivised to run at high capacity. This led to an oversupply of products, whose prices fell significantly as well as those for crude oil (see Figure 5.11).

One of the consequences of this was that Saudi Arabia introduced a clause into its sales contracts that would only allow for the crude oil to be refined by the original purchaser. Transfer of ownership is prohibited (without the express permission of the original seller) and, as a result, there is no actively traded market for Saudi crude oil.

5.6.5 Pricing sources

When pricing crude oil contracts, participants need to be aware of the current term structure of prices. There are a number of companies that specialise in compiling and publishing reference prices based on market activity, with Platts or Petroleum Argus being the mostly widely referenced. A number of Far Eastern contracts are referenced to the Asian Petroleum Price Index (APPI), which is published twice weekly.

5.6.6 Pricing methods

There are a number of different approaches to establishing the price of a crude contract as follows:

- *Official selling prices*: This was a traditional method of pricing oil where governments would announce the price for the sale of crude for a fixed period of time such as one year.
- *Fixed price*: Here the price to be applied has been bilaterally negotiated at a given level. Anecdotally, it is believed that about 90 to 95% of crude oil sold is on a long-term fixed price basis and therefore the spot market makes up no more than 5 to 10% of the market.

- *Floating price*: This uses a price quoted by companies such as Platts or Petroleum Argus, which is not fixed in advance. The process to determine the actual price is specified in the contract and may be the average of prices covering a short period around the delivery date.
- *Differential to a marker crude*: This is where a particular crude oil is quoted as a differential to one of the marker crudes noted above. The differential could move according to a variety of market factors and could either be positive or negative. For example, a crude oil that produces a higher yield of gasoline would be in greater demand during the summer months and the differential may therefore increase. Equally, a crude oil that yields a higher proportion of heating oil may be in greater demand in the winter months, again affecting the size of the differential.
- *Futures price*: This might be relative to a futures price on a particular date or an average of prices over a previously agreed period. It should, however, be noted that a futures market does not exist for every type of crude.
- *Exchange for physicals*: This pricing method allows two counterparties to a physical trade to fix a price using the futures market. A simple numerical example of this approach will be outlined in Chapter 6.

5.6.7   The term structure of oil prices

Prices for future delivery as represented by the forward curve will experience either "contango" (forward prices higher than spot prices) or "backwardation" (forward prices lower than spot prices).

Although something of a generalisation, commodity sectors such as crude oil and base metals are more prone to backwardation. This contrasts with precious metals, which mostly experience contango. One explanation of this is the availability of the commodity above ground. In the gold market a large amount of gold is held above ground and storage costs are relatively small. However, with crude oil it is relatively expensive to store the commodity (about 20% of the cost of a barrel), which discourages its storage. As a result, an increase in demand may not be met from existing stocks, as it will need to be extracted and refined. Given the time lag, spot prices rise relative to forward prices and may push the market into backwardation.

Backwardated markets are characterised by:

- a scarcity of the commodity;
- low inventories;
- volatile prices as a result of low inventories;
- a strongly rising price;
- a "fear" premium.

Contango markets are characterised by:

- a glut of the commodity;
- high levels of inventory;
- relative price stability;
- general price weakness;
- a "complacency" discount.

5.7   TRADING CRUDE OIL AND REFINED PRODUCTS

5.7.1   Overview

Why are crude oil and the refined products traded?

At a very simple level trading opportunities can arise for a variety of reasons:

- A producer has crude oil available to sell on the open market.
- Demand exists within the supply chain (e.g. at the refinery level) for a particular crude oil.
- A crude oil with a particular quality is in demand.
- A trader has identified the possibility of making money.

In an article in the *Financial Times* [12], it was noted that BP produced about 2.6 million barrels of crude oil per day (b/d), refined 4 million b/d and sold some 5.88 million b/d of refined products at its 29,000 service stations and other distribution points around the world. In order to balance this demand and supply, BP will buy and sell both crude oil and the refined products on an ongoing basis, and this provides the first definition of trading: buying and selling to balance supply and demand.

Who participates in trading?

Typical market participants include:

- national oil companies
- producers
- refiners
- integrated oil companies
- financial institutions.

What risks arise from buying and selling in the physical markets?

Over time a crude oil trader will end up with a portfolio of crude oils. The portfolio will comprise a variety of different exposures; such as:

- crudes priced on different bases (e.g. fixed; floating; futures prices);
- different grades of crude that may be priced off a differential to a certain marker crude;
- crudes that will be bought/delivered on different dates;
- crudes that need to be bought/delivered in different locations;
- different volumes.

This gives a second perspective on trading: the mitigation or transformation of the market risks that arise in the process of buying and selling crude oil. These risks can be managed by using derivatives.

View-driven trading activities

The third and final trading perspective relates to market participants that may wish to express a view on price movements without necessarily having an underlying economic exposure to manage. Here the motive is to make money from an anticipated move in some market variable. Possible strategies include taking views as follows:

- *Direction of the price*: The trader buys the commodity if the price is expected to rise and sells it when the price is expected to fall.
- *Grade differentials*: There is an expectation that the differential to a marker crude will change.
- *Shape of the forward curve*: The trader expects a change in the demand and supply fundamentals at different delivery points.
- *Freight rates*: Rates change due to a sudden change in demand at a certain geographical location.
- *Relationships between different markets*: The trader takes a view on a particular price relationship that might exist between two markets. One example of this is the price of Brent crude compared with the price of WTI. Traditionally WTI has traded at a premium to Brent but this relationship has been known to change for a number of reasons, such as:

  - declining North Sea output in a period of growing demand;
  - maintenance of oil rigs in the North Sea that might lead to a temporary reduction in output;
  - high levels of US stocks exerting downward pressure on WTI prices;
  - civil disruption in Nigeria. (This particular crude is perceived to be a substitute for North Sea oil so a reduction in output in the West African nation could lead to an increase in the demand for Brent.)

- *Price volatility*: Option traders will execute option strategies to exploit the perceived riskiness (i.e. the implied volatility) of the crude oil market. In a similar vein, certain option strategies are designed to profit from current volatility of the market, such as gamma trades.

How are oil products traded?

Trading of crude oil and the refined products can be undertaken by a variety of mechanisms. There may be a physical trade, an over-the-counter trade forward or an exchange-traded future. The forwards and futures trades will require physical settlement unless they have been set up to be cash settled or closed out prior to expiry. It is possible to buy options for physical delivery and swaps are also used extensively in the market, but these will always be cash settled. Option trades may not only be used as a mechanism to obtain or dispose of supplies but also as a mechanism to exploit the magnitude of price movements.

Arbitrage: a question of definition?

Arbitrage is a word that is often misused in many markets, although in the end its interpretation is just a question of definition. True arbitrage is the opportunity to buy a commodity at a certain price and sell it in the same or another market at a higher price to make a risk-free profit. It is sometimes confused with a spread trade, where the motive is to exploit an expected change in the relationship between two related, but ultimately different, commodities.

A possible true arbitrage for crude oil would involve:

- buying a particular oil in one geographical market;
- knowing what crude products the particular grade could produce and the total associated revenues – this would establish the value of the crude to buyer in the delivery location;
- adding the cost of freight to the final destination;
- adding any associated costs (e.g. insurance costs, costs of financing cargo while in transit);
- ensuring that the income from the final sale at the location of delivery is greater than all of the associated purchase costs.

Although often referred to as arbitrage trades, the following examples are designed to exploit the movement of a price differential between two related commodities. As such they are really spread trades:

- *Geographical spreads*:   Price of Brent crude vs price of WTI.
- *Demand and supply price relationships*:   Also known as the "crack spread", this relates the income generated by refinery outputs of products, to the cost of the refinery inputs of crude oil. There are a number of variations of this trade and one example is the gas oil "crack". The price of gas oil can be broken down into a Brent component and a gas oil crack.

$$\text{Gas oil price} = \text{Brent price} + \text{Gas oil crack}$$

  If gas oil is trading at USD 72 per bbl and Brent is trading at USD 60, the gas oil crack (the difference between the two prices) would be USD 12 per bbl. In very simple terms, the gas oil crack spread presented here could be interpreted as the refiner's profitability from taking a barrel of crude and converting it into a higher-value refined product. This gas oil crack is not a fixed number and will change depending on the relative demand and supply of the two constituents.
- *Seasonal price relationships*:   The price of gas oil (which is usually in greater demand in the winter for heating purposes) against gasoline (which is usually in greater demand during the summer months).

These types of spread trade could be executed by buying and selling in the physical market but it is more likely that they will be executed using derivatives to avoid the need for physical delivery.

There are a large number of crude oil markets and each has its own quoting conventions, contract types and liquidity issues. There are however, arguably, two key global physical markets, namely those for North Sea oil and West Texas Intermediate.

5.7.2   North Sea oil

North Sea crude oil is made up of a variety of different grades, which include:

Brent Blend	Forties	Oseberg
Ekofisk	Statfjord	Flotta

For many years the representative price of North Sea oil was Brent Blend, a mixture of crude oils from several different wells. As production in the North Sea declined, however, the definition of the reported price for the commodity was widened to include activity in a total of four crudes: Brent Blend, Forties, Oseberg and Ekofisk (BFOE). This ensured that the quoted price was reflective of actual market activity and Forties, Oseberg and Ekofisk were selected as they were considered to have very similar characteristics to those of Brent Blend.

There are a variety of instruments available to trade North Sea oil and they include:

- Dated Brent
- Brent Forwards
- Contracts for Difference
- Brent futures.

The majority of physical oil transactions are OTC and occur directly between counterparties according to bespoke contracts. Despite this, it should be noted that there are standardised forms of physical contracts in the OTC market, particularly in the forward market. The latter are typically traded up to 3 months in advance, hence there is a certain degree of overlap between the cash forwards price curve and the futures price curve.

For example, the following hypothetical prices quoted in early March of a particular year would be representative of a typical term structure:

Dated Brent	USD 65.01
Brent Forwards	
Brent (April)	USD 66.41
Brent (May)	USD 67.91
Brent (June)	USD 68.71

Dated Brent

One of the reasons for the continued popularity of Brent as a marker crude is the fact that is sometimes considered a "spot" contract and allows for the pricing of short-dated crude oil cargoes. However, the term "spot" in relation to the crude oil market warrants further description, as the term would normally be associated with immediate delivery. For Brent, normal market practice rarely deals with cargoes bought or sold for delivery in less than 10 days. Consequently, the Dated Brent prices quoted on a particular day are a reflection of the trading activity, which covers a period 10 to 21 days in the future. So the price given above on 7 March is based on deliveries for the period 17 to 28 March. This means that the spot price on a certain date covers market activity in three crudes (Brent Blend, Forties, Oseberg) encompassing an 11-day period starting in 10 days' time. The price quoted for Dated Brent is a rolling price assessment, so that on each day the activity period will shift to cover a new 11-day period.

It should be noted, however, that the above example describes how a price for Dated Brent would be assessed for publication by a price reporting company such as Platts. The pricing of a physical cargo on a floating basis, using Dated Brent as the benchmark, would be based on an average of prespecified published Dated Brent prices around the time of loading.

A typical Dated Brent contract would be for delivery, on an FOB, fixed price basis, at Sullom Voe in the Shetland Isles for a cargo of 600,000 bbl with a tolerance of ±1%.

Brent Forwards

Forward contracts lock in the price at the time of contracting of a commodity for delivery at a future point in time, but beyond 21 days in the immediate future. Somewhat confusingly, forward contracts in Brent may be referred to in several different ways as:

- Brent Forwards
- Paper Brent (due to fact that the contract may well be cash settled)
- Cash BFOE
- Paper BFOE
- 21-day cash BFOE
- Cash forwards.

For simplicity, these types of contract will be referred to as forwards. The price quotation for this type of forward represents the value of a cargo for physical delivery within the month specified by the contract. This means that, at the point of contracting, the exact date on which the oil will be loaded on board the ship is not known. It has become known as the 21-day market due to the fact that buyers are notified 21 days in advance of the loading dates for their cargoes.

Assume that on 7 March of any year, a Brent Forward is executed for delivery in May. In the month prior to delivery (April in this case) the managers of the loading installation will list the dates in May when the contract seller can load oil. This set of dates is referred to as the "laycan", which is a 2- to 3-day window where the buyer can arrange for a vessel to arrive for loading. For example, the loading dates may be 1st–3rd, 10th–12th, 20th–22nd and 26th–28th. In the Brent Forward market the contract seller has the right to nominate any of the loading dates as long as they give the contract buyer the requisite 21 days' notice. If the parties to the trade do not wish the deal to go to physical delivery, it will have to be cash settled or "booked out" to use the industry jargon.

If the seller on 17 April wished to nominate a particular set of delivery dates to physically settle the forward, he would no longer be able to use the first set (1–3 May) due to the minimum requirement to give 21 days' notice. Cargoes for delivery on that set of dates would be classified and traded as Dated Brent. Table 5.6 (page 134) illustrates the main features of the Bent Forward contract, which although OTC in nature does have an element of standardisation within the market. Reference may sometimes be made to partial contracts, which describe a forward contract with "standard" terms apart from the fact that the trade size will be less than the 600,000 barrels.

Contracts for Difference

Brent Contracts for Difference (CFDs) are one-period swaps that give a user exposure to the differential in price between a Dated Brent and a Forward Brent Contract. However, this differential is not the current difference between Dated Brent and a particular Forward Brent Contract. (In some markets these types of contract are referred as "dated to frontline" contracts in that they may offer exposure from the maturity of the spot contract to the first futures month.)

CFDs quotes represent the difference (either positive or negative) between the current second month forward quote and Dated Brent for a stated future period, in USD per bbl.

Therefore the CFD quote represents the value of time between the maturities of the two contracts. The quote for a given period will change as the relative demand and supply for the two constituent components evolves. The relationship could therefore be expressed as follows:

CFD quote = Forward Dated Brent minus Second month Brent Forward

Rearranging the formula gives:

Forward Dated Brent = CFD plus Second month Brent Forward

Another interpretation of the equation is that buying a CFD and taking a long position in the second forward month will lock in the purchase price for Dated Brent at a certain time in the future.

Say it is early March and the following prices are being quoted in the Brent market:

Dated Brent	65.00–65.02
Brent Forwards	
Brent (April)	66.40–66.42
Brent (May)	67.90–67.92
Brent (June)	68.70–68.72
Contracts for Difference	
CFD 1 week March 06/10	−2.01/−1.99
CFD 2 week March 13/17	−1.60/−1.58
CFD 3 week March 20/24	−1.41/−1.39
⋮	
CFD 8 week April 24/28	−0.35/−0.33

The normal market size for Brent CFDs is between 50,000 to 100,000 bbl and they are traded with weekly maturities out to 8 weeks. They can also traded for bi-monthly and monthly periods. Similar to any contract for difference, the counterparties agree a fixed differential at the point of the trade and then subsequently settle on the actual differential (sometimes referred to as the "floating" rate) at the contract maturity. Settlement at maturity is the average of the differentials published daily over the week covered by the contract.

CFDs are quoted on a bid–offer basis (see Table 5.5), so when the market is in contango, the quote is negative and the CFD bid price is greater than the offer. This ensures that when the implied forward price for Dated Brent is derived it will follow the normal convention of low bid, high offer. A market in backwardation will result in a positive CFD quote with the bid price lower than the offer.

The fact that the CFD quote may be negative combined with the use of ambiguous phrases such as "spread widening" and "spread narrowing" can make the analysis of CFDs confusing.

To illustrate the principles, consider an example of a CFD quote of +USD 1.50/+USD 1.55. If a trader believed that the differential would increase (i.e. become more positive), then he would buy the CFD at the offer side of the market as a market user. If at settlement the actual differential had increased to USD 1.75, a payment of USD 1.55 would be made

Table 5.5   Interpreting a CFD quote

	Bid	Offer
Market maker	*Buy*	*Sell*
	• Pay quoted differential ("fixed") • Receive actual differential ("floating") • Profits if actual differential is more positive/less negative than quoted differential	• Receive quoted differential ("fixed") • Pay quoted differential ("floating") • Profits if actual differential is less positive/more negative than quoted differential
Market user	*Sell*	Buy
	• Receive quoted differential ("fixed") • Pay quoted differential ("floating") • Profits if actual differential is less positive/more negative than quoted differential	• Pay quoted differential ("fixed") • Receive actual differential ("floating") • Profits if actual differential is more positive / less negative than quoted differential

and a payment of USD 1.75 received, representing a USD 0.20 net receipt per barrel. If it is assumed that the deal were executed on a notional basis of 50,000 barrels, this would equate to a cash settlement of USD 10,000 (50,000 barrels × USD 0.20).

Now consider that the quote is −USD 2.10/−USD 2.05. Once again it will be assumed that the trader believes that the differential will increase (i.e. become less negative) and so decides to buy the CFD at the offer side of the market. If at settlement the actual differential had increased to −USD 1.85, the terms of the contract necessitate making a payment of −USD 2.05 and receiving a payment of −USD 1.85. But a payment of a negative sum is actually a receipt as two negatives make a positive! A receipt of a negative sum would therefore represent a payment and the trader would be a receiver of USD 0.20 per barrel, which makes the two examples consistent.

The previous CFD example focused on the use of the instrument to exploit how the relative prices of Dated Brent and Brent Forward were expected to evolve. CFDs can also be used as a mechanism to hedge a position in Dated Brent if it is assumed that it is early March and a trader has agreed to buy a cargo of crude that will be priced on a floating basis using Dated Brent. Since he has not yet taken delivery of the crude, he is said, in market jargon, to "short crude for forward delivery". The cargo will not be loaded until the 21–23 March and the invoice price will be based on an average of Dated Brent prices centred on the loading date. The trader looks at the price screen and notes that the current value for Dated Brent is USD 65.02. He is concerned that the price of Dated Brent will rise and so decides to hedge his exposure. He could use the April forward to hedge the exposure, but runs a risk that the price of the forward may not track the movements in Dated Brent used to price his physical contract ("basis risk").

To hedge this exposure the trader will have to:

- Buy a CFD that covers the week in which the physical cargo will be priced; or
- Take out a long position in the second month Brent Forward contract from which the CFD is priced.

Using the figures quoted earlier, the trader's position using market user rates would be:

- Long one cargo of BFOE loading 21–23 March; priced at an average of Dated Brent around the time of loading.
- Buy a CFD for the week 20–24 March; priced at −USD 1.39.
- Long one Brent Forward for May delivery at USD 67.92.

Since mathematically the CFD quote is the forward Dated Brent value minus the second month Brent Forward, we can back out the forward Dated Brent price

$$-USD\ 1.39 = (Forward)Dated\ Brent - USD\ 67.92$$
$$Forward\ Dated\ Brent = 67.92 - 1.39 = 66.53$$

Buying the CFD and going long the second month forward is now economically equivalent to buying Dated Brent on a forward basis and locking in a purchase price of USD 66.53.

If it is assumed that the contract is to be settled (i.e. the week ending 24 March), the following prices are assumed to prevail:

- The average of published Dated Brent price over the 3-day loading period used to settle the physical contract is USD 69.50.
- The CFD settlement price for the week of 20–24 March is −USD1.30. The trader receives USD 0.09 per barrel. Given that the value of Dated Brent is known and a settlement value for the CFD has been established, the value of the Brent Forward for May delivery can be backed out. Since:

$$CFD = Dated\ Brent - Brent\ Forward$$

then given an agreed settlement value for the CFD at −USD 1.30 and a Dated Brent value of USD 69.50, the Brent Forward for May delivery can be calculated as:

$$USD\ 70.80 = USD\ 69.50 + USD\ 1.30$$

- The Brent Forward contract for May delivery is closed out on a cash-settled basis at USD 70.80, generating a profit of USD 2.88. The total cost per barrel is therefore USD 69.50 − USD 2.88 − USD 0.09 = USD 66.53. This was the price that the trader was able to lock in at the start of the transaction.

This may seem somewhat complex and so in order to make the hedging of the physical exposure easier, the purchaser may opt to go for a futures based pricing agreement, which could then be hedged by purchasing the same futures contract.

Brent Futures

There is also an active exchange-traded futures market that allows for crude oil to be traded for delivery in a specified future month for delivery at a particular location. As with any futures contract, it will have standardised terms and conditions. The main Brent contract is traded on the InterContinental Exchange (ICE). The contract is physically deliverable with an option to cash settle at expiry. Similar to most forward-dated contracts for crude, a period rather than a specific date is traded. Although the future settles against crude for delivery FOB Sullom Voe, there are mechanisms available (e.g. Exchange for Physicals), which allow for counterparties to deliver or receive oil at locations and on dates of their own choosing.

Trading in the Brent Futures contracts ceases at the close of business on the business day immediately preceding the 15th calendar day prior to the first day of the delivery month. Contracts are available for maturities out to six years, but the longer-dated contracts may offer different degrees of liquidity. The futures contract settles against the ICE Futures Brent Index, which is the weighted average of the prices of all confirmed 21-day BFOE deals (i.e. Brent Forwards) throughout the previous trading day for the appropriate delivery months.

A feature of the futures price is that it is used to construct an index termed BWAVE (Brent Weighted Average). This is an index price published on a daily basis that represents a weighted average of all futures trades executed for each maturity. This index has, over time, become a popular benchmark for some oil-producing companies (e.g. Saudi Aramco) that export crude into the European market. Saudi Aramco originally sold crude oil into Europe on the basis of Dated Brent, before switching to a single futures price and then eventually moving to the BWAVE index.

Table 5.6 compares the main features of the three main types of Brent contract.

Table 5.6 Summary of exchange-traded futures contracts

	Dated Brent	Brent Forward	Brent Futures
Exchange or OTC	OTC	OTC	Exchange
Underlying asset	Brent Forties Oseberg Ekofist	Brent Forties Oseberg Ekofist	Brent Forties Oseberg Ekofist
Pricing point	FOB Sullom Voe	FOB Sullom Voe	FOB Sullom Voe
Exposure period	10–21 days post trade	1st–31st of each quoted calendar month; greatest liquidity in near dated contracts	Consecutive calendar months out to about 6 years
Loading date	Specific date agreed in contract	Nominated by seller; range of dates during delivery month	Settles against the 21-day Brent Forward market
Standard size (bbl)	600,000	600,000	1,000
Settlement	Physical	Physical/cash	Physical/cash

5.7.3   US crude oil markets

The main crude oil traded in the USA is West Texas Intermediate (WTI). This is usually quoted for delivery at Cushing, Oklahoma, although Platts does provide quotes for alternative locations such as Midland, Texas. There is a range of other crude oil markets, however, with different delivery locations that include:

- West Texas Sour (delivered into Midland Texas)
- Light Louisiana Sweet (St James, Louisiana)
- Mars (Clovelly, Louisiana)
- Alaska North Slope (Long Beach, California).

Physical WTI price quotations are driven by the pipeline companies' requirement that all deliveries for a given month be notified by the 25th of the previous month. So for the period of 26 March to 25 April the quoted price on any single day is a representation of crude oil transactions to be delivered during the month of May. On 26 April, for example, the price will be reflective of transactions to be delivered during June. As a result of this market convention the distinction between the concepts of spot and forward becomes blurred. To illustrate the principles, let us assume that on 7 March the following prices for different delivery dates are observed for WTI (USD per bbl):

April	USD 61.25
May	USD 62.56
June	USD 63.23

The price quoted for April delivery reflects trades executed that day for delivery during the month of April.

Futures on crude oil and a number of related petroleum products are offered on NYMEX, with maturities extending to 5 years. Their light, sweet, crude oil contract is physically deliverable by pipeline at Cushing, with each lot consisting of 1,000 barrels. The contract may well be physically settled by pipeline delivery and so is also expressed as a US gallon equivalent (42,000 US gallons). The contract specification issued by the exchange describes the delivery period as follows:

All deliveries are rateable over the course of the month and must be initiated on or after the first calendar day and completed by the last calendar day of the delivery month.

Source: NYMEX

This implies that the seller will deliver the required physical throughout the month in question.

Under the Alternate Delivery Procedure, buyers and sellers matched by the exchange prior to maturity, may vary the terms of delivery from those described in the contract specification.

Despite allowing for physical settlement the vast majority of NYMEX and ICE futures positions are closed out before contract expiry, which means that buyers sell out of their positions at prevailing market prices while sellers do the opposite. Closing out of positions occurs even in situations where market participants do wish to buy or sell physical quantities.

This is because the standardised terms of futures delivery are usually too restrictive for physical market participants.

Although the contract is commonly referred to as being based on WTI, the exchange actually allows a variety of crudes to be delivered against the contract. There are some restrictions on the crudes that can be delivered to ensure that they are close substitutes, so the sulphur content cannot exceed 0.42% by weight and the gravity must be between 37° and 42° API. This makes the following domestic crudes deliverable:

- West Texas Intermediate
- Low Sweet Mix
- New Mexican Sweet
- Oklahoma Sweet
- South Texas Sweet.

The contract also allows for a variety of foreign crudes to be delivered under similar principles. However, the seller receives a certain cash discount or premium to the final settlement price to reflect a quality differential. The crudes and their respective differentials are:

- UK Brent (30c per barrel discount)
- Norwegian Oseberg blend (55c discount)
- Nigerian Bonny Light (15c premium)
- Nigerian Qua Iboe (15c premium)
- Colombian Cusiana (15c premium).

Because a seller now has the option to deliver a variety of crudes, the prices of the different crudes become tied together by arbitrage relationships. Since it would be theoretically possible to buy Brent and deliver into a WTI contract, the price differential between the two crudes should never exceed the costs of shipping Brent across the Atlantic.

Table 5.7   Summary of NYMEX contract specifications

	West Texas Intermediate (WTI)	Brent crude	Heating oil	Gasoline
Contract size	1,000 barrels	1,000 barrels	42,000 gallons (1,000 barrels)	42,000 gallons (1,000 barrels)
Quote	USD and cents per barrel	USD and cents per barrel	USD and cents per gallon	USD and cents per gallon
Minimum price fluctuation	0.01 USD per barrel	0.01 USD per barrel	0.0001 USD per gallon	0.0001 USD per gallon
Traded periods	Current year and the next 5 years	Current year and the next 5 years	18 consecutive months	12 consecutive months
Delivery/Settlement	Physical	Cash	Physical	Physical

Source: NYMEX.

NYMEX also offers contracts on a number of refined products such as heating oil (sometimes referred to as No. 2 fuel oil), which can be used to hedge diesel fuel and Jet Fuel exposures as well as a gasoline contract.

The different types of energy futures contracts offered by NYMEX are summarised in Table 5.7

5.8 MANAGING PRICE RISK ALONG THE SUPPLY CHAIN

5.8.1 Producer hedges

In the following examples, structures that are unique to crude oil are emphasised. To avoid repetition, interested readers are referred to Chapter 4 on base metals for generic vanilla and exotic option strategies.

Exchange-traded futures

Although the use of futures would appear to be straightforward, there is the possibility that an element of basis risk may exist. Basis risk is used to describe a number of different situations, which include:

- using futures in one product to hedge an underlying exposure in another (e.g. using gas oil futures to hedge a Jet Fuel exposure);
- a mismatch between the timing of the exposure and the protection period covered by the future;
- termination of a futures hedge prior to maturity, where there is an underlying physical exposure; here the basis risk is that the cash and futures price has not moved in parallel, resulting in a hedge that is not 100% efficient;
- physical delivery of the commodity in a location that differs from that used to price the hedging instrument;
- quality differences between the physical exposure and that specified by the hedging instrument.

Consider an example of a US oil producer who in early December is seeking to hedge the price risk of his planned production in the first quarter of the following year. He has agreed to sell 50,000 barrels a month to a refiner for the first 3 months. The contract will be settled on a floating rate formula with the final agreed price based on the average of quoted Platts prices, published daily in the month preceding the delivery of the crude oil. So for the 50,000 barrels to be delivered on the first business day of January, the price paid by the refiner will be the average of the Platts WTI prices published daily in December. The February delivery will be based on the average of January prices and a March settlement will be based on the average of February prices.

If the producer was concerned about a fall in the price of WTI, then he could sell three lots of 50 futures contracts to mitigate the risk. In a perfect world each futures contract would have a maturity that matches the underlying physical deliveries. However, it is not that simple with the WTI contract. His actual physical exposure will be priced at the average of December's cash prices and will not be finalised until January. At that point in time, the January WTI future will have expired. (The WTI contract expires 3 business days prior to the 25th calendar day of the month preceding the delivery day.) Hence he may choose to hedge the December price movements using a February contract, which will mature towards the end of January.

Because the price exposure of the physical sale and the future cover different time periods, the producer runs the risk that the cash and futures prices will not move in tandem – which is an example of basis risk. Fortunately for the hedger, the chances of futures and cash prices decoupling, i.e. the basis risk, is usually far less of a concern than the absolute price risk.

The following example illustrates the concepts. On 1 December a producer enters into a long-term contract whereby he agrees to sell forward 50,000 barrels per month of WTI crude oil for the 3 months of Q1 of the following year according to a price equal to the Platts assessed price for WTI at Cushing on the first good business day of each month. The producer's physical traders fear that cash prices may decline during the three Platts assessment pricing days (also known as the pricing windows), resulting in lower revenues.

In order to hedge its exposure to the pricing windows at the start of each month, the producer decides to initiate a short hedge by selling a strip of futures contracts, which will be "prompt" (i.e. nearest maturity) futures contracts on the respective pricing days. Hence to hedge its January, February and March sales, it sells February, March and April NYMEX WTI futures. On the pricing days in question the prompt month futures position is bought back at the prevailing market rate in order to unwind the hedge. Some time after the pricing date the producer delivers the 50,000 barrels of oil and receives a cash amount based on the Platts assessments in return. Table 5.8 shows the outcome of the hedging programme and the effective price realised by the producer. The table shows that the producer was able to lock-in an average price of 68.28 USD per bbl for its sale and that this outperformed an unhedged position that would have yielded a lower average price over the same period. On

Table 5.8 Producer hedge using WTI futures

Date	Physical	Futures	Futures gain/loss (USD per bbl)	Effective Price (USD per bbl)
Dec. 1	Sells 50,000 barrels forward Platts cash price = 68.37	Sells 50 lots per month of WTI: February = 69.67 March = 70.04 April = 70.63		
Jan. 1	Platts cash price = 67.93	Buy 50 lots February = 69.32	(69.67 − 69.32) = 0.35	(67.93 + 0.35) = 68.28
Feb. 1	Platts cash price = 67.55	Buy 50 lots March = 69.29	(70.04 − 69.29) = 0.75	(67.55 + 0.75) = 68.30
Mar. 1	Platts cash price = 68.79	Buy 50 lots April = 71.15	(70.63 − 71.15) = −0.52	(68.79 − 0.52) = 68.27

Average Platts cash price = (67.93 + 67.55 + 68.79)/3 = 68.09 USD per bbl

Average effective price = (68.28 + 68.30 + 68.27)/3 = 68.28 USD per bbl

Table 5.9 Evolution of the basis

	February futures	March futures	April futures
Initial value for basis	$68.37 - 69.67 = -1.30$	$68.37 - 70.04 = -1.67$	$68.37 - 70.63 = -2.26$
Value of basis at close-out of future	$67.93 - 69.32 = -1.39$	$67.55 - 69.29 = -1.74$	$68.79 - 71.15 = -2.36$

the other hand, had prices evolved in a positive direction then they would have locked-in its sales revenues at the expense of being able to benefit from a price rise. On this occasion we have assumed that the physical oil contract was priced at a single point in time.

In some contracts the physical contract would be based on an average of prices over a period to reflect the loading period. In this case the futures position would have to be unwound in equal amounts as the physical contract is priced. So if the physical contract is priced as the average of prices over a 5-day period, then one-fifth of the futures hedge would have to be unwound daily.

It is important to note that the effective sale price of 68.28 USD per bbl was not quite equal to the prevailing cash price at the time the hedge was initiated (68.37 USD per bbl). This is because cash prices and futures did not always move in tandem during the period in question.

The basis can be quantified as the spot price minus the future price and its evolution for this particular trade is documented in Table 5.9. In all the examples the basis decreased (i.e. became more negative).

The basis at the close-out can also be used to determine the effective price paid for the crude oil using the relationship:

Original futures price *plus* Basis at close-out = Effective price of crude

To illustrate, consider the physical consignment to be delivered in January. The original February futures price was 69.67 USD and the basis on close-out was −1.39 USD. This would infer an effective sale price for the crude of 68.28 USD, which indeed was the case.

In executing this hedge the producer took on the risk that the cash WTI price would weaken even further relative to the prompt WTI futures contract. The producer was willing to take this risk having determined that the basis between cash WTI and futures was far less volatile than the outright cash price. That is, he would achieve a less favourable sale price if the basis decreased or became more negative. For example, on the close-out of the February future, the effective sale price would only have been 67.67 USD if the basis had been −2 USD.

Crude oil swaps

A crude oil swap could be used to transform a specific price risk faced by a client. Let us say that a producer has a contract to sell oil on an ongoing basis at a fixed price. The producer believes that the price of crude will rise and so wishes to benefit accordingly. The refiner enters into a crude oil swap where a fixed price per barrel (say USD 50) is paid a cashflow based on an agreed index, such as Dated Brent. The fixed cashflow to be paid will be based on the weighted average of futures prices that cover the exposure period. The producer's intention is to use this swap cashflow to offset the fixed income of selling the crude. The net effect is that the producer ends up selling crude oil on a floating rate basis.

Although somewhat ambiguous, the market may use the terms "buy" and "sell" in relation to the swap instrument. Here we will define the purchase of a swap as an instance where an entity pays a fixed price and receives the floating or variable index. Selling a swap will be defined as a receipt of fixed against a payment of floating.

The swap transaction presented here covers an exact calendar month with the fixed price set at USD 50.00 payable by the producer. The floating index will be based on a straight average of Dated Brent prices published daily by Platts over the period of the contract month. At the end of the calculation period let us assume that the average of Dated Brent prices is USD 49.50 and that the contract was executed on 70,000 barrels. Just like all swap contracts, when cashflows are timed to coincide, a single net payment is due. The producer would therefore be a payer of USD 0.50 per barrel. When translated into a cash amount (there is no physical delivery of crude oil under the swap) this would equate to USD 35,000 (70,000 barrels × USD 0.50). Table 5.10 summarises the main types of swap and their respective settlement prices.

Table 5.10 shows certain swaps which mirror the underlying physical markets with respect to particular locations and delivery modes, e.g. Barges FOB Rotterdam. In the case of such a price assessment, the first criteria refers to the type of delivery vessel (Barges), the middle term (FOB, Free on Board) relates to how the delivery will be priced, while the third criteria refers to the delivery location (Rotterdam).

Dealers who enter into long-dated swaps in an illiquid product may be forced to hedge he exposure using crude oil futures. This will give them what is sometimes referred to as a "crack position" (i.e. an exposure in a refined product against crude oil).

Table 5.10 shows the main type of fixed for floating swap by product basis, and there are a number of alternative ways in which the cashflows can be calculated:

- *Fixed price vs quoted futures price*: These "futures swaps" are usually traded against the "front" month and might be applicable for those who have priced their physical deliveries against either basis but wish to transform it to the other. Due to the expiry dates of the futures, which are typically during a month rather than at the end, the price of a swap will be calculated as the weighted average of two futures. The March Brent swap, for example, prices from the last 11 days of the April futures contract and the first 11 days of the May futures contract.
- *Index price vs index price*: This might be executed as a deal based on two different indices. A possible example might be Dated Brent against Urals. This is a similar concept to Brent CFDs. A swap done on these indices would be structured in the traditional fixed vs floating format but the fixed price will be based on a differential between the two indices. Mathematically it can be shown that the fixed rate for a swap covering a given period is the weighted average of the futures prices that cover the same period. The weights are discount factors of the same maturity.

  For this type of swap the fixed price would be derived from the differential between the relevant futures prices. The floating payment will be based on the actual differential that is observed over the agreed payment period for the swap.

  A possible scenario of when someone would use this type of swap would be where a refiner buys a cargo of Urals and decides to hedge it with Brent futures given the

Table 5.10 Frequently traded crude oil and refined product swaps

Underlying commodity	Settlement price
Brent	Average of daily settlement price of prompt ICE futures contract
Dated Brent	Average of daily published Platts assessment
WTI	Average of daily settlement price of prompt NYMEX futures contract
Dubai	Average of daily published Platts assessment
Tapis	Average of daily published Asian Petroleum Pricing Index assessment
Gasoline 10 ppm 95 Ron Barges FOB Rotterdam	Average of daily published Argus assessment
NYMEX gasoline	Average of daily settlement price of prompt NYMEX futures contract
ICE gas oil	Average of daily settlement price of prompt ICE futures contract
NYMEX heating oil	Average of daily settlement price of prompt NYMEX futures contract
Gas oil 0.2% sulphur barges FOB Rotterdam	Average of daily published Platts assessment
Gas oil 0.5% sulphur cargoes FOB Singapore	Average of daily published Platts assessment
Fuel oil 3.5% sulphur barges FOB Rotterdam	Average of daily published Platts assessment
Fuel oil 1.8% sulphur cargoes FOB Singapore	Average of daily published Platts assessment

Note: For the gasoline contract, 10 ppm indicates there are 10 parts of lead per million.

absence of a futures market in his particular cargo. To hedge the basis risk that exists between the two cargoes the refiner enters into a swap to lock in the differential between Urals and Dated Brent. Although it may seem easier for the hedger to do a fixed/floating based purely on the price of Urals, this in reality would not be executed due to poor liquidity. The hedger is then exposed to a change in the Dated Brent–Brent Futures differential.

- *Index price vs futures price*: This type of swap would be quoted as an index price against a futures price.
- *Crude oil vs products*: Equally there may be swaps based on different refined products. For example, the swap could involve the exchange of cashflows based on the

price of crude oil against one of the refined products such as gasoline. Equally, the contract might be structured with cashflows based on the price of fuel oil, against that of electricity.

5.8.2 Refiner hedges

Hedging the crack spread using exchange-traded futures

Refiners will be buyers of crude oil and sellers of refined products. Given the nature of their different inputs and outputs, they are exposed to a change in the differential between the two prices. This is sometimes referred to as the "crack spread", which derives it name from the refining process where the crude oil is "cracked" into a variety of different outputs. The crack spread measures the income earned from the sale of refined products to the cost of crude oil.

Figure 5.12 shows generic refinery margins in different geographical locations. They are based on a single crude oil appropriate for that region and optimised refined product yields based on a generic refinery configuration, also appropriate for each region. The margins are expressed a semi-variable basis in that all variable costs (e.g. energy costs incurred in the production of the products) are included. A positive margin is one where the income received from the sale of the refined products is greater than the cost of buying the crude oil.

The refiner can hedge against a fall in this margin by fixing the spread using a future, OTC forward or an option. One of the most popular strategies in this area is the 3:2:1 futures crack spread. This is a single transaction that is composed of three crude oil futures, two gasoline futures and one heating oil contract. This reflects the fact that, broadly speaking, a typical refinery configuration will be such that a barrel of crude will yield twice as much

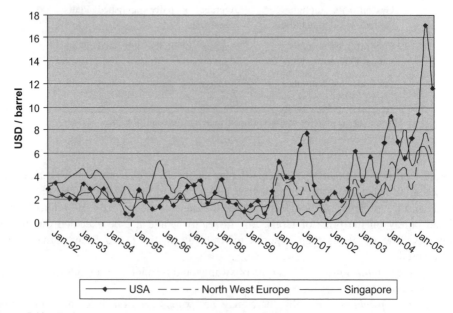

Figure 5.12   Refining margin by geographical region (USD per barrel) (1992–2004)

gasoline as it will heating oil. As a result, every three barrels of crude will yield two of gasoline and one of heating oil. Although refineries will also produce fuel oil and naphtha, there is no futures market for these products and so the exposures cannot be easily hedged.

To hedge a decline in the margin the refiner would sell the crack spread, which would involve a purchase of the requisite number of crude oil contracts and the sale of refined product contracts (gasoline and heating oil). Note that the action of selling or buying the spread refers to the nature of the refined product transaction. The spread will usually have a time dimension to reflect the speed with which the crude oil is refined. Hence the refiner may sell longer-dated refined product futures than the purchased crude oil future.

Although the futures hedge will fix the refining spread, it is by no means a perfect hedge, as the refiner runs two secondary basis risks. The first relates to differences in the delivery location between the physical transaction and derivative hedge. This will be reflected in the price of the different contracts and there is no guarantee that they will move in tandem. For example, assume that a US refiner decides to buy crude oil for delivery on the US Gulf Coast (USGC) with a similar quality as that of the WTI future (e.g. Bonny Light). He is likely to sell his gasoline output also for delivery at the same location (USGC). If futures are used to hedge the refining margin, the crude oil contract will be priced for delivery at Cushing while the gasoline contract is based on delivery at New York Harbour (NYH). This means they have exposure to the Cushing/USGC price differential on the crude oil exposure and NYH/USGC price differential on the gasoline contract. The second source of basis risk lies in the quality of the underlying physical products and that specified in the futures contract.

Hedging the crack spread using OTC swaps

It is assumed that a refiner is proposing to hedge its production revenues for a future fourth quarter. In the physical market it agrees to purchase 480,000 barrels of Brent crude oil according to a uniform pricing schedule based on the daily Platts Dated Brent assessment in October, November and December. In addition to this, the refiner agrees to sell 480,000 barrels of its refined products according to several other published assessments over an identical time frame. The details of the refiner's production profile is given in Table 5.11.

For the sake of simplicity it has been assumed that there are no waste products in this refining process although, in practice, this would not be the case. We will also assume that the refiner is unwilling to execute a futures-based transaction, as it does not want to be exposed to the basis risks. Furthermore, the refiner wishes to hedge its entire slate of products rather than those where a traded market exists.

It is possible to execute an OTC swap on the margin between the weighted basket of products in Table 5.11 and Dated Brent. Liquid swap markets exist for each of the production

Table 5.11 Hypothetical refiner's production profile

Product	% of total output	Pricing quote
Naphtha	3	Platts Cargoes CIF North West Europe
Gasoline	41	Argus 10 ppm 95 Ron Barges FOB Rotterdam
Gas oil	35	Platts 0.2% Sulphur Barges FOB Rotterdam
Fuel oil	21	Platts 1% Sulphur Barges FOB Rotterdam

Table 5.12   Derivative conversion factors

Product	USD per bbl to USD per metric tonne
Naphtha	8.90
Gasoline	8.33
Jet Fuel	7.88
Gas oil	7.45
Fuel oil	6.35

Note: To convert a quantity expressed in USD per barrel to USD per metric tonne, multiply by the appropriate conversion factor.

constituents, which means that the price of this "margin swap" can be derived as follows:

$$\text{Refinery margin} = (0.03 \times \text{Naphtha} + 0.41 \times \text{Gasoline} + 0.35 \times \text{Gas oil} + 0.21$$

$$\times \text{Fuel oil}) - \text{Dated Brent}$$

The fixed price on the swap is in essence a weighted average of the component swap prices, less the price of a Dated Brent swap. The weights applied to the refined products represent the refiner's relative production percentages.

In the European markets, refined product prices are quoted in USD per metric tonne while crude oil is quoted in USD per barrel. Refinery margins are quoted in USD per barrel, which means that the refined product swap prices must be expressed on the same basis. In the derivatives markets it is standard practice to use the conversion factors given in Table 5.12.

The refiner fears that margins will fall by the time the fourth quarter arrives and so enters into a margin swap based on a notional of 160,000 barrels per month for the quarter in question. We will assume that the fixed rate has been set at USD 7.24. The refiner sells the swap receiving a fixed price of USD 7.24, while paying a floating rate.

Five good business days after each month in the fourth quarter, the refiner pays or receives a cash amount depending on the difference between the fixed price of the swap and the average monthly refining margin implied by the various published prices. Accordingly, whatever it gains or loses in the physical market is offset under the swap. The result is a hedged position and secured revenues. Table 5.13 shows how this is achieved and that the net margin achieved is equal to the fixed rate on the swap.

5.8.3   Consumer hedges

Consumers of crude oil are largely refineries as most end users are more interested in the final refined product. As a recap, Table 5.14 shows the main refined products, their uses and applicable industry sectors.

Consider an example of an airline company based in Europe offering flights to a variety of different global locations. At the start of the year the airline asks a number of companies to tender for the delivery of Jet Fuel to different airports from which they operate (e.g. London Heathrow). The airline has an ongoing need for Jet Fuel and so is seeking a fixed number of barrels per month to be delivered. The tender price will be based on a floating formula and will settle against prices published by Platts. A normal method of pricing the Jet Fuel will be based on an "average of month" basis. This means that at the end of each

Table 5.13 Refinery margin hedge using OTC swaps

Date	Physical	Swap
Sep. 15	Agrees to sell 160,000 barrels per month in Q4 at average of daily published assessments. Delivery/settlement on 5th business day after month end	Sells 160,000 barrels per month in Q4. Refinery margin Swap = 7.24 USD per bbl
Nov. 5	Average margin according to October published prices = 6.82 USD per bbl Cash received = (160,000 × 6.82) = 1,091,200 USD	Swap settlement: = 160,000 × (7.24 − 6.82) = 67,200 USD
Dec. 5	Average margin according to November published prices = 6.03 USD/bbl Cash received = (160,000 × 6.03) = 964,800 USD	Swap settlement: = 160,000 × (7.24 − 6.03) = 193,600 USD
Jan. 5	Average margin according to December published prices = 8.11 USD per bbl Cash received = (160,000 × 8.11) = 1,297,600 USD	Swap settlement: = 160,000 × (7.24 − 8.11) = −139,200 USD

$$\text{Effective sale price} = \frac{(1{,}091{,}200 + 964{,}800 + 1{,}297{,}600 + 67{,}200 + 193{,}600 - 139{,}200)}{480{,}000 \text{ barrels}}$$
$$= 7.24 \text{ USD per bbl}$$

Table 5.14 Refined products and their main applications

Refined product	Major uses	Industry sectors
Jet Fuel	Air travel, military	Logistics
Road diesel or heating oil	Road haulage, farming, space heating	Airlines Couriers
Naphtha	Petrochemical feedstock	Utilities Railways
Gasoline/petrol	Road transport	Shipping
Heavy fuel oil	Seaborne transport, power generation, asphalt	Chemicals Heavy industry

month, the price paid will be an arithmetic average of the Jet Fuel price quoted daily in Platts. However, there are a number of different quoted Jet Fuel prices depending on the delivery location. These may include the US Gulf Coast, North West Europe (NWE), the Mediterranean and Singapore. The tender will require the selling company to state what the all-in cost of delivery to the airport will be. The additional cost of transportation to the airport will be expressed as a premium to the conventional delivery location. So the quote may come back from the seller as "Average of month based on a reference price of Platts CIF NWE plus a premium of USD X per barrel to cover transport costs".

Using swaps to transform a floating exposure into fixed

If, during the year, the airline is concerned about a rise in the price of Jet Fuel, it could enter into a commodity swap to cover part of the exposure. In April the company executes the following cash-settled Jet Fuel swap with an investment bank:

Commodity	Jet Cargoes CIF NWE (Cost, Insurance Freight, North West Europe)
Payer of fixed	Airline
Payer of floating index	Investment bank
Period of swap	Three months commencing 1 October
Fixed price	USD 650 per tonne
Notional amount	10,000 tonnes per month
Settlement	Monthly
Price source	Platts European
Floating reference price	Spot price for Jet Cargoes CIF NWE, published daily
Reference price calculation	Arithmetic average of the floating reference price over each month

At the end of each month the average of all of the daily spot prices is calculated and compared to the fixed price. If the average price is greater than the agreed fixed price of USD 650 per tonne, the airline will receive a cash payment based on this amount multiplied by the agreed number of tonnes. If the average price is the same as the fixed price, then no settlement takes place. If the price of Jet Fuel is on average lower than the fixed rate then the airline will make a payment for the difference to the bank, based on the differential. Settlement under the swap is normally 5 good business days after the last day of the traded month. The payment or receipt under the swap combined with the purchase of the physical commodity will result in a fixed price of USD 650 per tonne. It is important to note that, in this example, the terms of the swap matched exactly the terms of the airline's physical purchases.

Hedging Jet Fuel exposure using gas oil futures

Owing to chemical similarities it is market practice to price a physical Jet Fuel contract as a differential to gas oil. Jet Fuel normally trades at a premium to gas oil as it must meet higher quality specifications. However, this relationship can break down in certain cases where supply and demand fundamentals are such that gas oil is more sought after than Jet Fuel. The pricing relationship between the products can be expressed as:

$$\text{Jet Fuel} = \text{Gas oil} + \text{Jet differential}$$

If gas oil is trading at USD 72 per bbl, it can be converted to a tonnage equivalent by multiplying by 7.45 (see Table 5.12), to give a figure of USD 536.40. If the quoted price of Jet Fuel is, say, USD 586.40 per tonne, the "Jet Diff" is USD 50.00.

It is possible to hedge a Jet Fuel exposure using gas oil futures due to the existence of a liquid futures market. In the gas oil – Jet Fuel relationship, gas oil has traditionally been the main price driver, and as the Jet Fuel differential increased from the historic levels of the mid-USD 20 to USD 60, so gas oil has moved from USD 250 to USD 650. Thus, if a trades hedged in gas oil, it is likely that he would capture most of any Jet price movement.

A possible way of pricing a physical delivery of Jet Fuel could be:

Physical Jet Fuel = Prompt gas oil futures price at delivery + Fixed Jet Differential

+ Transport costs to delivery location

To hedge this exposure the airline can buy the requisite number of gas oil futures and, with the other two elements of the physical contract fixed, it will be able to lock in a known future cost.

Hedging Jet Fuel exposures using gas oil futures and a basis swap

There is an active OTC market for basis swaps that allow an end user to transform exposure in one product to that of another, i.e. an underlying exposure to gas oil can be transformed into a Jet Fuel exposure. These swaps are quoted on a bid–offer basis and are quoted as a fixed against a floating differential, in the same manner as a Brent CFD. The fixed price is calculated as the difference between gas oil and Jet Fuel.

In this example, we will assume that the airline buys its Jet Fuel requirements in the spot market on a variable price basis (e.g. an average of quoted Platts prices plus a premium for delivery to a particular location). To hedge the exposure the airline decides to use a combination of gas oil futures and a basis swap. It buys the gas oil future with the same maturity as the underlying exposure at the equivalent of USD 536.40 per tonne. At the same time it enters into a Jet "diff swap" at a quoted level of +USD 45. The swap is bought in the sense that the agreement is requiring the airline to pay a USD 45 fixed amount per tonne at expiry in return for receiving the average difference between the actual gas oil price and Jet Fuel price over the agreed period of the swap.

The combination of the two deals (buy the gas oil future, buy the "Jet diff" swap) hedges the two components to which they were exposed under the terms of the physical. Under this pricing agreement the buyer is exposed to a change in the price of gas oil and the Jet differential since Jet Fuel is priced from gas oil. The net effect of the transaction is that the airline locks in the price of its Jet Fuel purchase at USD 581.40 per tonne.

Assume that at maturity the following market conditions exist. The gas oil future is trading at USD 550.00 per tonne and the Jet differential has narrowed to USD 40. From the relationship presented earlier linking gas oil to Jet Fuel, we can infer that Jet Fuel is now trading at USD 590 per tonne. The airline will make a USD 13.60 profit on the close-out of the future but will have to make a net payment of USD 5 under the swap. The airline buys Jet Fuel at USD 590 per tonne to which they add the USD 5 loss on the swap but subtract the USD 13.60 profit under the future. The net cost is USD 581.40, equal to the locked-in value established at the point of executing the gas oil future and buying the swap.

Natural Gas

Find gas once and you're forgiven; find gas twice and you're fired.

Old industry adage

SYNOPSIS **The purpose of the chapter is to outline the different structures that exist in a number of natural gas markets, how and why natural gas is traded and a description of the most common derivative structures.**

A short introductory section outlines *how natural gas is formed* and *the different ways in which it is measured*. A key influence on the industry is the impact of *deregulation and subsequent re-regulation* and how it has impacted *the structure of the physical supply chain*. Since natural gas markets tend to be more local in nature than those for say crude oil, the impact of regulation will differ between countries. An overview of the experience of the USA, the UK and Continental Europe in this respect is outlined.

The section on *the demand for and supply of natural gas* considers where the commodity is found, how much of it is left and where it is consumed. The growing importance of *Liquefied Natural Gas* is also discussed.

Since the natural gas market does not have a global pricing benchmark, the difficulty in *defining price* is considered. Some *factors that influence the demand and supply for natural gas* are highlighted and *the importance of crude oil* in pricing contracts in some markets is discussed.

The *motivations for trading natural gas* as well as *the main locations where it is traded* are introduced and from this *the main derivative products* used to manage the associated price risk are analysed.

6.1 HOW NATURAL GAS IS FORMED

Natural gas is a fossil fuel, the main constituent of which is methane (CH_4). Oil and natural gas, which are frequently found together in the same deposits, are formed from the decay of vegetation and animals. Over time geological processes turned these remains into reservoirs of hydrocarbons, trapped by overlying impermeable rock strata.

Natural gas that is discovered with crude oil is often referred to as "associated gas" but is classified as "non-associated gas" when found separately. Although the actual composition of natural gas varies between reservoirs, a distinction can be made between "wet" and "dry" gas. Wet gas has a high proportion of other gaseous substances such as ethane, propane and butane, referred to collectively as natural gas liquids or NGLs. Dry gas is natural gas without these associated substances. After natural gas has been extracted from the ground the NGLs are removed and can be sold separately. For example, ethane is the key input in the production of plastics. The processing of natural gas also removes any water and hydrogen sulphide and adds a smell for safety purposes, as methane in its naturally occurring form is odourless.

6.2   MEASURING NATURAL GAS

The most common measure of the *volume* of natural gas is a cubic metre, which is normally expressed as m^3. In the USA the convention is to use imperial measures such as cubic feet (cf). As these measures are quite small, they are often multiplied by sizing factors such as a thousand (M; 10^3), million (MM; 10^6), billion (b; 10^9) and a trillion (t; 10^{12}). These measurements are taken assuming normal temperatures and pressures.

The *energy* content of natural gas is measured in a variety of ways. The calorific value of natural gas measures the amount of energy produced when a fuel is burnt. One calorie measures the amount of energy required to raise 1 gram of water by 1 degree Celsius. A joule is an alternative measure and 1 calorie equals 4 joules. A kilowatt is equal to 3,600,000 joules and is often expressed as a rate. For example a kilowatt-hour is equal to 1 kilowatt of power expended for 1 hour. Larger businesses and institutions sometimes use the megawatt hour (MWh). The energy outputs of power plants over long periods of time, or the energy consumption of states or nations, can be expressed in gigawatt hours (GWh).

In the USA the most common measure of energy content is the British Thermal Unit (Btu). It is defined as the amount of heat that is required to raise the temperature of 1-pound weight of water by 1 degree Fahrenheit. Another common measure in the UK market is the therm, which is equivalent to 100,000 Btu or about 97 cubic feet. In the European natural gas markets a variety of different measures can be used. These include therms, megawatt hours or gigajoules.

6.3   THE PHYSICAL SUPPLY CHAIN

One of the effects of natural gas deregulation has been to increase the degree of competition along the physical supply chain. The traditional monopolistic supply chain has been restructured so that different functions can now be performed by different entities. While some companies may be vertically integrated performing a number of functions along the supply chain, others may just operate "upstream" in exploration and production or "downstream" in the trading and supplying of gas.

6.3.1   Production

The first part of the physical supply chain is the exploration and production of natural gas from either an offshore or an onshore location. If the natural gas is produced offshore it has to be gathered from various rigs and piped ashore. The point at which the natural gas reaches the shore is generically referred to as the beach terminal. A significant number of the producers will be the oil majors, but there may also be a number of smaller independent producers in operation. There will also be a number of onshore production facilities but the process will essentially be similar. Before onward transportation this "wet" natural gas will have to be processed to separate the natural gas element (i.e. methane) from the other naturally occurring natural gas liquids. The resultant "dry" gas is then delivered into the pipeline system.

6.3.2   Shippers

The advent of re-regulation has allowed third party access (sometimes called "open access" in the USA) to the National Transmission System (NTS) and also saw the emergence of a new role within the supply chain – that of the shipper (sometimes referred to as marketers, particularly in the USA). They are licensed wholesalers who buy natural gas from the producers at the shore terminals for onward delivery along the main pipeline to end consumers. The ownership of designated shippers is diverse. They may be affiliated to natural gas producers, electricity companies or maybe financial trading companies such as Barclays Capital. The shippers/marketers will perform a variety of different roles:

- They may buy natural gas from producers and then find sellers.
- They may sell natural gas to customers and then source the supply.
- They may arrange for the transportation of natural gas along the network pipeline.
- They must inform the natural gas transporter (e.g. National Grid Gas in the UK) where the natural gas will enter the pipeline and where it will exit is achieved by a process of nomination. A shipper can nominate gas to be delivered into the system, out of the system, or to simply change the title of gas within the system.
- For natural gas to be shipped along the main high-pressure pipeline, the shipper has to acquire sufficient entry capacity to permit the flow and then nominate the amount it wishes to deliver. Equally to remove natural gas, exit capacity needs to be booked. Entry and exit capacity can be booked directly with the system operator, and can be auctioned as well as being traded in a secondary market.
- Generally speaking natural gas can enter the system from offshore or onshore production facilities or storage. It exits the system into local distribution networks, storage facilities or is delivered to large industrial users. As part of their daily responsibilities the shippers must ensure that their daily operations balance – that is, the amount of natural gas injected into the system equals the amount withdrawn. Financial penalties are incurred by shippers who fail to balance their demand and supply.

6.3.3 Transmission

Once onshore the natural gas has then to be transported along a large high-pressure pipeline to either a natural gas retail supplier or directly to a wholesale consumer. By transporting it under pressure a greater volume of natural gas can be moved. In order to keep the natural gas moving along the pipelines there will be a number of compressor stations that ensure that the natural gas remains pressurised. A retail natural gas supplier will arrange for the natural gas to be delivered to the end user along lower pressure pipes that join the high-pressure pipeline.

One of the consequences of re-regulation was the realisation that new entrants to the market would not be willing to build competing large-scale national transportation infrastructure. In the USA there are over 150 pipeline companies operating about 285,000 miles of pipeline, 65% of which is interstate. Most natural gas users receive their gas from a supplier that is often referred to generically as a local distribution company (LDC). Depending on the degree of deregulation in the market, the LDC may operate in a specific geographical area or may be free to offer services throughout a specific marketplace. In the USA the delivery points to LDCs are sometimes referred to as "citygates" and are often used as pricing points for buyers and sellers.

In the UK National Grid Gas is the company that manages 4,200 miles of the main high-pressure pipeline – sometimes referred to as the National Transmission System (NTS). It is a private company (also sometimes referred to generically as the Transmission System

Operator or TSO) but operates under a licence granted by the UK regulator. Its role is to deliver natural gas and it can only buy or sell natural gas for purposes of managing the integrity of the pipeline. It is obliged to follow the terms of the "Network Code", which is a framework that dictates how it will operate and the nature of the relationship it has with the users of the network such as shippers. The Network Code enshrines a principle that is common to re-regulated markets, which is the principle of third party access. Third party access allows certain companies (shippers) to have access to the pipeline network in order to facilitate the movement of natural gas on behalf of producers or consumers. There are also a number of independent natural gas transporters who have built extensions to the NTS to supply certain customers not served by the main network.

Natural gas leaves the NTS on a continual basis either directly to large industrial users (such as power stations), storage facilities or into one of a number of Local Distribution Networks into which the UK is grouped. Once within the regional network the natural gas can be routed towards the final consumer.

One of the key responsibilities of the transmission system operator is to ensure that the system is balanced. This is done as a three-stage process. Firstly, there is the nomination process, where the shippers are required to inform the TSO as to the how much natural gas will be delivered, over what period and the entry and exit points. The TSO will then confirm the nomination after they are sure that sufficient capacity exists within the network. The final stage in the process is the scheduling by the TSO of all the confirmed nominations based on defined priorities.

Although the act of balancing the network will be performed by the TSO, the shippers will be incentivised through monetary penalties to ensure that the amount of natural gas entering the system matches the amount of natural gas exiting. The transmission system operators have a number of available options to ensure that the volume of natural gas within the pipeline is kept within acceptable limits. For example, they could utilise production contracts to supply natural gas that include a clause that allows for the contracted amount to be increased above the stated amount. This additional amount is referred to as the "swing". The existence of adequate storage facilities is also important so that natural gas could be withdrawn at short notice. A third tool that could be used is interruptible supply contracts with large industrial consumers. Here the customer is willing to accept that his supply of natural gas may be curtailed in periods where demand is high. In exchange the consumer will receive some form of financial compensation.

6.3.4 Interconnectors

Interconnectors are large pipelines that link Great Britain to mainland Europe, Northern Ireland and Norway. As production in the North Sea declines, the importance of the interconnectors will increase, as the UK will be forced to import more natural gas.

6.3.5 Storage

Excess natural gas can be stored in large underground caverns, above ground facilities or within the pipes on the transportation network (a process referred to as "line-packing"). By raising and lowering the pressure on any pipeline segment, a pipeline company can use the segment to store gas during periods when there is less demand at the end of the pipeline.

Using line-packing in this way allows pipeline operators to handle short-term fluctuations in demand.

Underground cavities are created by drilling down into salt layers, adding seawater to dissolve the salt and then pumping in natural gas to force out the water. Depleted oil or natural gas reservoirs are also used for this purpose. Natural gas can also be stored in a liquefied form (LNG), which reduces the amount of space occupied.

Storage is sometimes classified as either base or peak load. Base load storage is more strategic in nature, and although the facilities may be large in size, the rate at which the gas can be extracted is low. Natural gas reservoirs that have been depleted are a popular choice for this sort of facility. Peak load facilities are more tactical in nature and are designed to allow smaller amounts of gas at a faster rate. Salt caverns are commonly used for peak storage needs.

In a re-regulated market storage facilities are run on a commercial basis with capacity being sold off to third parties. The availability of storage capacity relative to demand will have an important impact on the price of natural gas [1]. For example, in Europe it has been estimated that France has about 90 days of its average natural gas demand available in storage, Germany 76 days, Italy 60 and the UK 13. In terms of peak demand, the UK storage capacity would be equivalent to about 7 days of supply. If capacity is scarce relative to demand, a cold spell of weather could cause natural gas prices to rise steeply. In general terms, excess natural gas is injected into storage during warmer periods and withdrawn in colder times.

6.3.6 Supply

Under monopoly style natural gas structures, the final consumers would have virtually no choice as to who provided their natural gas supply. In the natural gas markets that have been re-regulated, consumers should be free to choose the provider of their natural gas supplies. This freedom of choice also extends to the suppliers who can choose the source of their natural gas and arrange with a shipper to ensure its delivery.

6.3.7 Customers

Distinction is usually made between two different types of customer. Retail consumers would typically include households, shops and offices whereas very large industrial customers would cover such as power stations that may buy directly from either shippers or producers. In some cases the large industrial users may have separate arrangements to receive their supplies by a specific "offtake" from the national pipeline system. However, within the industrial capacity there will be larger customers who have an arrangement whereby their supply can be interrupted or where the agreement to supply gas is "firm".

6.3.8 Financial institutions

Within a re-regulated framework and the growth of traded markets, financial institutions play an increasingly important role. They perform a variety of different functions.

Traditional lending banks who have lent to upstream producers will have taken on an element of commodity risk. If they cannot offset that risk, they may seek out an institution with natural gas trading capability in order to manage the price risk.

The majority of the *oil producers* (e.g. BP, Shell) will have very sophisticated natural gas trading and risk management operations and will act as trading counterparties to many of the banks. However, the banks will be able to offer their range of services to smaller or new entrant producers who may be attracted into the market as a result of deregulation.

Utilities will have large demand and uncertain consumption forecasts and will also have significant volume and price risk based on weather and natural gas consumption. As a result, they require structured natural gas contracts that provide them with flexibility.

Major *industrial natural gas consumers* are chemical companies, building products, glass, steel manufacturers and fertiliser manufacturers. It may also be possible to aggregate smaller loads and manage the natural gas price risk centrally where an entity has a multisite operate.

Traders and hedge funds will use the natural gas market to implement view-driven strategies using the suite of physical and derivative products.

6.4 DEREGULATION AND RE-REGULATION

The emergence of natural gas as a tradable commodity has come about as a result of deregulation in some countries. This, however, does not mean that the various markets have became unregulated, but rather that a new set of regulations have emerged.

Prior to re-regulation, gas markets were characterised as monopolies where one entity would purchase virtually all of the domestic production, transport it to its end destination and sell it to a final consumer. Agreements to buy and sell were primarily based on long-term, fixed price contracts, often linked to the price of oil. In the USA prior to deregulation, the natural gas producers would sell to pipeline companies who then transported and sold it either to large industrial users or to local distribution companies for onward sale to the general public. The prices charged by producers to the transportation companies and the amounts paid by the local distribution companies were regulated at the federal level. The retail consumer was protected against monopolistic practices by state regulation.

6.4.1 The US experience

The first country to introduce competition into their domestic natural gas market was the USA. In the very early days of the industry it was regulated at a local level but as intrastate pipelines, and then interstate pipelines, started to develop there was no effective method of overseeing the industry. The origins of formal federal regulation were set out in the Natural Gas Act of 1938, which recognised that while the movement of natural gas along major interstate pipelines was a natural monopoly, it required an element of regulation. The act concerned itself with the setting of rates for the transportation of natural gas along interstate pipelines but did not specify any particular regulation of producer prices. Wellhead price regulation came about in 1954 in a legal case (Phillips Petroleum Co. vs Wisconsin). As a result of this law suit the Federal Power Commission (who regulated interstate natural gas sales at the time) imposed price ceilings on the amount that producers could charge, which remained in place until 1978. There were three effects of the Phillips decision:

- Since the sale price for which natural gas could be sold was regulated, there was little incentive for the producer to devote extra capital to expand exploration.
- The price of intrastate gas was not subject to the same regulation and so created a bias, which encouraged producing states to sell it locally rather than nationally. This created natural gas shortages in the mid-1970s in some states.

- As a result of the Middle East Oil embargos in the 1970s, natural gas became a more attractive energy substitute. Combined with the relatively low price ceilings imposed by the regulator, the demand for natural gas increased substantially.

The next significant act was the Natural Gas Policy Act of 1978, which aimed to create a single market for gas that did not favour intrastate over interstate sales and would allow market forces to determine the price of natural gas. The act also saw the Federal Power Commission replaced by the Federal Energy Regulatory Commission (FERC). However, the complete "unbundling" of natural gas services continued via a series of orders issued by the FERC and federal legislation. In 1985 FERC Order 436 (sometimes referred to as the "open access order") required that natural gas pipelines provide open access to transportation services albeit on a voluntary basis. However, it was the Natural Gas Wellhead Decontrol Act of 1989, that effectively led to the restructuring of the natural gas industry and encouraged market-determined gas prices. This meant that large-scale consumers of natural gas were able to negotiate prices directly with producers and contract separately for its transportation. FERC Order 636 issued in 1992 made the voluntary unbundling of services outlined in Order 436 compulsory. This order stated that the pipeline companies had to separate their transportation and sales functions to give the customer greater choice as to the sale, transportation and storage of natural gas.

The overall impact for the USA was that producer prices were no longer subject to regulation and were driven by the fundamentals of supply and demand. Producers and consumers could contract directly with the pipeline companies no longer taking possession of the natural gas. They would now only offer transportation as a service to another company. It also gave rise to a range of new services such as shipping and trading.

6.4.2 The UK experience

In the UK the natural gas market was subject to major deregulation and re-regulation from the mid-1980s (e.g. the Gas Acts of 1986 and 1995). Prior to this time the market had been dominated by a single monopoly – British Gas. The company was initially privatised and by the late1990s had demerged with a series of separate companies performing different roles (e.g. BG focusing on extraction; National Grid Gas maintaining the transportation network and Centrica supplying natural gas to retail customers under the British Gas brand). The industry's upstream activities (e.g. exploration and production) are regulated by the DTI (Department of Trade and Industry) while the downstream activities (e.g. consumer supply) are currently regulated by OFGEM (Office of Gas and Electricity Markets).

6.4.3 Continental European deregulation

The entire European market is regulated by a series of directives that should eventually be introduced as law within each member state country. The second Gas Directive of 2003 (which repealed the first Gas Directive of 1998) has the principal objective of creating a single unified market for natural gas. This was complemented by the Gas Regulation of 2005, which expanded on many of the issues outlined in the 2003 Directive. The Directives require each country within the EU to restructure its natural gas industry in order to allow consumers greater choice as to who will supply their natural gas. The Gas Directives covered a variety of issues such as:

- Unbundling of services provided by integrated companies
- Security of supply
- Infrastructure
- Designation of the transmission system operator to run the high-pressure pipeline network
- Fair access to transmission networks
- Access to storage
- Distribution of natural gas to customers
- National regulation.

One of the consequences of this deregulation was a wave of attempted and successful mergers as many of the market participants believed that the only way to compete in an enlarged market would be through economies of scale. This would (in theory) allow them to service a large and geographically diverse range of clients and possess the ability to compete with the large eastern European suppliers such as Gazprom.

Inevitably any market will evolve according to local conditions and at different speeds. However, a number of common features have evolved for countries that have introduced an element of competition:

- Prices are now determined more by conditions of demand and supply than by long-term contract.
- Monopolistic structures have been replaced by the unbundling of functions allowing new companies to enter the market, and offer greater competition.
- New functions have evolved to meet the demands of the new structures (e.g. shippers).
- A new set of regulations has evolved for different elements of the physical supply chain. For example, in the UK the "Network Code" outlines the relationship between the owners of the National Transmission System (NTS) and the Gas shipping companies who in a deregulated market are now able to administratively arrange for natural gas to be moved along the pipeline.
- New traded markets allow the management of natural gas market price risk (both OTC and on an exchange-traded basis)
- There is greater movement of natural gas across international borders in both gaseous and liquefied forms.

6.5 THE DEMAND AND SUPPLY FOR GAS

6.5.1 Relative importance of natural gas

One of the most authoritative reviews of the energy market is produced annually by BP [2]. Unless otherwise referenced, the statistics in this section are derived from the *BP Statistical Review of World Energy 2006*. The annual review provides statistics in relation to the consumption of energy by fuel type. It defines primary energy sources as:

- Oil
- Natural gas
- Coal
- Nuclear Energy
- Hydro Electric.

Table 6.1 shows energy consumption figures for the main geographical locations, which are expressed in a common unit – million tonnes oil equivalent (MMtoe).

The trade in natural gas is characterised by a number of different features:

- Domestic markets, where natural gas is moved by pipeline.
- The exporting and importing of natural gas internationally by pipeline.
- A global liquefied natural gas (LNG) market.

Not surprisingly oil is still the most popular fuel source followed by coal and then natural gas.

6.5.2 Consumption of natural gas

In terms of geographical consumption the statistics presented in Table 6.1 may obscure individual country usage. The USA consumes the largest amount of energy (2,336 MMtoe) with China (1,554 MMtoe) the second largest. In terms of natural gas consumption the USA is again the largest consumer (634.5 billion cubic metres – bcm) followed by the Russian Federation (405 bcm). Figure 6.1 illustrates the consumption of natural gas by region.

Table 6.1 Consumption of primary energy by region (million tonnes oil equivalent)

	Oil	Natural Gas	Coal	Nuclear Energy	Hydro Electric	Totals
North America	1,133	697	614	209	149	2,801
South and Central America	223	112	21	4	142	501
Europe and Eurasia	963	1,010	538	286	187	2,984
Middle East	271	226	9	0	4	510
Africa	129	64	100	3	20	317
Asia Pacific	1,117	366	1,648	125	167	3,424
TOTALS	**3,837**	**2,475**	**2,930**	**627**	**669**	**10,537**

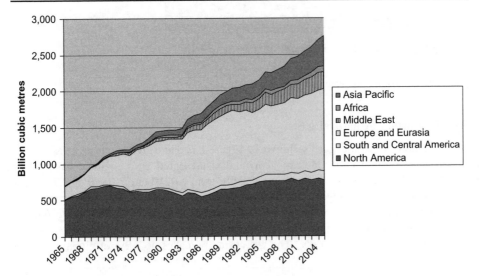

Figure 6.1 Consumption of natural gas by region, 1965–2005

6.5.3 Reserves of natural gas

Table 6.2 shows the three countries with the largest reserves (in trillions of cubic metres; tcm). In contrast, the USA accounts for only 3.0% and the UK 0.3% of total proven reserves. Proven reserves by region are shown in Figure 6.2.

Table 6.2 Proven natural gas reserves

Country	Amount	Percentage of global reserves
Russian Federation	48	26.6%
Iran	27	14.9%
Qatar	26	14.3%

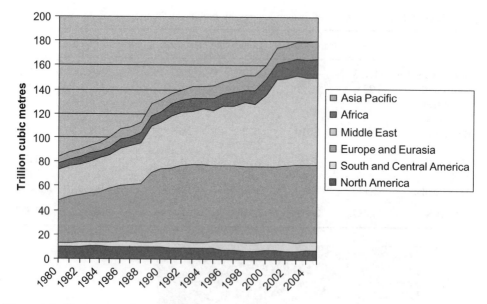

Figure 6.2 Proven natural gas reserves 1980–2005

6.5.4 Production of natural gas

The production of natural gas is shown in Figure 6.3. Here the graph is measured on a different scale (billion cubic metres; bcm) and is presented on a regional basis. Overall production of natural gas has been rising steadily from 1,021 bcm in 1970 to 2,763 bcm in 2005. Table 6.3 gives the highest individual producers of natural gas.

The countries mentioned previously with the highest proven reserves tend to only contribute a relatively small proportion of current production. Iran contributes 3.1% of the overall production and Qatar 1.6%. The UK currently makes up 3.2% of global production.

Table 6.3   Natural gas production

Country	Percentage of global production
USA	19.0%
Russian Federation	21.6%

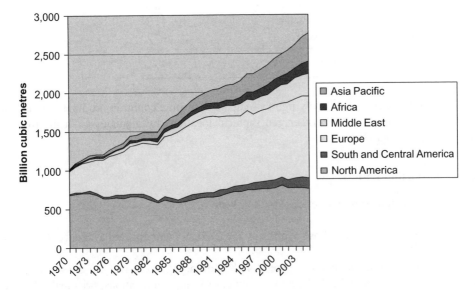

Figure 6.3   Natural gas production 1970–2005

6.5.5   Reserve to production ratio

One key concern often expressed in relation to energy is that, given that fossil fuels are finite in nature, how long will it be until the resource runs out? The reserve to production ratio (R/P ratio) divides the level of proven reserves at the end of the year by the production in that particular year. The result is the number of years that the reserves would last if production were to continue at that level. Table 6.4 indicates the figures for the end of 2005. It should be remembered that a variety of different estimates are available, which will often widely differ as a result of the different assumptions made.

In the UK, the Offshore Operators Association [3] (UKOOA) argues that although nearly 2,000 billion cubic metres (bcm) have been recovered from the North Sea since 1965 there could be up to 1,500 bcm still remaining. According to the UKOOA, gas production peaked in 2000, at an average of 297 million cubic metres (MMcm) per day. They also point out that the country consumes between 200 and 250 per day during the summer, rising to 350 MMcm per day in an average winter and up to 450 MMcm per day on a very cold winter's day. This shortfall is usually met by removing gas from storage or overseas imports.

Table 6.4 Reserves to production ratio

Country	Years
North America	9.9
South and Central America	51.8
Europe and Eurasia	60.3
Middle East	>100
Africa	88.3
Asia Pacific	41.2
Globally	65.1
Oil	40.6

The overall demand and supply figures indicate that some countries are likely to become more reliant on imports from other geographical locations by pipelines or in the form of liquefied natural gas (LNG).

6.5.6 Exporting natural gas

The largest pipeline exporters of gas in 2005 were:

- The Russian Federation, whose exports of 151.28 bcm were directed at France, Germany, Italy and Turkey.
- Canada, whose pipeline exports were 104.18 bcm, going exclusively to the USA.
- Norway, who exported 79.46 bcm to a number of European locations, principally France, Germany and the UK.
- The Netherlands exported 46.75 bcm principally to France and Germany.
- Algeria, who shipped 39.08 bcm under the Mediterranean to Italy and Spain.

From this it is unsurprising to see that the largest four importers of gas via pipelines were:

- USA   104.21 bcm
- Germany   90.70 bcm
- Italy   70.99 bcm
- France   36.20 bcm.

6.5.7 Liquefied natural gas

Countries dependent on gas, but for geographical reasons cannot receive it via a pipeline, must resort to receiving gas as LNG [4]. This is not a competing product to natural gas; it is merely an alternative method of distribution. In liquefied form natural gas occupies 1/600th of the space it would in gaseous form, making it more viable to transport over longer distances. To create LNG, the gas is cooled below its freezing point of $-161°C$ ($-260°F$) and other constituents such as oxygen and carbon dioxide are removed to leave a gas that is virtually pure methane. Once converted the gas can be transported in specially adapted ships to LNG terminals in any geographical location, where the conversion process is then reversed. However, converting natural gas to LNG is a complex process that requires a substantial infrastructure, that is expensive and may take many years to construct.

The annual production of gas in LNG form is expected to increase from its current levels, particularly for countries with high consumption rates relative to their own domestic supplies. The biggest importers of LNG are:

- Japan   76.32 bcm
- South Korea   30.45 bcm
- Spain   21.85 bcm
- USA   17.87 bcm

The largest exporters of LNG are:

- Indonesia   31.46 bcm
- Malaysia   28.52 bcm
- Algeria   25.68 bcm
- Qatar   27.10 bcm

Most European countries will become increasingly reliant on imports over the coming years as their own domestic supplies decline. Four main suppliers currently meet this demand: Russia (supplying 40%), Algeria (10%), the Netherlands (13%) and Norway (22%). LNG will provide a method of diversifying supply allowing gas to be imported from more distant locations such as the Middle East or Nigeria.

In the USA, 80% of demand is met from domestic supplies. The residual demand is met through cross border pipelines, principally with Canada. Another growing area of supply for the USA is liquefied natural gas but, as of late 2005, the USA only had four LNG terminals although 30 facilities were being planned.

6.6 GAS PRICE DRIVERS

6.6.1 Definitions of price

Before considering the factors that influence the price of natural gas, it is perhaps useful to reflect on what this term actually means. From a retail perspective the price of natural gas may vary (due to changes at the wholesale level) but will be influenced by regulatory considerations. However, the price of natural gas at the wholesale level will be influenced by a very different set of factors. In a highly monopolistic natural gas industry, contracts to buy or sell natural gas may well be long term, bilateral and fixed price in nature. The use of a "take or pay" contracts might exist, meaning that if a buyer did not take the agreed volumes he would have to pay a fee. Although aspects of these types of pricing structure may persist in a re-regulated market, there is now a greater possibility that the price will be based on fundamental considerations of demand and supply.

As with any commodity there will be different prices for delivery of natural gas in different maturities. However, although there may be a common set of delivery maturities, there will be different sources for reporting prices of deals executed. In order to ensure the efficient settlement of a variety of contracts (especially derivatives), the emergence of a single credible and accepted benchmark reference is key, and for the energy markets there are a variety of different possible sources. For example, such an index should be representative of market conditions at a particular time and the market should be considered to be liquid (defined as the ability to execute a transaction without significantly moving the price). Some contracts may be settled against a price quoted on a futures exchange such as ICE or NYMEX. Other popular price sources are privately owned price reporting publications such as the *European Spot Gas Markets* (ESGM) published by Heren [5] and *Inside FERC*, published by Platts [6] for the US market.

The ESGM reports a variety of different prices, which include:

- Monthly and daily price indices for a variety of locations (e.g. NBP, beach locations and continental hubs such as Zeebrugge).
- Quoted prices that cover natural gas for delivery day-ahead, weekend, working days next week, the balance of the month, monthly, quarterly and annually.
- Price differentials for all of these delivery months for NBP natural gas against delivery at a beach terminal (e.g. Bacton, Fergus).

Inside FERC reports:

- Spot prices of natural gas delivered to a variety of pipelines.
- Spot prices for different market centres.

6.6.2 Supply side price drivers

On the supply side of the price equation there are a number of key issues.

Current levels of domestic production and proven reserves

For some countries the balance between the levels of domestic production and imports will have a big impact on price. For example, the UK became a net importer of natural gas from continental Europe in 2005, which introduced a new set of price dynamics such as increased sensitivity to changes in the price of crude oil. If the amount of natural gas to be extracted falls below initial expectations, this may exert upward price pressure.

Production outages due to accidents or weather

For example, US natural gas production, which is very concentrated in the Gulf of Mexico, was severely disrupted in 2005 due to Hurricane Katrina. Within this category it would be appropriate to include the closing of fields for maintenance during certain times of the year when demand is expected to be low.

Available infrastructure

Like many commodities there is a limit to the flexibility of supply due to the fact that infrastructure projects will require a long time to complete. Interconnectors are large international pipelines used to transport natural gas. If the price of continental natural gas is higher than that in the UK, there is an incentive to deliver natural gas into Europe, while the opposite will hold true if the price of UK natural gas is higher than that seen on the continent. The size and timing of planned infrastructure projects, such as storage facilities, new interconnectors and LNG terminals, may influence prices for delivery of natural gas in the future. For example, in mid-2006, the UK had only one interconnector across to Belgium. However, two new interconnectors were opened in the latter half of the year linking the UK with Norway and Holland, with a second interconnector to Norway planned to open in 2007/08. Combined with planned LNG facilities, the total import capacity of the UK will be able to meet about two-thirds of current consumption.

One particular day shortly after the opening of the Langeled Norwegian pipeline a combination of warm weather; a major shipment of LNG to the UK, a shortage of storage capacity and a large delivery to test the interconnector caused a surplus of supply. The National Grid Gas reported that 344 million cubic metres were available compared with estimated demand of 234 million cubic metres. This led to suppliers paying buyers to take up the excess with the price of gas reportedly falling to *minus* 5 pence per therm [7].

Security of natural gas supplies

This can be interpreted as either the availability or reliability of natural gas supplies and is a key factor for those countries that are reliant on imports of natural gas. The security of supply is enhanced by the existence of a diversified source of supply, adequate transmission infrastructure and sufficient storage facilities. Traditionally western Europe has been able to source its natural gas supplies from four key areas:

- The North Sea (from UK, Norwegian and Dutch owned fields)
- Onshore European natural gas fields
- Russia
- Algeria.

In late 2005 and early 2006 the issue caused substantial price volatility and was a key consideration in the European market. Firstly, the price of UK natural gas rose steeply as supplies from Europe via the interconnector fell. A number of reasons were cited for this disruption including an accusation by the EU government of anticompetitive practices by continental European natural gas participants. There was a suggestion that market participants acted to limit supplies from the regulated countries surrounding the UK in an attempt to drive up prices. A counter argument was that UK producers had oversupplied the market in previous years and had cut back production, which had also led to a rise in price. This was later compounded by a shutdown of one of the main UK storage facilities for a 3-month period.

At the same time a dispute arose between Russia and Ukraine [8] over the price to be paid for Siberian natural gas. For many years Russia had been supplying a number of surrounding countries at subsidised prices. However, in early 2006 Russia decided to increase the price charged for the natural gas. The Ukraine objected claiming that it was Moscow's attempt to punish them for developing closer ties with the West.

As tension rose, Russia reduced the flow of natural gas into the pipeline by an amount equal to Ukraine's usage. This had a knock-on effect to the rest of Europe, as the pipeline used to transport the natural gas was the key route through which countries such as Italy and Germany were supplied. The incident was almost repeated in 2007, this time with respect to Belarus, but closure of the gas pipeline was averted shortly before the deadline. The incidents highlighted a general issue that a producer of natural gas will not always have complete control over the pipeline system if it runs across a number of countries. As a result it will be exposed to an element of political risk. One of Russia's planned infrastructure projects is a pipeline under the Baltic Sea to feed directly into the German market, thereby bypassing neighbouring states.

However, history shows that using energy supplies as a political tool is a risky strategy for the selling country as it can often encourage end users to seek either alternative sources of supply or indeed energy substitutes. It has been argued that the oil embargos of the 1970s, which caused the price of crude oil to rise steeply, was one of the contributory factors that led to the usage of natural gas an energy substitute. This substitution effect combined with government policies that aimed to reduce the reliance on crude oil usage led to a fall in demand and a subsequent fall in the price. Similarly, a dispute between Italy and Algeria in the 1980s led to a substantial drop in natural gas exports and the associated revenues for the North African country.

6.6.3   Demand side price drivers

The demand side of the market is driven by:

- *Seasonal demand or weather:* The main component of natural gas demand is domestic for heating and cooking requirements and so a change in the weather may lead to a change in demand.
- *Degree of domestic competition between suppliers:* As the choice of suppliers increases, the price of natural gas should fall (all other things being equal).
- *Electricity generation:* Natural gas is seen as an environmentally attractive fuel to run electricity power stations, and as the electricity market has deregulated this has further spurred the growth of natural gas.
- *Exports:* Since the UK is now linked to the rest of Europe via a series of pipelines, it is possible to export gas to other countries if there is an increase in demand.
- *Storage injections:* Typically natural gas is injected into storage in the summer, when demand is relatively lower.

6.6.4   The price of oil

The linkage between the price of natural gas and crude oil ("gas to oil pricing") stems from a number of reasons and affects both regulated and re-regulated markets. The linkage exists for a number of reasons:

- The fact that both energy sources are often found together and so by linking the price of natural gas to oil energy companies would not be incentivised to produce one source over another.
- The early natural gas finds in Europe were valued based on alternative fuels, which commercial and domestic consumers had used prior to this time. As a result natural gas contracts for industrial consumers tended to be linked to the price of fuel oil, power generation contracts to the price of fuel oil or coal, domestic supply contracts to the price of gasoil. In some cases contracts could also be linked directly to the price of a particular crude oil (e.g. Brent).

- When natural gas became more of a substitute for oil, natural gas price rises became indexed to the changes in the oil price to ensure that it remained attractively priced and retained its market share.
- For some end users there is an element of substitutability between different fuel sources, so relative pricing becomes important.
- Since oil-based products are mature liquid markets, they provide an attractive relative pricing source in geographical locations where natural gas markets are considered illiquid. This was particularly relevant when banks were lending to large exploration and production projects. In order to ensure there were sufficient cashflows to service the debt, this led to the development of long-term natural gas sales contracts that were indexed to oil-based products.

One interesting illustration on the role of oil prices within a deregulated market is the situation faced by the UK. Many large industrial consumers and power stations can operate using either natural gas or oil-based products. As a result the gas – oil price link will have an indirect impact on the price of natural gas. Additionally, as the UK becomes more reliant on overseas European imports, its main source of supply will be from a variety of different countries within Europe. Since a significant proportion of natural gas contracts in Europe are indexed to the price of crude oil, and if natural gas is imported via the interconnector, the price charged to the purchaser will be influenced by the price of oil.

Using values published as part of the *BP Statistical Review of World Energy* the correlation coefficient between the price of natural gas in different locations and crude oil is given in Table 6.5.

A report published by the European Commission in 2006 [9] into competition in the European gas markets highlighted more detail about the nature of oil indexation in the region. It noted that supply agreements were characterised by long-term contracts of between 15 and 20 years in duration and generally included a pricing formula that was indexed to a variety of different fuels.

There is no single indexation formula that applies across all markets but there may be common elements to the supply contracts in which they are embedded:

- A predefined maturity, say, 10 or 20 years.
- A "take or pay" clause that requires the buyer to take delivery of an agreed quantity of gas or to pay for it even it is not required.
- The price of natural gas in these contracts is usually recalculated every one to three months.

A hypothetical indexation formula might have the following characteristics. Let us assume that a gas supplier was fixing his prices with a large industrial consumer as of 1 November

Table 6.5   Correlation between price of crude oil and natural gas

Price of European natural gas and crude oil	0.8927
Price of British natural gas and crude oil	0.9627
Price of Henry Hub natural gas and crude oil	0.9438
Price of LNG and crude oil	0.9066

Annual sampling dates: European natural gas, 1984–2005; British natural gas, 1996–2005; US natural gas, 1989–2005; LNG, 1985–2005.

2006. There will be a base price for the natural gas, which may be adjusted by the average price of the chosen oil-based product (e.g. fuel oil) that prevailed over a 3-month period with a one-month lag. In this example, the pricing window would extend from 1 July 2006 to 30 September 2006. The contract price would then be valid for, say, a 3-month period to 1 February 2007. This would link the price of natural gas to the price of oil, but with the effect of being both lagged and damped by the averaging process. This indexation formula would be referred to as a "3−1−3". The end formula will normally include adjustments to ensure that the final price takes account of the fact that the prices of the different oil products, expressed in units of volume rather than units of energy, may be traded in a different currency and may have different thermal properties.

The EC report (2006) suggested that about 75% of all contracts were indexed and the most popular oil-based products were light fuel oil, gas oil and heavy fuel oil. This figure did vary according to the region of natural gas production. In the UK the figure was closer to 20% with the main pricing basis being either market determined or one that was linked to the rate of inflation. In the Netherlands, Norway and Russia, the indexation patterns were revealed that about 80% of production was indexed to heavy and light fuel oils.

As a result it would be reasonable to say that deregulated markets are characterised by longer-term contracts, with take or pay clauses and prices indexed to oil-based products. Deregulated markets would have a wider range of contract maturity from within-day contracts to longer-term contracts (but not as long as those seen in regulated markets). Prices are more likely to be indexed to the fundamental demand and supply factors for natural gas. It would seem likely that the influence of crude oil and the refined products will continue to exert an influence over EU pricing structures since the Netherlands, Norway and Russia supply about 60% of Europe's natural gas needs. The advent of a re-regulated market will not necessarily signal the immediate end of the influence of oil on natural gas prices given that contracts indexed to oil tend to be very long term in nature.

6.7   TRADING PHYSICAL NATURAL GAS

One of the impacts of moving from a monopolistic structure characterised by long-term fixed pricing agreements, is the move to shorter-term trading arrangements. The motivations for trading natural gas can be explained within the context of the risks faced by different elements of the physical supply chain.

6.7.1   Motivations for trading natural gas

Producers will be concerned about maximising their revenues and meeting their contractual supply commitments. If they are unable to produce natural gas to meet their requirements they may be forced to enter the market to meet their requirements. Additionally, if they have flexibility to increase their production they may be tempted to produce more if they believe they will be able to earn a high price. They may be faced with a number of different supply contracts with different maturities that they may or may not be able to meet from their existing production. Additionally, the contracts may be priced in a variety of different ways (e.g. fixed, floating, oil indexation). This may motivate them to enter into derivative contracts to mitigate the associated risk.

The flip side of this are the *consumers* of natural gas who will be trying to ensure that they can supply sufficient gas at the most cost efficient price. Similar to the producers, they will be faced with a variety of market risks that they may wish to mitigate.

Since *shippers* are responsible for ensuring that their demand and supply commitments are in balance, they may be forced into the market to buy and sell natural gas. The *TSO* will be responsible for ensuring that, overall, the system is in balance and so may need to buy and sell natural gas to achieve this.

With respect to *storage*, one of the popular strategies that are used by traders and consuming utilities is to buy natural gas when it is cheap (e.g. in the summer months), in anticipation that the revenues generated at its eventual point of sale will exceed all associated costs.

Financial institutions will offer risk management solutions to those entities along the physical supply chain. As such they will be take on a particular risk that they will then seek to offset at a profit by trading with similar institutions. For example, they may identify an opportunity to arbitrage the price of natural gas in two different locations (e.g. the UK National Balancing Point (NBP) vs Zeebrugge).

6.7.2   Trading locations

The trading will be executed either on an exchange or over-the-counter basis. For example, within the UK there are two main organised exchanges, the IntercontinentalExchange (ICE) and the on-the-day commodity market (OCM) both of which will result in physical delivery if the contracts are held to maturity. Over-the-counter trading is a mix of either physically or financially settled contracts.

6.7.3   Delivery points

Within any natural gas market, agreement has to be reached on where the transfer of natural gas ownership will occur. As a result, a number of popular delivery locations have evolved that are either physical or virtual in nature.

There are over 30 major market hubs in the USA of which the most commonly cited delivery point is the Henry Hub in Louisiana. It is the physical meeting point for 16 intra- and interstate pipelines, where a significant proportion of natural gas is taken from various production points in the Gulf of Mexico and fed to a number of states through the East Coast, Midwest and up to the Canadian border. Although it is possible to buy and sell gas in any location, the price may be quoted as a spread (referred to as the location differential) to the Henry Hub figure. In addition, the US market makes reference to the concept of "citygates", which are the locations at which the local distribution companies receive natural gas from a pipeline and are also pricing points.

In a similar vein the Zeebrugge hub is a common delivery location in continental Europe as it represents the physical junction of a number of international pipelines. If the hub is physical in nature, it is likely that there will be a range of other facilities available to the market participants such as storage and treatment. Other physical hubs in Europe include Baumgarten in Austria and Emden in Germany.

In the UK there is a virtual delivery point referred to as the National Balancing Point (NBP), which is a notional point within the national transmission system through which all natural gas is deemed to flow and about which all natural gas is required to balance. The

Dutch national transmission company has created something similar to the UK, which is referred to as the Title Transfer Facility (TTF).

6.8 NATURAL GAS DERIVATIVES

6.8.1 Trading natural gas in the UK

Over-the-counter (OTC) trades broadly encompass four different types of transaction. NBP spot and forward transactions, beach contracts and interconnector trades. These trades can vary in their maturity; for example NBP trades are quoted from "within day" out to 3 years. Each counterparty will undertake to make trade nominations to the system operator on the quantity of natural gas and the period of the performance to which it relates. An NBP transaction could also be executed such that the buyer and seller will trade the right of ownership of natural gas within the National Transmission System (NTS). Since the natural gas is already within the NTS, the system operator will simply have to make an adjustment to the accounts of the two shippers on the quantity traded.

Beach trades are bilateral contracts where the purchase or sale will take place at a specified natural gas terminal where it is brought ashore from a production facility. These deals are executed for natural gas transactions outside of the NTS and can be useful for a shipper who is looking to resolve an anticipated system imbalance. Interconnector trades for delivery at, say, Zeebrugge will operate in a similar fashion.

One of the key requirements of the Network Code is that shippers are required to balance their daily injections with daily deliveries at the NBP. If actual natural gas usage is not equal to the amount nominated, the shipper will be out of balance. The system will be long natural gas if too much is delivered or the withdrawals ("offtake") are less than expected. The system will be short natural gas if the shipper didn't deliver enough or the offtake was more than expected. This imbalance can be anticipated by the TSO by matching nominations made by different shippers to buy and sell natural gas. There are a number of ways in which the system can be brought back into balance:

- Shippers can obtain or dispose of natural gas in the "on-the-day commodity market" (OCM).
- Shippers trade with producers outside the NTS using beach contracts.
- The system operator can buy or sell natural gas on the OCM if they believe an imbalance will occur and settle retrospectively with a particular shipper.
- The system operator or shippers use contracts to extract natural gas from storage.
- Certain clients have agreements whereby their supply can be interrupted.

6.8.2 On-the-day commodity market

The OCM was set up as part of the re-regulation process of the UK Natural gas industry to help to manage system imbalances. Access to this 24-hour electronic market is restricted to the system operator and licensed shippers. Transactions can be executed between these counterparties for either balancing purposes or for pure trading motives. This regulated market currently has two different segments, the day-ahead market and the within-day OCM. The day-ahead market offers four different types of contract:

- Individual days

- Balance of the week
- Weekend strip
- Working days next week.

The within-day OCM offers three types of transaction. A *locational trade* allows for the purchase or sale of natural gas that is at specific points on the NTS. A *physical trade* allows for the purchase or sale of physical natural gas at the NBP. *Title trades* represent a change of ownership of natural gas that is already at the NBP.

If National Grid Gas is required to buy extra natural gas to make the system balance, an imbalance charge is subsequently made to the offending shipper at what is referred to as a System Marginal Price (SMP). On the OCM the "SMP buy" is the highest price at which the system operator bought natural gas for the system, while "SMP sell" is the lowest price at which natural gas was sold out of the system. A related concept is the System Average Price, which is a volume weighted average of all buy and sells.

6.8.3   Exchange-traded futures contracts

In the UK a natural gas futures contract was first listed in January 1997. It can be used for a variety of reasons:

- To help to manage an entity's natural gas price exposure.
- As a means of taking exposure to the gas market without necessarily having an underlying exposure. In this case the investor would simply close-out the futures position prior to expiry.
- The futures market can also be used as a means to obtain or dispose of supplies to the natural gas market as all of the contracts will result in physical delivery at the NBP if held to maturity.

Table 6.6 highlights the main features of the UK natural gas future traded on the ICE and the Henry Hub natural gas futures traded on NYMEX.

One of the roles that exchanges often fulfil is a pricing benchmark against which OTC transactions can settle. One example of this is ICE natural gas index. It is an unweighted rolling average of the front month settlement price calculated and published at the end of each trading day. The final value for the contract is set after the close of trading on the date on which the front month contract expires (i.e. two business days prior to the first delivery day of the expiring contract).

If a the contract traded on the ICE is not closed-out prior to its expiry, the counterparties will be expected to go to full delivery in equal measure on each individual day in the contract for an amount equal to the number of lots remaining open at the expiry of the contract. The basic foundation is the *day contract*, which can be traded for individual days out to 7 days ahead. A natural gas day runs from 06:00 to 05:59 the following day. *Month contracts* are strips made up of individual and consecutive calendar days, the total number of which is dependent on the number of days in the particular month. These contracts will be listed out to 11 months in the future. A *balance of the month* contract is made up of a series of daily, physically settled contracts for the remaining number of days within a particular calendar month. Each day, the number of contracts within the transaction will reduce by one. *Quarter contracts* are strips of 3 individual and consecutive calendar months. However, the

Table 6.6   Contract specifications for UK and US natural gas futures

	ICE	NYMEX
Contract size	Minimum of 5 lots of 1,000 therms per lot of natural gas per day	1 lot
Unit of trading	1 lot equals 1,000 therms of natural gas per day	1 lot equals 10,000 million British thermal units (MMBtu)
Quotation	The contract price is in sterling and in pence per therm	US dollars and cents per MMBtu
Minimum price fluctuation	0.01 pence per therm	$0.001 (0.1c) per MMBtu ($10.00 per contract)
Maximum daily price fluctuation	There are no limits	$3.00 per MMBtu ($30,000 per contract) for all months. Trading at the limit for 5 minutes will lead to temporary cessation of activity for 5 minutes
Contract description	• Season contracts • Quarter contracts • Month contracts • Balance of month contracts • Day contracts	72 consecutive months commencing with the next calendar month
Last trading day	The *month, quarter and season* contracts cease trading at the close of business on the last but one business day prior to the start of the next contract delivery period. The *balance of month* contract ceases trading at the close of business on the last but on business day prior to the last but one calendar day of the contract delivery period. The *day contract* ceases trading at 16.00 on the business day prior to the delivery day	Three business days prior to the first calendar day of the delivery month
Delivery	Physical at the UK National Balancing Point	Physical at the Sabine Line company Henry Hub in Louisiana

Source: ICE; NYMEX

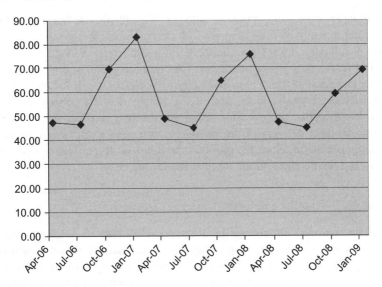

Figure 6.4 Term structure of UK natural gas futures prices
Source: Data sourced from Bloomberg.

contracts are standardised to given time periods (e.g. January – February – March) rather than being, say, a negotiable set of consecutive months. *Season contracts* are strips of 6 individual and consecutive contract months. Season contracts are specified as either April through to September or October through to March.

An example of the term structure of natural gas futures prices is shown in Figure 6.4. Forward prices are not predictors of future spot prices but represent the prices for delivery of natural gas at future specified dates. The data also indicates very clearly the seasonal nature of natural gas prices; prices are higher for winter than for summer delivery. The European Commission (2006) noted in its survey of the European gas markets that although market-determined prices such as the ICE exhibited seasonality, very long-dated gas contracts did not display the same properties as they were based on indexed formulae that were often calculated using trailing averages.

On NYMEX the central contract is a series of single monthly contracts for delivery of natural gas at Henry Hub. However, the exchange has recognised that there are a number of other natural gas pricing points in the USA and Canada, and therefore offers a number of "basis swap futures" that are quoted as price differentials between about 30 different pricing points and Henry Hub. For example, if a natural gas consumer wanted to hedge the cost of natural gas for delivery at a different location than Henry Hub, he would be exposed to a basis risk. That is the price he would pay for the delivery of his physical natural gas could be different than that received under a Henry Hub delivered future.

6.8.4 Applications of exchange-traded futures

Hedging the purchase cost of natural gas

Let us assume that a UK industrial consumer of natural gas has an agreement with a producer to receive natural gas on a regular basis. However, the price agreement that is used is based on the prevailing spot price at the time of delivery. We will assume that the producer is not prepared to enter into a fixed price contract with the consumer, and the consumer decides to buy a single month natural gas future on the ICE for delivery in 3 months' time. The price quoted for this future is 44 pence per therm. The consumer decides to close-out the futures position at the last possible moment to avoid physical delivery (the ICE future expires on the last but one business day prior to the start of the contract delivery period). We will assume that on that date the price achieved for selling the future is 48p per therm. If we assume that the consumer takes delivery of the natural gas at the same price from his supplier, his cost will be 48p per therm minus the profit on the future of 4p per therm. This gives a cost of 44p per therm, a sum equal to the original futures price.

Futures calendar spreads for natural gas storage operators

For those companies who run storage facilities, they will either be storing natural gas on behalf of another entity within the supply chain or can buy natural gas for their own account in order to exploit a favourable move in market prices. If there is excess storage capacity, it may be possible to generate an arbitrage profit. Recall from Chapter 1 on pricing that the forward price of any asset is the spot price plus the cost of carrying an underlying position for the duration of the hedge. This cost of carry would be driven by such elements as the cost of financing the purchase of the underlying and the cost of its storage. If the cost of storage in a facility is less than the value embedded within the forward price, it may be possible for the storage operator to execute an arbitrage trade.

For example, let us assume that the storage operator has identified that he will have excess capacity in 1 month's time for a period of 1 month. Let us also assume that the price of natural gas for 1- and 2-month delivery is 50p per therm and 55p per therm respectively. If the storage operator was to buy the natural gas for forward delivery in 1-month and simultaneously sell it forward for delivery in 2 months, he would make a profit if the associated costs of taking physical delivery of the natural gas in 1 month's time and holding are less than the price differential earned from the futures trades. This strategy is referred to as "going long the calendar spread". That is, the trade is the simultaneous purchase of a short-dated futures contract with the sale of a longer-dated futures contract. The use of exchange-traded futures by the various entities along the supply chain for natural gas is summarised in Table 6.7.

Exchange for physicals

An exchange for physical (EFP) represents a mechanism that will allow two entities to use the futures exchange as a means of fixing the price for a physical supply contract without using the exchange to fulfil delivery. Let us take an example of a producer of natural gas who has agreed to supply 50,000 therms per day to an end user for the month of August. We will assume that both sides are unable to agree on the price terms and so agree to use the EFP mechanism. EFPs need to be registered prior to the maturity of the particular futures contract to which they relate and so they agree to register this trade 15 business days prior to the contract maturity. We will assume that 5 business days later the producer enters the ICE futures market and sells 50 lots (1 lot = 1,000 therms) at the prevailing price of 44p per therm.

Table 6.7 Potential applications of exchange-traded futures

Participant	Nature of price exposure	Action
Producer	Exposed to falling prices	Sell futures
Shipper/Marketer	• If long natural gas, exposed to falling prices	Sell futures
	• If short natural gas, exposed to rising prices	Buy futures
Traders	Similar to shippers	Buy/sell futures
Storage	• If long natural gas, exposed to falling prices	Sell futures
	• If holding excess storage capacity held	Buy short-dated futures, sell long-dated futures
Consumer	Exposed to rising prices	Buy futures

The consumer will do the opposite trade (i.e. sell 50 lots) but can choose the timing of the trade to any point after the registration of the EFP, but prior to maturity of the future. There is no requirement for the two parties to execute the trades at the same time. We will assume that the consumer executes the purchase leg the following day when the futures price has risen to 46p per therm. Since neither party wants to use the exchange as a mechanism for delivery of the natural gas, they agree a nominal price to close out their futures positions, which will also be used to settle the physical contract. We will assume that they agree the futures close-out price to be 45p per therm. So, from the producer's perspective they have:

• Sold the future at 44p per therm
• Closed out futures position at 45p per therm
• Delivered the natural gas to consumer at 45p per therm.

From the producer's perspective the net income on the transaction is 44p per therm. This is calculated as the money received from the consumer for the physical natural gas (45p per therm) less the 1p per therm loss on the futures transaction. From the perspective of the consumer he will have bought the futures at 46p per therm and will close-out at the agreed price of 45p per therm to make a 1p loss. He takes delivery of the natural gas at the agreed close-out price of 45p per therm resulting in a net cost of 46p per therm. In both instances the price paid or received for the natural gas was determined by the price at which the initial futures position was executed.

6.8.5 Over-the-counter natural gas transactions

OTC contracts can be separated out into two main types: physical or financial. Physical natural gas transactions will involve the delivery of natural gas, whereas financial contracts will be cash settled.

Physically settled contracts: Fixed price contract

The following term sheet indicates the typical terms for a physical contract that is executed at a fixed price:

Seller	Barclays
Buyer	Client
Trade date	29 November 2005
Supply period	06:00 1 March 2006 to 06:00 1 September 2006 (184 days)
Daily quantity	25,000 therms
Total quantity	4,600,000 therms
Price	Forty five spot five five (45.55) pence per therm

In this contract the seller is responsible for delivering to 4.6 million therms over a 6-month period in equal amounts per day (i.e. 25,000 therms per day). This type of contract includes a clause that outlines the compensation that either party would have to pay if it fails to perform as part of the contract. The market has adopted a common set of terms and conditions (published in 1997) to ensure that transactions are based on uniform standards. Assume that the client is unable to receive the contracted amount, then the seller would have to dispose of the natural gas in the marketplace. The compensation that either side of the contract would face for a breach of contract is based on the system marginal price (SMP) traded on the OCM.

Physically settled contracts: Floating price contract

Here the price is not fixed but will be based on an agreed mutual index. A typical term sheet, linked to the day ahead price quoted by Heren, might appear as follows:

Seller	Barclays
Buyer	Client
Transaction date	29 November 2005
Supply period	06:00 30 November 2005 to 06:00 1 December 2005
Supply quantity	400,000 therms
Price	A price expressed as a price per therm equal to the Index Price.
Index price	For delivery on a business day, that day's price as stated in pence per therm of natural gas for the "day ahead". For delivery on a day which is not a business day, that day's price as stated in pence per therm of natural gas for the "weekend"; each as published in the column NBP under the heading "ESGM Price Assessment" in the issue of British/European Spot Gas Markets, the Heren report published on the business day immediately preceding that day of delivery.

For a US floating contract the terms might appear as:

Seller	Barclays
Buyer	Client
Transaction date	2 December 2005

Delivery period	Each calendar day from and including 09:00 central standard time 1 January 2006 to and including 09:00 hours central standard time 31 January 2006
Contract quantity	6,000 MMBtu per calendar day in the delivery period
Price	A price expressed as a price per MMBtu equal to the Index Price
Index price	"NATURAL GAS S LOUISIANA (HENRY HUB) INSIDE FERC" meaning the contract price will be a price stated in USD per MMBtu of natural gas, calculated on the first business day of the calendar month following each month in the delivery period, published under the heading "Market Center Spot Gas Prices (per MMBtu): South Louisiana: Henry Hub Index in the issue of Inside FERC for such calendar month.

A BTU is a British Thermal Unit, which is a measure of energy used in the US market. The notation MMBTU stands for one million units.

Another variation of this type of structure is to link the price to an exchange-traded future. A hypothetical UK transaction linked to the price of the ICE future would have the following terms:

Seller	Barclays
Buyer	Client
Transaction date	24 March 2005
Supply period	06:00 hours 1 July 2005 to 06:00 hours 1 August 2005 (31 days)
Daily quantity	20,000 therms
Total supply quantity	620,000 therms
Contract price	"Natural gas – ICE – Monthly index" meaning the contract price will be a price stated in pence per therm of natural gas, calculated as the average of prices per therm of natural gas published on the ICE on each day of the calendar month preceding the prompt calendar for delivery in the prompt calendar month.

In this contract a single price will be applied to each of the daily deliveries but is not agreed at the time of the trade. The price applied will be based on the daily average of a month's futures price, in the month prior to delivery.

It is, of course, possible to execute an option for physical delivery. For example, a client may decide to buy a put option, which would give them the right to sell natural gas for delivery at the NBP. Indicative terms might look as follows:

Option trade
Transaction date	28 September 2005
Seller	Barclays
Buyer	Client
Option style	European

Option type	Put
Expiration	23 December 2005
Strike price	35p per therm
Premium	GBP 0.00675 per therm
Total premium	GBP 27,202.50

If the client exercises the put, then Barclays will buy natural gas from the client under a pre-agreed set of terms, an example of which is given as:

NBP trade

Buyer	Barclays
Seller	Client
Supply period	06:00 hours 1 January 2006 to 06:00 hours 1 February 2006
Daily quantity	130,000 therms

If the option is not exercised then the seller simply collects the premium. The premium cost is calculated as 130,000 therms per day for 31 days at £0.00675 per therm. Options on UK gas can trade with implied volatilities that range from 40 to 90% and are structured with Asian-style (i.e. averaging) payoffs.

6.8.6 Financial/Cash-settled transactions

Cash-settled transactions are attractive to either producers or consumers where they wish to separate the physical delivery or receipt of the natural gas from the associated price risk. Additionally there may be traders and hedge funds who will not hold a shipping licence but wish to take price exposure to the market without the need to trade in the underlying instrument.

Natural gas swaps

The most popular type of transaction would be a natural gas swap, which can be used for a variety of purposes:

• To manage the basis risk of delivering natural gas at different physical locations. This could be achieved by entering into a swap where the cashflows are linked to prices in different delivery locations.
• To transform the price risk of a physical purchase or sale (e.g. from a fixed to floating exposure).
• As a means of exploiting a potential view on a rise in a natural gas price.

Take, for example, a hedge fund that decides it wants to take exposure to the underlying price of UK natural gas. It decides to enter into a natural gas swap, with a maturity of 6 months, starting one year after it has been traded. The swap will involve an exchange of cashflows, where one will be fixed (say 70p per therm) and the other will be based on an index price taken from Heren. The floating index would typically be the daily unweighted average of day-ahead prices quoted by Heren. The floating side of the swap can also be based on the arithmetical average of a futures price, such as the nearby price of the ICE UK natural gas futures.

The cashflows will be exchanged on a monthly basis and will be based on a notional quantity of 30,000 therms per day, to give a total of quantity of 5,460,000 therms. Settlement of cashflows would take place 5 business days after the end of the monthly calculation period. By way of example, let us assume that at the end of one of the settlement months the daily average of prices quoted by Heren was 66.56785 (the accuracy of the calculations would be stated in the deal confirmation and may extend to 5 decimal places). We will say that the hedge fund is the payer of the fixed rate and receiver of floating, and there are 31 days in the month. The cashflows to be exchanged are therefore:

Fixed cashflows

35,000 therms × 70p × 31 = GBP 759,500

Floating cashflows

35,000 therms × 66.56785p × 31 = GBP 722,261.17

Net payment by the hedge fund is the difference between the two cashflows – GBP 37,238.83. By paying fixed on this transaction the hedge fund is effectively taking the view that the price of UK natural gas will, on average, be greater than 70 p per therm.

Swaps can also be used to transform the price risk of buying or selling natural gas at a particular location. Take the following US locational basis swap:

Trade date:	16 January 2006
Effective date	1 October 2006
Termination date	31 March 2006
Notional quantity	4,000 MMBtu per calendar day in each calculation period
Calculation period	Each consecutive calendar month, from and including the effective date, to and including the termination date
Payment date	In respect of each calculation period, the fifth business day following the last pricing date in such calculation period

Floating amount A

Floating amount A	Payable by the client
Reference price	NATURAL GAS – TEXAS (HSC/BEAUMONT)
Specified price	The index price for spot delivery
Source	*Inside FERC*
Pricing date	The first commodity business day during the calculation period

Floating amount B

Floating amount B	Payable by Barclays
Reference price	NATURAL GAS – HENRY HUB – NYMEX plus spread
Spread	Minus USD 0.1500 per MMBtu
Specified price	Settlement price for the calendar month and year corresponding to the calculation period

Source   NYMEX
Pricing date   The last commodity business day on which the relevant
                  futures contract is scheduled to trade on the exchange.

There could be a number of motivations as to why this transaction could be executed. Basis risk with respect to the natural gas market is where the price in one location moves by a different amount to that elsewhere. This basis risk is often expressed as a spread differential to the NYMEX future, which settles at Henry Hub. If we assume that natural gas to be delivered for a certain date at the Houston Ship Canal–Beaumont is USD 6.85, while the NYMEX futures contract for the same delivery is USD 7.00. The basis differential for HSC–BEAUMONT would be minus 15 cents to the NYMEX futures contract.

Since the bank will be less interested in actually owning the underlying, it may wish to take a view based on how the locational spread may evolves over time. Looking at the direction of the cashflows above, the bank will make a profit if the basis differential tightens. Imagine that the differential moves to NYMEX minus USD 0.10. The bank could take an offsetting position where it receives NYMEX less the USD 0.10 and pays HSC–BEAUMONT. The net result is that the HSC–BEAUMONT cashflows cancel out and the bank receives more on the incoming NYMEX cashflow than it has to pay out.

If the client has an underlying exposure to natural gas priced at HSC–BEAUMONT, the swap will allow it to transform the exposure to that of Henry Hub. So if the client is selling natural gas, the price it receives will be paid away under the swap and it will be a net receiver of Henry Hub minus USD 0.15.

Option strategies

In terms of option-based strategies, the various single option strategies presented elsewhere could be applied within the natural gas market (see, for example, Chapter 4 on base metals).

One product that links the swap market to the option market is an option on a swap – a swaption. Some of the terminology for this product can be confusing but it is common to describe swaptions as being either "payer" or "receiver" transactions. A buyer of a receiver swaptions has purchased the right to pay a fixed price (and therefore receive a variable cashflow) in a swap. If neither counterparty wishes to enter into the swap at the point of exercise it is possible to cash settle the transaction at the point of expiry. Here the terms of the swap agreed under the option are marked to market at the swap rates that prevail at the time of exercise. The resulting net present value of the cashflows is then paid to the counterparty for which the deal has value.

Take the following example:

Option contract
Option buyer   Client
Option seller   Barclays
Option maturity   1 month

Swap contract
Swap maturity   1 year
Payment frequency   Monthly for both fixed and floating
Total notional amount   4,800,000 MMBtu

Notional per month	400,000 MMBtu
Fixed price	USD 8.50 per MMBtu
Floating price	Final settlement price for NYMEX futures contract corresponding to the calendar month of the swap settlement

Another popular strategy not yet considered is a *corridor*, which comprises a combination of options. Assume that there is a consumer of natural gas that wishes to buy insurance against a steep rise in price. He can buy a call option with the strike placed out-of-the money and then finance this by the sale of another option. In previous examples (e.g. the aluminium producer analysed in Chapter 4, on base metals) the sold option had been of the opposite type (i.e. an OTM put with a strike set to achieve zero premium) but in a corridor the sold option is the same type but with a higher strike.

Let us assume that the consumer is faced with the following market conditions:

Trade date	1 March 2006
Effective date	1 April 2006
Maturity	30 April 2006
Notional amount	1,750,000 MMBtu
Reference price	Near month NYMEX future (i.e. April 2006)
Current futures price	USD 6.74 per MMBtu
Pricing date	The penultimate business day on which the futures contract is scheduled to trade on the exchange
Premium payment date	5 business days from trade date
Settlement date	5 business days after maturity date
Settlement method	Cash settled

Options on North American natural can trade with implied volatilities that could range from 40 to 120%. An OTM European-style call option to cover the period 1 April to 30 April 2006, priced with an implied volatility of 50% and a strike of USD 7.00, would cost USD 0.35 per MMBtu. Since the option has been written on a notional of 1,750,000 MMBtu, this would give a premium cost USD 612,500. This could be partly financed with the sale of a call option with a higher strike. The higher strike option will not completely recoup the premium on the purchased option as this could only be achieved if both options had exactly the same strike (a somewhat pointless exercise). Let us assume that the consumer decides to sell an OTM call with the strike set at USD 7.50 – a level he does not believe will trade. For simplicity, we will assume that it has been priced at the same level of implied volatility. The premium on the option would be USD 0.20 per MMBtu, to give a total income of USD 350,000. The net cost to the trader is therefore USD 0.15 per MMBtu or USD 262,500 on the entire position. Settlement on the purchased call option will be:

$$\text{Max}(0, \text{Underlying price at expiry} - \text{Strike price})$$

Settlement on the sold call option will follow the same logic, except that the seller will face increasing losses as the expiry price rises above the strike price.

The effect of the strategy will be that as long as the underlying price is below the strike of the purchased call, the consumer will buy the natural gas at the prevailing market price

Table 6.8   At expiry payoff of consumer corridor strategy

Underlying price ($ per MMBtu)	Cost of purchasing the natural gas	Settlement on purchased call option ($7.00 strike)	Settlement on sold call option ($7.50 strike)	Net premium cost	Net purchase cost of natural gas
5.00	(5.00)	0.00	0.00	(0.15)	(5.15)
5.50	(5.50)	0.00	0.00	(0.15)	(5.65)
6.00	(6.00)	0.00	0.00	(0.15)	(6.15)
6.50	(6.50)	0.00	0.00	(0.15)	(6.65)
7.00	(7.00)	0.00	0.00	(0.15)	(7.15)
7.50	(7.50)	0.50	0.00	(0.15)	(7.15)
8.00	(8.00)	1.00	(0.50)	(0.15)	(7.65)
8.50	(8.50)	1.50	(1.00)	(0.15)	(8.15)

plus the net premium cost. Between the two strikes the consumer will pay a fixed price equal to the strike of the purchased call plus the net premium cost. Above the strike of the sold put the net purchase price will increase, but still be less than the prevailing underlying price. This is shown in Table 6.8, which analyses the "at expiry" situation for the consumer, assuming both options are cash settled. We will assume that the consumer has agreed to buy the natural gas at the same price at which the option will be settled.

7

Electricity

One of the biggest surges in the electricity in the UK occurred at the end of an international soccer match in 1990 when England lost to Germany. Demand soared by 2,800 megawatts, which was equivalent to more than a million kettles being switched on as the English drowned their sorrows with the answer to all of the world's problems – a cup of tea.

Source: National Grid

SYNOPSIS **The purpose of the chapter is to describe a number of electricity markets and the nature of the most popular derivative products**.

The first part of the chapter includes a *description of electricity, how it is produced and how it is measured*. Each market for electricity will be structured in a different manner but *a generalised overview of a physical supply chain* is outlined.

From this the *main drivers of the wholesale price* of electricity are outlined, which includes an overview of how *regulation* has shaped the evolution of the *physical supply chain*. Since electricity is a secondary source of energy, the difference between the price of the input (typically natural gas or coal) and the output is often expressed as either a *"spark"* a *"dark" spread*. The *cost of emitting carbon dioxide* is now a key consideration when generating electricity, and so the adjusted spreads are calculated.

The trading of electricity is still evolving in many countries and the present structures that exist in Scandinavia, the USA and the UK are detailed.

The chapter concludes with a *description of the main derivative products* (forwards and swaps) that are used in the electricity markets.

7.1 WHAT IS ELECTRICITY?

All matter is made of atoms, the core of which is called a nucleus. This nucleus is made up of protons and neutrons and is surrounded by electrons. If electrons move from one atom to another a current of electricity is created.

In itself electricity is fairly useless to our everyday use. It is nearly always converted into a different kind of energy at its end point of consumption. It is converted into heat to cook food or boil water or into light and sound energy in order to watch TV or listen to the radio.

Electricity is made by converting different forms of energy. Not much electricity exists naturally in the environment and it is almost impossible to capture or store. What does exist on Earth are many forms of stored energy mainly in the form of plants and fossil fuels, which can be converted into electrical energy. It is also possible to convert movement energy from wind and waves and light energy into electrical energy. Changing one form of energy into another is termed transformation, while moving energy from one location to another is called energy transfer.

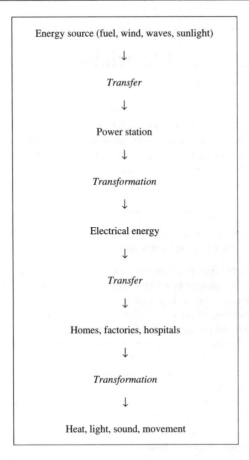

Figure 7.1   Flow diagram

Figure 7.1 summarises the path of energy from source to useful form.

7.1.1   Conversion of energy sources to electricity

Fuels

Inputs such as fossil fuels or nuclear fuel are used to boil water. The resulting steam is used to drive a turbine, which in turn drives a generator, which produces the electricity. The generator works by 'electromagnetic induction'. This is the rotation of a wire within a magnetic field, which induces an electric current. An old-fashioned bicycle dynamo works in much the same way as it transforms movement energy into electrical energy, which is then transferred to the bulb and transformed into light energy.

Solar energy

Heat energy is absorbed by solar panels and used to heat water into steam. The steam is then used to drive a turbine which produces electricity in a similar manner to above.

Wind, wave, hydroelectric and tidal energy

Movement energy is used directly to drive a generator. In this case there is no need to boil water to turn a turbine.

7.1.2   Primary sources of energy

Electricity is sometimes referred to as a secondary source of energy as it must be created from some primary source. The primary fuel sources used in electricity generation include:

- Natural gas
- Nuclear power
- Coal
- Oil
- Water
- Wind.

The choice of fuel will be dependent on how efficiently it generates electricity, the cost of the fuel itself and any waste products that may result from the process. The main fuels used in electricity generation in the USA and the UK are shown in Table 7.1.

The UK is heavily reliant on natural gas as the primary source of fuel, while US production is dominated by coal. The latter is understandable given that the USA has 25% of global coal reserves and accounts for 25% of all global coal consumption.

One of the reasons why natural gas is a popular primary fuel is that it has a relatively high thermal efficiency. Thermal efficiency relates the electrical energy produced to the energy content of the input as in every step of electricity generation some energy is lost. Burning fuel to boil water is particularly inefficient since a lot of energy is lost in the form of heat. Take, for example, a fossil fuel fired power station, where a common sight is the enormous clouds emerging from their towers. This is mainly steam taking energy in the form of heat straight out into the atmosphere.

Table 7.1   Fuels used in electricity generation*

Fuel source	USA	UK
Natural gas	16%	40%
Coal	51%	33%
Nuclear power	20%	19%
Residual fuel oil	3%	1%
Hydropower	7%	1%
Other fuels	2%	3.5%
Electricity imports	–	2.5%

Source: EIA, Digest of UK Energy statistics.

*Figures for the USA are for 2003, UK is for 2004; other fuels include geothermal, solar, wind power and biomass. Figures may not add up to 100% due to rounding differences.

For example, in a combined cycle natural gas power station, the thermal efficiency reaches about 47%. This means that for every 100 units of natural gas used as a fuel source, only 47 units are converted to usable electrical energy. The least thermally efficient energy source is coal (about 36%), then nuclear power (about 38%).

There are some significant regional differences in the selection of the primary fuel source. In Norway production of electricity is virtually 100% hydropower based. In years where there is excess rainfall the country can supply its surrounding neighbours (Sweden, Denmark and Finland) with a cheap source of electricity. However, when the reservoirs are low, Norway will import electricity from its neighbours who are more reliant on conventional primary fuel sources.

7.1.3 Commercial production of electricity

Although the general principles of electricity generation are universal, the actual design of power stations may vary. Three possible generation methods are:

- Combined heat and power (CHP)
- Combined cycle gas turbine (CCGT)
- Open cycle gas turbine (OCGT)

A CHP station is one that typically uses natural gas to produce electricity but also allows the steam and hot water that is produced at the same time to be captured for other uses.

A CCGT is an energy efficient system where initially one turbine generates electricity from the gas produced during the combustion of the primary fuel source. The hot gases are then passed through a boiler and the steam that is produced drives a second turbine that generates electricity.

An OCGT generates electricity from gas produced during fuel combustion. This method of generation is not regarded as being particularly efficient but OCGT plants can increase their load very quickly and hence tend to be used as a reserve to respond to sharp increases in demand.

7.1.4 Measuring electricity

Consumption of electricity is measured in two ways. When reference is made to electrical power the unit of measurement is a watt. Since a watt is a relatively small amount of power it is more common to express it as a kilowatt (1,000 watts) or a megawatt (1 million watts). The higher the watt or kilowatt rating of a particular electrical device the more electricity it requires. If an electric light bulb is rated at 100 watts it is describing an instantaneous quantity; it is consuming at any split second 100 watts.

However, a consumer of electricity will not want to use the commodity over a split second but over a period of time, which means that the quantity has to be expressed as a rate. The amount of electricity generated or used over a period of time is measured in watt-hours (Wh). This is determined by multiplying the number of watts used or generated by the number of hours, which is then divided by 1,000. For example, ten 100-watt light bulbs burning for 1 hour would consume 1,000 Wh, which is equal to 1-kilowatt-hour (1 kWh) of electric energy.

If someone wanted to have access to a generation resource he might decide to buy a power station with a capacity of 100 MW. However, if he wanted to use this amount of electricity for 1 hour, he would buy 100 MWh. Other measurements of electrical energy in ascending order are:

- Megawatt hours (MWh = 1,000 kWh)
- Gigawatt hours (GWh = 1,000 MWh)
- Terrawatt hours (TWh = 1,000 GWh)

Another unit of measurement to which reference will be made later is the volt, which measures the force being used to push electrons around a circuit. Technically this "force" is called potential, which is measured using the unit volt. Potential can be thought of as the steepness of a hill that electrons run down. The steeper the hill (i.e. the higher the current) the faster they roll.

7.2   THE PHYSICAL SUPPLY CHAIN

Just like natural gas, regulation has played a major role in shaping markets in each geographical location. As with natural gas there has been substantial deregulation followed by re-regulation in a number of markets. This has resulted in each electricity market developing its own conventions. However, there are a number of common themes from which it may be possible to describe in general terms how a re-regulated market may be structured. For example, a common theme in the process of deregulation is the unbundling, along the supply chain of the different functions that were traditionally performed by a single fully integrated utility. In the UK, which is regarded as one of the most deregulated markets in the world, the result is that there is significant competition in the generation and supply of electricity but not in its transmission and distribution.

According to a report by the European Commission (2006), the physical supply chain for electricity can be broken down into a number of different components:

- The production of electricity (generation)
- The transport of electricity on high voltage lines (transmission)
- Transportation on low-voltage lines (distribution)
- The marketing of electricity to final consumers (supply)
- The buying and selling of electricity on wholesale markets.

The following descriptions outline the key functions of the main participants in the physical supply chain of electricity.

Electricity generators

These will be the companies who build and run power stations that produce electricity. There may be a mixture of producers of different size and varying degrees of integration. Some producers may operate a portfolio of different plants in different locations using different fuels and technology. At the other end of the spectrum there may be independent power producers who do not have any transmission capabilities and do not sell on to the retail market. They may operate within a defined area supplying electricity to wholesale buyers.

The transmission system operator

Having produced the electricity it has to be transmitted to the end user, usually by means of high-voltage wires mounted on overhead pylons. Transmission lines link the generators to the distributors. The network of transmission lines is referred to collectively as the grid with the transmission system operator (TSO) being ultimately responsible for ensuring its efficient and reliable operation. TSO responsibilities vary by jurisdiction but can include:

- The coordination and scheduling of transmission transactions.
- Responsibility for ensuring that the demand for, and the supply of, electricity are balanced on an ongoing basis; since electricity cannot be stored, demand and supply must balance instantaneously or the lights will go out.
- Managing generation in system emergencies.
- Managing generation reserves.
- Ensuring that new transmission facilities are built when and where they are required.
- Coordinating transmission payments.

Electricity distribution businesses

As electricity cannot be delivered into a home directly from the high-voltage network, a series of substations around the network will transfer the electricity onto a lower voltage local network before its final delivery.

Suppliers

These will be the companies that will sell and bill customers for the electricity they use. They will make use of the distribution networks to supply energy to the end consumer. In some cases wholesale customers with a significant demand may agree a supply contract directly with the producer.

End customers

They can be either domestic users or large and small business customers. Each of the participants in the supply chain will want to be compensated. As an indication, in the UK the final price paid by the domestic consumer can be spit down approximately into:

The cost of generation	43%
Transmission	3%
Distribution	24%
Supply	30%

7.3   PRICE DRIVERS OF ELECTRICITY

Electricity must be produced when it is demanded. As a result the spot price for electricity is very dependent on actual physical delivery. If there are problems with physical delivery, such as transmission constraints, this could lead to volatile prices. However, since it is impossible to store electricity a high price today does not mean a high price tomorrow.

If the demand exceeds the supply of electricity, then the lights will go out (a black out). However, there may be instances where there may be a momentary excess of demand over supply, which may cause the lights to dim or flicker. This is referred to as a "brown out".

The four main users of electricity are:

- Domestic (e.g. lighting and appliances)
- Industrial (e.g. manufacturing)
- Commercial (e.g. office buildings)
- Transportation (e.g. railways).

Electricity markets are essentially local markets given the fact that generation and supply is generally limited to a certain geographical location. However, the markets are subject to global influences as the primary fuel sources may need to be imported and the cost of carbon emissions needs to be taken into account.

Demand for electricity is related to the concept of load. Load is defined as the amount of power carried by a system or the amount of power consumed by an electrical device at a specified time. This demand will vary considerably according to the time of day, the day of the week, the season of the year and the climate. Generators will therefore create a load profile or load shape that describes the pattern of electricity demand over a given period of time.

Generating companies may operate different types of power stations according to different types of demand or load. A baseload generating unit is used to generate power at a flat rate around the clock. Baseload is the minimum amount of electrical power delivered or required over a period of time at a steady state. A peak load generating unit is used to meet the requirement during periods of greatest demand on the system. Intermediate load generating units meet systems requirements that are greater than base loads but less than peak loads.

When constructing load curves (a representation of demand in a particular generation period), account has to be taken of:

- the type of end user (e.g. residential, commercial and industrial) and the electricity is used;
- the time of day;
- the time of year;
- the geographic region (for example, in the USA, the demand for electricity peaks in the summer with the exception of the northern states and Florida).

Figure 7.2 shows the global generation of electricity over the period 1990–2004. Generation in Europe has remained stable but there has been an increase in growth in North America and Asia. Once again the dominant theme in the Asia Pacific region has been the growth in generation in China. In 1990 the country generated 621 TWh and by 2004 this had risen to 2,187 TWh.

Like many commodity markets, participants will be buying and selling electricity for a variety of different maturities resulting in a forward curve. Like any forward curve it is simply the clearing price where demand equals supply for different maturities in time. Also like many commodity markets, it will display backwardation albeit on a seasonal basis. Typically power prices in the UK and Europe will be higher for winter delivery than those for summer. However, traditional forward pricing relationships cannot be applied to electricity markets due to the inability to borrow, lend or store electricity, and the relevant demand and supply factors are considered below.

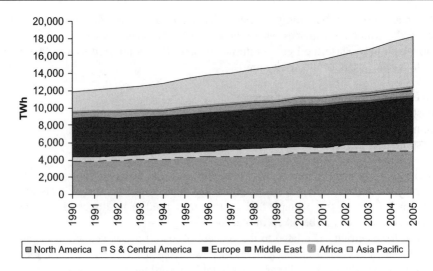

Figure 7.2 Global electricity generation
Source: BP Statistical Review of World Energy 2006.

7.3.1 Regulation

The European experience

The impact of regulation on pricing relationships cannot be ignored as it continues to shape electricity markets around the globe. Within Europe, the First Electricity Directive of 1996 removed legal monopolies by allowing large electricity customers the ability to choose their source of supply. It also set out the principles whereby vertically integrated companies were required to allow third parties access to their transmission and distribution networks. It also started the process of unbundling (i.e. legal separation) of the activities performed by these vertically integrated companies. In effect, it introduced a distinction between the regulated part of the market (i.e. the network operations) and the competitive elements (generation and supply). The Second Electricity Directive and the Cross Border Electricity Trading Regulation (both introduced in 2003) developed many of the themes of the earlier legislation. One of the biggest provisions of these directives was the requirement that the electricity market in each country would have to be open to all households by a certain date.

There have been some other EU-related regulations that have impacted the electricity market. The Directive on Security of Supply and Infrastructure (2005) requires that the member states work to ensure that there is an appropriate level of network security. Environmental issues in relation to carbon emissions were addressed in the Emissions Trading Directive of 2003 and will be considered in depth in Chapter 10. In 2001 the EU issued the Renewable Electricity Directive, which mandated member states to increase the amount of electricity consumed from renewable sources to 22% by 2010.

The American experience

Although it is possible to generalise about the structure of an electricity supply chain, the USA power industry has fragmented into a number of different markets with no overarching structure. In some areas of the USA, there are open, competitive, wholesale and retail markets while others have a more regulated framework.

The supply of electricity in the USA has traditionally come from one of three sources:

- Utility companies that may be owned by shareholders or the local municipality. The utilities have responsibility for a specific geographical area and would typically operate along all parts of the physical supply chain. Historically they may also have supplied other household services such as natural gas, water and telecommunications. If the entity is a municipal utility, one or more local governments may run it, depending on the area it serves. Although utilities still exist in a deregulated market it is more likely that they will only be involved in one particular aspect of the market, such as retail distribution.
- Rural co-ops set up to provide electricity to remote locations. This type of company is owned by the customers it serves.
- Federally owned power agencies that may have been established to sell power that was generated from infrastructure projects paid for by the government (e.g. hydro-related). One example is the Tennessee Valley Authority, which was set up in 1933 to help the region to develop during the Great Depression. One of its original responsibilities was to provide electricity to homes and businesses in the region.

The overall direction for the electricity industry is determined by the passage of Federal law. The Federal Energy Regulatory Commission (FERC) regulates the industry at the wholesale level. FERC's main areas of responsibility include the activities of Independent System Operators (ISOs), Regional Transmission Organisations (RTOs), some aspects of generation, and the wholesale trading of power.

Regulation at the state level encompasses areas such as vertically integrated utilities and competition in the retail sector. Municipal utilities will either be regulated at state or local government level, while electricity co-ops are regulated by their own elected boards.

The US markets have evolved at different rates throughout the country but, typically, once the traditional model of a single entity operating along the entire supply chain is subject to deregulation, the development of independently owned generation emerges, providing the incumbent utility – which at this stage of reform is the single buyer of power – with more competition. Typically, the next stage of development in the market allows large consumers to choose their source of supply. This gave rise to Independent System Operators (ISOs) that manage the transmission of power over a given area. As competition increases, electric marketers have emerged, buying and selling electricity between wholesale participants. The final stage of development occurs when the retail buyers are free to choose their supply of electricity.

North American Electric Reliability Council

NERC is responsible for ensuring the reliability, security and adequacy of the bulk power system in the USA, Canada and parts of Mexico.

NERC is owned by its eight members who devise the individual rules under which the different system operators work together. These members are known as regional reliability councils and are, in turn, made up of members from each segment of the electricity industry. The regional reliability councils are:

- Western Electricity Coordinating Council (WECC)
- Midwest Reliability Organization (MRO)

- Southwest Power Pool (SPP)
- Electricity Reliability Council of Texas Inc. (ERCOT)
- Northeast Power Coordinating Council (NPCC)
- ReliabilityFirst Corporation (RFC)
- Southeastern Electric Reliability Council (SERC)
- Florida Reliability Coordinating Council (FRCC)

In 2005, the US government introduced the Energy Policy Act, which will lead to the creation of the Electric Reliability Organization (ERO). The ERO will have the authority to develop and enforce mandatory standards for the reliable operation and planning of the wholesale electricity system in the North American region. At the time of writing (early 2007) it seems likely that NERC will evolve to take on this role, with oversight from FERC. The ERO will delegate authority to the different regional entities, giving them the responsibility to propose and enforce reliability standards.

7.3.2 Demand for electricity

Economic activity

Similar to crude oil an increase in economic activity will tend to lead to an increase in the use of electricity.

Weather

For example in the USA, seasonal demand for electricity will increase during the summer as more households switch on their air-conditioning units. Elements of weather that affect the demand for electricity will include the absolute temperature, the level of humidity, the amount of cloud cover and expected rainfall.

Human activity

The time of day will determine if the demand for power is heavy or light. Normal working hours are typically defined as peak time, while off peak covers evenings, nights and early morning. In the same vein the day of the week will impact demand. When buying or selling power, weekends can be traded separately and may be classified as a lower usage time period. Extending the argument further, power can be traded in "blocks" of months to represent the different seasons, which in the electricity market are broadly defined as winter and summer.

End user

Suppliers will also differentiate between whether a customer is retail or industrial in nature. Typically retail customers will be greater users of electricity at the weekend, while during the week industrial users will be the greatest source of demand.

Special events

There may also be odd events that will cause a sudden surge. For example, the UK TSO (National Grid Electricity Transmission) has to deal with what they refer to as "TV pick up". This a short but sometimes dramatic increase in demand that occurs at the end of certain TV programmes such as soap operas and sporting events. In their preparation for the 2006 soccer World Cup, the demand forecasters collected a lot of information to develop an accurate picture of demand. This included the timing of the match and whether it would coincide with sunset, if extra time was a possibility and what alternative TV options would be scheduled to be shown after the match.

Efficiency improvements

As technology improves a number of household appliances have increased their efficiency of consumption, leading to a decrease in their use of electricity (all other things being equal).

7.3.3 Supply of electricity

Physical capacity

There are a number of different factors that could be included in this category.

- The type of available generation (i.e. coal or natural gas), which will determine the cost of generation and have an influence on the price paid for electricity in any period.
- The operating "health" of available generation, which might be reflected in the amount of required maintenance work on plants or mechanical failure.
- Limits on the physical capacity of electricity transmission that could restrict the amount of power imported into or exported from a particular geographic region.

One relationship that many traders will try to monitor is the way in which the reserve margin of a particular market changes. This is defined as the actual amount of available generation capacity relative to peak demand, and is normally expressed as a percentage. For example, in the USA, FERC suggests that capacity margins should average 15% to 17%. Generally speaking there is an inverse relationship between the reserve margin and the wholesale price of electricity.

Interconnections

The term can be used to refer to individual transmission lines that link different markets in one geographical location (e.g. the USA) or more commonly to the overall capacity provided by the various lines (sometimes undersea cables) that run between two countries. The UK has an interconnector with France and so, in theory, a difference in price between the two countries should result in power being directed to the highest price location. The interconnector between the two countries is approximately 70 km in length with 45 km of cable underwater. The capacity of such interconnectors affects the ability of the country or region to import and export electricity.

Fuel prices

Like all traded products, the balance between supply and demand will determine the market price. However, it could be argued that, in the short-term, demand for electricity is somewhat inelastic in its response to changes in price. For example, a domestic user will switch on a light without much consideration for the actual cost. So if the short-term price were to increase significantly for one generating period, it is unlikely that this would have a material effect on the end user as most domestic consumption, and a significant proportion of industrial and commercial consumption, is based on tariffs that do not change rapidly.

As a result, it is the activities of the generating companies that determine the short-term price for electricity. Suppliers wishing to buy electricity will seek out the lowest cost source of generation, such as wind and hydro. Once generation capacity in this sector is reached, buyers will then purchase their supplies from the next cheapest source, which will typically be nuclear powered. After this, electricity will be provided by installations using either coal or natural gas as their primary fuel input. Consequently, the price of electricity will be driven by the price of the particular fuel used at the point where demand equals supply – the so-called "marginal fuel".

Typically coal and gas generators are the marginal sources of electricity generation and their activities will have a significant impact on the market price. In addition, and depending on which market is being analysed, the cost of emitting carbon may also influence the price of electricity.

- *Electricity and natural gas*: An increase in the price of electricity, all other things being equal, should lead to an increase in the price of natural gas. However, the same relationship may not hold the other way around. At any point in time, generation capacity that uses the cheapest marginal fuel will be running near capacity. However, demand is unlikely to be met by generation powered by a single fuel source and so the more efficient plants that use the alternate marginal fuel will be switched on. It will be the price of the fuel input used by these generators that will determine the market price of electricity. So if natural gas prices are low relative to coal, installations using this fuel input will always be on. In order to supply the marginal demand, coal fired installations will be used. If the price of gas rises but is still below coal, the increase is unlikely to have an impact on the price of electricity.

  Conversely if gas is the more expensive than coal a rise in its price will have a greater impact on the price of electricity.

- *Electricity and coal*: The effect of coal on the price of electricity may be country specific. For a country such as the UK that imports coal from overseas, a rise in the price of electricity is unlikely to have a significant effect on its price since it is being purchased in a global market that will be subject to a multitude of different price drivers.

  The impact of an increase in the price of coal will depend – like natural gas – on whether it is the marginal fuel. If it is the marginal fuel, then an increase in the price of coal will lead to an increase in the price of electricity. However, if coal is comparatively cheap compared to natural gas, then an increase in the price of coal will have a weaker effect on the price of electricity.

There is also a positive correlation between coal and natural gas in that a rise in coal prices will cause generators to demand more natural gas, pushing up its price.

Participants' bidding behaviour

In markets where electricity is priced using an auction process, the bidding behaviour of the participants may have an effect on the clearing price.

7.3.4 Factors influencing spot and forward prices

The previous list of price drivers was presented without any context of time. In their report on the energy sector, the European Commission (2006) noted that market participants rated the following factors as being key price determinants for different maturities:

> *Short-dated maturities*
> Plant availability
> Fuel prices
> Precipitation
> Wind speed
> Interconnector availability
> Temperature
> Price of carbon emissions
> *Long-dated maturities*
> Forward fuel prices
> New generation capacity or retirement of existing capacity
> Water reservoir levels
> Weather trends
> Interconnector capacity
> Price of carbon emissions
> Economic growth.

The report also argued that a risk premium would be embedded within the forward price to reflect the value to participants of the certainty of cashflow that a forward contract would offer over an unknown future spot price. This component could be either a premium or a discount but the report argues that in practice it is more likely to be a premium.

The shape of the forward curve, similar to natural gas, is distinctly cyclical in nature. Figure 7.3 shows the monthly forward prices of power in the UK, Germany and France in early December 2006.

7.3.5 Spark and dark spreads

Since the main sources of fuel input to produce electricity are natural gas and coal a producer of electricity is caught between two markets. They run the risk that the price of their input exceeds the price of their output. This relationship is captured in two key price relationships.

The "spark spread" is measured as the price of electricity minus the price of natural gas. This effectively measures the relationship between what is produced (electricity) and the main fuel input (natural gas). It is also possible to measure the "dark spread", which relates the price received for electricity to the cost of producing it by using coal. Although it would appear to be a simple calculation, the different energy sources will be measured in different ways. The convention is to express the spread in currency units per MWh, which means that in calculating the spark spread, natural gas, which will be expressed in therms for the UK market or British Thermal Units (Btus) for the US market, will need to be converted into an equivalent MWh value. In addition, the thermal efficiency of the input needs to be taken into account. Recall from an earlier section that thermal efficiency relates the electrical energy produced to the energy content of the input. When calculating the spark spread the market

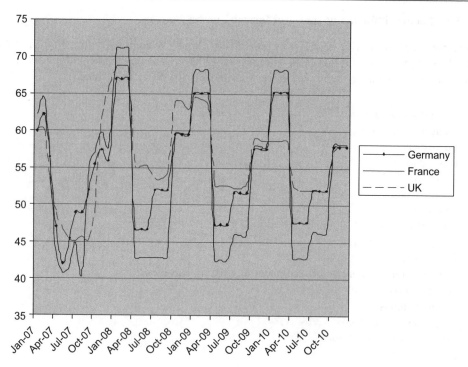

Figure 7.3   Forward prices for UK, French and German power (monthly maturities)
Source: Barclays Capital.

convention is to use a thermal efficiency of 49.13%. That means that for every 100 units of natural gas that are used in production, only 49.13 units are converted into usable electricity. To calculate the dark spread a thermal efficiency of 36% is applied.

In simple terms, the spark spread can be calculated as:

Raw spark spread = Price of power − (Price of input fuel/Thermal efficiency)

However, with the advent of the emissions trading, the raw spark spread is adjusted to include the cost of emitting carbon into the atmosphere as represented by the cost of a carbon credit.

Adjusted spark spread = Raw spark spread − (CO_2adjustment × CO_2price)

This adjusted spark spread is sometimes referred to as the "clean spark spread". The dark spread adjusted for the cost of emitting CO_2 is referred to as the "clean dark spread"(!)

The CO_2 adjustment is the number of metric tonnes of carbon dioxide emitted into the atmosphere to produce 1 MWh of electricity. A figure of 0.42 would be typical for natural gas, while the figure applied to coal is 0.85.

The following is a full worked example of how the numbers are derived. Let us assume that the cost of day-ahead electricity in the UK is quoted at £34.50 per MWh and that day ahead gas for delivery at the UK National Balancing Point is 36p per therm. The first step is to divide the price of gas by 100 to express it in £ per therm; the value is therefore £0.36. To convert therms into MWh, the market uses a value of 0.0293071 per therm, so dividing by this value returns a figure of £12.28 per MWh. This is the cost of the input fuel in the electricity generation process.

The next step is to take account of the fuel efficiency, which involves dividing the fuel cost in £per MWh by 0.49131. This returns a value of £25.00 rounded to 2 decimal places. The unadjusted or raw spark spread is therefore £34.50 − £25.00 = £9.50.

Let us assume that the cost of emitting 1 tonne of CO_2 was quoted at £10.75. Since the CO_2 adjustment is 0.42 this equates to a cost of £4.52 per tonne of electricity produced. The spark spread adjusted for the cost of emitting carbon would therefore be £9.50 − £4.52 = £4.98.

A similar exercise can be performed for the dark spread. Here the assumption is that steam coal has a heat content of 12,000 Btu per pound weight, which equates to 7 MWh per tonne. So, to obtain the price per MWh for a short tonne of steam coal, its price is divided by 7.

Assuming the same prices for UK electricity as in the previous example, and using a coal price of USD 71.15 per short ton (API #2 1 Monday Coal Forward; a short ton is 0.907 of a metric tonne), converted at a spot exchange rate of £1 = $1.90, gives a sterling price of £37.45 per tonne. The price expressed in equivalent units of MWh would therefore be £5.35. Using a thermal efficiency of 36% gives the following dark spread:

$$\text{Raw dark spread} = £34.50 − (£5.35/0.36) = £19.64$$

The "clean" dark spread is calculated using the same value for CO_2 emissions as in the previous example, but assuming a higher CO_2 adjustment of 0.85 (recall that coal generates more carbon dioxide in the production of 1 MWh of electricity). The cost of emitting 1 tonne of CO_2 is assumed to be £10.75.

$$\text{"Clean" dark spread} = £19.64 − (0.85 \times £10.75) = £10.50$$

If the spread is positive, buying gas and selling electricity will be profitable. However, if the spread were to go negative, an electricity producer who has bought gas forward on a fixed basis and has sufficient flexibility within his generation capacity may be encouraged to sell the natural gas back to the market.

More importantly it will indicate the increasing impact of the price of carbon on the price of power. This effect varies between markets, depending on the source of primary fuel in generation. For example, the impact of the price of carbon is greater in Germany than in the UK, given that Germany has a greater proportion of coal-fired power generators.

The spreads could be used either by financial institutions to express a view on the differential between the two types of power or could be used by generators to lock in a particular margin. If an electricity producer were to sell the spread (sell electricity, buy natural gas) it would allow him to lock into an advantageous physical margin for future delivery. The exposure could be subsequently unwound by executing a reversing position to buy back the spread. This would have to be executed using OTC forwards as electricity futures are notoriously illiquid.

7.4 TRADING ELECTRICITY

7.4.1 Overview

The main participants in the trading of electricity are utility companies, generators, suppliers, industrial consumers and financial institutions (e.g. banks and hedge funds). The country that has the largest population with a wholesale market for the trading of electricity is the USA. However, trading in this country has fragmented into a variety of different regional markets that have evolved in different ways due to the influence of State and Federal regulations.

In Europe, a report by the European Commission (2006) highlighted that the largest consumers of electricity in Europe are (in descending order) Germany, France, the UK, Italy and Spain. It also reported that less than 0.2% of electricity required to meet demand was imported, making the region virtually self–sufficient in terms of production.

7.4.2 Markets for trading

Broadly speaking, participants in a liberalised market will either procure or dispose of their electricity using either OTC or exchange-traded agreements. The majority of deregulated participants (e.g. generators and suppliers) will manage their respective commitments using bilaterally negotiated contracts. These contracts can cover a variety of generation periods and be agreed well in advance of a particular maturity. Equally OTC contracts (including derivatives) can be used by market participants to express particular views on the market that are not linked to physical positions.

The other trading mechanism available to participants is the exchange-traded transaction. In the wholesale power markets there are two main types of exchange: those specifically related to trading physical power, and multi-asset class exchanges that trade electricity derivative products as part of a wider suite of risk management instruments. Popular power exchanges include Nord Pool in Scandinavia, EEX in Germany, OMEL in Spain and GME in Italy. In these transactions market participants transact anonymously using the exchange as a central counterpart.

Derivative exchanges such as NYMEX offer electricity futures as part of their product portfolio. However, electricity derivatives are notoriously illiquid and have never reached the critical mass enjoyed by other similar contracts.

7.4.3 Motivations for trading

Generally speaking the participants will be either be looking to manage the physical exposure inherent within their daily operations, or simply to express a view on the direction of a particular market. The physical market for trading electricity is focused on:

- short-term trading in real time
- day ahead
- weekly
- monthly
- seasonal contracts.

The first two time frames are generally considered to be spot transactions, while the remaining categories would be viewed as forward transactions.

The European Commission (2006) highlighted that from the generators' perspective they are aiming to sell their generation output and optimise the operation of their generation portfolio. They noted that the majority of production would be sold forward, whereas optimisation of generating capacity is carried out on the spot markets (i.e. day-ahead or within-day markets). At the other end of the spectrum, retailers will buy the vast majority of electricity forward. The report noted that some of the larger electricity companies were trading not only to manage their own commitments but also to express views on market movements.

7.4.4 Traded volumes: spot markets

The EU Commission (2006) noted that large differences existed in terms of traded volumes in the different European spot markets. Their analysis focused on trades executed on the power exchanges and those that were brokered on the DTC market. In the Spanish market they estimated that spot trades executed on the domestic power exchange were equal to 84% of the national electricity consumption with negligible amounts being traded on the OTC brokered markets. By comparison, the respective figures in the UK were 2.17% and 8.6%. The differences can be partially explained by local market structures that may require users to trade via the exchange.

7.4.5 Traded volumes: forward markets

In terms of volumes in the forward markets the EU report highlighted three countries where forward trading (either exchange-traded or OTC) exceeded 100% of national electricity consumption. The three countries were Germany (639%), the Netherlands (548%) and the UK (146%).

7.5 NORD POOL

Nord Pool [1] is a Nordic power exchange in Oslo that has been set up by four Scandinavian countries (Denmark, Norway, Sweden and Finland) who operate in a liberalised power market. The Nordic power markets cooperate on a number of operational issues although there are Transmission System Operators (TSOs) in each country. The effect of this cooperation is that they create a large regional interconnected grid that facilitates the supply of electricity between each of the countries. The market participants trade as if there were a single interconnected transmission system serving all of the four countries.

As with most liberalised markets a number of common characteristics are present:

- There is competition in both the generation and the supply of electricity.
- A regulated power exchange exists that allows certain market participants to trade electricity in a variety of maturities.
- The power exchange is not the only mechanism to procure/dispose of electricity and is complementary to any bilaterally negotiated OTC contracts. Nord Pool estimate that they capture about 32% of the total Nordic consumption of electricity.
- A range of products has emerged to facilitate the trading of electricity.

The Nord Pool Group consists of a number of entities that include:

- *Nord Pool Spot AS* – this is the physical spot market for Nordic electricity, sometimes referred to as the Elspot market.
- *Nord Pool Financial Market* – a cash-settled derivative market offering exchange-traded derivatives or exchange-settled OTC contracts.
- *Nord Pool Clearing ASA* – the clearing house for the exchange.

The main responsibilities of Nord Pool are to:

- provide a reference price for electricity that will allow the settlement of a variety of trades;
- operate a physically settled spot market;
- organise a cash-settled "financial products" market;
- act as the counterparty to all trades entered into via the different Nord Pool markets;
- report the volumes to be consumed or delivered to the relevant TSO for trades executed on the exchange.

7.5.1 The spot market: Elspot

It is likely that market participants will have entered into a series of bilateral commercial contracts to deliver and consume electricity. However, generators can offer to supply in excess of their existing commitments and consumers are free to vary their demand load. The Elspot market [2] is the location where market participants will be able to buy and sell physical electricity to optimise their respective generation and consumption capacities.

The spot market for Nordic power is for next day physical delivery. Power is traded in blocks of one hour to cover the entire 24 hours of the day ahead. The price for each hour of actual generation is based on an auction process. Market participants will review how much they plan to produce or consume on the bais of existing contractual commitments and prevailing market conditions. They will then submit, by midday, a schedule of price and volume pairs for each hour. This expresses in MWh the amount they are willing to consume or produce. All of the participants' schedules are aggregated to construct demand and supply curves. The price at which the two curves intersect will form the market price, which should result in a balanced system. Once the system price has been determined the participants are notified as to the volume and price of their commitments the following day. Nord Pool spot acts as a central counterparty for all trades executed on the exchange. It becomes the buyer to all sellers and the seller to all the buyers, with all of the contracts being legally binding.

Although the system price calculated by the exchange should be applied to all areas of the network, there are instances where the physical capacity of the system cannot cope with the resultant demand and supply. This is sometimes referred to as grid congestion, and may occur where the demand to receive electricity is greater than the physical capacity to supply it. To ensure that the system is able to deliver, the area that suffers the congestion will have a different price from the rest of the network.

7.5.2   Post spot: the balancing market

To allow for the possibility that demand and supply profiles will change, the Elbas market (serving Finland, Sweden and some areas of Denmark) has emerged that will allow participants to fine-tune their positions after the closure of the spot market. This market is sometimes referred to as the "hour ahead" balancing market as it allows participants to balance their positions for a particular operating hour.

7.5.3   The financial market

The Nord Pool financial market [3] executes standardised futures, forwards and options that are financially settled rather than physically settled. The exchange lists futures out to about 6 weeks and then forward style contracts out to about 4 years. The main difference between the contracts relates to the daily mark to market requirements of each contract. The exchange also allows for the trading of European-style options.

The possibility that the system may experience more than one price for a given generation hour due to the possibility of system congestion, leaves the participant open to an element of basis risk. If he has bought or sold power forward using a Nord Pool contract, the contract will settle against the system-wide price set in the spot market for that particular generation period. If there is congestion in a particular area, the participant runs the risk that the price he pays for the physical commodity differs from the physically settled forward. As a result, the exchange has introduced contracts for difference that would allow a participant to mitigate this possibility.

7.5.4   Real-time operations

As well as operating a spot, balancing and financial market there is also a real-time market for the system operators to balance demand and supply during each generation period. The bids and offers submitted by the participants for this market will be to increase or decrease generation or consumption in addition to any commitments entered into in any of the exchange's other markets. It is also used to establish the price to be applied to any imbalances; instances where the contractual amount to demanded or supplied varies from that actually consumed or delivered. To illustrate the concept a simplified example is used. We will assume a scenario where a power generator has agreed to sell 100 MWh to a consumer for a particular hour of generation. Due to operational problems the generating company only produces 80 MWh during the period but the consumer uses his full expected amount. The consumer pays the generator for the full 100 MWh at the agreed price. However, the generator was in deficit by 20 MWh, which the system operator will have had to source in real time from an alternative supplier. The cost incurred by the system operator is passed onto the generator at such a level that he will not enjoy any financial benefit from not meeting his contractual commitments. Typically in this scenario the generator will be charged an amount higher than the amount that was received for the original sale contract.

7.6   UNITED STATES OF AMERICA

7.6.1   Independent System Operators

Prior to deregulation, the operation of the grid may well have been performed by the existing utility, Federal power agency or municipal utility. One of the key elements of deregulation, however, is to allow new market participants access to the transmission system. To ensure that any electricity supplied is done in an unbiased manner based on market-driven factors, Independent System Operator (ISOs) were set up with responsibility for the daily operation of the transmission system.

The ISO's responsibilities will vary from area to area but may include:

- Managing the competitive wholesale electricity market that will determine the price for any particular generation period.
- Forecasting the demand for electricity for each generation period.
- Scheduling generation to meet demand by deciding which generating facilities would be used during any given period.
- Adjusting the generating schedules as a particular period approaches.
- "Ramping" up or down generation units in real time to ensure that demand and supply are always in balance.
- Ensuring that any technical issues over the performance of the grid (e.g. system outages) are resolved.
- Providing supporting services (sometimes referred to ancillary services) to ensure the smooth running of the system. For example, the ISO must ensure that sufficient reserve capacity is available to draw upon at any given time. An example of this type of service is a spinning reserve, where a participant is willing to provide extra electricity to the system for a short period and at short notice.

Each ISO will also determine how the market participants will settle their accounts for electricity bought and sold in the auction process. The exact process is subject to approval by FERC and, as applies to many aspects of the market, there is no single approach. In some areas participants may settle with the ISO while in others they may settle via a third party hired by the ISO, referred to as a scheduling coordinator.

Depending on the location and the geographical region covered, the entity performing these functions may be described as a Regional Transmission Organisation (RTO).

Example of market structure

PJM (the acronym derives from the fact that the company has its roots in Pennsylvania, New Jersey and Maryland) manages the electricity transmission services for 51 million people, covering 13 states and the District of Columbia. The company was first formed in 1927 when two utilities in Pennsylvania and one in New Jersey agreed to share resources. Since then its area of responsibility has increased significantly and it is now classified as a Regional Transmission Organization (RTO), whose main responsibility is to ensure the safe and reliable operation of the transmission system in the regions it serves. Its area of responsibility encompasses over 56,000 miles of transmission lines and about 165,000 MW of generating capacity. PJM is responsible for:

- The coordination of the movement of electricity in its designated region.
- Ensuring the reliability of the grid.
- Administration of a competitive wholesale market.
- Planning the expansion of transmission and generation.
- Invoicing of market participants for all electricity bought and sold.

In any generation period, PJM schedules movements of electricity, including:

- Electricity scheduled for generation that was agreed between market participants based on bilateral transactions.
- Electricity bought and sold on the day-ahead market.
- Real-time purchase or sales to balance actual supply and demand.

7.6.2 Wholesale markets in the USA

The main way in which electricity was traditionally priced in the USA was through a mechanism that allowed for the costs of operation to be covered, as well as providing for an acceptable return for investors.

In a deregulated market, the balance between demand and supply determines prices. There are two main pricing mechanisms in operation. Participants can agree to either buy and sell electricity based on a mutually arranged price as part of a bilateral negotiation, or set the price according to an auction process organised by the relevant ISO.

In the auction-based process, prices are set for each generation period, but the price in any one period may be significantly different from the price in the previous period. For example, if generating capacity is suddenly lost there could be a substantial increase in price until sufficient reserve capacity can be brought online.

Those entities supplying end customers indicate how much energy they require and how much they are willing to pay; generators indicate what they are willing to supply and the price they will charge. The auction process sets the price for any particular period as the highest generating price submitted, such that all demand is satisfied. The following is a simplified example of how the system operates. Assume that in one single period of generation the demand to receive electricity is 1,000 MW and there are four generators (I to IV). Each of the generators has the capacity to provide 250 MW but the prices at which they are willing to supply differ due to the type of fuel used in the generation process. Accordingly, the prices offered by the generators are:

- Generator I: USD 60
- Generator II: USD 65
- Generator III: USD 70
- Generator IV: USD 75

In this case supply and demand are matched in terms of volume, and the clearing price for this period is USD 75. This is the highest price accepted from all available generators such that demand is equal to supply. All of the generators are paid this amount irrespective of how much they bid in the auction process; the same price also applies to those demanding the electricity. In the event that the price that the end users are willing to pay is below the generation prices in the auction, the market will not clear in the day-ahead markets and the ISO will not schedule any generation. If, during the generation period, a user takes electricity it has not already acquired, it will have to pay the real-time imbalance price.

Congestion occurs when lower priced generation is available on one part of the grid but, owing to physical constraints, cannot be delivered into a particular location. As a result, the receiving area must source its generation from local facilities that will be more expensive and different prices will apply in each location for that generation period. This pricing technique is referred to locational marginal pricing. A congestion charge is a cost that is charged by an ISO to a participant who wishes to utilise a congested transmission path. It is the difference between the two prices in locations where locational marginal pricing is in effect. In many ISO models the sender will pay congestion charges but it is also possible for the receiver of electricity to pay, depending on the market in which he is operating. Financial Transmission Rights are instruments auctioned by a system operator and represent an agreement whereby the ISO will compensate a participant if an actual congestion charge is greater than a previously agreed level.

When electricity is traded on a wholesale basis, the contracts are physically settled for delivery at a pre-agreed location. Some examples of these locations include:

- *Pacific North West*
  Mid-Columbia (Mid-C)
  California/Oregon border (COB)
  Nevada/Oregon border (NOB)

- *California*
  NP 15
  SP 15

- *Desert SW*
  Mead
  Palo Verde
  Four Corners

- *Gulf/Texas*
  ERCOT seller's choice
  ERCOT North
  ERCOT South
  ERCOT West
  ERCOT Houston
  Entergy

- *Midwest/North East*
  NEPOOL
  NY Zone A
  NY Zone G
  PJM
  Cinergy
  AEP

7.7 UNITED KINGDOM

7.7.1 Neta

In March 2001 the New Electricity Trading Arrangements [4] (NETA, but pronounced as "neeta") were introduced with the result that in the first few years about 3.5 GW of excess generating capacity was mothballed and prices fell considerably.

NETA was designed to ensure that those entities wishing to buy or sell electricity should be able to freely negotiate bi- or multilateral contracts either on an OTC basis or on a recognised exchange. NETA included provisions for:

- A mechanism that allows for the balancing of demand and supply by the transmission system operator.
- Delivery of electricity to a single notional point, avoiding the need for a multitude of different delivery locations.
- The development of short-term power exchanges that will allow market participants to adjust their demand and supply requirements. For example, APX Power UK allows members to manage their within-day balancing requirements.
- OTC derivative markets that allow participants to hedge the exposures of varying maturities.
- A settlement process to charge those entities that have not delivered or received their contracted power.

Contracts to buy and sell electricity are made bilaterally through direct OTC negotiations or via recognised exchanges. Electricity is bought and sold for half-hour periods and contracts can be struck for periods in the future. This type of trading will continue until "gate closure", which is 1 hour before the specific generation period. Once a contract has been made the two parties are required to notify the system operator of the terms of the deal (but not the price). This will allow any imbalances to be identified after the specified period. An imbalance occurs when there is a difference between their actual physical outcome with the trades that they had contractually agreed.

Each day the generators and suppliers of electricity are required to submit an "initial physical notification" to the balancing mechanism. This is what they are expected to produce or consume per half-hour period the following day. They will also indicate if they are willing to deviate from these levels of production/consumption and at what price.

Prior to gate closure, generators and suppliers must deliver a final physical notification to the system operator, which represents an expectation of how much they will supply and consume. This is the time at which the generators and consumers will additionally indicate how much they are willing to deviate their production from this indicated level. This is done by submitting bids and offers, which represent the amount and price that they are willing to vary production from their final physical notification. Any single participant may submit a variety of bids and offers for a single period, indicating the level at which he will be prepared to operate and the associated price he is willing to pay or receive.

During the one-hour period after gate closure, and during the actual generation period, the transmission system operator will aim to resolve any imbalances between production and consumption on a real-time basis. The imbalance can be managed by utilising the extra flexibility to consume or produce by the market participants from their notified levels. The system operator may also be faced with spikes in demand, power station failure or perhaps physical capacity problems of the transmission grid.

During the half-hour generation period, power will be delivered or consumed in accordance with the underlying contracts agreed by the producers and consumers. After this period any imbalance is calculated by reconciling what was supposed to be generated or consumed with what was actually consumed. Any surplus or deficit is charged back to the guilty party by the imbalance system based on the prices the system operator was faced with when trying to resolve the imbalance.

Imbalances occur for a variety of reasons:

- Traders of electricity may buy more, or less, energy than they have sold.
- Generators may producer more, or less, energy than they have sold.
- The customers of suppliers may consume more, or less, energy than the supplier has purchased on their behalf.
- Failure of generation equipment.
- Scheduling errors.
- Output variances due to ambient temperatures; energy can be "lost" during transmission due to factors such as temperature.

In 2005 NETA was expanded to include Scotland and was renamed BETTA (British Electricity Trading and Transmission Arrangements).

7.7.2   UK trading conventions

The EFA calendar

Trading periods for UK power is based on the Electricity Forward Agreement (EFA) calendar. This is a common calendar, which breaks down a year into 12 months each containing 4 or 5 weeks, with every week allocated a particular number. As a result of this process some anomalies arise. In some years (for example, 2009), there will be 53 weeks in the EFA calendar. Week 53 in the 2009 EFA calendar runs from Monday 28 December 2009 to Sunday 3 January 2010.

At the highest level the trading year is broken down into two seasons with summer defined as EFA April to EFA September and winter as EFA October to EFA March. The year is also expressed in quarters:

Quarter 1 = EFA January to EFA March

Quarter 2 = EFA April to EFA June

Quarter 3 = EFA July to EFA September

Quarter 4 = EFA October to EFA December

Equally it is possible to break down the EFA trading year into a series of individual EFA months, but it should be recalled that the trading calendar does not follow the regular

Gregorian calendar in that a particular month (e.g. December 2009) may include dates from other months.

Every prenumbered week will be broken into EFA days, with a day starting at 23:00 on the previous night to 23:00 on the day in question. Each EFA day is divided into 6 EFA blocks of 4 hours each:

$$\text{Block 1 } 23:00 \text{ to } 03:00$$

$$\text{Block 2 } 03:00 \text{ to } 07:00$$

$$\text{Block 3 } 07:00 \text{ to } 11:00$$

$$\text{Block 4 } 11:00 \text{ to } 15:00$$

$$\text{Block 5 } 15:00 \text{ to } 19:00$$

$$\text{Block 6 } 19:00 \text{ to } 23:00$$

Each of these blocks could be referred to in abbreviated fashion using WD to denote that the block occurs during a weekday or WE for a weekend. So WD3 would relate to a weekday time period covering 07:00 to 11:00, while WE5 would cover a weekend time period extending from 15:00 to 19:00.

To further complicate matters, each day could be further subdivided into a number of half-hour periods to reflect the actual physical generation patterns. Block 1 of a particular trading day includes the 47th and 48th half-hour periods of the previous day and periods 6 to 6 of the particular calendar day in question. This structure would be the same for the remaining EFA daily blocks. These half-hour periods are referred to as settlement periods.

7.7.3 Load shapes

For contracts that will cover a day or more, definitions of how much power is going to be delivered is usually stated on the contract. This is sometimes referred to as the "load shape".

- *Baseload*: This type of contract provides for the delivery of a constant volume of power on each and every half hour that the contract covers.
- *Peak load*: Contracts specifying this load shape require the delivery of power between 7am and 7pm (EFA half hours 15 to 38 inclusive; EFA blocks WD3 to WD5) on weekdays only, which should reflect the period of highest demand. Peak load also covers holidays, but does not include weekends.
- *Off peak*: This covers all other periods outside the peak load definition. Expressing this in EFA blocks implies that it will cover WE1 to WE6 on both Saturday and Sunday plus WD1, WD2 and WD6 on weekdays.
- *Extended periods*: An extended period would be extension of one of the above three standard load shapes. This is constructed by adding WD6 to a peak load contract.
- *Overnights*: These cover the periods WD1 and WD2 (weekdays) or WE1 and WE2 (weekends).
- *Extra weekend contracts*: Permutations in this area would cover the peak hours ("weekend peaks") or be in the form of extended contracts ("weekend extended peaks").

7.7.4   Examples of traded products

A combination of all these concepts allows us to consider a number of products:

- *November peak load* – this will be 07:00 hours to 19:00 hours, Monday to Friday, from the first day of EFA November to the last day of EFA November inclusive.
- *December baseload* – this will be 23:00 hours to 23:00 hours, 7 days of the week, the last day of EFA November to the last day of EFA December inclusive.
- *Summer peak load* – this will be 07:00 hours to 19:00 hours, Monday to Friday, the first day of EFA April to the last day of EFA September inclusive.
- *Summer baseload* – this will be 23:00 to 23:00 hours, 7 days of the week, the last day of EFA March to the last day of EFA September inclusive.
- *Winter peak load* – this will be 07:00 hours to 19:00 hours Monday to Friday, from the first day of EFA October to the last day of EFA March inclusive.
- *Winter baseload* – this will be 23:00 hours to 23:00 hours, 7 days of the week, from the last day of EFA September to the last day of EFA March inclusive.

7.7.5   Contract volumes

When power is traded in the UK market it may be quoted in MW, which is sometimes referred to as the contract capacity, contract unit or unit of power.

A megawatt is an instantaneous quantity of electricity. If I were to switch on a light bulb that consumes 100 watts, it is consuming 100 watts of power at any given time that it is on. A megawatt-hour is the volume of power produced or consumed during a particular hour. So if the light bulb is switched on for an hour it will consume 60 watt-hours or 60/1,000,000 megawatt-hours. A MWh can be thought of as the rate of delivery of power.

In trade confirmations the volume per settlement period (e.g. every half hour in the UK) and the total contracted volume (sum of every half hour) will be stated in MWh not MW. A couple of examples may help to clarify this point.

Trade 1: "Winter peak load 20 MW"

This should be interpreted as:

- *Duration*: Each half-hour period from 07:00 to 19:00 on Monday to Friday, from the first day of EFA October to the last day of EFA March inclusive. This is a total of 24 half-hour periods per weekday.
- *Total contracted volume*: This is calculated as 20 MW × 12 hours × 5 days × 26 weeks = 31, 200 MWh.
- *Daily volume*: This is calculated as 20 MW × 12 hours = 240 MWh.
- *Volume per settlement period*: This is the amount to be delivered in each half hour period of generation and is equal to 10 MWh.

Trade 2: "Summer base load 100 MW"

This should be interpreted as:

- *Duration*: Each half hour from 23:00 on the last day of EFA March to 23:00 on the last day of EFA September. The contract delivers for 24 hours a day or 48 half-hour generation periods.
- *Total contracted volume*: This is calculated as 100 MW × 24 hours × 7 days × 26 weeks = 436,800 MWh.
- *Daily volume*: This is calculated as 100 MW × 24 hours = 2,400 MWh during each EFA day.
- *Volume per settlement period*: This is the amount of electricity to be delivered in each of the 48 half-hour blocks and is equal to 50 MWh.

7.7.6 Contract prices and valuations

Although transactions are entered into with the quantity expressed in MW, prices are agreed in £/MWh. So when valuing a contract the total contracted volume (MWh) is multiplied by the price to find the value of the contract. Take, for example, Trade 1 outlined above. If the contract had been traded at £14 per MWh, the total value of the contract would be expressed as

$$£14 \text{ per MWh} \times 31,200 \text{ MWh (total contracted volume)}$$

If the contract price in Trade 2 had been negotiated at £15 per MWh, the total contract value would be calculated as

$$£15 \text{ per MWh} \times 436,800 \text{ MWh} = £6,552,000$$

7.8 ELECTRICITY DERIVATIVES

7.8.1 Electricity forwards

Unlike other markets that use a forward curve for pricing contracts for delivery at different points in time, the fact that electricity cannot be stored means that the traditional methods of pricing a forward contract (i.e. spot price plus net carry) does not apply. As a result, expected levels of supply and demand determine the forward price. Additionally, the forward price may move independently of the spot price, as there is no mechanism for arbitraging the market. Thus, if a forward contract is perceived to be trading "rich" to some notion of theoretical value, it is not possible to sell the electricity forward, buy it for spot delivery, store it for a given period and then use it to fulfil the forward obligation.

Over-the-counter forward deals may be attractive for a variety of reasons:

- Price certainty is achieved.
- Avoids the need to buy in a volatile spot market.
- Physically settled transactions can be a useful tool to secure supplies.
- Can be executed on a paper basis with an investment bank so that the supply and the risk management can be separated.
- Can be used to speculate on movements in the market.
- Certain financing transactions may require the end user to use forwards to give certainty of revenues.

Table 7.2 Form for delivery

Total supply period		Applicable days							From CET	To CET	Contract capacity (MW)	Contract quantity (MWh)	Contract price (EUR/ MWh)	Total amount (EUR)
Start	End	Mon	Tue	Wed	Thu	Fri	Sat	Sun						
3 Aug 2006	3 Aug 2006				X				08:00	20:00	50	600	60	36,000

A fixed price power forward is fairly straightforward in terms of how the contract will be set out. Although each contract will vary, the basic terms will be similar. For example, the following criteria need to be specified for a physically settled transaction:

- Trade date
- Buyer
- Seller
- Type of governing contract
- Price
- Volume
- Load shape
- Delivery schedule
- Delivery point

The contracts will often contain a schedule outlining the detail of the supply. Take, for example, the transaction in Table 7.2 for delivery on the RTE Grid in France.

The contract fixes the price for delivery of 50 MW for 12 1-hour periods to give a total contract amount of 600 MWh. At an agreed fixed rate of EUR 60 per MWh, the total value of the contract is set at EUR 36,000. The contract also highlights some features of trading in the continental European markets that differ from those in the UK:

- Trading is done according to the regular calendar.
- The power day begins at midnight and ends at midnight.
- Baseload is defined as 00:00 to 24:00; peak load covers 08:00 to 20:00; off peak is 00:00 to 08:00 and 20:00 to 24:00. Although these times and shapes are common across many of the European markets, there are some exceptions such as the Dutch market where peak load is defined as 07:00 to 23:00.

Take another example for delivery in the UK:

Trade date	3 August 2006
Seller	Barclays
Buyer	Counterparty
Contract	Day ahead (i.e. 4 August 2006)
Shape	Base load
Hourly volume	50 MWh
Total volume	1,200 MWh
Contract price	GBP 33.50 per MWh

Table 7.3   Form of Contract

EFA month	Start date	End date	Contract price (£/MWh)	EFA block settlement volume (MWh)					
				WD1	WD2	WD3	WD4	WD5	WD6
Aug 2006	3 August	4 August	33.50	200	200	200	200	200	200

Recall that the EFA day can be broken down into 6 blocks of 4 hours. Since the agreed hourly volume is 50 MWh this will result in 200 MWh being delivered in each block (Table 7.3). The total volume will therefore be 1,200 MWh, giving the contract a rounded-down value of £40,200 (1,200 MWh × £33.50 per MWh).

Floating price forwards

Also sometimes referred to as "index price forwards", these allow the parties to the trans-action to deliver a given amount of MW at a given time period in the future at a price that will be set at the point of delivery based on an agreed market price index.

7.8.2   Electricity Swaps

Electricity swaps can be used for a number of reasons but typically they would allow a user to transform the risk exposure on a bilateral contract to a different basis. Alternatively they could be used to express a particular view on the market. For example, a supplier may have agreed a floating price supply contract with a generator but wishes to transform his exposure so that he pays on a net basis a fixed price. In this case he could receive a floating cashflow from a swap provider to negate the underlying exposure with the gener-ator and in return pay a fixed price. Equally, based on the same parameters, a generator could also transform his risk by paying floating and receiving fixed under the terms of a swap.

As an example, take the following termsheet based on an EFA winter baseload contract:

Trade date:	23 November 2006
Effective date	Last day of EFA September 2007
Termination date	Last day of EFA March 2008
Total notional quantity	87,360 MWh
Notional quantity per calculation period	20 MWh per delivery date multiplied by the number of delivery dates during such calculation period.
Delivery date	Daily
Calculation period	Monthly
Payment dates	The 10th business day of the calendar month
Fixed price payer	Barclays
Fixed price	£65 per MWh
Floating price payer	Counterparty
Floating price	Unweighted arithmetic average of an agreed reference index published daily.

Reference index   Electricity – London Energy Brokers' Association
                                        (LEBA) UK Power indices: 8–9 index (a
                                        volume-weighted average of all day-ahead baseload
                                        trades executed in London by a number of contributing
                                        brokers between 8am and 9am)

The total notional quantity is calculated as

$$20 \text{ MWh} \times 24 \text{ hours} \times 7 \text{ days} \times 26 \text{ weeks} = 87,360 \text{ MWh}$$

Although this particular swap settles against a day-ahead index, there are a variety of other indices that exist for UK power swaps, all published by the LEBA. They include:

- Working days
- Monday to Friday peak
- All days.

Continental European power swaps will have a number of key features with differences to reflect local market conventions. The main markets that will be traded include France, Germany, Spain, Scandinavia and the Netherlands. However a number of generalisations can be made about their structure.

There will be a stated maturity such as 6 months in as the frequency with which the cashflows will be paid. This will usually be monthly and is referred to as the calculation period. The contract will outline the particular load shape, which may typically include:

- Baseload: 24 one-hour periods from 00:00 to 24:00
- Peak load: 12 one-hour periods from 08:00 to 20:00
- Off-peak: 12 one-hour periods from 00:00 to 08:00 and 20:00 to 24:00 Monday to Friday; 24 one-hour periods from 00:00 to 24:00 Saturday and Sunday

Payment is made in arrears after each calculation period, usually with a lag, which could be either 5 days or 20 days.

In terms of the "price" of the swap, the fixed rate per MWh will be stated as well as the counterparty responsible for making the payment. For continental power swaps the floating payment may typically be based on hourly prices. The counterparties to the trade would agree a notional quantity for each hour of generation expressed in MWh, which is applied to the floating price derived from the agreed source. The floating payment made at the end of each calculation period is the sum of these monetary values.

Therefore, as an example, take a 92-day baseload contract with an agreed notional quantity of 6 MWh for each hour of generation. At the end of each month the counterparties would have to take the hourly price observations, apply them to this notional quantity and add them up to calculate the floating amount. The total notional quantity for the contract would be equivalent to

$$13,248 \text{ MWh} (6 \text{ MWh} \times 24 \text{ hours} \times 92 \text{ days})$$

The typical hourly indices against which the contracts settle are:

- *Germany*: The price per MWh for delivery on the German high-voltage grid, in the price area RWE grid, stated in euros and published EEX on their website www.eex.de under the heads for electricity "spot market, area prices (Date, Hour)".
- *France*: Also hourly priced, and expressed in euros per MWh for delivery on the RTE high voltage grid, with a price published by Powernext SA; www.powernext.fr.
- *The Netherlands*: For delivery on the Tennet high-voltage grid with a price published by the Amsterdam power exchange; www.apx.nl.
- *Spain*: For delivery on the Spanish high-voltage grid with a price quoted by OMEL; www.omel.es.

Documentation

Physically delivered UK power deals are governed by the Grid Trade Master Agreement (GTMA). Physically delivered continental European power deals are governed by the European Federation of Energy Traders General Agreement (EFET). An International Swaps and Derivatives Association (ISDA) agreement will govern all financially settled deals, irrespective of where they are traded.

8

Plastics

It is now estimated that each person in the developed world consumes on average more than their body weight in plastics a year.

Quote from *Risk* magazine [1]

The purpose of the chapter is to describe how plastic is made, which factors impact its price and how the market risk associated with buying and selling plastic can be managed using derivatives.

I suspect for many readers it may have been a long time since they studied chemistry and so *the basic physical structure of plastics* is documented in the first part of the chapter. This also serves as a useful introduction to some of the technical terms used in the industry such as *monomers* and *polymers*.

The next section outlines the *commercial supply chain* for plastics, which starts with either crude oil or natural gas to produce the monomer building block. This is then polymerised before being manufactured into an end product.

The main *drivers* that affect the price of plastic are outlined, followed by *a description of the main derivatives*. At the time of writing, the main derivative market was centred on the futures contracts offered by the LME. As liquidity improves, it is expected that more OTC structures will gradually emerge.

8.1   THE CHEMISTRY OF PLASTIC

Plastic is a general term used to describe different chemical structures. At a very basic level, plastics are formed when carbon and hydrogen atoms are combined in different ways. Groups of atoms bonded together form molecules which, when linked together in different ways, yield plastics that have different physical properties.

Hydrocarbons (i.e. molecules of hydrogen and carbon) are classified as either monomers or polymers. A monomer (*mono* = one) is a building block molecule, which could be chemically reacted to make molecules with longer chains. A polymer (*poly* is Latin for many) is a number of individual monomers chemically joined by a bond to form a single structure. For example, the simplest of plastics is polyethylene (sometimes referred to as polythene), which is made up of ethylene/ethene [2] monomers. The chemical structure of an ethylene monomer is expressed as:

where C indicates carbon atoms and H indicates hydrogen atoms.

An ethylene molecule has two carbon atoms, which are joined by a double bond. Double bonds are relatively easy to break, allowing a new atom or molecule to join the original structure.

When it is chemically reacted with other ethylene molecules a polymer chain is formed to make polyethylene. Chemically, polyethylene is written as $[C_2H_4]_n$ where the subscript n is used to denote an integer that determines the length of the polymer chain. The chemical structure of polyethylene (a polymer) is expressed as:

$$*\left[\begin{array}{cc} \overset{\displaystyle H}{\underset{\displaystyle H}{|}} & \overset{\displaystyle H}{\underset{\displaystyle H}{|}} \\ C & C \end{array}\right]_n *$$

where C indicates carbon atoms H indicates hydrogen atoms, and n is an integer that determines the length of the polymer chain.

Although hydrogen and carbon are the two main building blocks, other elements (such as fluorine, chlorine, iodine and bromine) can be added to the monomer conversion process to change the physical characteristics of the resultant polymer. For example, at the monomer level, if chlorine were to replace one of the hydrogen atoms in ethylene, the result is chloroethene (vinyl chloride), which is C_2H_3Cl. After polymerisation, it will form polyvinyl chloride or PVC. PVC has a higher tensile strength, but a lower melting point, than polyethylene.

Because there are thousands of different hydrocarbons it is often convenient to divide them into categories. One such category is alkenes, of which ethylene is an example. Alkenes generally have a simple chemical structure, are cheap to make and are relatively easy to polymerise. Alkenes are also sometimes referred to as "olefins" and their polymers (such as polythene and polypropylene) "polyolefins".

8.2   THE PRODUCTION OF PLASTIC

In the previous section we described the chemical composition of polyethylene and its main monomer building block, ethylene. Here we will describe the main sources of ethylene and how plastic is produced.

Plastics can be manufactured from a variety of hydrocarbons, which are extracted from either crude oil or natural gas. There are a variety of hydrocarbons that can be used in plastic production, which include:

- ethylene – C_2H_4
- propylene – C_3H_6
- butene – C_4H_8

The most common building block is the monomer ethylene, introduced in the previous section, which can be derived from either crude oil or natural gas.

8.3   MONOMER PRODUCTION

8.3.1   Crude oil

As crude oil has very limited applications by itself, it is refined to produce a variety of products. Chemically, crude oil is made up of many different hydrocarbon structures that are then separated (using a process known as fractional distillation) into different components denoted by the length of their carbon chains. Examples of refined short-chain molecules are ethene, propene and butene, which are also monomers that can be used to make plastic. Longer chain carbon molecules such as naphtha can also be used as part of the plastic production process. Naphtha can then be broken up (using a process known as steam cracking) to yield a number of different products such as high-grade petrol and ethylene.

8.3.2   Natural gas

Once extracted from the ground, natural gas will be processed to remove any impurities and then separated into its component elements, referred to collectively as natural gas liquids (NGLs). These include:

- ethane
- propane
- methane
- butane
- pentane

Once the ethane (C_2H_6) is collected, it is steam-cracked to produce ethylene. This is then polymerised to become polyethylene, which is sometimes referred to as polyethene or simply polythene.

However, there is a trade-off between the two routes to produce ethylene. Producing ethylene from natural gas is cheaper but yields a smaller amount; producing ethylene from crude oil is more expensive but returns a higher yield. Geographical access to the raw materials has also played a role. Where low-cost access to natural gas is possible it is usually the feedstock of choice for the production of ethylene and polyethylene.

8.4   POLYMERISATION

The next step is polymerisation, which involves reacting ethylene with a catalyst. The choice of the catalyst at this point will impact the final polymer produced as it restructures the bonds that link the carbon and hydrogen atoms. The resultant polymer will be in the form of:

- pellets
- film
- resin
- powder.

8.5   APPLICATIONS OF PLASTICS

Once a particular polymer has been made it has to be fabricated into a final usable product for purchase by a consumer. Listed below are a number of well-known polymers with examples of some of their day-to-day applications:

- *Polyethylene (PE)*:   Low-density polyethylene is used for food bags and squeezy bottles. High-density polyethylene is used for detergent bottles, refuse bags and shopping carrier bags. The London Metals Exchange (LME) futures contract is based on linear low-density polyethylene. The term "linear" simply refers to the fact that the carbon atoms are "ordered" in a straight line, which results in a polymer that takes up less physical space.
- *Polypropylene (PP)*:   When rigid it can be used for caps and other closures; when in flexible form used for films for confectioneary and tobacco.
- *Polyethylene terephthalate (PET)*:   Used for soft drink containers, squeezy bottles and oven safe food trays.
- *Polyvinyl chloride (PVC)*:   Use for thin films, clothing, bottles and cartons.
- *Polystyrene (PS)*:   Used for compact disk cases, cartons and medicine bottles.
- *Polytetrafluoroethylene (PTFE)*:   This has non-stick applications, such as kitchenware.

Once formed a polymer is said to be thermoset or thermoplastic. The term "thermo" refers to the effect of heat while the terms "set" and "plastic" refer to how the polymer reacts to the heat. A polymer that is described as a thermoplastic is one where the application of heat will cause the product to change shape but will not lead to any change in its chemical composition. This would allow the material to be remoulded back into its original shape or may allow for recycling. Examples of this are polythene and nylon. A polymer that is described as being a thermoset is where the application of heat alters not only the shape but also its chemical composition. This means that once it has been melted it cannot be remoulded and will solidify irreversibly – it is "set". Examples in this category include polystyrene and PTFE.

Thermoplastics, which constitute the greater demand of the two categories, can be converted into a final product using a number of processes that include:

- *Injection moulding*:   The plastic is fed into a heated chamber whereupon it softens into a fluid. It is then injected into a mould and cooled until it solidifies. The mould can be removed or the object can then be removed from the mould. This technique is used in the production of butter tubs and yoghurt containers.
- *Blow moulding*:   By this method, Molten plastic in the shape of a tube is formed. Using compressed air, the tube is then blown to fill the insides of a chilled mould. This method is used to make items such as bottles or tubes.
- *Extrusion*:   In this process the plastic is heated in a chamber and, when in molten form, is pushed through an opening called a "die". The shape of the opening will allow the plastic to cool and set in a particular form.

Some polymers may undergo further processing once they are formed to give them specific qualities that are suited to specific jobs. For example, rubber can be vulcanised (i.e. heated with sulphur) to make it stronger and more resistant to heat.

8.6 SUMMARY OF THE PLASTICS SUPPLY CHAIN

When considering the structure of the plastic production process, there are, broadly speaking, two different types of *producer*. An example of an *integrated* producer would be a large oil major that can extract crude oil or natural gas and send it for *refining*. After refining the manufacture of monomers and polymers will follow. A *non-integrated* producer would be a buyer of monomers for the production of a particular type of polymer. From that point a *converter* will purchase a particular polymer either directly from a producer or from a *distributor* and manufacture an end product for use by an *end consumer*. *Traders* will act as a counterparty to different entities in the physical supply chain to facilitate the purchase and sale of different polymers and to offer a variety of risk management services.

8.7 PLASTIC PRICE DRIVERS

In many respects the market factors that influence the price of plastics share much in common with those that influence commodities generally. Since crude oil and natural gas play a significant part in the production of plastic, the factors that influence those commodities will also have a knock-on influence to the plastics markets.

The key price drivers for the market include:

- *Cost of crude oil and natural gas*: Since the basic feedstock of the entire process is crude oil or natural gas, the final price of plastic will be heavily influenced by price movements in this sector.
- *Environmental concerns*: Very often the proposed construction of a new petrochemical site in a particular location raises issues surrounding the impact on the environment. This may delay the building of a new facility and add further to the existing capacity constraint. There is also the issue of recycling. In general, plastics are not easy to recycle, as they are often complex and composite materials, which could increase the cost. However, those that can be recycled will act as an extra source of supply.
- *Production capacity*: If the price of a commodity experiences a sharp increase in price, economic theory tells us that the production should respond accordingly. This does not take into account the fact that there may often be a substantial lag if there is a need to invest to expand any existing facilities. Here lack of production capacity could include not only the refining of crude oil or natural gas but also the polymerisation capacity.

  One concept that links the first two price factors together is the regional cost of the feedstock relative to the available capacity. Since hydrocarbons are cheaper to produce in the Middle East there is expected to be a gradual trend to site new refining and polymerisation plants in this region. Given the difficulty of building the equivalent facilities in the West it would seem that reliance on the Middle East for energy is only likely to increase.
- *Production disruption*: This could be due to a variety of reasons such as natural disasters or labour disputes. For example, in 2005 following a number of severe hurricanes on the US Gulf Coast, a number of production facilities were closed down and US demand was met by an increase in imports from Asia.
- *Economic cycle*: If the economy is experiencing a boom period then there will be a general increase in production with an associated uplift in the demand for plastics.

- *Level of existing inventories*:   If prices are rising due to increased demand and production has been unable to respond immediately, the excess has to be met through existing inventories.
- *Technological progress*:   As technological improvements have taken hold, the possibility of substituting plastic for other materials has increased. For example, in the beverage industry, cans have gradually been replaced by PET containers, which have become lighter, stronger and more tolerant to heat.
- *Strength of the US dollar*:   Similar to most commodities, plastics are quoted in USD. A strengthening dollar will make plastics relatively more expensive in domestic currency terms, and vice versa.
- *Emerging markets demand*:   Again, similar to most metals, the rapid economic expansion and the associated increase in demand of countries such as China and India will have a significant bearing on the price of the commodity.

8.8   APPLICATIONS OF DERIVATIVES

Arguably the key step in making plastics a tradable commodity was the creation of an exchange-traded plastics future. The LME initially listed two different types of contract, the polypropylene (PP) contract and the linear low-density polyethylene (LL) contract. As shown in Table 8.1, these two commodities account for about 40% of the thermoplastics market.

The Melt Flow Rate (MFR) is a measure of a plastic's viscosity (i.e. the ability of the plastic to flow). When heat is applied to a polymer it will change into liquid that, if it is a thermoplastic, can then be converted back to a solid in perhaps a different shape. As an example, the LL future allows for a MFR of about 1, which means that 10 grammes will travel 100 centimetre in 1 second.

Table 8.1   Plastic futures contract specification

Polypropylene (PP)	Linear low-density polyethylene (LL)
Contract features	
• Homopolymer general-purpose injection moulding grade, nominal melt flow rate 12 (−2/+3), "barefoot" (i.e. without any additives) • Raffia or fibre extension grade. Nominal melt flow rate 3.4 (+/−0.5). Additive free • General-purpose injection moulding grade. Melt flow rate 20 (+/−3). No additives. • All grades should be deliverable without premium or discount to each other	Linear low-density polyethylene (LL) butene copolymer general purpose blown film and blending grade, nominal melt flow rate 0.8 (−0.1/+0.4), without additives

Table 8.1 (*continued*)

Polypropylene (PP)	Linear low-density polyethylene (LL)
Delivery	
• Contracts to be deliverable monthly on a global basis. The seller will decide the choice of LME approved brand and the location (Houston, Antwerp/Rotterdam area and Singapore/Johor PTP) • Raffia only deliverable in Singapore/Johor PTP • General-purpose injection moulding grade only deliverable in Houston, USA	Contracts to be deliverable monthly on a global basis. The seller will decide the choice of LME approved brand and the location (Houston, Antwerp/Rotterdam area and Singapore/Johor PTP)
Packaging	
Standard delivery, 24.75 tonnes packaged on 18 pallets in 25-kilo bags, 55 bags per pallet, each pallet shrink or stretch wrapped and covered with plastic hood	Standard delivery, 24.75 tonnes packaged on 18 pallets in 25-kilo bags, 55 bags per pallet, each pallet shrink or stretch wrapped and covered with plastic hood
Applications	
Automotive, textiles, furniture, houseware	Packaging (plastic bottles, storage containers)

Source: The London Metal Exchange.

8.9   ROLES OF THE FUTURES EXCHANGE

A futures exchange has three principal roles:

1. It provides a central reference point for the pricing of commercial contracts for the underlying commodity.
2. It provides a series of instruments to allow participants to hedge an underlying exposure.
3. It provides participants with a source of supply for the underlying commodity or allows them to dispose of any excess inventory.

8.9.1   Pricing commercial contracts

One general feature of commodity products where no traded market exists is the lack of a transparent method for pricing commercial contracts. Up until the introduction of the futures contracts there were a number of price sources for pricing plastics that included the privately owned Platts, ICIS and the CMAI. These methods of reporting prices are done retrospectively on a weekly basis by polling market participants on their recent market activities. However, it seems likely that if the plastic contracts are a success, commercial contracts may follow the lead of the metals markets and move towards price-setting mechanisms based on the quoted LME price. A premium may be payable over the LME price to take account of factors such as the grade of the polymer and the delivery location. This practice would also allow both parties to the transaction to hedge their underlying price exposure using LME contracts, separating the underlying physical supply contract from the contract that hedges the price exposure.

As was hinted at in Chapter 4 (base metals), the seller of an exchange-traded commodity may have an embedded option within the contract. If a seller is required to deliver the physical commodity to satisfy a futures obligation, he will seek to buy the commodity in the cheapest location. Polyolefins (e.g. polyethylene and polypropylene) are produced globally with the lowest price being seen in Asia. The seller of the contract will therefore seek out the cheapest source of the commodity to deliver into the contract, and as a result, the exchange-traded price will reflect this situation. In some futures markets this is referred to as the "cheapest to deliver" option.

If an underlying commercial contract is being priced on the basis of a price quoted by ICIS, Platts or CMAI but hedged using LME futures, this introduces an element of basis risk. That is, the price on which the underlying transaction is based does not move by the same amount as the hedging instrument. However, if the prices quoted by the various sources differ significantly, it may be possible for an arbitrageur to buy (sell) the physical commodity at the lower (higher) non-LME price and sell (buy) the LME contract. This would gradually force the different prices to converge.

However, basis risk is an umbrella term, which could be applied in a number of contexts. Two other examples of basis risk could also impact the effectiveness of a hedged transaction. The first relates to the chemical composition of the underlying commodity to be hedged. The LME contract is for polymers in a "semi processed" state; that is, the commodity is in a form that would allow a converter to transform the material into a final end product. If a counterparty wished to use the LME contract to hedge an exposure to a "customised" polymer, there is no certainty that the prices of the two contracts would move in unison.

Another example of basis risk is the delivery destination of the underlying commodity. The futures price is for delivery in Houston, Antwerp and Singapore. If the underlying commercial contract is priced for delivery in a different location, the price may differ from that quoted on the LME. If demand for plastic in a certain geographical location has increased, then delivery to that particular locale may attract a premium over the LME price.

8.9.2 Hedging instruments

Ultimately the process of hedging allows an entity to protect the economic value of some underlying exposure.

In an earlier section we had outlined a simplified physical supply chain for the plastics industry. Futures can be used at each stage of the process depending on the nature of the

Table 8.2 Price exposure and futures strategies for the plastics supply chain

Supply chain role	Polymer price exposure	Futures transactions
Polymer producer	Falling prices	Sell futures
Converter	Rising prices	Buy futures
Distributor	Falling & rising prices	Sell/buy futures
End consumers	Rising prices	Buy futures
Traders	Falling and rising prices	Sell/buy futures

underlying exposure. Table 8.2 provides a recap of the supply chain, the nature of the price exposure and whether they are likely to be buyers or sellers of futures.

Reference is sometimes made to price-fixing hedges and offset hedges. A price-fixing hedge will be a transaction that is not transaction specific and is designed to alter the overall price risk of a commercial exposure. On the other hand an offset hedge will be based on a specific transaction and can be thought of as a micro hedge.

Price-fixing hedge

The manufacturer of any product may be faced with a situation where the required raw materials may not be priced until their actual receipt. This means that the company is exposed to a possible change in its profit margins. As a pre-emptive action the manufacturer could buy futures whose maturity coincides with the pricing date for the underlying commodity. Since the futures is not being used as a source of supply, the transaction could be closed-out by taking an equal and opposite position shortly prior to maturity.

Let us assume that a manufacturer of plastic water bottles has an ongoing need to buy linear low-density polyethylene. He doesn't feel he is able to pass on any extra costs to the end user of the water bottles and so decides he needs to lock in his costs to maintain his margins.

Looking at the prices for the futures contract in early March, he notes that the June futures contract is trading at USD 1,185 per tonne and so decides to buy one future at this price. The final settlement price for this futures contract will be set on the last business day of the month preceding its expiry month (i.e. the last business day in May). Actual settlement (i.e. exchange of cash for commodity) will take place on the third Wednesday of each futures expiry month (i.e. the third Wednesday of June in this example). Since the manufacturer does not want to take physical delivery of the commodity, he will therefore need to take an offsetting by 31 May (assuming it is a good business day).

Let us also assume that the manufacturer decides to close-out the futures position at the end of May when the price for June delivery is at USD 1,250 per tonne. Recall from the appendix that the final futures price will be the same as the spot price prevailing at the same time. Having bought the future at USD 1,185 and sold it at USD 1,250, the manufacturer has made a profit of USD 65 per tonne. As was shown in Chapter 4 (base metals), the manufacturer will not receive this payment by the variation margin system but will have it paid on the exchange-appointed settlement day (the third Wednesday of the delivery month). If the manufacturer can time the close-out of the futures contract with the pricing of the physical commodity, the mismatch between the two prices should not be significant. This does, however, assume that the underlying contract is priced on the basis of the LME rather than, say, an alternative source such as ICIS.

If the purchase of physical had been based on the LME price as of 31 May, then the net cost to the manufacturer would be USD 1,250 less the USD 65 dollars profit per tonne on the future. That gives a net cost of USD 1,185, which is equal to the price of the original purchased future. This ignores any premium that may have been negotiated to the LME price for quality differentials and delivery to a specific location.

The hedger can simultaneously execute a series of futures contracts for delivery in sequential months, if he knows that there will be a regular underlying physical exposure. This is described as a strip of futures.

Offset hedge

An offset hedge is where the future is used to protect the value of a specific transaction. Let us assume that a distributor has agreed to sell some PP in 2 months' time. The distributor has agreed a fixed sale price with the customer based on today's 2-month LME futures price (USD 1,055) plus a margin. The distributor is not obliged to hedge this exposure but runs the risk that the cost of the raw material will rise prior to the promised delivery, eroding any profit margin. As a result he decides to buy futures at the current price.

Let us assume that the long futures position is closed-out shortly before expiry to avoid physical delivery. We will also assume that the price of the plastic has risen to USD 1,100 per tonne. This will result in a profit of USD 45 per tonne on the futures contract. The distributor goes into the physical market and buys the requisite amount of polymer, paying the prevailing price, which we will also assume to be USD 1,100. The net position of the distributor is:

- *Futures transaction*
  Futures bought @ USD 1,055
  Futures sold @ USD 1,100
  Net futures profit and loss = USD 45 profit per tonne
- *Underlying commercial contract*
  PP sold to customer at USD 1,055 + Margin
  PP bought at USD 1,100
  Net physical profit and loss = USD 45 loss per tonne + Margin

The effect of this futures hedge is to lock in the agreed margin with the customer. Once again the example assumes that physical purchase of the PP is priced according to the LME to avoid basis risk.

8.9.3 Source of supply/disposal of inventory

Although 99% of all futures contracts are closed out prior to expiry, the exchange can be seen as a source of polymer or as a way for an entity to dispose of any excess inventory it may be holding.

The LME subsequently introduced three new contracts that became effective in June 2007. The contracts were regional in nature (Asia, Europe and North America) for each of the PP and LL contracts. This resulted in a total of six new contracts. The regional contracts were identical with respect to the general specification and delivery points to their existing equivalent global contract. The exchange also increased the number of "prompt" dates, widening the range of eligible dates at the shorter end of the price curve. The main benefit is that they will allow better correlation with physical prices in each region and offer potential arbitrage opportunities. It is hoped that the changes will bring increased liquidity and volumes.

8.10   OPTION STRATEGIES

At the time of the launch of plastics contracts the LME did not implement an option contract. Their argument was that they wanted liquidity to develop in the underlying futures market so that an option trader would be able to hedge any option exposure. However, entities that operate along the supply chain could obtain option-based price protection from the OTC market.

Rather than repeat material covered elsewhere, the interested reader is referred to Chapters 3 and 4 for a discussion of the range of different OTC option strategies that are possible. Chapter 3 (gold) reviews option strategies from a producer perspective, while Chapter 4 (base metals) analyses the strategies through the eyes of a consumer.

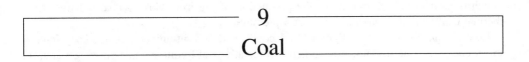

9
Coal

At the industry's peak in the first quarter of the twentieth century, collieries employed 1m miners. Today only six underground mines and a handful of opencast mines are operating with a workforce of fewer than 5,000'.

Quote from *Financial Times* on the state of the UK mining industry

SYNOPSIS The purpose of this chapter is to outline the most common derivative structures seen in the coal market.

The chapter will be of interest to those who are new to the coal market and are unfamiliar with the market or the hedging structures that are commonly traded. However, the chapter has been structured such that the detail on the market merely provides a context around which the discussion of the derivative structures is placed. As a result, those readers who wish to "cut to the chase" can start in the final section.

The chapter starts by *defining the different varieties of coal*. Then the discussion develops to consider the *demand and supply for coal*. The next section describes the *main participants* in the coal market and the nature of their market risks. From this the different *factors that will influence the price of coal* are highlighted and analysed. The final section presents the *main derivative structures* that are used in the coal market. These comprise futures, swaps and swaptions. Although vanilla options are also traded in the market, these are not covered in the chapter to avoid repetition with materials presented in previous chapters.

9.1 THE BASICS OF COAL

Coal, like crude oil, is a general term that is used to describe different types of a particular commodity. The World Coal Institute [2] (WCI) defines coal as:

...a combustible, sedimentary organic rock, which is composed mainly of carbon, hydrogen and oxygen. It is formed from vegetation which has been consolidated between other rock strata and altered by the combined effects of pressure and heat over millions of years to form coal seams.

The type of coal recovered depends upon the length of time it has spent in formation, as well as the temperature and pressure to which it has been subjected. Often coal is classified as being either low or high rank, which are terms that can be used to describe the properties of each type. High-rank coals encompass anthracite and bituminous coals. These coals will have a higher energy and lower moisture content. Domestic and industrial consumers use anthracite, which makes up about 1% of the world's reserves, primarily for heating purposes. Bituminous coals (52% of the world's reserves) can be broken into two main types: thermal or "steam coal" and metallurgical or "coking coal". Thermal coals are used in power generation and cement manufacture, while metallurgical coals are typically used in the manufacture of iron and steel. Coking coal is used in coke ovens to produce coke, which is used in blast furnaces for the production of pig iron. Coking coal is harder than thermal coal and consequently trades at a premium.

Lower rank coals include lignite ("red coal") and sub-bituminous coals. They have a lower energy and higher moisture content. Applications of lignite include power generation, while sub-bituminous coals are used in power generation and cement manufacture.

The International Energy Agency [3] (2006) defines coal in a different manner, categorising it as either hard coal or brown coal.

Hard coal with a high thermal value ... is economically suited to international trade, with characteristics making some coals suitable for metallurgical (coking) uses. Brown coal (lignite) has a much lower thermal value ... and is suitable mainly for power generation locally or to a lesser extent for briquette manufacture.

9.2 THE DEMAND FOR AND SUPPLY OF COAL

Figure 9.1 shows the primary energy supply by fuel and illustrates how this has evolved over time.

Over the period the total amount of energy consumed in each category has increased from 4,055.88 million tonnes of coal equivalent (Mtce) to 5,467.89 Mtce. However, the percentage of energy consumption attributable to coal has fallen from 22.4% in 1973 to 20.4% by 2005. The percentage that crude oil contributes to the overall supply mix has also experienced a fall, while the contribution of both nuclear and natural gas has increased. Figure 9.2 shows the coal reserves by region and type in million tonnes.

The five countries with the highest reserves and their associated reserves to production (R/P) ratio are shown in Table 9.1. Figures are for commercial solid fuels only; i.e. bituminous coal and anthracite (hard coal) and lignite and brown (sub-bituminous) coal. The R/P ratio is the reserves at the end of a year divided by that country's production.

Figure 9.3 shows how the nature of coal production has evolved since 1973 with the split between "hard coal" (i.e. higher rank coals) and "brown coal" (lower rank coals). The figure

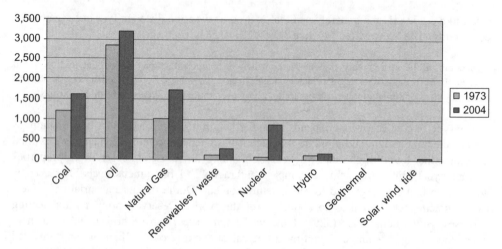

Figure 9.1 Total primary energy supply by fuel, OECD total
Source: from International Energy Agency (2006) *Coal Information*.

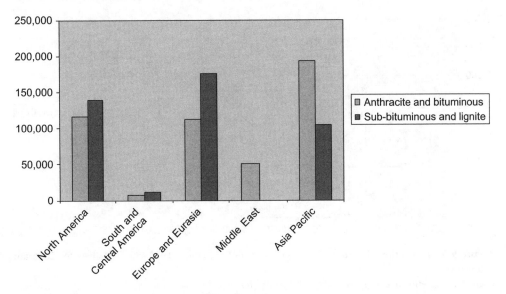

Figure 9.2   Regional Coal Reserves (million tonnes)
Source: BP Statistical Review of World Energy 2006.

Table 9.1   Reserves to production ratio

Country	Share of global reserves	R/P ratio (years)
USA	27.1%	240
Russian Federation	17.3%	>500
China	12.6%	52
India	10.2%	217
Australia	8.6%	213
Globally	100%	155

Source: BP Statistical Review of World Energy 2006.

indicates that production of coal has increased over the period, but production is dominated by the higher rank coals.

Figure 9.4 shows the regional production of coal expressed in million tonnes of oil equivalent. Unlike crude oil, supply is not concentrated in a relatively narrow geographical region. The graph indicates that Asia Pacific is the largest individual producer of coal with the majority of this being accounted for by China, Australia, India and Indonesia.

The regional consumption of coal (again in million tonnes of oil equivalent) is shown in the Figure 9.5. Just five countries – China, USA, India, Russia and Japan – account for over 73% of world consumption.

Figure 9.6 illustrates the main exporting countries and their associated volumes. The four largest exporters (in descending order) are:

• Australia
• Indonesia

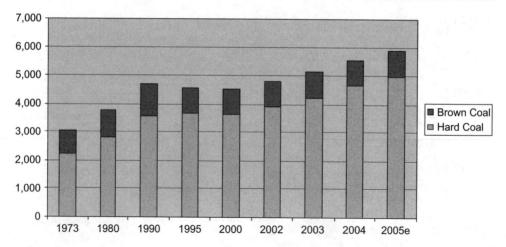

Figure 9.3 Production of hard and brown coal in million tonnes, 1973–2005. (Values for 2005 are estimates)
Source: International Energy Agency (2006) *Coal Information*.

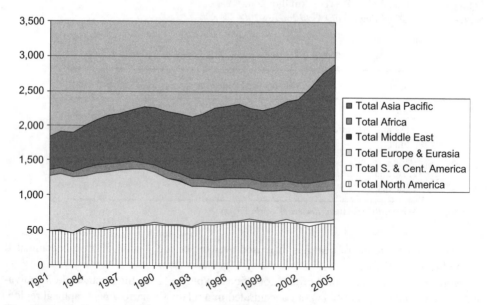

Figure 9.4 Regional production of coal (millions tonnes oil equivalent)
Source: BP Statistical Review of World Energy 2006.

- Russia
- South Africa

Figure 9.7 illustrates the major importers of coal in 2005. Of the eight countries listed it would be reasonable to conclude that the market for coal can be categorised by oceans: the Pacific and the Atlantic. Figure 9.8 illustrates some of the major flows of hard coal (i.e. higher rank coals) in 2005.

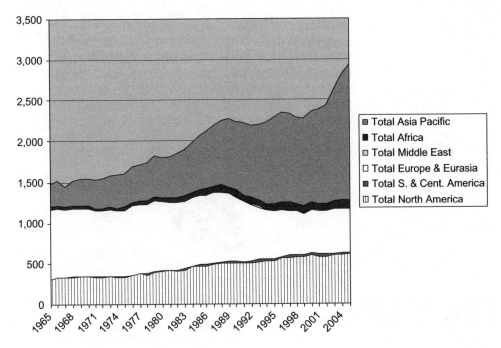

Figure 9.5   Regional consumption of coal
Source: Statistical Review of *World Energy 2006*.

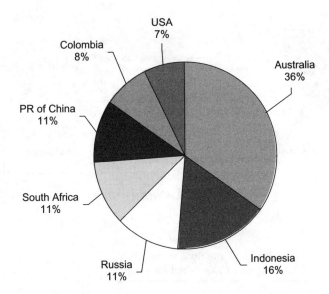

Figure 9.6   Major hard coal exporters (millions of tonnes, 2005 estimates)
Source: International Energy Agency (2006) *Coal Information*.

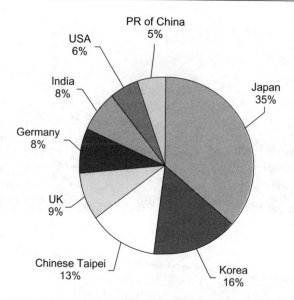

Figure 9.7   Major hard coal importers (millions of tonnes, 2005 estimates)
Source: International Energy Agency (2006) *Coal Information*.

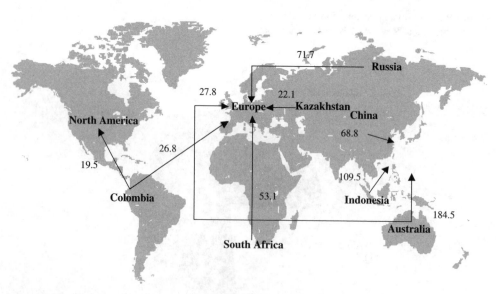

Figure 9.8   Major flows of hard coal (millions tonnes) 2005
Source: International Energy Agency (2006) *Coal Information*.

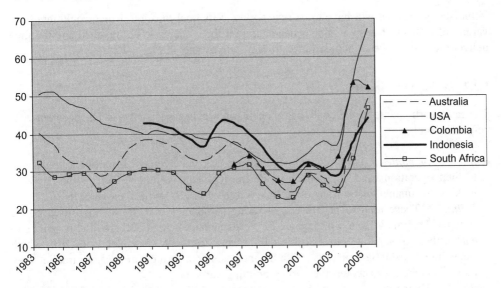

Figure 9.9   Steam coal over the period 1983–2006
Source: International Energy Agency (2006) *Coal Information.*

Figure 9.9 illustrates the movement of the price of steam coal over the period 1983 to 2005 for five major markets (average export unit values in USD per tonne).

The growth in the production and consumption of coal has been "fuelled" by the following factors:

- Increased demand for energy globally.
- Coal is cheaper per kilowatt-hour than competing energy sources such as natural gas and crude oil.
- The fuel is relatively safe to transport and costs less to move than oil or natural gas.
- There are substantial reserves available. According to the *BP Statistical Review of World Energy 2006*, coal had a reserves to production ratio of 155 years at the end of 2005, compared to 40.6 and 65.1 years for crude oil and natural gas, respectively.

9.3   PHYSICAL SUPPLY CHAIN

9.3.1   Production

The two methods of extracting coal are by underground or surface ("open cast") mining. Although more coal can be recovered from a given deposit by surface mining than from underground mines, the majority of coal is extracted from underground mines. The WCI note that there are regional variations to this, with surface mining in Australia accounting for 80% of production, while in the USA it makes up about 67% of production.

Similar to most commodities that are extracted from the ground, it will not be in a form that will be immediately usable. Depending on the physical form of the coal upon its extraction, it may require crushing in order to have an end product that physically manageable. The coal is also cleaned and will have any impurities removed.

Inevitably the coal will have to be transported to its final location, which could involve a variety of different transport modes depending on the distance to be travelled and the final delivery location. These include lorries, trains, barges and ships.

9.3.2 Main participants

The main participants in the coal supply chain, and their associated risk management concerns, include:

- *Mining companies*: Large companies will use risk management solutions to add value to their operations and will tend to trade in significant volumes. Other mines may be looking for financing solutions often linked to coal prices and FX movements.
- *Utilities*: These tend to be power-generating companies that operate coal-fired power stations. They may have a preference to use financially settled derivative transactions to enable them to separate out the physical delivery from the associated price risk, which can exhibit substantial volatility. With the increasing concern over emissions trading, they must also take into account the cost of emitting carbon.
- *Banks*: Their trading activity with other financial desks creates liquidity for the market as a whole, thereby facilitating the development of risk management solutions. Equally, banks that have a trading capability will be able to offer a hedging solution to other lending banks that wish to offer risk management solutions to their clients without the need for a trading desk. Banks with a trading desk can also offer a mechanism for other banks to offset the market risk inherent within the issuance of commodity-linked investment structures.
- *Industrial companies*: Cement producers are major coal consumers and the cost of the raw material can contribute a significant amount to their overall costs. Steel producers use coking coal but financial markets only trade thermal coal. This is the best available hedge but is not perfect in that the hedger has an exposure to basis risk (i.e. the risk that the price of the two commodities does not move in the same direction).

9.4 THE PRICE OF COAL

Steam coal is not a homogeneous product and, as such, a number of benchmarks have evolved based on standardised specifications surrounding the ash, sulphur and energy content. The main pricing locations from which indices have evolved are:

- Central Appalachia (USA)
- Powder River Basin, Wyoming (USA)
- Europe ARA (Amsterdam, Rotterdam, Antwerp)
- Richards Bay (South Africa)
- Newcastle (Australia)

Not all of these locations, however, are traded internationally.

Similar to crude oil, the distinction between the concept of spot and crude is somewhat blurred. For example, Platts [4] quotes prices for delivery in the prompt month, the prompt month plus one, three forward quarters and forward calendar year for certain coals.

9.5 FACTORS AFFECTING THE PRICE OF COAL

Electricity industry

Since electricity represents one of the largest uses of coal, an increase in the electrification of a country (e.g. India) will have an impact on price. Although in this instance it may be tempting to suggest that the same would be true of China, this is one instance where China has abundant reserves of coal, which it can use to meet this demand.

Planned capital expenditures for the building of new coal-fired power-generating facilities will influence perceptions of the future balance between demand and supply. For example, in the USA it is expected that the proportion of electricity to be generated from coal will rise from 50% in 2005 to 60% by 2030 [5].

Electricity production margins

The main fuels used to produce electricity are natural gas and coal. If the price of natural gas rises relative to coal, then it may encourage producers to switch. With the advent of allowances for installations that emit carbon dioxide, the cost of polluting now has to be taken into consideration. This cost is now also expressed in terms of the "dark spread" and "clean dark spread" [6].

Technology

As a result of the increased environmental concerns, much money has been spent on improving the performance of coal at the point of consumption while aiming to reduce the undesirable environmental side effects. The efforts to clean coal either involve the way in which it is prepared prior to its consumption or by fitting equipment to power stations to reduce undesirable emissions such as sulphur. Another focus of the technology has been to increase the thermal efficiency of coal by fitting more efficient boilers that reduce the carbon dioxide emissions.

Another perspective on the role of coal is its use within fuel cell technology [7]. Since hydrogen does not occur in a natural form in large quantities it would probably have to be manufactured (which, of course, would consume more energy) and one possible source is coal.

Environmental issues

Coal is perceived as a significant polluter of the environment and any associated regulation that may hinder its production or consumption could have an adverse effect on its market price. Methane, which is formed alongside coal, is released when the coal is mined and is classified as a greenhouse gas. Additionally, when coal is burnt it releases pollutants such as carbon dioxide, ash and oxides of sulphur and nitrogen (SO_x and NO_x).

Freight costs

Although not all coal is traded internationally, the price of coal will be influenced by the cost of transport to an end location. The major bulk commodities shipped internationally are iron ore, coal, grains, alumina and bauxite. To serve this demand there is a relative modest fleet of ships numbering about 6,000, of which only 1,800 are capable of carrying the larger loads. Unlike other commodities, an increase in demand can result in a relatively quick response in that it might only take about two years to build a new vessel.

Economic expansion

As an economy expands there may be an increase in the demand for coal. Take, for example, the economic expansion of China, which has led to an increase in the demand for steel. This has led to an increase in demand for coking coal to fuel the blast furnaces used in the production process.

Coal quality

The heat and sulphur content are considered the primary determinants of steam coal. For example, coal mined from the Powder River Basin in Wyoming is more popular with utilities as it has a lower level of sulphur. Combined with the fact that is mined from open cast pits, it is cheaper and cleaner than coal extracted from the Appalachian Mountains [5].

One of the main value drivers of coal is its calorific value. Similar to the concept of a crude oil assay, a sample of coal needs to be checked in laboratory conditions to ensure that it is in line with the specifications defined in a contractual supply agreement. Although the calorific value of coal is affected by a number of factors, the amount of the moisture in the coal will impact the measure. Some coal contract specifications include the terms "net as received" (NAR) and "gross as received" (GAR). When coal is quoted on a GAR basis the associated calorific value (sometimes known as the upper heating value) is the gross calorific value obtained under laboratory conditions after all the moisture has been removed. Quoting on a NAR basis refers to the net calorific value obtained in boiler plants and is known as the lower heating value. The difference between the two would be the heat of the water vapour produced.

Mining related issues

Since coal is extracted from the earth there are a number of factors that could influence the price of coal. These were outlined in the Chapter 4 on (base metals) and include:

- Capital spending and exploration
- Production disruption
- Production costs.

Whether the coal is mined from open cast or underground sites will influence the cost and drive the economics of production. For example, in the UK, estimates [8] suggest that the country has about 188 billion tonnes in reserves but only produces 20 million tonnes – a substantial fall from the 220 million tonnes that was produced in 1950. Part of this fall is attributable to the fact that the reserves are deep underground and therefore uneconomical to mine.

In some countries, such as Russia, the coal may need to be transported over significant distances to reach the final point of consumption. Related to this is the availability of logistics at the points of loading and discharging. Equally, since coal is often shipped by rail, derailments and subsidence on the line may have an impact on supply.

Competing fuel costs

Liquefaction is the process by which coal is transformed into a liquid. The resultant liquid fuel can be refined to produce fuels or other oil-based products such as plastic. The conversion from coal to oil is believed to be economic at about USD 35.00 [9] per barrel of crude.

In a similar vein gasification converts coal into synthetic gas, which can then be used by power stations to generate electricity. Coal, water and oxygen are mixed in a gasifier, which acts like a high-pressure cooker. The combination of heat and pressure chemically breaks down the coal to produce synthetic gas, while impurities such as sulphur are removed. This "syngas" can be burnt to drive a gas turbine for the production of electricity. As an undesirable side effect the gasification process produces carbon dioxide, but technology is evolving to capture this and bury it underground.

Influence of financial institutions

The entrance of banks, hedge funds and institutional investors could be significant. An increase in investment interest could result in an upward influence on the price, while the trading activities of the banks and hedge funds could provide enhanced liquidity with respect to the provision of risk management structures for the physical supply chain.

9.6 COAL DERIVATIVES

Estimates of the size of the coal market vary but one crude method of assigning a monetary value is to take the volume produced each year and multiply it by the prevailing market price. Using a production figure of 5 billion tonnes and a market price of about USD 60 per tonne, this would imply a value of USD 300 billion.

The derivatives market for coal is a fraction of this amount with notional values totalling about USD 100 billion. In most derivative markets, this figure would be a multiple of the physical market, suggesting that there is still potential for the market to expand.

The vast majority of transactions are financial swaps, but vanilla options are also traded. Financial Coal swaps have been trading in the OTC markets for about 5 years. The indices traded in the markets reflect the three key locations for seaborne thermal coal. There are also the indices for which only a forward market exists. Two of these locations are sources of coal (South Africa and Australia) and the third is a consuming location (Europe). The indices [10] are:

- *TFS API*[TM]*2*: This is a CIF (cost, insurance, freight) price for delivery in Rotterdam, which is an average of certain prices published by Argus and the McCloskey group.
- *TFS API*[TM]*4*: This is a FOB (free on board) price for delivery from Richards Bay, South Africa. This index derives its value from prices quoted by Argus, the McCloskey group and the South African Coal Report.
- *GlobalCoal Newcastle index*: This price relates to coal originating in Newcastle, Australia [11].

Within the context of the coal market API does not refer to the density of the material but simply stands for average price index. This reflects that the index is complied from a number of different observations and the final price is a simple average of these prices. The number (i.e. 2 and 4) that follows the acronym has no significance apart from allowing practitioners to distinguish between the two different pricing locations.

Driven by the liberalisation in the electricity markets across Europe, the utilities, who are the biggest users of financial swaps on coal, have been faced with less predictable load factors and are, therefore, moving away from using the 1-year fixed price supply contracts, which were the norm. This has led to an increase in hedging requirements using price indices.

Prices for coal are considered to be relatively volatile, but still are at the lower end of competing fuel sources. The following ranges of implied volatilities are indicative:

API2 Rotterdam	25–35%
API4 Richards Bay	20–25%
GlobalCoal (Newcastle)	18–25%
Crude Oil	25–50%
Natural Gas (US)	40–120%
Natural Gas (EUR)	40–90%

9.6.1 Exchange-traded futures

Exchange-traded coal futures do exist and one example is the Central Appalachian Coal future traded on NYMEX. The contract specification is detailed in Table 9.2.

The IntercontinentalExchange® (ICE) lists two exchange-traded futures:

Rotterdam Coal Futures	API 2
Richards Bay Coal Futures	API 4

The main features are:

- Both contracts are cash settled against the applicable Argus/McCloskey Coal Price Index report.
- The contract trades in lots of 1,000 tonnes, with a minimum trade size of five lots (5,000 tonnes).
- The contract is expressed in USD per tonne with the minimum price movement of 5 cents per tonne.
- The contract availability is for six consecutive month contracts, six consecutive quarters (January–March, April–June, July–September and October–December), five consecutive seasons (Summer is April–September, winter October–March) and two consecutive calendar years. For all of the contracts with a maturity greater than one month, they are constructed using a strip of individual and consecutive months.
- The monthly contracts cease trading on the close of business on the last Friday of the contract delivery period. The quarter, seasons and calendar years cease trading at the close of business on the last Friday of the first month contract in that quarter/season/calendar year.

Table 9.2   Coal futures specification

Trading unit	1,550 tons of coal
Price quotation	US dollars and cents per ton
Trading month	The current year plus the next three calendar years. A new calendar year will be added following the termination of trading in the December contract of the current year
Minimum price fluctuation	$0.01(1 cent) per ton
Last trading day	Trading terminates on the fourth to last business day of the month prior to the delivery month
Delivery	Delivery shall be made FOB buyer's barge at seller's delivery facility on the Ohio River between Mileposts 306 and 317 or on the Big Sandy River, with all duties, entitlements, taxes, fees and other charges imposed prior to delivery paid by the seller
Contract delivery unit	The seller shall deliver 1,550 tons of coal per contract. A loading tolerance of 60 tons or 2%, which ever is greater, over the total number of contracts delivered is permitted
Heat content	Minimum of 12,000 Btu per pound, gross calorific value with an analysis tolerance of 250 Btu per pound below
Ash content	Maximum of 13.50% by weight with no analysis tolerance
Sulphur content	Maximum of 1.00% with analysis tolerance of 0.050% above
Moisture content	Maximum of 10.00% with no analysis tolerance
Volatile matter	Minimum of 30.00% with no analysis tolerance
Hardness/Grindability	Minimum 41 Hardgrove Index with three-point analysis tolerance below. Hardness measures how difficult it is to pulverise coal for injection into the boiler flame
Size	Three inches topsize, nominal with a maximum of 55% passing one quarter inch square wire cloth sieve or smaller to be determined on the basis of the primary cutter of the mechanical sampling system

Source: NYMEX.

9.6.2   Over-the-counter solutions

Coal swaps

Arguably, the most popular OTC solutions in the coal markets are swaps and swaptions on coal. Take, for example, the risk profile of a large Australian coal producer. Like many others, the company sells the majority of its production through traditional long-term contracts, with the balance sold against an index (API 2 for delivery in Rotterdam) on a floating basis. They have chosen this particular index-pricing basis for their exports as they have access to very favourable shipping rates. However, this gives the company exposure to a fall in the price of coal. As part of its risk management strategy it is willing to swap this exposure into a fixed price if it believes that the "price" (i.e. the fixed element of the swap) is at an attractive level. It decides to enter into a swap with the following terms:

Trade date	October 2006
Effective date	June 2007
Maturity	September 2007
Total notional quantity	15,000 MT (metric tonnes)
Notional quantity per period	5,000 MT
Settlement dates	Each month in arrears
Payment date	5 business days after settlement date
Fixed price payer	Bank
Fixed price	USD 60.00
Floating rate payer	Client
Reference floating price	Coal–TFS API^{TM}2–Argus/McCloskey's
Tenor	Monthly price

With the company receiving the floating index on their underlying physical exposure but paying the same index under the terms of the swap, the net effect is that the two floating exposures cancel, leaving the producer paying a fixed cost of USD 60.00 per metric tonne. This presumes, however, that the date at which the floating price is fixed for the swap coincides with that of the physical exposure. If not, the company is faced with an element of basis risk.

In this scenario the producer sells most of his production under long-term fixed price agreements. As a result of the steep rise in natural gas and crude oil witnessed in the early twenty-first century, coal became relatively more attractive with demand increasing accordingly. This had an obvious knock-on effect and the price of coal also increased. Since many coal-producing companies had sold their production forward at a fixed price, they were unable to take advantage of this price change. A possible solution would be to enter into a coal swap to receive of a floating index price and pay fixed. The net effect of this would have been to leave the producer as a net receiver of the floating index, allowing him to benefit from the rise in the price of coal.

In the previous example the cashflow exchanges took place on a monthly basis. This would be useful as a hedge for a producer who is selling a regular amount of coal per month over the period in question. However, the swap could also be structured as one 3-month contract. Here the contract is most likely acting as a cash-settled forward transaction, where the price is fixed at the start of the period but settled in arrears. For example:

Trade date	October 2006
Effective date	June 2007
Maturity	September 2007
Total notional quantity	15,000 MT (metric tonnes)
Notional quantity per period	15,000 MT
Settlement date	One 3-month period paid in arrears
Payment date	5 business days after settlement date
Fixed price payer	Bank
Fixed price	USD 60.00
Floating rate payer	Client

Reference floating price	Coal–TFS^{TM} API2–Argus/McCloskey's
Publication source	Argus/McCloskey's coal price index report
Tenor	3-month price at start of period

A common feature of OTC coal swaps is that the agreements will include a currency conversion provision, which allows for the payment of cashflows to be denominated in a currency other than USD. For example, a contract that makes the cashflow payments in either GBP or EUR may be based on the average exchange rate for the particular settlement period (e.g. monthly, as in the above example). The price source is usually an independent reporting service such as Reuters.

Coal swaptions

Another popular trade in the market is the coal swaption (e.g. an option on a coal swap). A possible termsheet for such a trade might appear as:

Option trades	
Trade date	September 2006
Expiry	December 2006
Option style	European
Option seller	Bank
Option buyer	Client
Premium per MT	USD 1.85
Total premium	USD 27,750

Underlying transaction	
Effective date	Start December 2007
Maturity	End March 2007
Total notional quantity	15,000 MT (metric tonnes)
Notional quantity per period	5,000 MT
Settlement dates	Each month in arrears
Payment date	5 business days after settlement date
Fixed price payer	Bank
Fixed price	USD 60.00
Floating rate payer	Client
Reference floating price	Coal–TFS^{TM} API2–Argus/McCloskey's
Tenor	Monthly price

Motivation for using swaptions

The rationale for the trade will be different depending on the end client. If the client is a producer or consumer of coal, then it is most likely that the motivation will be to hedge, on a contingent basis, some form of underlying exposure. For example, the terms of the underlying swap are identical to those presented in the first swap example. In that scenario we had argued that in that scenario a producer selling on a variable rate basis could receive a fixed price to transform his exposure to a falling coal price. A possible motivation to buy this swaptions is that his believes the price of coal will rise but cannot afford his view of the market to be wrong.

10
Emissions Trading

For most of the Earth's history the planet has been either very cold, by our standards or very hot...
Ice-core studies show that in some places dramatic changes happened remarkably swiftly: temperatures
rose by as much as 20°C in a decade.

Quote from *The Economist* [1]

SYNOPSIS **The purpose of this chapter is to outline the chief aspects of the climate change debate and to document the features of the emissions trading markets.**

Emission trading has linkages to previous chapters on power although it can be read on a standalone basis. Much has been written about climate change, some of it very technical, some of it highly politicised. The aim of the chapter, however, is to present the principle issues in a non-technical manner in order to provide a context for the description of emissions trading.

There is a short description on the *science of climate change* in the first section, which includes a description of the *carbon cycle*. From this the possible *consequences of global warming* are presented and, to provide balance, some of the *arguments against climate change* are outlined.

Climate change will be forever associated with the *Kyoto Protocol* but the lead up to this point and subsequent developments are vital to the understanding of how the market works. A description of the *Kyoto mechanisms* is presented, which develops into a discussion of *which factors influence the price of emissions*.

Europe is home to the largest emissions market in the world, and so the salient features of *the EU trading scheme* are outlined. The final section details the features of *the most popular OTC traded instruments*.

10.1 THE SCIENCE OF GLOBAL WARMING

10.1.1 Greenhouse gases

The earth is warmed by energy radiated by the sun. Although some of this is reflected back into space, a significant proportion will reach the surface of the earth. Most of the energy is absorbed by the earth's surface but some is reflected back into space in the form of infrared radiation. This infrared radiation, however, may not directly exit into space, as its eventual escape maybe blocked by "greenhouse gases" (GHG) that make up about 1% of the atmosphere. The main greenhouse gases are:

- Carbon dioxide (CO_2), which is generated as a result of burning fossil fuels and by the respiration of humans and animals.
- Methane (CH_4), which may be released when mining for coal or searching for natural gas and oil. It can also be generated by landfills and livestock.
- Nitrous oxide (N_2O), which can be generated by burning fossil fuels or it may be found in fertilisers.

- Hydrofluorocarbons (HFCs) and perfluorocarbons (PFCs), which are produced by refrigeration and air-conditioning units.
- Sulphur hexafluoride (SF_6), which is used in a variety of manufacturing processes.

The main focus of the climate change debate to date has been on carbon dioxide emissions. As a result, it is common to express the amount of these other GHGs in terms of tonnes of CO_2 equivalent (CO_2e).

Greenhouse gases (GHGs) are not inherently bad as they trap heat and maintain the planet some 30 degrees Celsius warmer than it would otherwise be. Most GHGs do occur naturally, but their volume is increasing as a result of human activity. Electricity generation accounts for about a quarter of global emissions, mainly due to the fact that coal is still a significant primary fuel input. The second largest source of emissions is deforestation, which accounts for about 18% of emissions, followed by agricultural activities and transport, each contributing about 14% to the total figure [2].

10.1.2 The carbon cycle

The carbon cycle describes the possible pathways a carbon atom takes through the different components of the ecosystem. A convenient starting point is the atmospheric content of carbon dioxide. Carbon atoms may be retained in the air until eventually they will be absorbed by green plants, combined with water and turned into starch. This could occur over a matter of hours or hundreds of years.

The carbon atom is now part of a large starch molecule, and there are two possible pathways the atom may now take:

- It may be used by the plant in respiration, thus releasing the carbon atom back into the atmosphere as carbon dioxide.
- The starch molecule may be further processed and become part of the plant in the form of wood or other plant cells or molecules.

If the carbon becomes part of the plant, it then may take one of three possible pathways:

- The plant may die and be decomposed by bacteria in the soil, thus releasing the carbon as carbon dioxide back into the atmosphere.
- An animal may eat the plant.
- If the plant is burnt (either directly or as a fossil fuel), carbon dioxide is released back into the atmosphere.

If eaten by an animal (as part of a larger organic molecule such as fat, carbohydrate or protein) it will then follow one of three pathways:

- The carbon is used in respiration and released into the atmosphere as carbon dioxide.
- The carbon becomes part of the animal having been used to build protein, fat or carbohydrate.
- The carbon remains in the state it was eaten, is undigested and is passed out of the animal as faeces, which will be broken down by micro-organisms and the carbon they contain will be released once more as carbon dioxide into the atmosphere.

From here we start to "recycle" in that the animal may die or be eaten by another animal and again the carbon atom can follow several different pathways. The carbon will always eventually end up in the atmosphere as carbon dioxide, which is why the system is called a "cycle", even though it does not really follow a single, simple pathway.

The science of global warming is complex in that the effect of rising temperatures may well be accompanied by other changes in climate. These changes, which are referred to as "feedback loops" include:

- the amount of cloud cover
- levels of precipitation
- wind patterns
- rising sea levels
- an intensification of the water cycle increasing the risk of droughts and floods
- a change in the duration of the seasons.

10.1.3   Feedback loops

Although some of these changes may give rise to cooling effects, such as increased cloud cover that may block out sunshine; others may exacerbate the rise in temperatures. For example, if the Siberian permafrost were to melt, exposing the peat surface beneath, there would be an increase in the amount of methane released into the atmosphere.

Man-made aerosols, which are microscopic particles that reflect sunlight back out into space, may offer some temporary cooling effect but have their own side effects such as a reduction in air quality.

10.2   THE CONSEQUENCES OF GLOBAL WARMING

The debate over global warming has evolved from whether the earth is getting warmer to one that tries to identify the extent to which human activity has contributed to the warming: referred to as anthropogenic activity.

One concern is that human activity has led to the "enhanced greenhouse effect", whereby the GHGs in the atmosphere have become denser than normal. According to the fourth Intergovernmental Panel on Climate Change [3] (IPCC) report, the concentration of carbon dioxide increased from a pre-industrial value of 280 parts per million (ppm) to 379 ppm by 2005. The latter value exceeds ranges observed over the last 650,000 years, which have varied from 180 ppm to 300 ppm and a suggestion is that at the current rate of increase the concentration will have reached 800 ppm by the end of the century [1]. Some scientists also argue that the CO_2 being currently emitted could remain in the atmosphere for up to 200 years, suggesting that any action taken to reduce these levels would not have an effect for a very long time.

The consequences of global warming are believed to include:

- An increase in temperature
- Melting of polar ice caps
- A rise in the sea level
- More events of extreme weather and

- Changes in ocean currents (for example, the possibility that the Gulf Stream may "switch off" causing a fall in temperatures in northwest Europe).

As a result of the increased CO_2 levels, the earth's surface is predicted to rise by 1.4 to 5.8 degrees Celsius by 2100. Taken in context, the temperature of the earth rose by 0.7 degrees Celsius since 1900 [4].

10.2.1 The Stern Report

The Stern Report [5], which was published in 2006, came to the following conclusions.

- Over the last 30 years temperatures have been rising by 0.2 degrees Celsius per decade and all of the 10 warmest years on record have occurred since 1990.
- A doubling of pre-industrial levels of greenhouse gases is very likely to lead to a rise of between 2 and 5 degrees Celsius and that this level of greenhouse gases will be reached somewhere between 2030 and 2060.
- If annual greenhouse emissions remain at their current levels, concentrations of these gases would be more than three times their pre-industrial levels by 2100, leading to an increase in temperatures of between 3 and 10 degrees Celsius.
- There is a significant risk of temperature increases above 5 degrees Celsius by the early part of the next century if emissions grow at their current rate.
- A temperature increase of 5 degrees Celsius would be outside the experience of human civilisation.

10.2.2 Fourth assessment report of the IPCC

The fourth assessment report of the Intergovernmental Panel on Climate Change was made in February 2007 [3]. In the third assessment report they concluded: "Most of the observed warming over the last 50 years is likely to have been due to the increase in greenhouse gas concentrations." The term "likely" was used to indicate a probability of occurrence greater than 66%. In the fourth report they concluded: "Most of the observed increase in globally averaged temperatures since the mid-20th century is very likely due to the observed increase in anthropogenic greenhouse gas concentrations." The report defined "very likely" as having a probability of occurrence of more than 90%.

The main findings of their fourth assessment report included the following observations:

- The concentration of carbon dioxide, methane and nitrous oxide in the atmosphere as a result of industrialisation now exceed pre-industrialisation levels.
- The increase in carbon dioxide is attributed primarily to the usage of fossil fuel and land-use change. Methane and nitrous oxide concentrations are primarily due to agriculture.
- There is a very high confidence (at least a 9 out 10 chance of being correct) that the net effect of human activities since 1750 has been to cause an increase in warming.
- Warming of the climate system is beyond doubt, and is evidenced from increases in global average air and ocean temperatures, widespread melting of snow and ice and rising global average sea level.

- For the next two decades a warming of about 0.2 degrees Celsius per decade is projected.
- Emissions at or above current levels would lead to further warming that would very likely be greater than that experienced during the twentieth century.
- Even if greenhouse gas concentrations remain at current levels, the effects of human-related activities would continue for centuries.

10.3 THE ARGUMENT AGAINST CLIMATE CHANGE

Nobody knows just how much carbon dioxide the world is going to produce in the future. Nobody knows just what it will do to the temperature. Nobody knows just how temperature rises will affect the world economy.

The Economist (4 November 2006)

Although there has been a growing consensus that human activities have contributed significantly to the warming of the earth, there is still an undercurrent of disagreement on the subject. The main reasons for disagreement are as follows:

- Climate change has been defined solely in terms of the study of the effect of greenhouse gases. It is claimed that solar activity is a significant contributor to the climate and that there is a possibility that a reduction in the sun's activity could lead to significant cooling [6].
- Just because the majority of people believe in something, this does not necessarily mean that it is right [7].
- The main research that supports the current majority theory is not independent and is being funded by those with an interest in propagating the current consensus view.
- Obtaining funding for scientific research that may contradict global warming is difficult to procure [8].
- As a result of the current concern over climate change, a new industry has developed, which many individuals and institutions have an interest in perpetuating.
- Any information that may contradict current thinking is not given the prominence that it deserves. For example, those arguing against the extent of anthropogenic activity point out that:

  - The earth underwent a similar period of warming from 1918 and 1940 [9].
  - The earth actually cooled from the 1940s to the 1970s. This is countered, however, by the argument that this was caused by the cooling effect of sulphur in the atmosphere, generated by industrial activity, which is now in decline [9].
  - Crops in areas normally associated with warm temperatures have been ruined by unseasonably cold weather [6].
  - Some areas in East Antarctica are becoming colder [9].
  - Between 1998 and 2005, global average temperatures did not increase [9].

- The choice of language in the predictions is too vague:

Since the early 1990s, the columns of many leading newspapers and magazines, worldwide, have carried an increasing stream of alarmist letters and articles on hypothetical human-caused climate change. Each alarmist article is larded with words such as "if", "might", "could", "probably", "perhaps", "expected", "projected" or "modelled" [9].

- Even with a high probability of an event occurring the margin for error is still significant: "a 10% uncertainty in any theory is a wide open breach for any latter – day Galileo or Einstein to storm through with a better idea" [6].
- The science is too complex to model and predict. The contrary argument says that the climate will change naturally, sometimes predictably sometimes unpredictably. The changes could be gradual, while others will be shorter and difficult to explain.
- The time frames over which climate judgements are made are often selective. For example, over 90% of the last 2 million years the climate has been much colder than it has been today, and if looked at from this perspective the planet is actually emerging from an ice age.

A report on the economics of climate change issued by the UK House of Lords Select Committee on Economic Affairs [10] (prior to the publication of the fourth Intergovernmental Panel on Climate Change report) included the following comments:

- There was concern about the objectivity of the IPCC process in that some of the scenario analyses and summary documentation was influenced by political considerations.
- Some of the positive aspects of global warming were downplayed in the third IPCC report.
- The preoccupation of setting emissions targets at an international level was not an effective method of addressing the climate control issues. "The Kyoto Protocol makes little difference to rates of warming, and has a naïve compliance mechanism which can only deter countries from signing up to subsequent tighter emission targets."

10.4   HISTORY OF HUMAN ACTION AGAINST CLIMATE CHANGE

10.4.1   Formation of the IPCC

The first world conference on climate change took place in 1979 but it was not until 1988 that the World Metrological Organisation and the United Nations Environment Programme established the Intergovernmental Panel on Climate Change (IPCC). The IPCC reviews published research on the issue of climate change and issues influential assessments on a periodic basis; to date they have issued reports in 1990, 1995, 2001 and 2007.

10.4.2   The Earth Summit

The IPCC's first report in 1990 formed the basis of negotiations for the United Nations Framework Convention on Climate Change. The text of the convention was launched in June 1992 at the Rio de Janeiro "Earth Summit". The convention identified a number of countries referred to as "annex I parties" which comprised the industrialised nations that were members of the OECD in 1992 plus countries that were deemed to be in transition (e.g. the Russian Federation). This listing would eventually determine how many countries needed to ratify the subsequent Kyoto Protocol for this to become legally enforceable.

10.4.3 The Kyoto Protocol

The second IPCC assessment report concluded, on the balance of available evidence, that human activity was having an effect on the climate and that this would pose a threat to human and economic development. These results paved the way for the development and signing of the Kyoto Protocol in December 1997. The Protocol set individual, legally binding targets for a number of industrialised countries (referred to as "annex B" countries) willing to take steps to curb their emissions of greenhouse gases [11].

For the Protocol to be legally binding it had to be ratified by an agreed number of developed countries who were determined to be responsible for the majority of global emissions in the industrialised world. Only those countries that ratified the protocol became parties to the treaty but ratifying the Protocol did not require the signatoris to adopt legally binding emissions targets unless they were annex B countries.

The Kyoto Protocol outlined a variety of mechanisms that would allow countries to meet their commitments. Each of the countries for which the Kyoto protocol is legally binding has been assigned an emission limitation or reduction target. The emission targets vary from country to country and range from a cut of 8% to an increase in 10% of a baseline value measured from 1990. Despite the different target ranges, the overall aim of the accord is an overall reduction in greenhouse gases by 5% in the 2008–2012 period.

The Protocol outlines three mechanisms to help to achieve this aim.

- Emission-trading schemes
- Clean development mechanism
- Joint implementation.

Two of the mechanisms are project based, while the third is a market-based mechanism. These mechanisms, however, were never intended as the only way in which countries would tackle emissions. In addition, countries are expected to pursue policies that would encourage an overall reduction in the levels of emissions.

Emission trading schemes

One example of this is the European Union Emissions Trading Scheme (EU ETS), which was set up to operate initially from 2005 to 2007 and in its first phase was a pre-Kyoto agreement. The second phase of the scheme will run from 2008–2012, to coincide with the Kyoto period.

The market for trading emissions involves the purchase or sale of the right to emit an agreed amount of a specified pollutant. Emission-trading schemes are sometimes referred to as "carbon markets" as carbon dioxide is the mostly widely produced greenhouse gas. Participants can use the mechanism to acquire rights in order to meet their emission targets.

Under the terms of the Kyoto Protocol these rights are referred to as "assigned amount units" (AAU) where 1 AAU is equal to 1 tonne of CO_2e. Hence, if an installation had emitted 100 tonnes CO_2e in 1990, then over the Kyoto period of 2008–2012 it would be faced with a target of, say, 92 AAU. If the installation chose to emit more than this amount, it would either have to buy the necessary allowances in the market or invest in technology to reduce its level of emissions. Within the EU scheme, these allowances are termed EUAs (European Union Allowances), and are either allocated or auctioned by regulators.

The EU ETS is an example of what is known as a "cap and trade" scheme. A national regulator allocates allowances to different sectors and then individual eligible firms. The regulator will be responsible for monitoring compliance within the limits and will also enforce penalties for non-compliance.

Clean development mechanism

The CDM represents investment by an annex B country in a developing country that will result in measurable long-term climate change. CDM projects, which became effective in 2005, must reduce emissions below those emissions that would have occurred in the absence of the project.

These projects are monitored and certified by the UN, who will then issue credits on an annual basis equal to the amount by which emissions have been reduced.

These credits are referred to as certified emission reductions (CERs). The CERs generated by such project activities can be used by eligible entities in annex B countries to help to meet their emissions targets under the Kyoto Protocol, or may be traded in a secondary market.

Typical projects include:

- Energy efficiency schemes
- Methane capture
- Fuel switching (e.g. from coal to gas)
- Capture and destruction of certain industrial gases.

The projects are being currently undertaken primarily in China, India, Brazil and South Korea. Projects can be registered with the UN for 10 years (non-renewable) or for 7 years, with the possibility of renewal for a further 7 years. The option to renew will only be granted if the so-called "baseline" conditions have not changed. Take, for example, a project that is designed to reduce the emission of HFCs and is registered for an initial period of 7 years. If, after the fifth year, the host government introduces a law that requires the mandatory control of all HFCs, the project cannot be renewed for the second 7-year period. However, the host government will still be able to claim allowances for the remaining 2 years of the initial period. Credits are allocated on an annual basis for the reduction in emissions subject to their verification. If the installation attempting to cut emissions goes out of business, subsequent credits will not be issued.

It would seem reasonable to assume that if there were an increase in the number of CERs issued, this would lower the price of allowances. However, this is unlikely to happen as in subsequent compliance periods the overall cap on emissions will be set at progressively lower levels. This should restore the increase in demand for allowances, increasing their price. As of early 2007 there were nearly 600 registered CDM projects and nearly 40,000,000 CERs have been issued. On current estimates, the UNFCC estimates that nearly 800,000,000 CERs will be generated until the end of the Kyoto period in 2012 [12].

Joint implementation

In the joint implementation (JI) mechanism, one annex B country invests in an emission reduction project in another annex B country. The costs of cutting emissions in the target country is cheaper than in the investing country. This allows for the transference of allowances from the target country to the investing country. These allowances are referred to emission reduction units (ERUs) but unlike the clean development mechanism there is no overall change in emissions. The JI mechanism takes effect from 2008 to coincide with the Kyoto period.

10.4.4 From Kyoto to Marrakech and beyond

After Kyoto a series of further conferences were held to establish the operational aspects of the Kyoto Protocol, all of which were adopted in the Marrakech Accords of 2001. The Kyoto Protocol eventually came into force on 16 February 2005 after the requisite number of countries had ratified the agreement. As of mid-September 2006, 164 countries and the European Community had ratified the Kyoto Protocol. However, the USA and Australia have indicated that they will not be ratifying the Protocol. To date there has been no addition to the provisions of Kyoto beyond 2012, although the EU has indicated that their ETS will extend beyond this period.

Critics of Kyoto argue that even if it is fully implemented it will not change the concentration of greenhouse gases by much and that action to combat climate change should focus on controlling the increasing demand for transport and electricity in countries such as India and China.

10.5 PRICE DRIVERS FOR EMISSIONS MARKETS

Economic growth

As an economy expands it is likely that production of carbon and other industrial gases will increase. For action on global warming to be truly effective, an overall global limit on the amount of greenhouse gases produced would be needed. Politically this would be exceptionally difficult to achieve, as expanding countries such as India and China are unlikely to agree.

Supply of allowances

In phase I of the EU ETS, allowances were freely handed out, a process referred to as "grandfathering", but many of the recipient power generators raised electricity prices by the market value of the carbon permits they held. This boosted their profits by up to £800 million [13].

In April 2006, the EU ETS published their first reports of actual emissions for the previous year. The reports indicated that the level of actual emissions were at least 95 million tonnes lower than the available supply of allowances. This caused prices to collapse from a high of about EUR 31 to EUR 9 in a short period of time. Part of this is due to the fact that there was not much historical information on the amount of actual pollution the installations were emitting. So, as a result, the original allocation of allowances was made on a judgemental basis.

Demand for allowances

The choice faced by installations subject to emission targets is whether they should invest in technology to reduce their emissions, therefore being able to sell any surplus allowances, or to simply buy their allowances from another market participant. For example, the aviation sector will be included in the EU ETS from 2011 onwards and this is expected to increase the demand for allowances. Although aviation is a relatively small source of greenhouse gases (about 3%), it is expected to grow at a significant rate.

It also seems likely that many countries will miss their Kyoto targets, which will increase the demand for allowances. However, the resultant price effect will also be a function of the time remaining before the end of the compliance period.

Type and "vintage" of emissions to be traded

In the first phase of the EU ETS, allowances cannot be carried over, therefore contracts for delivery in phase II trade at a different price. Since the first phase of the scheme was oversupplied with permits relative to the amount emitted, many observers believe that the price of phase I allowances will gradually tend towards zero.

Credits earned from the CDM (i.e. CERs) will be allowable in the second phase of the ETS and can be used to meet emission targets. Although the extent to which these credits can be used will be subject to limits, their availability will have an impact on the price of emission allowances. An increase in the amount of CERs that can be used by an installation to meet its totals should have a negative impact on the price of EUAs. This is because firms will be able to submit more CERs as part of their compliance requirements, thus lowering the demand for EUAs, leading to a fall in price.

If CERs are expensive to produce, then it is likely that there will be higher demand for EUAs, resulting in an increase in price.

The potential emergence of new carbon markets in countries such as Japan or Canada will eventually lead to the migration of CERs to the highest priced location.

Weather patterns and fuel prices

Since one of the biggest sources of emissions is power generation, weather patterns and fuel prices will influence the price of allowances. If a generator has the ability to substitute different fuel sources, such as coal or natural gas, they may compare the carbon-adjusted dark and spark spreads to determine the optimum fuel source. So if the price of natural gas were to increase, combined with a period of cold weather, a generator may be encouraged to switch to coal as the primary fuel input. Since coal generates more greenhouse gases the generators would need to buy more allowances to cover the increased use of the commodity. This should then drive up the price of allowances, the cost of which would be passed on to consumers in terms of a higher electricity charge.

Intuitively, there is a positive correlation between the prices of carbon and the prices of both power and gas. There is a negative correlation between the price of coal and the price of carbon.

Penalties for non-compliance

Penalties are determined by each country or region. Fees for non-compliance in the EU scheme have been established but, irrespective of the charge, any breach of the targets will need to be made up in the following year.

Alternative sources of electricity production

The cost of emissions will be affected by the planned increase in alternative low-carbon technologies such as nuclear power and renewable sources. If such technological changes are expensive, this will lead to an increase in the demand for allowances.

Regulation

Factors that might affect the price of allowances could include:

- The stringency of a national allocation plan.
- Whether project-based credits can be included and the extent to which they could be used.
- Whether allowances or credits can be carried over between compliance periods.
- The perceived strength of the compliance regime used to police a particular scheme.

Linkages with other energy markets

In an article entitled *The Energy Revolution*, Bond (2007) provides an interesting insight into the linkages that exist between different energy markets and the price of carbon. He argues that the early part of the twenty-first century may "be seen as an inflexion point in the global economic order". He points out that the market is signalling that the supply of conventional energy sources needs to be increased but political sentiment is moving away from the reliance on hydrocarbon-based fuels.

Put bluntly the world has simultaneously discovered that the supply of energy may not match future demand and that the type of energy currently supplied is incompatible with survival. Market prices signal the need for dramatic increases in the supply of hydrocarbon-based energy, while political shifts signal the need for an equally dramatic decrease in the use of hydrocarbon-based energy.

Furthermore, he argues that the global economy needs to invest heavily in the energy infrastructure to meet a projected 50% increase in demand over the next 30 years. To avoid the worst consequences of global warming, however, there needs to be an 80% cut in energy supplied from fossil fuels to alternative sources.

Bond points out that a positively sloped forward curve (i.e. a market in contango) signals a longer-term excess of demand over supply; a curve in backwardation would therefore be indicative of a shorter-term imbalance between markets (demand exceeding supply) and a longer-term excess of supply over demand. Relating this to the different energy markets he notes that the forward curves for the energy markets that emit the most CO_2 are in contango while the curves for cleaner energy are backwardated.

From this observation we can deduce that as yet, the markets do not believe that policy changes will successfully reduce global demand for the dirtier fuels in favour of cleaner energy sources.

10.6   THE EU EMISSIONS TRADING SCHEME

10.6.1   Background

At first sight the carbon market would appear to function as any other. There are buyers and sellers with the market clearing at a level where demand is equal to supply. Unlike other markets, however, the commodity being traded – the certified absence of carbon emissions – does not exist.

The EU ETS is designed to cut greenhouse gases and is mandatory for all member states. As a result, 25 countries and more than 11,000 installations fall within its scope. The initial trading period covered the years 2005 to 2007, while the second phase coincides with the Kyoto period of 2008–2012. Under the Kyoto protocol the EU accepted that regionally it would cut its emissions to 92% of its 1990 levels.

The scheme is based on a number of fundamental principles:

- It is a "cap and trade" system.
- The initial focus will be on reducing carbon dioxide emissions from industrial installations.
- The scheme will operate in phases, which will allow for reviews and the possible widening of its scope in terms of gases and participants.
- National allocation plans will be developed periodically.
- Compliance with the rules of the scheme will be monitored.
- The scheme recognises the project-based schemes outlined in the Kyoto Protocol (CDM and JI) and also has provisions for establishing links with compatible schemes in other countries and regions.

The actual amount by which each country will cut its emissions varies. Some countries will be allowed to emit more than its 1990 levels while others have been set a more aggressive target than the 8% overall cut. The EU arrangement, where different countries are allowed to emit at different levels, is sometimes referred to as the "burden sharing agreement". This agreement incorporated a wide choice of targets, ranging from a 28% reduction for Luxembourg to a 27% increase for Portugal.

The EU also passed a "linking directive" that allows companies and states to use credits from Kyoto's project-based mechanisms to help to comply with their scheme obligations. The directive allows for the possibility of recognising other trading schemes outside the EU. The EU ETS was the first scheme in the world to recognise that CERs, ERUs and EUAs were all equivalent. However, a CER is not converted into an EUA but is considered fungible for compliance purposes. Credits from nuclear facilities, land use, land-use change and forestry activities are not recognised.

In phase I the activities covered included power and heat generation industries. These included combustion plants, oil refineries, coke ovens, iron and steel plants and factories making cement, glass, lime, bricks, ceramics, pulp and paper. In this phase of the scheme, a size threshold was applied based either on production capacity or output. However, airlines and transport were excluded from phase I.

Phase II will run for 5 years from 2008 to 2012, and although there is no current internationally agreed plans for the post-Kyoto period, the EU has indicated that the emissions trading scheme will continue. In phase II of the scheme, member states will be able to unilaterally decide if they wish to include other gases in addition to carbon dioxide, and the aviation industry will be included from 2011 onwards.

10.6.2 How the scheme works

The EU commission is responsible for passing the requisite legislation, which establishes the rules for the scheme. The commission will set guidelines for the way in which individual countries allocate their allowances and will establish the criteria for monitoring and reporting the actual amount emitted. It will also establish a central registry, which will record all the information sent to it by the national authorities.

Each of the member states will set up a national authority, which in the UK will be the Department for Environment, Food and Rural Affairs (DEFRA). The national authority will allocate the allowances to the individual installations and establish an electronic registry to record the holdings and any transfers that may take place as a result of trading activities. The authority will also be responsible for monitoring and verifying the actual amount emitted, and will enforce any penalties that may be due as a result of non-compliance.

Operators of installations covered by the scheme must have a permit to emit greenhouse gases. Each installation will be allocated EU allowances (EUAs) either free of charge, or by a state-organised auction. One EUA gives the holder the right to emit 1 tonne of CO_2e. The scheme should cap the amount of allowances such that a scarcity will emerge and therefore give rise to a traded market. Those that emit less than their allowances will be able to sell the excess on the market, while those who emit more will need to either buy units from the market or invest in technology that will reduce their emissions. Although the allowances are only allocated to plants that are covered by the scheme, they can be held by anyone (e.g. investment banks) to facilitate the emergence of a traded market.

By 31 March in each year, installations subject to emissions targets must submit a report that verifies how much they emitted in the previous year. By the end of the following month the installations must surrender allowances equal to the amount they emitted during the previous year. These allowances are then cancelled and cannot be used again. Installations that do not have enough allowances to cover their emissions will be fined €40 per tonne of CO_2e and must cut emissions in the following year by an amount equal to the excess. In the second phase of the scheme it is envisioned that the penalties for failing to meet this targets will rise to €100 per tonne of CO_2e.

10.6.3 Registries and logs

For a trading mechanism to become effective there is a need to document compliance and, as such, national registries have emerged to fulfil this role. The registry will typically record:

- CO_2 allowances and units that are allocated to and held in accounts for eligible installations;
- annual verified installation emissions;
- the movement of allowances to and from accounts;
- annual compliance status of installations.

In the EU these will be consolidated at a regional level into the Community Independent Transaction Log, which will extract information from different national registries such as the Environment Agency in the UK, which will administer the UK registry. These national and regional logs will eventually be consolidated at the international level with the establishment of an International Transaction Log expected in mid-2007.

10.6.4   National Allocation Plans (NAPs)

A NAP outlines the total volume of allowances to be allocated for a given multi-year period. This is split down into annual figures and details the allocation to each sector and installation. The key points of the UK NAP for the period 2008–2012 [14] are:

- The UK will allocate 246,175,995 allowances per annum during the period amounting to a total of 1,230,879,990.
- Although this represents an increase in allowances from the first phase of the EU scheme, it can be accounted for by the fact that the scope of the second phase has widened.
- Large electricity producers will bear the brunt of the reduction in allowances against "business as usual" levels.
- Allowances will be allocated at the sector level and then between installations within the sector.
- The government will allow the use of project credits although there will be limitations on their usage.
- 7% of phase II allowances will be auctioned.
- A number of allowances will be set-aside in a "new entrant reserve" to be allocated free by to installations that commence or extend operations that fall within the scope the scheme.

10.7   EMISSION DERIVATIVES

In their annual *State and Trends of the Carbon Market*, the World Bank [15] estimated that, overall, the monetary value of the global aggregated carbon markets was over USD 10 billion in 2005. By the end of the third quarter of 2006, they estimated that the value had increased to nearly USD 21.5 billion. In volume terms, the market traded 324.31 million tonnes of CO_2 (MMtCO$_2$e) equivalent in 2005, rising to 763.90 MMtCO$_2$e by the third quarter of 2006.

Within the allowance market, which, by the third quarter of 2006, was estimated at just over USD 19 billion, the vast majority of activity was attributed to the EU ETS (USD 18.8 billion). The report identified three other markets for trading allowances in operation:

- New South Wales market in Australia

- Chicago Climate Exchange – a voluntary but legally binding scheme in North America.
- The UK ETS, launched in 2002 prior to the EU scheme.

There is also the prospect of markets in other areas, particularly in the USA where, although there is little political will at the national level, there are a number of regional schemes willing to support the Kyoto principles. These include:

- The Regional Greenhouse Gas Initiative, due to become effective in January 2009 and will be run by seven states in the North East region of the USA.
- In the US Western States there are plans to start a market in 2011 that will encompass California and Oregon.

Whereas EUAs can only be used by corporates within the EU ETS, CERs are a global carbon currency that are fully bankable and can be used across time lines by corporates and governments. The market for project-based transactions, estimated by the World Bank at USD 2.4 billion by the third quarter of 2006, was dominated by activity in the Clean Development Mechanism. The report notes that over the period 2003 to 2006:

- About two-thirds of the purchased CDM and JI credits have been made by European entities.
- Japan has accounted for approximately one-third of all purchases.
- Private buyers tend to predominate rather than governments.
- The sales of credits have mostly originated from China and India.
- Many of the CDM projects have been designed to capture HFC, which is an industrial gas significantly more potent than carbon dioxide.

Although CDMs have been created and sold they cannot be used to offset carbon emissions until the Kyoto period starting in 2008. They have tended to trade at a discount to allowances of about 25% as a result of the uncertainty regarding the extent of their usage. Equally, since many projects may have long payback periods, companies have been wary of investing if there are uncertainties as to whether the credits will be recognised after the Kyoto period.

Transaction examples

The market for EUAs comprises a number of different instruments:

- Spot and forward transactions, which are both physically settled
- Financially settled swaps
- Investment products.

EUAs can be sold on a spot basis with delivery occurring 2 days after trade date and payment made usually 5 days after delivery.

By convention, the EUA forward market has adopted a single annual settlement date of 1 December in any particular year. The selection of this settlement date was, to an extent, somewhat arbitrary but is logical in that compliance is an annual end-of-year requirement. There would be little need to buy an allowance in January and hold it for the remaining part of the year, as this would simply create an additional financing cost. However, since the commodity is 100% fungible, the cost of an EUA for settlement between two different years in the same compliance period could be accounted for using standard forward pricing techniques.

Assume that the forward price for delivery in December 2008 is trading at €20 and that 12-month Euribor is 5%. All other things being equal, the December 2009 contract should trade at €21.0139. The difference between the two contracts of €1.0139 can be accounted for by the time value of money principles. So if one were to buy the December 2008 contract and hold it for one year, one would have to borrow the purchase price at current interest rates, incurring a charge over the year of €1.0139 (€20 × 5% × 365/360).

Although the EUAs can be used to meet compliance with the emission targets, traders will also be looking for opportunities to execute transactions. Some simple trading strategies might include the following:

- *Identifying a mispriced contract*: Say, for example, a trader believed that a 2009 contract was not trading at its "fair value" and was considered expensive. The trader could buy a 2008 contract and sell the 2009 contract forward. This is called "buying the 2008/2009 spread". The trade could then be closed-out when the trader believed that prices had come back into line. Alternatively, the trader could take delivery of the 2008 contract, finance the holding for a 12-month period and then use it to meet the commitment created by the sale of the 2009 allowance.
- *Geographic arbitrage*: If the price of an EUA is different in two geographical locations, a trader could buy and sell to exploit the differential.
- *Phase I/Phase II spreads*: This was a popular trade used to take views on the price differential between allowances in two different phases of the EU scheme. If a trader believed that the spread between the two contracts was mispriced, he could initiate a strategy that would involve the purchase of the contract that was considered to be underpriced and the sale of the one believed to be overpriced.
- *EUA/CER spread*: CERs are quoted and traded as a percentage of EUAs. Spread trades can be initiated if a trader believes that the percentage discount to the EUA is fundamentally justified. For example, if the trader believed that the percentage is too high (i.e. CERs are too expensive to some notion of "fair value") the trader would sell the CER and buy the EUA.

Trades are executed on a standardised number of allowances: 10,000, 25,000, 50,000 and 100,000 being typical. So a hypothetical term sheet for a forward deal may appear as:

Seller	Bank A
Buyer	Company B
Allowance type	EU Allowance
Trade date	March 2007
Compliance period	2008–2012
Number of allowances	25,000
Purchase price	€14.00
Total purchase price	€350,000
Delivery date	1 December 2008
Settlement	Physical

The transaction is physically settled in that it requires the crediting and debiting of an account at the applicable registry.

An extension of the physically settled spot and forward transactions is a process known as "inventory monetisation"; it is also sometimes referred to as asset-backed financing. Under the terms of this transaction, a corporate can use its inventory of EUAs to borrow money at an attractive rate. This is an instrument that has been used in a number of different financial and commodity markets for many years.

Under the terms of the deal two separate transactions will be executed simultaneously as a single package. The first deal is a spot transaction where the corporate sells its inventory of allowances to the investment bank. Under the terms of the second deal, the corporate agrees to buy the back the same volume of allowances for forward delivery. The prices at which the two transactions are executed are determined using the time value of money principles. Assuming that a corporate decides to use this mechanism to borrow money for a one-year period for a holding of 1 million allowances, a trader at the investment bank calculates that the 12-month forward price of the contract is €15, meaning that, the amount the corporate will have to repay at the end of the period will be €15,000,000. The amount that the corporate can therefore borrow at the start of the period is simply the present value of this sum. The trader sees that 12-month Euribor is at 5.00% and so decides to apply a margin of 0.50% to this rate. The present value of the forward proceeds is therefore €14,173,693, which is calculated as €15,000,000/(1 + 0.0575 × 365/360). The impact of the deal is that the corporate is effectively borrowing at a rate of 12-month Euribor plus 0.50%.

This trade would be advantageous to the corporate if it normally borrows money at a rate greater than 0.50% over 12-month Euribor. The profit to the bank depends on the strength of its balance sheet. To be able to finance the loan to the corporate, the bank will have to borrow in the money markets and if it can achieve this at, say, Euribor without any spread, it will also be able to profit.

Emission swaps are financial in nature because they are cash settled. They are only effective for one day and will involve an exchange of cashflows fixed for floating. In some respects they are similar to the single day contracts for difference that are popular in the equity markets.

An indicative set of terms is shown below:

Trade date	March 2007
Effective date	1 December 2008
Termination date	1 December 2008
Pricing date	1 November 2008
Delivery date	1 December 2008
Commodity	EU Allowance
Total notional quantity	25,000
Fixed rate payer	Company A
Fixed price	€14.00
Floating price payer	Bank
Reference price	LEBA–Carbon–Index on the designated pricing date for the relevant delivery date. Reference price source reported on Telerate
Settlement	Cash

A swap contract would be useful if a participant wanted price protection but did not require physical delivery. Equally, the contract would be useful for those participants who wished to express a view on the movement of allowance prices. It is financially settled, as it does not require ownership of an allowance to be transferred. The participants agree a cash settlement amount based on the difference between two prices.

In early 2007 contracts for delivery in December 2007 swap contracts were trading at less than €1.00 per allowance, reflecting the belief that the first phase of the EU market was oversupplied. Since allowances could not be "banked" for use in the second phase, their price was expected to decline towards zero.

There is also a market in CERs, which are classified as being primary or secondary. A primary CER is a credit expected from a CDM project, but has yet to be issued. A secondary CER is a credit that has been issued and traded. Secondary CERs are priced off EUAs for the same maturity but trade at a slight premium to primary CERs. Essentially, a trader will discount the price of an EUA for a particular delivery by an amount that reflects the perception of the risks associated with the CER. As a rule of thumb, CERs tend to trade in range of 75–90% of the price of EUAs.

CERs tend to trade at a discount to the EUA for a variety of reasons:

- *Delivery risk*: As of the time of writing (early 2007) the International Transaction Log (ITL) had not become fully operational. This will eventually link the central registry for recording CDMs with the registries in each individual country. As a result, all CERs that have so far been created are sitting in a temporary holding account in the CDM registry and cannot be transferred out to an account in the respective national registry.
- *Kyoto eligibility criteria*: Although the Kyoto Protocol established a reduction in emissions from 1990 levels, no AAUs have actually been granted, as no one is sure exactly how much carbon dioxide was being emitted in 1990. As a result, CERs cannot be transferred from one country to another.
- *Credit risk*: CERs are granted annually from certified projects but if the installation that was the focus of the project goes out of business, no subsequent CERs will be issued.
- *Limitation on usage*: Each country has a cap on the proportion of compliance that can be met by the use of CERs. In the UK this has been set at 10%.

Forward CER transactions will resemble the form outlined in the previous EUA example. However, the allowance type is defined as an eligible CER but includes a provision entitled "delayed delivery". This reflects the fact that (as of early 2007) with the ITL non-operational it was not possible to deliver CERs into the respective registries. Delayed delivery effectively postpones the delivery of the credit until these operational issues have been resolved.

Structured swaps have also evolved to allow participants to benefit from the spread that exists between CERs and EUAs. For example, a corporate could enter into a swap where it can exploit the difference between the relatively higher price that was paid for EUAs and the price of a lower CER. This swap would allow the corporate to meet its emissions targets by using CERs up to the allowable limit but also receive a cash payment. The terms of this "phase two strip" deal would appear as:

EUA buyer	Investment bank
EUA seller	Corporate
CER buyer	Corporate
CER seller	Investment bank
Volume/Notional	Y tonnes

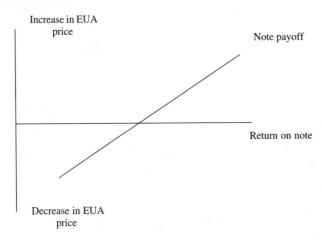

Figure 10.1 Payoff from CER or EUA note

Delivery dates	1 December annually from 2008 to 2012 inclusive
Price	Agreed at outset, fixed for entire deal
Payment date	5 days after delivery

There are two different ways in which the bank could quote the price of the transaction:

- Five bids on the EUAs and five offers on the CERs (one bid–offer spread for each individual year).
- One bid price for the EUAs and one offer for the CERs (one single bid–offer spread applicable to each year).

The typical volume per annum would be equal to the counterparty's annual limit of CERs that he can use. On each of the due delivery dates, EUAs and CERs would be electronically transferred into the other party's registry account. Barclays would then make a payment 5 days after the receipt of EUAs. This payment would be the difference between the agreed price differential of the EUAs and the CERs.

With the prospect of the second phase of the EU ETS being overall short of allowances, there is an expectation that the demand for allowances will exert upward pressure on prices. As a result, some simple investment packages emerged to allow investors access to the market, without the need to physically hold the allowance.

In their original form the structures have a linear payoff (sometimes referred to as a "delta one exposure") that was not capital protected. Diagrammatically, the payoff from the structure would be as shown in Figure 10.1.

The instrument would be, say, a 5-year structure based on phase II allowances that will pay off on the basis of the difference between the price of EUAs at the start of the period and the price of EUAs at maturity.

11
Agricultural Commodities and Biofuels

A change in supply typically means a short-term change in price, but a change in demand typically means a change in the long term price.

Futures magazine (November 2006)

SYNOPSIS **The purpose of the chapter is to describe a number of "soft" agricultural markets and how they are being increasingly used to produce ethanol. A number of exchange traded and OTC derivative structures are also detailed.**[*]

Over the years a substantial amount of literature has been produced about agricultural products and their associated derivatives. Traditionally they focused on the use of:

- Exchange-traded futures for personal investment or speculation
- Derivatives for the hedging of a direct exposure to the change in agricultural prices.

This chapter aims to review some of the *"soft" agricultural markets* and then show how they are evolving as a result of the increased demand for alternative fuel sources such as *ethanol*.

   The chapter concludes with an overview of the main *exchange-traded and over-the-counter derivatives*.

   Readers interested in the application of futures to hedge a pure agricultural exposure on this type of focus are referred to the different commodity exchanges, such as the Chicago Board of Trade. In addition, many of the structures already considered within this book could be adapted for the agricultural market.

11.1 AGRICULTURAL MARKETS

11.1.1 Physical supply chain

The physical supply chain for grains such as corn and wheat would typically start with private farmers who would grow the crop. They would store this temporarily in their own silos before selling it to a larger commercial entity referred to generically as a grain elevator (even though, strictly speaking, a grain elevator is a term used to describe a building used to store grain before onward shipment). These larger commercial entities would include companies such as Cargill who would then sell the grain to a food producer, who would convert the commodity into a product that could be consumed by an end user.

---

[*]Unless otherwise referenced, the data in this chapter has been sourced from the *Commodity Refiner*, published in the fourth quarter of 2006 by Barclays Capital.

11.1.2 Sugar

Global sugar production of sugar for 2006–2007 has been estimated at 149 million tonnes, while consumption for the same period was approximated at 148 million tonnes. Unlike the other two grains to be analysed in this chapter, consumption has not significantly exceeded production in recent times and stock levels have been fairly stable.

The main producer of sugar is Brazil, accounting for about 20% of global volumes. This has increased substantially from about 1986/87, when it accounted for 8% of global production. The second largest producer is India (15%) followed by the EU (12%) and China (7%). In terms of exports, Brazil accounts for 41% of the world's total raw and refined sugar trade.

The largest consumers are, by region, India accounting for 14% with Asia (excluding China) accounting for 18%, followed by the EU and Latin America (both 12%).

11.1.3 Wheat

There are a number of varieties of wheat, but its main use is in the production of flour, which is then used in foods such as bread and pasta. Global production of wheat for 2006–2007 has been estimated at 585 million tonnes, while consumption for the same period has been estimated at 613 million tonnes. Consumption has exceeded production in five of the last six years pushing inventories down by 41% in the same period. These stockpiles are at their lowest levels since the early 1980s [1].

In terms of production by region, the EU accounts for 20% of the global total. The second largest producer is China at 18%, followed by India (12%), United States (9%) and Russia (7%).

In term of consumption by country, the single biggest consumer of wheat is China, which accounts for 16% of the global total. From a regional perspective the EU consumes 19% of all wheat. India accounts for 12% of all global consumption while the figure for the USA is 5%.

11.1.4 Corn

Traditionally corn (sometimes referred to as maize) has been used as a feed for livestock. However, it does have applications for human consumption such as sweeteners for soft drinks, but with the increase in the price of oil, farmers have been tempted to direct their output towards the production of ethanol.

Global production of corn for 2006–2007 has been estimated at 689 million tonnes, while consumption for the same period has been estimated at 724.1 million tonnes. Similar to wheat, consumption has exceeded production in five of the last six years pushing inventories down by nearly the same margin (i.e. 40%).

The largest producer of corn is the USA, which accounts for about 41% of the global total. China is the second largest producer, accounting for 20% of the total, with the next largest being Brazil and the EU (both 6%).

The United States consumes about 33% of global production, while the respective values for China, the EU and Brazil account for 20%, 7% and 6%. The USA is also the world's largest exporter of corn, making up 70% of the total volume.

Corn used for ethanol production in the USA has risen strongly from a level of 1% in 1980 to 22% in 2006. This percentage is expected to increase as new ethanol facilities are built.

11.2   ETHANOL

If you look at the ethanol landscape worldwide, the US and Brazil are like Kuwait and Saudi Arabia.
Fabrizio Vichichi (*Financial Times*, 26 January 2006)

11.2.1   What is ethanol?

Ethanol has the simplest chemical structure of the hydrocarbons within the family of alcohols. In chemistry alcohol is used to describe a hydrocarbon with an —OH group attached to a carbon atom. Ethanol is just one of many alcohols, although the words are sometimes incorrectly and interchangeably used in the media.

When ethanol is produced for fuel, the goal is to maximise the strength and minimise the impurities. As a result, the primary production inputs such as corn and sugar cane are chosen for their ease of cultivation and their high carbohydrate levels.

Initially the corn or other crop is mashed and then heated to destroy any bacteria or other microorganism that may interfere with fermentation. The mash is then cooled and yeast is added. The yeast feed on the mash, releasing carbon dioxide and ethanol. Since carbon dioxide is a gas, it bubbles out of the fermenting mash leaving the ethanol behind. At this stage the ethanol contains many impurities which, along with any water, are removed by distillation. Any remaining impurities are removed by using a molecular sieve.

Proponents of ethanol produced from sugar cane argue that when used as a fuel it is environmentally friendly; the carbon dioxide produced from burning it is neutralised by the carbon dioxide absorbed by plants while it is being grown. However, counter-arguments point out that the increased demand for sugar cane in Brazil may encourage production to expand into environmentally sensitive areas such as the Amazon. Critics also argue that some of the current technology used to produce ethanol requires a substantial power input, which may offset any perceived environmental benefits.

Attention has now turned to "cellulosic" ethanol, which uses a variety of other materials such as waste plant material to produce the ethanol, without as many side effects.

World production for ethanol was estimated at 10.7 billion gallons in 2004 and had risen to 12.1 billion gallons by 2006 [2].

11.2.2   History of ethanol

Arguably the first significant use of ethanol as a biofuel was in Brazil in the 1970s. At the time Brazil imported 90% of its crude oil, so the government acted to reduce the impact of rising prices [3]. Through a series of subsidies to sugar mills, ethanol was promoted as an alternative fuel source. By the 1980s new car production was focused almost exclusively on cars that ran purely on ethanol. However, this first boom was short lived as a result of a combination of factors:

• The country struggled to produce sufficient sugar cane to meet demand.

- The government lifted price controls on the price of the fuel at the pumps, leading to an increase in price.
- The vehicles had a mediocre performance.
- An increase in the global price of sugar encouraged producers to switch back to using the raw material to make refined sugar.
- The subsequent price collapse of crude oil made gasoline relatively attractive.

However, in 2003 the country introduced "flex-fuel" cars, which operated either on ethanol or petrol or a mixture of the two fuels. By 2006 estimates suggested that 50% to 75% of all domestic new car sales were of the "flex-fuel" variety and that about half of the country's sugar cane crop was being used for domestic ethanol production [4]. As a result of their knowledge and experience gained in the 1970s and also the relatively low-cost nature of their ethanol operations, Brazil has become known as the "Saudi Arabia of biofuel".

In the USA, ethanol is mainly produced from corn. Currently, to make it competitive with gasoline, users enjoy some degree of tax relief, which is due to finish in 2010. In addition to consumption subsidies, farmers receive government funding to encourage production. Since 1980 US ethanol producers have enjoyed protection from Brazilian ethanol by way of an import tariff of 54 cents a gallon. As the demand for ethanol has increased there has been increased investment in production facilities. These additional production facilities were expected to increase US output by 2.6 billion gallons a year, raising total output to about 7 billion gallons by mid-2007 [5].

The demand for ethanol in the USA was boosted when the government banned the gasoline additive MBTE (methyl tertbutyl ether) for environmental reasons. As a substitute, ethanol is now added to gasoline to a maximum concentration of about 10%. Beyond this level most normal internal combustion engines experience operating difficulties unless they have been specially converted.

In Europe ethanol is produced from wheat, barley and rye and, similar to the USA, producers enjoy the benefit of an import tariff. About 1 million tonne of wheat was used to make ethanol in Europe in 2005 but this is expected to increase eight-fold by 2009 [6].

One of the main stumbling blocks to the global usage of ethanol as a source of fuel for transport is the cost of developing a retail distribution network. Additionally, questions have been raised about how feasible it would actually be to produce ethanol in sufficient quantities to replace the current reliance on gasoline as the amount of land required to produce sufficient quantities would be enormous. This could influence the amount of land dedicated to grow corn and feed, which would impact other parts of the food supply chain.

One side effect of this increase in demand for ethanol was the usage of futures at the Chicago Board of Trade (CBOT) as a mechanism to obtain physical supplies of the commodity. Whereas only about 1% of all futures contracts normally go to delivery, in mid-April 2006, 70% of all expiring contracts were physically settled [7].

11.3 PRICE DRIVERS

11.3.1 Weather

A strong harvest will increase the amount of the product coming to the market. In this respect the key factor is weather. A very hot summer – or indeed a very cold one – may have an adverse effect on the size of the harvest.

11.3.2   Substitution

Following the sharp rise in energy prices during the early part of the century, the interest in ethanol had a subsequent effect on the demand for its primary production inputs, which include sugar, corn and soybean. The demand for ethanol produced from corn is believed to be economical using current technology when crude oil is trading at about USD 60 a barrel.

A related biofuel is biodiesel, which can be produced from renewable resources such as soybean or palm oil. Biodiesel has a number of advantages that makes it attractive [8]:

- It can be used in existing diesel engines.
- It can be blended with normal diesel.
- It is environmentally very friendly, emitting a lower amount of carbon than conventional fuels.

11.3.3   Investor activity

With the growing interest in ethanol, large flows of speculative money have moved into the futures market driving up prices, which, all other things being equal, should exert upward pressure on the spot price. With the general increase in investor interest in commodity indices such as the S&P GSCI®, the "rolling" of the index's constituent futures (see Chapter 12) will influence the shape of the forward curve.

11.3.4   Current levels of inventory

The level of stockpiles is an indication of the balance between demand and supply and as such will have an impact on price.

11.3.5   Protectionism

Inevitably when considering the nature of agricultural commodities the issue of tariffs and subsidies will arise. Subsidies will have an effect on where and how much is produced, while import tariffs may be designed to protect a domestic industry for social or political reasons. For example, acreage switching due to differing grain subsidies is a factor monitored by some traders.

Subsidies to farming usually take the form of either an income supplement or a minimum price guarantee, and this has led to international trade disputes such as that seen between the USA and Europe. The EU has long operated a Common Agricultural Policy to support its farmers and has used a number of trade barriers to minimise the competition faced by domestic suppliers.

11.3.6   Health

The demand for certain soft commodities such as sugar may also be affected by a growing awareness of a number of health-related issues. For example, a change in the way that food is packaged may result in a change in dietary habits if the amount of sugar is made more visible. Additionally, the development of sugar substitutes may result in a fall in demand.

11.3.7   Industrialising countries

No commodity price analysis would be complete without some mention of India and China. As both countries continue to urbanise, it is likely that diets will evolve to include more processed foods with higher sugar content and more protein; and this should lead to an increase in the demand for corn as a feed for livestock.

11.3.8   Elasticity of supply

In the energy and metals chapters it was noted that the supply side responses to an increase in demand showed that additional production could not be immediate owing to the time needed to construct the required infrastructure. However, with respect to the agricultural sector the response time is determined by the relatively short period it takes to plant and harvest a particular product.

11.3.9   Genetic modification

Genetically modified crops are now very common and result in greater crop yields and more effective resilience to disease. However, not all areas of the world (e.g. the EU) will accept such grains.

11.4   EXCHANGE-TRADED AGRICULTURAL AND ETHANOL DERIVATIVES

There a number of competing exchange-traded agricultural futures contracts and a sample of three traded on the Chicago Board of Trade (CBOT) are listed in Table 11.1. The exchange publishes a substantial amount of literature covering many aspects of their use, which is available from their website (www.cbot.com).

Although there are many different "species" of wheat, the USA produces six different types:

- Hard Red Winter
- Hard Red Spring
- Soft Red Winter
- Durum
- Hard White
- Soft White

The spring/winter classification relates to when they are planted with most of the production being based in the mid-west and eastern states.

Among the different uses of corn in the USA, yellow corn is used as a feedstock and for the production of starches.

Table 11.1 Futures contract specification for corn, wheat and ethanol

	Corn	Wheat	Ethanol
Contract size	5,000 bushels	5,000 bushels	29,000 US gallons (approximately one rail car)
Deliverable grades	No. 2 yellow at par, no. 1 yellow at $1\frac{1}{2}$ cents per bushel over contract price, no. 3 yellow at $1\frac{1}{2}$ cents per bushel under contract price	No. 2 soft red winter, no. 2 hard red winter, no. 2 dark northern spring and no. 2 northern spring at par; no. 1 soft red winter, no. 1 hard red winter, no. 1 dark northern spring and no. 1 northern spring at 3 cents per bushel over contract price	Denatured fuel ethanol as specified in the American Society for Testing and Materials Standard D4806 for denatured fuel ethanol for blending with gasolines for use as an automotive spark ignition engine fuel plus California standards
Tick size	$\frac{1}{4}$ cent per bushel (USD 12.50 per contract)	$\frac{1}{4}$ cent per bushel (USD 12.50 per contract)	One-tenth of 1 cent ($0.001) per gallon (USD 29 per contract)
Price quote	Cents per bushel	Cents per bushel	Dollars and cents per gallon
Contract months	December, March, May, July, September	December, March, May, July, September	All calendar months
Last trading day	The business day prior to the 15th calendar day of the contract month	The business day prior to the 15th calendar day of the contract month	The 3rd business day of the delivery month
Last delivery day	Second business day following the last trading day of the delivery month	Seventh business day following the last trading day of the delivery month	Second business day following the last trading day of the delivery month

Source: Chicago Board of Trade.

11.5 OVER-THE-COUNTER AGRICULTURAL DERIVATIVES

OTC contracts such as swaps exist for agricultural products such as wheat, corn and sugar. Ethanol contracts have been slow to emerge and are still relatively illiquid. Similar to examples in previous chapters, they can be used for a number of reasons that include:

- Transforming an underlying price exposure from floating to fixed or vice versa.
- Taking a directional view on the price of the commodity without having to take physical delivery.

The swap may cover a single period in the future with the exchange of cashflows being based on the classic "fixed for floating" model. A hypothetical term sheet may appear as:

Commodity	Corn
Trade date	August 2007
Effective date	1 November 2008
Termination date	30 November 2008
Notional amount	700,000 bushels
Fixed price payer	Counterparty
Fixed price	USD 3.5000 per bushel
Floating price payer	Barclays
Reference price	Corn–CBOT; the arithmetic average of the daily settlement price of the first nearby month futures contract over the period of the swap

OTC swap contracts for wheat will be very similar in structure and also settle against the Chicago Board of Trade price. This is a similar situation to the base metals market, where commercial contracts are linked to the LME price. This allows the hedger to ensure that the price on which the physical contact is based is the same as that used for the applicable hedging instrument. The issue of basis risk was covered in Chapter 5 (crude oil) and Chapter 8 (plastics).

Options on agricultural products are well established and readers interested in different structures are referred to the examples documented in Chapter 3 (gold) and Chapter 4 (base metals).

12
Commodities Within an Investment Portfolio

Empirical evidence has shown that commodities as an asset class add significantly to the diversification within a portfolio given their negative correlation with financial assets.

SYNOPSIS **The purpose of this chapter is to outline the role of commodities within an investment portfolio**.

This chapter will be of interest to those who:

- wish to invest in the asset class but are unsure of how the different instruments work;
- are already invested in commodities but would like to deepen their understanding of the market and raise their awareness of other investment opportunities;
- are employed on the "sell side" of the financial sector and wish to further their understanding of the suite of products being sold to the investment community.

The chapter begins by defining the main *investor types* and then outlines *the principal benefits of investing in commodities*. The discussion develops the relative merits of the types of commodity exposure. A significant amount of money invested in the market is referenced to *commodity indices*. The sources of the index returns, such as the roll yield, are analysed. The most common method of taking exposure to a commodity index is by use of a *total return swap* and the chapter includes a fully-worked example.

As the investment community has become more confident in the "vanilla" mechanisms of commodity investment, the range of *structured investments* has widened. A number of structures are presented, and, where possible, decomposed into their constituent parts. The chapter concludes by presenting *a framework for analysing commodity investments*.

The chapter does not include details of a number of popular "view-driven" option strategies such as straddles and strangles as they are not unique to commodities and have been extensively documented in other texts. The interested reader is referred to the bibliography for further details.

12.1 INVESTOR PROFILE

The range of potential commodity investors is broad and includes:

- *Retail sector*: The most popular choice of instrument would either be a mutual fund/unit trust or an exchange-traded fund (ETF).
- *Real money accounts*: This sector encompasses institutional investors (e.g. mutual fund/ unit trust fund managers, insurance companies and pension funds) who have restrictions on their ability to borrow. Their investment activities are longer term in nature and are characterised as being one of "buy and hold".
- *Commodity Trading Advisers*: These investors typically use futures to gain exposure to a particular sector of the commodities market. Their investment activities may not be restricted to just commodities and may include exposures in other asset classes.

- *Hedge funds*: These are also sometimes referred to as "leveraged" accounts as they typically are allowed to borrow in order to finance their activities.
- *Investment banks*: Although perhaps more associated with shorter-term trading activities, any position they hold implies that they are managing a portfolio.

12.2   BENEFITS OF COMMODITIES WITHIN A PORTFOLIO

12.2.1   Return enhancement and diversification

Over a 35.5-year period commodities have generated returns greater than those offered by traditional financial assets (see Table 12.1) although they do display a greater degree of price variability.

Table 12.1   Correlation coefficients between different financial assets; January 1970 – June 2005

	S&P TR	S&P GSCI® TR	JPM US GB	US 3M T-Bill
Return	11.12%	12.30%	8.06%	6.41%
Volatility	16.84%	19.75%	9.61%	1.58%
Sharpe ratio	0.279	0.309	0.162	–

Key:
- S&P TR = Standard and Poors GSCI total return index.
- S&P GSCI® TR = Goldman Sachs Commodity Index total return.
- JPM US GB = JP Morgan Government Bond total return index. (Figures for volatility and return are annualised.)
- Sharpe ratio: a measure that relates the return on an asset over and above the return on a risk free asset, relative to its risk (i.e. its standard deviation) of the asset

Source: Barclays Capital.

One of the main benefits of commodities is that they are negatively correlated with financial assets and therefore act as a powerful portfolio diversifier. Over the same 35.5-year period the correlation coefficients between commodities and the financial assets listed in Table 12.1 were:

Equities	−0.28
Bonds	−0.10
Treasury Bills	−0.01

12.2.2   Asset allocation

Barclays Capital tried to determine the optimal allocation of commodities within a portfolio [1]. Using standard portfolio optimisation techniques it considered the impact of adding commodities on a pro-rata basis to a balanced portfolio comprising 45% equities, 45% fixed income and 10% cash. It concluded that an allocation of 25% in commodities yielded the highest Sharpe ratio. The model portfolio consisted of 25% commodities, 34% equities, 34% bonds and 7% cash.

This allocation was then back-tested to 1970 against the non-commodity portfolio (i.e. the 45/45/10 portfolio allocation) and the results indicated that the commodity-based portfolio yielded a higher absolute return over the period.

12.2.3   Inflation hedge

Research by Barclays Capital confirmed the perception that commodities are positively correlated with inflation [1]. However, this is not surprising as many inflation indices have a commodity component.

12.2.4   Hedge against the US dollar

Commodities returns are negatively correlated with the value of the US dollar, as most are internationally denominated in USD. Since 1975 the correlation between the annual returns of the S&P GSCI® Total Return Index and the Federal Reserve US Dollar Index has been −0.30 [1].

12.3   METHODS OF INVESTING IN COMMODITIES

There are a number of ways in which one can invest in commodities, each of which has advantages and disadvantages. Thus, one could

- purchase a commodity generating or consuming asset (e.g. a power station);
- buy shares in companies whose business is commodity related (e.g. mining companies);
- buy the physical commodity;
- buy futures;
- enter into total return swaps;
- buy structured OTC transactions.

However, one of the main attractions of derivatives is that is possible to take a bearish view on a commodity without actually selling the underlying asset. For example, selling futures or paying the return on a total return swap would achieve this result.

12.3.1   Advantages and disadvantages

An investor may be motivated to purchase a large generating or consuming asset but this would require him to devote considerable time to its management.

Some investors may choose to buy equities in companies that operate along the physical supply chain. As a result they will not be taking a pure commodity exposure and may be taking on non-commodity risks, such as the market's perception of the company's management.

Buying the physical commodity may be difficult for many investors, as the issue of storage will need to be considered. Equally there will be an upfront outlay of cash, which will have to be financed.

Futures offer an advantage over the physical commodity, as the investor will only be required to finance the initial margin payment, which will be smaller than the outright cost of the commodity. However, since the contracts are typically denominated in USD, futures create a foreign exchange exposure to non-USD investors. Another advantage of futures is that it allows the investor to take a bearish view on a commodity by selling the future; something that may be difficult in the physical market. The investor will also be faced with the issue of selecting the appropriate maturity to trade. This gives rise to "curve risk", which is the risk that the forward curve may move in a particular way such that it may have an unanticipated effect on the value of a particular futures position. If the investor decides to trade in a future that is physically settled, he must also monitor his exposure to ensure that at maturity he does not make or take delivery.

As a result of the drawbacks of these different ways of investing, many are now turning to over-the-counter bespoke structures that will remove many of the logistical issues highlighted above. For example, the return to the investor can be paid in his domestic currency – a process referred to in the market jargon as "quantoing". However, OTC structures are not without risk; for example, if an investment is taken out with an entity with a poor credit rating, there is always the possibility that the counterparty will be unable to meet its obligations.

12.4 COMMODITY INDICES

Instead of linking the payout on an investment to a single commodity, a popular technique has been to link the payout on the instrument to a commodity index. Arguably the most popular index for investment purposes is the S&P GSCI® with anecdotal estimates [2] in 2006 suggesting values being benchmarked against it, ranging from USD 25 billion to USD 100 billion. The index was launched in 1991 and was the first major commodity index designed to meet investor demand for commodities as an asset class. Although the index includes a diverse range of commodities, there is a very large concentration in energy-related products (over 70%). The weights of the constituent commodities are determined annually by committee and driven by the US dollar value of global production over a 5-year period.

The return on the S&P GSCI® is based on futures, but since some investors may not be allowed to invest in leveraged structures, the returns are calculated in such a way that this effect is removed.

As a result, the S&P GSCI® represents an unleveraged long-only investment in commodity futures. Within the context of futures investing, leverage describes the ability to use a small amount of capital to control a much larger exposure. As an example, take a futures contract based on US crude oil (West Texas Intermediate). Buying one future requires the purchaser to take delivery of 1,000 barrels of crude at a fixed price. On 3 August 2006, the September 06 futures contract closed at a price of USD 75.46, implying that each contract had a monetary value of USD 75,460. According to NYMEX's website, the initial margin at that time was USD 4,725 for each contract. As a consequence the profits and losses on the futures contract will be magnified by a factor of 16 relative to the initial investment. This is calculated by dividing the contract value by the initial margin. This is an example of leverage.

The S&P GSCI® is actually composed of three indices, as follows:

- *Spot index*: This takes its value from price movements of the futures contracts included within the S&P GSCI®. To be able to replicate this exposure, an investor would have to buy the individual future contracts in the same proportion as the index.
- *Excess return index*: This incorporates the return on the spot index as well as any profit or loss obtained by "rolling" a hypothetical futures position as it approaches delivery. The value of this component reflects the fact that an investor who was replicating the return on the index by buying a futures contract would need to "roll" his exposure on an ongoing basis. Rolling the contract involves selling out of an existing long position as it approaches maturity and simultaneously buying whichever future is next to mature.

- *Total return index*: This incorporates the return on the excess return index as well as interest earned on a (hypothetical) fully collateralised contract position on all the commodity futures included within the S&P GSCI®.

We have seen that for every dollar invested in a futures contract the resultant exposure would be significantly larger. Using the WTI values presented earlier to create an unleveraged position, an investor would have to pay a sum equal to the value of the future's exposure (USD 75,460 in this case). However, since only USD 4,725 of initial margin is required, the index calculation assumes that the balance (USD 70,735) is placed in a risk-free investment such as US Treasury T-bills.

12.4.1 Explaining the roll yield

Most investors link their investment to the total return element of the S&P GSCI®. This means that the return will be based on three elements, namely:

- The change in price of the constituent futures
- The yield from rolling the future
- The yield on cash collateral in excess of the initial margin requirement.

In some respects the first and third elements of the return are easily understood. If futures prices rise and/or the yield on cash increases, an investor's return will rise. The roll yield arises from the possibility that certain commodities may experience prolonged periods of backwardation. To identify those commodities that are more prone to this type of price behaviour, it is convenient to group the main commodity markets under three headings:

- *Energy and industrial metals*: These markets are characterised by supply lags and are prone to tightness of supply.
- *Gold and precious metal*: In this case there are large above-ground stocks and, as such, any increase in demand can be met without unduly influencing the price of the metal.
- *Agricultural commodities*: The supply side can respond relatively quickly to any imbalances.

Overall the first category is more likely to experience backwardation, whereas it is less common in the second and third categories.

The generalised approach to pricing any forward contract irrespective of the asset class is expressed as [3]:

$$\text{Forward price} = \text{Spot price} + \text{Net carry}$$

From a commodity perspective, net carry is defined as:

$$\text{LIBOR} - \text{Convenience yield} + \text{Storage costs}$$

All other things being equal, if the only component of the relationship that changes is time itself, then the forward prices for a given maturity will converge towards the spot price.

As an example, assume that copper is trading at USD 7,790 per tonne for 3-month delivery while the spot price is USD 7,830. An investor could buy the future and, as a result of the passage of time, its price would rise to converge with the spot price, all other things being equal. If this were the case, at or very shortly before maturity, the future could be sold to generate a profit of USD 40 per tonne. The investor would retain an exposure to the copper market by simultaneously re-establishing a long position in the next 3-month contract, which, if the market is still in backwardation, will be at a lower price than the current spot price. If during the life of the future the spot price of copper rises, then this is an additional source of profitability. Equally, a fall in the spot price will reduce the profit on the position but the prices will continue to converge to provide a partial offsetting profit.

Rolling futures in a contango market will generate a negative yield, as the investor will be buying futures at a high price that will decline towards the prevailing spot price, all other things being equal.

12.5   TOTAL RETURN SWAPS

With a total return swap (TRS) the investor will receive a cashflow that takes its value from the movement of a particular index. In return, a variable cashflow will be paid that could be referenced to a variety of sources. If an investor wishes to express a bullish view on the commodity market, he will receive the index return. The TRS allows the investor to express a bearish return by paying the index return.

One of the features of a TRS is that the instrument does not require an initial outlay of cash. An instrument that does not require an upfront investment is sometimes referred to as being "unfunded". However, for investors who cannot enter into these types of note – as they technically represent a situation of infinite leverage – the notes are often designed as bond-like structures where the client is required to make an initial investment. In this case it would be termed a "funded" structure.

Sample termsheet

The following terms would be typical of a total return swap referenced to the S&P GSCI® commodity index.

Trade date	1 March 2006
Effective date	1 March 2006
Termination date	1 March 2007
Commodity index	S&P GSCI® total return index
Notional quantity	USD 100 million
Index amount payer	Bank
Calculation period	Monthly
Index amount	On each monthly payment date the index amount payer shall pay an amount calculated in accordance with the following formula:

$$\text{Notional quantity} \times \left(\frac{\text{Index}_m - \text{Index}_{m-1}}{\text{Index}_{\text{start}}} - \text{Fee} \right)$$

If the index amount is negative then the floating amount
payer shall pay to the index amount payer the absolute
value of the negative amount. For the purposes of
settlement m means the applicable index reset date in each
calculation period, which is defined as the first trading day
of each calendar month.

"$Index_m$" means the closing settlement price of the index for
the applicable index reset date; "$Index_{m-1}$" means the
closing settlement price of the index for the immediately
preceding index reset date; "$Index_{start}$" means 2922.42;
and "Fee" means 0.25% per annum (actual/365 basis) of
the notional amount, calculated over the actual number of
calendar days in each calculation period.

Floating payer   The client

Floating amount   On each monthly payment date the floating amount payer
shall pay an amount calculated in accordance with the
following formula:

$$ANQ \times \left[\prod_d \left(1 - \frac{91}{360} R_d \right)^{\left(\frac{-1}{91} \right)} - 1 \right]$$

where ANQ is the "adjusted notional quantity" determined
by the following expression:

$$\text{Notional Quantity} \times \left(\frac{Index_{m-1}}{Index_{start}} \right)$$

"R_d" means the T-bill Auction High Rate for day d; "d"
means each calendar day in the applicable calculation
period; and "T-bill Auction High Rate" on a particular day
means the auction high rate for 3-month US Treasury Bills
published on the most recent auction date prior to that
particular day.

Settlement of cashflows

The first period of the TRS covers 1 March 2006 to 3 April 2006 (1 April is a Saturday),
which is a period of 33 days. We will assume that the index at the end of the month is
2,955.33.

The cashflow referenced to the index is calculated as the percentage change in its value
less the agreed fee. The percentage increase in the index equates to a monetary payment of
USD 2,252,243. This is calculated as

$$USD \frac{200,000,000 \times (2,955.33 - 2,922.42)}{2,922.42}.$$

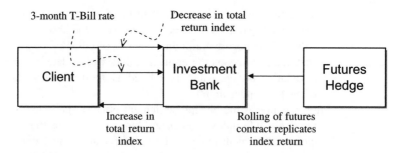

Figure 12.1   Total return swap

The agreed fee is 0.25% of the notional amount, which is equal to USD 45,205.48 (i.e, USD 200 million × 0.25% × 33/365). The total payable to the client under the index leg of the swap is therefore USD 2,207,037.52.

For ease of illustration let us assume that throughout the period the yield on the US Treasury Bills was 5.00%, which would make the floating payment equal to USD 924,639.57 (=USD 200,000,000 × 0.004623).

Where the payment dates for the two legs coincide, the market convention is to settle a net amount. The net amount payable to the client at the end of this period is therefore USD 1,327,603.

The total return swap is shown diagrammatically in Figure 12.1.

In the next period the cashflows will be calculated in a similar manner. Payments due under the floating side of the swap, however, will now be calculated on a different notional amount ("the adjusted notional quantity"). The notional amount is adjusted up or down by the change in the index relative to its original value. So the value for the second period would be USD 202,252,243 (=USD 200,000,000 × 2,955.33/2, 922.42). The rationale for adjusting the notional amount in this manner is to replicate the profits or losses that would be incurred if the investor had actually bought the underlying commodities.

The bank will hedge its exposure by entering into a series of trades in an attempt to replicate the return on the index. This is done by buying the relevant commodity futures in the proportion specified by the current weightings of the index. The total return swap incurs a cost of 0.25% to the client which, in effect, covers any hedging costs as well as providing a return.

The structure is not without risk to the client. A client who is receiving the index leg is exposed to a decline in its value and is also exposed to the credit risk of the structuring bank. Typically the structure is unsecured, so if the structuring bank were to default, the investor would no longer receive his cashflows.

There are a number of different ways in which the deal could be structured. For example, the swap could be in zero coupon form with only one set of cashflows being paid at maturity. Another alternative would be to link the index cashflows to the excess return component of the S&P GSCI® with the client only paying the hedge management fees.

12.6 STRUCTURED INVESTMENTS

12.6.1 Gold-linked notes

The gold-linked note can be structured to appeal to two different views on the direction of gold: bullish or bearish. Equally, investors who were unsure of the direction but believed that the gold price was likely to move significantly, could invest in both. In its original form it was targeted at high net worth individuals and therefore included a 100% capital guarantee.

The bullish part of the structure paid a fixed return of 5% (10.25% on an annualised basis) if the price of gold at the 6-month maturity point was 10% higher than the value at the start of the investment. The bearish element worked in a similar manner, as it would pay a fixed 5% return on the investment if the price of gold had declined by 10% from its original value.

The investor takes on two primary exposures. Firstly, he has a directional exposure to the price of gold and, secondly, an exposure to the implied volatility of gold due to the options embedded within the structure.

To achieve the capital guarantee, the investor's proceeds are used to buy a zero coupon bond that generates the required funds at maturity. As an alternative, the investor could use a cash deposit that repays an amount (principal plus interest) equal to the value of the initial investment.

To generate the fixed return of 5% on the investment, the difference between the investment proceeds and the cost of the zero coupon bond is used to buy European style OTM digital calls (for the bullish element) and European style OTM digital puts (for the bearish element). These digital options payout a fixed amount (in this case equal to 5% of the investment) if they are exercised at their expiry. Readers interested in understanding more on digital options are referred to Chapter 1.

12.6.2 Capital guaranteed structures

Capital guaranteed structures originally became popular in the equity market as a way of allowing the investor to participate in the upside of a particular index but with no loss of capital. This technology has been adapted for the commodities market and could be applied to single commodities, commodity indices or bespoke baskets.

Take, for example, a 5-year note linked to the S&P GSCI®. The return to the investor at maturity is expressed as:

$$\text{Notional} \times [100\% + \text{Participation rate} \times \max(0\%, \ \text{Index}_{\text{final}})]$$

where $\text{index}_{\text{final}} = P_{\text{final}} - P_{\text{initial}}$, in which

P_{initial} = commodity index value at inception and

P_{final} = commodity index at maturity.

This means that the investor will at least have his capital returned at maturity, plus a fixed percentage of any increase in the index (the participation rate). If the index falls below its initial value, the investor will have the initial value of his investment returned.

The note is constructed as follows. Let us say that the minimum investment is USD 100,000. The structuring institution deposits a sum of money today that will, on maturity, repay the initial investment. If we assume that a 5-year zero coupon investment yields 5%, the amount deposited today to earn USD100,000 in 5 years is USD 78,353 (i.e, $100,000/(1.05)^5$). The balance of the proceeds (USD 21,647) is then used to buy an index call option that will generate the upside return.

Let us assume that the S&P GSCI® is trading at 2,900 at inception and a 5-year option (assuming an implied volatility of 25%) on the index is priced at 497 index points. To "monetise" this option cost, a useful technique is to express the cost as a percentage of the current spot rate (which also happens to be the strike in this instance). This returns a value of 17.14%, which represents the percentage cost of the initial investment of an option whose payout is equal to 100% of any increase in the index. Applied to the investment proceeds, this gives an option cost of USD 17,140. Since the investor has USD 21,647 available to buy call options, this allows him to earn 126% (the participation rate) of the appreciation of the FTSE over the period (USD 21,647/USD 17,140).

From this analysis, it follows that the main determinants of the participation rate are zero coupon rates and implied volatility. If zero rates are high, the present value of the amount required to generate the principal will be lower, releasing more funds to buy call options. These options will be cheaper if implied volatility is low.

Since the investor is long a call option, his position is delta, gamma and vega positive. That is, the main source of an investor's profitability is an increase in (respectively):

- spot
- actual volatility
- implied volatility.

The participation rate can be increased using a number of different techniques. For example, the call option on the index could be replaced by a basket option, whose return is linked to a number of different commodities. In Chapter 4 on base metals, it was shown that the basket option would be cheaper due to the impact of correlation. This option, however, will give the investor an added exposure to correlation in addition to the delta and vega exposures. This correlation exposure is sometimes referred to as the "correlation vega" since the correlation value used to price the option will alter the value of the volatility input. Readers interested in the different techniques that could be used to alter the participation rate on capital guaranteed notes are referred to Kat (2001).

12.6.3 Combination structures

Half pipe copper note

Diagrammatically, the returns to the investor on this structure are shown in Figure 12.2. The note is structured with a capital guarantee so part of the investor's proceeds are placed on deposit for the maturity of the note such that the principal amount will be returned at maturity. The residual investment proceeds are then used to buy a package of options with

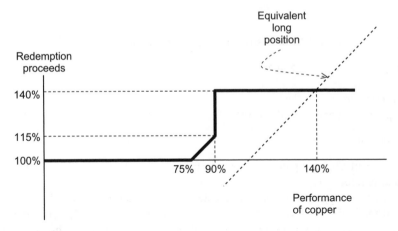

Figure 12.2 Half pipe copper note

100% participation, but whose strikes are set at a level to ensure that the residual proceeds are fully invested.

The final payoff to the investor is determined by the price of copper at maturity and is determined as follows:

- If the price of copper at maturity is less than or equal to 75% of its initial price, the investor will receive back 100% of his investment.
- If the price of copper at maturity is greater than 75% but less than 90% of its initial price, the investor will receive a payout according to the following formula:

$$\text{Notional} \times \left[100\% + \left(\frac{\text{Copper}_{\text{final}} - \text{Copper}_{\text{initial}}}{\text{Copper}_{\text{initial}}} \right) \right]$$

where $\text{Copper}_{\text{final}}$ = price of copper at maturity
$\text{Copper}_{\text{initial}}$ = price of copper at inception.

- If the price of copper at maturity is greater than or equal to 90% of its initial price the investor will receive back 140% of his investment.

The payoff on this structure can be replicated by the combination of the following options:

- The purchase of a call option with a strike set at 75% of the spot price at inception.
- The purchase of a digital call option with a strike set at 90% of the spot price at inception.
- The sale of a call option with a strike set at 90% of the spot price at inception.

The maximum payoff on the instrument is set at a level such that the net cashflow to the investor will be 40% of his investment. Buying a call at a strike of 75% and selling a call at 90% of the strike will result in a 15% profit if both options are exercised. With the payoff on the digital option set at 25% of its strike, the maximum payoff of 40% can be achieved.

Since there is a limit to the profit that the customer could earn, it would not be the most effective strategy for investors who were very bullish on the prospects for the market. From Figure 12.2 two it can be seen that if the price of copper at maturity were in excess of 140% of the initial spot price, the investor would have been better holding the underlying metal.

Bonus note

A hypothetical termsheet for this structure might appear as:

Maturity	5 years
Underlying	Copper
Annual coupons	None
Initial price of copper	USD 6,500

Redemption value:

- If the price of copper at maturity is less than its initial price, 100% of the investor's principal is refunded,
- If the price of copper at maturity is greater than or equal to its initial price but below 125% of the initial price (i.e. USD 8,125), the investor receives 125% of his principal.
- If the price of copper at maturity is greater than or equal to 125% of its initial value, the investor's payoff will be:

$$\text{Principal amount} \times \max (\text{Copper}_{\text{final}}, 150\%)$$

where $\text{Copper}_{\text{final}} = $ Initial copper price/Final copper price.

The return to the investor is shown diagrammatically in Figure 12.3.

The capital guarantee is generated by a zero coupon bond structure or a simple deposit with the principal plus interest repaying the original investment proceeds. Similar to the structures already discussed, the remaining balance is then invested in a package of options. The option structures that replicate this payoff are:

- The purchase of an ATM spot digital call option with a cash settlement at maturity equal to 25% of the strike price.
- The purchase of an OTM European call option with the strike set at 125% of the initial spot price.
- The sale of an OTM European call option with the strike set at 150% of the initial spot price.

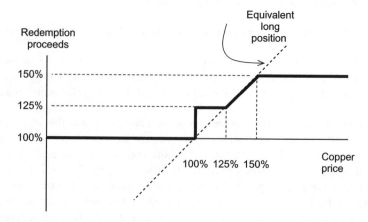

Figure 12.3   Bonus note

12.6.4 Non-combination structures

Himalaya note

A Himalaya note is a principal protected structure that is not based on directional views of the market but on relative performance. Take the following hypothetical terms:

Maturity	5 years
Underlying	Gold, aluminium, copper, Brent, natural gas
Annual coupons	None
Redemption value	100% + Max (5%, 40% × Maximum performance)
Observation period	Annually

Maximum performance is defined according to the following expression:

$$\text{Maximum performance} = \frac{\sum_{x=1}^{5} \text{Perf}_{\text{best}}^x}{5}$$

$$\text{Perf}_{\text{best}}^x = \frac{P_{(x)\text{observation}}}{P_{(x)\text{initial}}}$$

where $P_{(x)\text{observation}}$ = Price of the best performing remaining commodity on the xth observation date

$P_{(x)\text{initial}}$ = Price of the best performing commodity on the strike date.

After the annual observation date the best performing commodity is removed from the basket. To illustrate the concept, hypothetical annual prices for each of the commodities are listed in Table 12.2. All prices in the table are expressed in USD apart from natural gas prices, which are expressed in pence per therm; the percentage change is calculated from the initial price in year 0.

- In year 1, the best performer is Brent (7.84%), which is then removed.
- In year 2, the best performer is aluminium (8.21%), which is then removed.
- In year 3, the best performer is copper (8.51%), which is then removed.
- In year 4, the best performer is gold (2.92%), which is then removed.
- In year 5, the best (and only) performer is natural gas (2.70%).

The arithmetic average of these returns is 6.036%, 40% of which is 2.4144%.

Table 12.2 Hypothetical price performance of five assets over a 5-year period

Year	Gold	% change	Aluminium	% change	Copper	% change	Brent	% change	Natural gas	% change
0	685	–	1,876	–	6,543	–	51	–	48.89	–
1	650	−5.11	1,968	4.91	6,890	5.30	55	7.84	47.56	−2.72
2	700	2.19	2,030	8.21	7,005	7.06	58	13.73	49.23	0.70
3	720	5.11	2,104	12.15	7,100	8.51	66	29.41	44.56	−8.86
4	705	2.92	2,267	20.84	7,946	21.44	71	39.22	48.67	−0.45
5	716	4.53	2,607	38.97	8,203	25.37	75	47.06	50.21	2.70

Since the payoff on the option was defined as:

$$100\% + \mathrm{Max}\ (5\%, 40\% \times \mathrm{Maximum\ performance})$$

the investor will receive a cashflow equal to 105% of his investment.

There are variations on this structure such as the "Kilimanjaro", where the payout is based on the worst performing commodity over a given period. The commodity is then removed for all subsequent fixings.

Since this structure is taking a view on the relative performance of a number of commodities, one of key pricing inputs is correlation. In the Himalaya structure, the investor is long correlation; that is, if the price of one of the underlying assets increases, the prices of the other assets are also likely to increase. If this were the case, the size of the expected payoff at maturity would be greater, raising the value of the optionality. The investor is also long implied volatility. An increase in implied volatility widens the range of possible payoffs at maturity, increasing the possible size of the return.

12.6.5   Collateralised Commodity Obligations

The Collateralised Commodity Obligation (CCO) product was built on the popularity of Collateralised Debt Obligations (CDOs), which are bond-like structures that offer credit investors an enhanced return by redistributing the credit risk of a given portfolio.

Collateralised Debt Obligations

In general terms a CDO describes a structure where a special purpose vehicle (SPV) is set up with the sole purpose of buying a pool of financial assets which, for early structures, were typically bonds or loans. The purchase of the assets is financed by the issue of bonds to end investors, while the investors' returns are generated by the cashflows of the purchased assets.

The SPV is structured to ensure that it is bankruptcy remote and will have no prior operating history that could give rise to any additional future liabilities. It will also be restricted from performing activities such as merging with other entities or issuing more debt.

The SPV's is usually restricted to those activities that are considered necessary to facilitate the particular transaction for which it has been established. Typically these will include:

- The issuance of notes.
- The purchase of the underlying assets.
- Entering into an investment advisory agreement with a fund manager who will acquire and manage the pool of financial assets.

From an investor's perspective the three main credit-related issues are noted to be:

- *Default probability*: This is defined as the likelihood that an asset will default over a given period of time.

- *Default correlation*: This describes the tendency of assets to default together. It relates to the manner in which defaults within a portfolio are "parcelled out". For example, if the assets within the portfolio are described as being highly correlated, then the assets will tend to act as one single entity; the portfolio will suffer either very large losses or no losses at all. Low correlation implies that although the portfolio will suffer some losses, they are unlikely to be catastrophic.
- *Default severity*: Default severity is the loss in the event of a default occurring and is measured as the market value of the asset after default. Often reference is made to the recovery rate of an asset, which is the amount the investor will get back from the defaulted asset.

In the CDO structure the pool of financial assets purchased are typically higher yielding, lower credit rated while the issued liabilities are lower yielding more highly credit rated. The market sometimes describes this as "arbitrage" but since these structures are not risk free it would be more accurate to describe the process as one that offers the investor an enhanced return by redistributing the credit risk of the purchased pool of assets. The notes that are issued to investors are divided into different levels of risk with varying levels of return. In general terms, there are three tranches of securities: senior, mezzanine and equity. In the CDO structure the lower yielding, higher credit-rated assets are typically AAA rated, while the liabilities may be classified as sub-investment grade (e.g. less than BBB−). Investors in the equity tranche receive a dividend-like return (called an excess spread), which is only paid after the senior and then mezzanine bondholders are paid. The returns for the equity holders can be attractive, but the apportionment of principal losses starts from this lowest tranche and then increases upwards.

The CDO structure has a number of early repayment triggers to protect the bond investors from a deterioration in the underlying collateral pool. If the triggers are activated, then bondholders are repaid sequentially with the highest credit-rated notes being redeemed first (Figure 12.4).

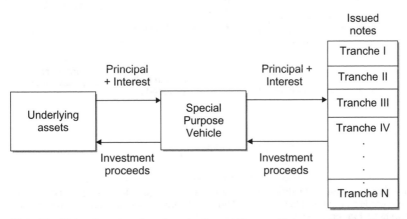

Note: The higher tranches (e.g. tranche I) would have a higher credit rating but a lower return. The lower tranches would have a lower credit rating but a higher return.

Figure 12.4   Collateralised Debt Obligation

Collateralised Synthetic Obligations

CDO structures in which the physical loans and bonds are replaced with a portfolio of credit default swaps, are usually referred to as Collateralised Synthetic Obligations (CSOs).

Credit default swaps are a form of credit insurance that involves the payment of a fee (referred to as a spread) by the buyer of credit protection, with the credit protection seller making a payment if a certain event of default (e.g. bankruptcy) occurs to a specific entity. Although the CSO structure is similar to the CDO, the return to the investor is generated in a different manner. Typically, the investor pays his investment proceeds to the SPV, who invests them in high-quality collateral to earn a rate of return. The investor, via the SPV, then sells credit protection on a portfolio of CDSs, which will generate an enhanced return. If any of the entities to which the CDSs are referenced default, the investor's principal is diverted from the collateral to make good the contingent payment due under the terms of the default swaps.

Collateralised Commodity Obligations

The CCO structure borrowed a number of features from the CSO. The structure is designed to create a note that gives investors exposure to an asset class, which may be difficult for them to access, along with an enhanced yield for a given level of risk.

The CCO structure may be linked to a variety of different commodities, and is illustrated in Figure 12.5.

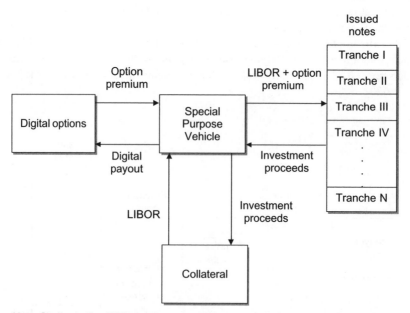

Note: Similar to the CDO structure, the higher tranches (e.g. tranche I) would have a higher credit rating but a lower return. The lower tranches would have a lower credit rating but a higher return.

Figure 12.5   Collateralised Commodity Obligation

Precious metals

- Platinum
- Palladium

Base metals

- Aluminium
- Copper
- Nickel
- Tin
- Lead
- Zinc

Energy

- WTI
- Brent
- Heating oil
- Gas oil
- Natural gas
- Unleaded gasoline

The investor's proceeds are put on deposit to earn LIBOR, which partly finances the investor's return. However, the main source of returns under the structure is generated by the sale of a portfolio of cash-settled European style digital options, written on a variety of commodities. This premium is paid to the investors in the form of an enhanced yield. The issued notes are structured as a number of different tranches ("slices"), typically rated from super senior to equity, with the spread to LIBOR (i.e. the enhanced yield) falling, the higher the credit rating.

The digital put options are struck on the money and will only be exercised if the price of the particular commodity is below the strike (sometimes referred to as a trigger level) at expiry. The trigger is typically set at about 50% of the initial spot price of the commodity. Although there may be 14 different commodities, there will be about 100 digital options within the note. Options for the same commodity have strikes set at different levels.

If triggered, the digital option payouts would be financed by the unwinding of the investor's collateral; this means that the CCO is not a capital guaranteed structure. Similar to the CDO structure, principal losses are incurred sequentially from the lowest tranches upwards. Unlike the CDO, however, the losses will not be crystallised until maturity, which means that all the coupons on the CCO will be protected.

12.7   ANALYSING INVESTMENT STRUCTURES

The variety of structured products presents the investor with a very wide range of possibilities. Some of the structures we have analysed can be decomposed into their constituent elements but the solutions that are modelled using Monte Carlo techniques can be very difficult to analyse. It is possible, however, to present a relatively simple framework that will allow an investor to analyse any product with which he is faced.

- Is the investor faced by any restrictions as to what type of structure he can execute? (The restrictions may be in relation to leverage or use of derivatives.)
- What is the nature of the investor's desired cashflow?
- What is the investor's view on expected market movements? (Their direction, magnitude and timing.)
- Do current conditions indicate a favourable entry point to the trade?
- What is the investor's attitude to risk? Is there a need for capital protection or is the investor willing to risk some loss of principal for an enhanced return?
- Is the investor comfortable with the risks of the proposed structure? Have all the applicable market risks been identified? (These may include an exposure to directional movements, changes to implied volatility or a price correlation between different assets.)
- Has the risk–return profile for a range of extreme market values been considered?

Glossary

AAU
Assigned amount units. Under the terms of the Kyoto agreement, an AAU allows the holder the right to emit 1 tonne of carbon dioxide.

Allocated gold
Gold that is stored on an allocated basis means that ownership of individual bars is clearly identified. The opposite is unallocated gold, where the metal is kept in a vault and ownership of a particular bar is not identified.

American option
An option that allows the holder to exercise their right to buy or sell at anytime prior to expiry.

Annex B country
Under the terms of the Kyoto agreement, annex B countries represented those nations who were willing to commit to legally binding targets to reduce emissions.

API
The density of crude oil is often expressed in terms of an API value. The scale was devised by the American Petroleum Institute and the lower the value the more dense the crude oil and vice versa.

Arbitrage
This describes a situation where an asset is trading at two different prices in the same market. This would allow a participant to buy and sell quickly to make a risk free profit net of any costs.

Argus media
An independent price reporting and energy news agency.

Asian Petroleum Pricing Index
This is a popular benchmark for pricing crude oils from Asian markets.

Assay
An analysis to determine the presence of a particular substance or component. Within the context of gold an assay will determine the percentage of the metal within a particular bar. In the crude oil market the process is used to determine the proportion of each refined product that can be made from a particular type of crude oil.

At-the money
An at-the money option is an option where the strike rate is equal to the current underlying market rate.

Average price option
An average price option is an option where the payout at expiry is linked to an average of market prices. An alternative averaging structure is where the strike is not fixed until maturity and is based on a pregreed series of market values.

Backwardation
A situation where longer dated forward prices are lower than shorter dated prices.

Balancing
Within the power and gas markets, the process of ensuring that the amount of the commodity entering the system equals the amount exiting the system.

Barrier option
A barrier option has all the features of a conventional option with the addition of a trigger or barrier. The trigger is placed in either the in-the- money or out-of-the money region and if it trades will activate ("knock-in") or deactivate ("knock-out") the option.

Basket option
A basket option is an option where the expiry payoff is linked to the performance of a number of different underlying assets.

Bermudan option
An option is described as being Bermudan in style if it can be exercised on one of a number of preagreed dates.

BFOE
Within the oil market this acronym stands for Brent Fortes Oseberg Ekofisk. It reflects the fact that North Sea Crude oil is made up of a series of different crude oils despite being often referred to simply as "Brent".

Binary option
A binary option is an option where the payoff, if exercised, is a fixed amount irrespective of how deeply the instrument is in-the-money.

Biofuels
A range of fuels whose production and consumption are relatively "environmentally friendly" (e.g. ethanol).

Borrow
Within the context of the base metals market, a borrow is a single transaction comprising two legs with different maturities. The first leg is a purchase and the second is a sale. The first leg could either be a spot or forward deal while the second leg matures at a later date. The party executing the transaction therefore has use of the metal for a specific period of time.

British thermal unit
A common measure of energy content used in the US natural gas markets. Defined as the amount of heat that is required to raise the temperature of one pound of water by one degree Fahrenheit.

Call option
A call option allows the holder the to buy the underlying asset if the option is exercised.

Cap and trade system
Within the context of emission trading a cap and trade system places a maximum amount on the amount of carbon dioxide to be emitted and allows market participants to negotiate the transfer of allowances at a market determined price.

Capital Guaranteed Structures
A capital guaranteed investment ensures that the buyer will always receive back their principal at maturity. This is usually achieved by diverting part of the investors' proceeds into a zero coupon bond that repays par at maturity. However, there is no third party guaranteeing repayment so it is more accurate to describe them as offering capital protection.

Carbon cycle
The carbon cycle describes the possible pathways a carbon atoms takes through the different components of the ecosystem.

CBOT
Chicago Board of Trade – a futures exchange. Merged with the Chicago Mercantile Exchange in July 2007 to become known as the CME group.

CERs
Certified emission reductions. These are credits issued under the clean development mechanism.

CIF
A price quoted as CIF, will include the Cost (of the product), Insurance and Freight.

Clearing House
In a futures market the clearing house is the entity that is the ultimate counterparty to any transaction. Ensures that all purchases and sales are matched and that all margins are collected.

Clean dark spread
The dark spread adjusted for the cost of emitting carbon dioxide.

Clean Development Mechanism
Under the terms of the Kyoto agreement the clean development mechanism represented one of the mechanisms to achieve a reduction in greenhouse gases. The mechanism encourages the investment in developing country projects which will be rewarded by the issuance of credits which could be used in order to comply with the Kyoto emission targets.

Contango
A contango market describes a situation where the price of a commodity for forward delivery is greater than the price for spot delivery.

Cost of carry
When holding a position in an asset, the cost of carry is the amount of income generated by the instrument less any expense incurred. If gold is purchased and held, the initial cost has to be financed by borrowing money. This borrowing cost can be offset by lending out the gold to earn a leasing fee. The cost of carry is the difference between the interest cost

and the leasing income. If the cost is greater than the income there is a negative cost of carry and vice versa.

Commitment of traders report
This is a report produced by the commodity futures trading commission that shows the position in the US markets for "commercial" and "non-commercial" users of futures.

Commodity Futures Trading Commission
The US regulator for exchange traded futures.

Commodity Trading Advisors
This is a group of investors who typically use futures as a means of gaining exposure to a particular market. Their activities may not be restricted to commodities and may encompass a wider set of asset classes.

Contract for difference
A contract for difference is a transaction that pays out at maturity a sum of money based on the current price of an asset relative to a value established at the trade date. Neither party to the contract is required to deliver the underlying asset. Sometimes referred to as a "cash settled forward" or a "swap".

Convenience yield
This is the premium that a consumer is willing to pay to be able to consume a commodity now rather than in the future.

Correlation
A statistical measure that indicates the tendency of two asset prices to move in the same or opposite direction.

Correlation vega
When pricing basket options, the correlation between the underlying assets is accounted for within the implied volatility input. Correlation vega measures how much the price of the option will change by for a small change in the correlation between the assets.

Cracking
The process of taking heavy hydrocarbon molecules and breaking them into lighter ones.

Crack spread
The crack spread measures the difference between the cost of crude oil and the income generated from the sale of the refined products.

Dark spread
The dark spread measures the difference between the cost of coal and income generated from the sale of electricity.

Delta
Delta measures the amount by which the premium of an option will change for a small change in the underlying price.

Density
Density is a measure of the number of molecules within a defined volume.

Derivative
A class of instruments that derive their value from an underlying asset price or index value. The derivative building blocks comprise futures/forwards, swaps and options.

Digital option
See binary option.

Discount factor
A discount factor can be used to present value any cash flow occurring at a future date.

Downstream
In the context of crude oil markets this refers to a series of activities at the end of the physical supply chain such as the distribution of refined products to end consumers.

Electricity Forward Agreement
A series of market conventions (e.g. calendar dates) that are used in the UK electricity market; also an agreement that fixes the price of electricity at some future date.

Elspot
This is the physical spot market for Nordic electricity, sometimes referred to as the Elspot market.

Emissions trading schemes
A market where allowances to emit carbon dioxide are traded between market participants.

Energy Reliability Organisation
In 2005, the US government introduced the Energy Policy Act, which will lead to the creation of the Electric Reliability Organization (ERO). The ERO will have the authority to develop and enforce mandatory standards for the reliable operation and planning of the wholesale electricity system in the North American region.

European option
An option where the holder can only exercise their right to buy and sell at expiry of the contract.

EUAs
European Union Allowances. These are emission allowances traded within the EU ETS.

EU ETS
The Emission Trading Scheme operated within the European Union.

Exchange Delivery Settlement Price
The final price of a futures contract.

Exchange for physicals
This is a technique used to price a physical commodity by using the futures market.

Exotic option
An option where the payoff does not resemble that of a European or American style option. Exotic options comprise a number of different products of which average rate ("Asians") and barriers are examples.

FERC
In the USA the overall direction for the electricity industry is determined by the passage of Federal law. The Federal Energy Regulatory Commission (FERC) regulates the industry at the wholesale level.

Fineness
A measure of the quality of gold. The greater the fineness, the purer the metal.

FOB
A price quoted on a "free on board" basis covers the delivery to a particular port and onto a ship although it is acknowledged that the buyer has responsibility for the goods once they pass over the ship's rail.

Forward
An agreement to fix the price for delivery of an asset at a preagreed date in the future.

Forward curve
A diagrammatical representation of the different prices for delivery of a commodity at different time periods.

Forward Rate Agreement
See contract for difference.

Funded/unfunded
In the context of investments, a funded structure requires an initial investment. An unfunded structure does not require any upfront investment.

Futures
A forward – style agreement traded on an organised exchange.

Gamma
The rate of change of delta with respect to the spot price.

GOFO
The gold forward offered rate.

Gold swap
An agreement that involves the sale (purchase) of gold for spot value and the simultaneous purchase (sale) of the gold for a forward maturity.

Heavy crude oil
A heavy crude oil has a high density, expressed as an API gravity.

Heren
A publisher of market information for the gas, power and carbon markets.

Hydrocarbons
Molecules consisting of hydrogen and carbon atoms.

Implied volatility
The volatility implied by an observed option price.

In the money
An option where the strike rate is more favourable than the underlying price.

Interconnector
A pipeline or transmission wire that links two different countries or regions.

IntercontinentalExchange
A futures exchange.

International transaction log
The central registry where all the certified emission reductions generated from the clean development mechanism will be recorded.

IPCC
Intergovernmental Panel on Climate Change was formed in 1988. Reviews published research on the issue of climate change and issues summary reports every 5 – 6 years.

ISDA
International Swaps and Derivatives Association; professional market body for the derivatives industry.

ISO
An Independent System Operator manages the transmission of power over a given area.

Joint Implementation
Under the terms of the Kyoto agreement the joint implementation mechanism represents the investment in an emission reduction project by one annex B country in another.

Knock-out/Knock-in
Within the context of barrier options a knock-out option is a contract that includes a barrier/trigger that if traded will deactivate the option; if a trigger leads an option to be activated it is referred to as a knock-in option.

Kyoto agreement
The Kyoto agreement, which was signed in 1997, established legally binding emission targets for the signatories. It was eventually ratified in 2005.

Lease rate
The rate at which gold can be lent or borrowed.

Lease rate swaps
A bilateral agreement to exchange cash flows where each leg is calculated on a different basis. Typically one of the legs will be a fixed rate and the other will be floating. Both legs derive their value from gold lease rates.

Lend
Within the context of the base metals market, this a single transaction with two legs, whereby the metal is sold for spot value with an agreement to repurchase it at some future date. The economic affect of the transaction is equivalent to the loan of the metal over the same period.

Leverage
The ability to use a small amount of capital to control a much larger exposure.

Light crude oil
Crude oil that has a low density.

Liquefied Natural Gas

In liquefied form natural gas occupies 1/600th of the space it would in gaseous form making it more viable to transport over longer distances. To create LNG it is cooled below its freezing point of $-161°C/-260°F$ and other constituents such as oxygen and carbon dioxide are removed to leave a gas that is virtually pure methane.

Load

Load describes how much electricity will be consumed by an electrical device at a given time. A baseload contract provides for the delivery of a constant volume of power. A peak load contract covers the period of highest demand. Off peak covers all other periods outside of the peak load definition, typically nights, weekends and holidays.

Loco London

Literally, "location" London. The price for gold is typically quote in terms of a certain level of quality for delivery in a particular location. The loco London price is the price for delivery of the metal in London.

London Bullion Market Association

The professional market body for the London Gold market.

London Good Delivery

These are a set of standards that define the exact nature of the gold that will be exchanged for delivery in London.

London Metals Exchange

An organised exchange where base metals and plastics can be traded.

Long

Can be used to describe either the purchase or existing holding of an asset.

Margin – initial and variation

Margins are incurred when executing futures transactions on an organised exchange. Initial margin is collected when a position is first opened and returned when the position is closed. Variation margin is based on the change in the value of the contract and is collected according to the terms set out by the individual exchange.

Marker crudes

Crude oil prices are often expressed as a spread to some benchmark or "marker" crude. The two key marker crudes are Brent and West Texas Intermediate.

Mean reversion

The tendency for the price of a particular asset to revert towards a long term average value.

Methane

Another name for natural gas.

Midstream

Within the context of crude oil this relates to a series of activities along the physical supply chain. Typically they include all the refining related activities.

Min-max

This is an option structure, which is constructed as the combination of the purchase (sale) of a call and the sale (purchase) of a put option with the strikes set at a level that result in a zero premium. Has the effect of setting the minimum or maximum values at which an asset could be bought or sold.

Monomer
A building block used in the production of plastic.

Naphthenic
A crude oil that has naphthenic properties is one that has a high viscosity but low flammability.

Natural gas liquids
When natural gas is extracted from the ground it will usually comprise of a series of different gases, which are then separated into their component parts. Collectively they are referred to as natural gas liquids.

NERC
North American Electric Reliability Council is responsible for ensuring the reliability, security and adequacy of the bulk power system in the USA, Canada and parts of Mexico.

Nord Pool
A Scandinavian Energy Exchange.

Notional amount
A value used to calculate the cash flows associated with a derivative transaction. Does not represent an actual cashflow itself.

NYMEX
New York Mercantile Exchange; a futures exchange.

Olefins/polyolefins
Because there are thousands of different hydrocarbons it is often convenient to divide them into categories. One such category is alkenes of which ethylene is an example. Alkenes generally have a simple chemical structure, are cheap to make and are relatively easy to polymerise. Alkenes are also sometimes referred to as "olefins" and their polymers (such as polythene and polypropylene) "polyolefins".

Options
An instrument that gives the holder the right but not the obligation to buy or sell an underlying asset at a preagreed price at a date in the future. Since the holder is acquiring a right, they will be required to pay a fee which is called a premium.

Organisation for Petroleum Exporting Countries
An organisation of eleven crude oil producing countries.

OTC
Over the counter; a transaction that is executed outside of an organised exchange.

Out of the money
An option where the strike rate is less favourable than the underlying market price.

Paraffinic
A chemical property of crude oil, which literally means "like paraffin".

Plain vanilla
A jargon phrase used to describe a very simple version of a particular structure.

Platts
A provider of information for the energy and metals markets.

Polymer
A polymer (poly is Latin for many) is a number of individual monomers chemically joined by a bond to form a single structure.

Pour point
A measure of the lowest temperature at which either crude oil or a particular refined product flows as a liquid under a given set of conditions.

Premium – 1
The fee payable when buying an option.

Premium – 2
In some markets commodities are traded as a spread to some benchmark. For products that have a higher quality their price is expressed as a premium to the benchmark.

Prompt date
The date for delivery of an asset.

Put – call parity
This concept links options to their underlying markets by creating an equality between puts, calls and the underlying asset. In a simplified form it states that the purchase of a call and the sale of a put with the same strike and same maturity will be economically equivalent to a long position in the underlying market.

Put option
An option that gives the holder the right but not the obligation to sell an underlying asset.

Quanto
The return from a quanto structure is based on an asset denominated in a foreign currency, however the actual cashflow that is paid to the holder is denominated in the investor's local currency removing all of the currency risk.

Regional transmission organisations
An independent system operator with regional responsibilities.

Ring
The part of the London Metal Exchange where physical trading of metal takes place.

Rolling
Rolling is the process whereby an investor sells a maturing futures, but to ensure their exposure is maintained, simultaneously buys a future with a later maturity.

Roll yield
When a futures market is in backwardation, longer dated contracts will be trading at a lower price to those with shorter maturities. If a longer dated contract is purchased and held to maturity then, all other things being equal, its price will rise allowing the investor to sell the contract at a profit.

S&P GSCI
Previously known as the Goldman Sachs Commodity Index, but was sold to Standard and Poors in early 2007. Widely acknowledged to be the most widely used measure for index-linked investment structures.

Shippers
Shippers are wholesale participants in the natural gas market who will be responsible for the movement of natural gas through the pipeline.

Short
The sale of an asset; can also be used to denote the need to buy something at a future date that is currently not owned.

Sour
Crude oil with a high sulphur content.

Spot
"Immediate" delivery of an asset. Depending the asset concerned this could be anything from the same day to several days in the future. Generally spot means delivery in two days time.

Strike
The price at which an asset is bought or sold if an option contract is exercised.

Swap
A bilateral, multiperiod agreement to exchange cashflows whose magnitudes are calculated or different bases. When the contract covers a single exchange it may be referred to as a "contract for difference" or a "cash settled forward transaction".

Swaptions
An option on a swap.

Sweet
Crude oil with a low sulphur content.

Synthetic
Within the context of derivative theory, it is often possible to combine instruments so that on a net basis they will possess the economic properties of another. For example, by buying a call and selling a put with the same strike and maturity the resultant position is economically equivalent to being long the underlying asset. That is, it is a synthetic long position.

Therm
A measure of energy used in the UK natural gas market.

Thermal efficiency
Thermal efficiency relates the electrical energy produced to the energy content of the input.

Theta
Measures by how much an option premium will change with respect to the passage of time, typically one day.

Total Return Swap
A transaction whereby an investor will receive a set of cash flows based on the return of a given asset or index. The transaction allows an investor to take exposure to the asset or index without having to actually buy it.

Upstream
Upstream describes a series of activities at the start of the physical supply chain and includes exploration and extraction.

Utilities
A company that provides a range of household services such as power and water.

Vega
Measures by how much an option premium will change with respect to a 1% change in implied volatility.

Viscosity
A measure of the ability of crude oil or a refined product to flow or its resistance to pouring.

Volatility
A measure of price variability.

Volt
Measures the force being used to push electrons around a circuit.

Warrant
Within the context of the base metals market, a warrant will denote ownership of metal stored within a warehouse.

Washington Agreement
This was an agreement between Central Banks detailing their planned future gold sales. First signed in 1999 and revised in 2004.

Watt
Unit of measurement of electrical power.

Watt hour
The amount of electricity generated or used over a period of time is measured in Watt-hours.

Zero coupon rate
A zero coupon instrument has only two cash flows; the initial outlay and the final repayment. A zero coupon rate measures the rate of return implied by these two values.

Notes

CHAPTER 2: RISK MANAGEMENT

1. Risk management from an institutional investor is the subject of Chapter 12.

CHAPTER 3: GOLD

1. www.lbma.uk.org.
2. The full list of standards can be found on the LBMA's website.
3. See World Gold Council's website www.gold.org.
4. See www.gold.org.
5. GFMS: *Global Gold Hedge Book Analysis*, Q4, 2004; Edition 9, February 2005.

CHAPTER 5: CRUDE OIL

1. Definition taken from annual general report.
2. *Financial Times* (30 May 2006) Energy: special report.
3. See, for example, *Commodities Now* (June 2006) Oil Sands, a short term solution to Middle East oil dependence? and *Financial Times* (8 November 2005) Safe deposit? Canada's oilsands can give much of the world a fresh energy source.
4. *Financial Times* (24 August 2005) Fuel shortage could mean a rocky road for diesel cars.
5. *Wall Street Journal* (29 September 2005) Refining incapacity.
6. See *Financial Times* (31 August 2005) Storm over the oil industry: a hurricane is another worry as production costs mount. Also *Financial Times* (1 September 2005) US refinery industry caught out by hurricane disruption.
7. *Financial Times* (25 April 2006) Security of supply raises fears of long-term contango.
8. *Financial Times* (31 August 2005) Storm over the oil industry: a hurricane is another worry as production costs mount.
9. *Financial Times* (15 August 2006) The dramatic knock-on effect of BP's Prudhoe shut-down.
10. www.opec.org.
11. Davis, M. (May 2002) *Dynamics of the oil forward curve*. Platts.
12. *Financial Times* (4 July 2006) Aggressive trading culture surfaces at BP.

CHAPTER 6: NATURAL GAS

1. See, for example, *Financial Times* (25 October 2005) Catan, T.: Pressure is building for more gas storage. Also *Financial Times* (5 January 2006) Catan, T.: Gas acquires new strategic importance as fuel of the future.
2. The report can be downloaded from the company's website, www.bp.com.
3. UK Offshore Operators Association (2003) *Security of Gas Supplies.*
4. See Barclays Capital (January 2006) *Coming Ashore. The Implications of Liquefied Natural Gas (LNG).* See also *Financial Times* (25 October 2005) Simensen, I.: Energy demand sets LNG market alight.
5. See www.heren.com.
6. See www.platts.com.
7. See *The Times* (18 September 2006) Norwegian link set to drive down prices; see also *Financial Times* (4 October 2006) Gas given away as surge from Norway causes price plunge.
8. *Financial Times* (3 January 2006) What the clash means for Ukraine: and for Europe.
9. European Commission (February 2006) *Energy Sector Inquiry.* Draft Preliminary Report.

CHAPTER 7: ELECTRICITY

1. Nord Pool (Summer 2003) *The Nordic Power Exchange and the Nordic Model for a Liberalised Power Market.*
2. Nord Pool (30 March 2006) *Trade at the Nordic Spot Market.*
3. Nord Pool (30 March 2006) *Trade at Nord Pool's Financial Market.*
4. Ofgem/Department of Trade and Industry (31 May 2000) *An Overview of the New Electricity Trading Arrangements VI.*

CHAPTER 8: PLASTICS

1. Quote taken from *Risk* magazine (July 2006) Needing plastic surgery.
2. Ethylene and ethene are different terms used to describe the same chemical structure. Differences in their usage may occur on a geographical basis. The slightly old fashion term of ethylene will be used throughout the text.

CHAPTER 9: COAL

1. *Financial Times* (18 April 2006), comments on the state of the UK mining industry.
2. World Coal Institute (2005) *The Coal Resource*
3. International Energy Agency (2006) *Coal Information*
4. Platts coal methodology (June 2006).
5. *Financial Times* (27 July 2006) Rail tries to keep supplies on track.
6. See Chapter 7 on electricity for worked calculations of these spread measures.
7. See Chapter 5 on crude oil for more on this topic.
8. *Financial Times* (15 August 2005) Brighter outlook in prospect for coal sector.

9. World Coal Institute (October 2006) *Coal – Liquid Fuels.*
10. TFS API is a trademark of Tradition Financial Services Ltd.
11. www.globalcoal.com.

CHAPTER 10: EMISSIONS TRADING

1. *The Economist* (9 September 2006) The heat is on: a survey of climate change.
2. *Financial Times* (31 October 2006) Change that is costing the earth.
3. www.ipcc.ch; Summary for Policymakers.
4. See www.unfccc.int and *The Stern Review* (2006) The economics of climate change.
5. *The Stern Report* (2006) The economics of climate change.
6. *Sunday Times* (11 February 2007) An experiment that hints we are wrong on climate change.
7. *Daily Telegraph* (16 October 2006) The consensus view is frequently very wrong indeed. Also *Sunday Times* (30 April 2006) Getting far too heated over global warming.
8. *Daily Telegraph* (16 October 2006) The consensus view is frequently very wrong indeed.
9. *Sunday Telegraph* (9 April 2006) There IS a problem with global warming . . . it stopped in 1998.
10. The Economics of Climate Change. House of Lords Select Committee on Economic Affairs. July 2005.
11. Kyoto Protocol to the United Nations: *Framework Convention on Climate Change.*
12. See http://cdm.unfcc.int/index.html.
13. *The Economist* (6 May 2006) Cleaning up.
14. EU Emissions Trading Scheme: *UK National Allocation Plan 2008–2012.* Department for Environment, Food and Rural Affairs.
15. The World Bank: *State and Trends of the Carbon Market 2006.* The World Bank published two documents, the first in May 2006 covering events in 2005 and an update in October 2006, which extended the data to the 3rd quarter of 2006.

CHAPTER 11: AGRICULTURAL COMMODITIES AND BIOFUELS

1. See *Financial Times* (5 October 2006) Tight supply and biofuel demand add spice to grain market.
2. See *Financial Times* (9 May 2006) Brake on biofuels as obstacles clog the road.
3. See *Financial Times* (28 February 2006) Flexibility on fuel gives manufacturers an edge.
4. See *Financial Times* (30 March 2006) Prices soar as Brazil's flexfuel cars set the pace.
5. See *Financial Times* (21 June 2006) Wind changes in favour of biofuels; and Elusive cornucopia: why it will be hard to rep the benefit of biofuel.
6. See *Futures* magazine (November 2006) What will move grains in 2007?.
7. See *Financial Times* (22 May 2006) Fears of ethanol shortage force rush for stocks.
8. See *Financial Times* (7 February 2007) US sees mileage in biodiesel.

CHAPTER 12: COMMODITIES WITHIN AN INVESTMENT PORTFOLIO

1. Taken from an internal Barclays Capital presentation in 2006 entitled *Investing in Commodities as an Asset Class*.
2. See Barclays Capital presentation in 2006 entitled *Investing in Commodities as an Asset Class*. See also *Risk* (November 2006) Contango.
3. See Chapter 1 on derivative pricing for more background on the pricing of forward contracts.

Bibliography

Banks, E. and Dunn, R. (2003) *Practical Risk Management*. John Wiley & Sons Ltd.
Bond, T. (2007) *The Energy Revolution*. Barclays Gilt: Equity Study.
Bossley, E. (October 1999) *Trading Natural Gas in the UK*. Oxford Institute for Energy Studies.
Christian, J. (2006) *Commodities Rising*. John Wiley & Sons Ltd.
Crabbe, P. (1999) *Metals Trading Handbook*. Woodhead Publishing Limited.
Cross, J. (2001) *Gold Derivatives: The Market View*. World Gold Council. (Available from the World Gold Council website.)
Crowson, P. and Sampson, R. (2000) *Managing Metals Price Risk with the London Metal Exchange*. London Metal Exchange.
European Commission (February 2006) *Energy Sector Inquiry*. Draft Preliminary Report.
Energy Information Administration (2003) *Derivatives and Risk Management in Energy Industries*.
The Economist (22 May 2003) The devil's excrement.
The Economist (30 April 2005) Oil in troubled waters.
The Economist (22 April 2006) Steady as she goes.
The Economist (12 August 2006) Oil's dark secret.
The Economist (9 September 2006) The heat is on: a survey of climate change.
Flavell, R. (2002) *Swaps and Other Derivatives*. John Wiley & Sons Ltd.
Galitz, L. (1996) *Financial Engineering*. FT Prentice Hall.
Geman, H. (2005) *Commodities and Commodity Derivatives*. John Wiley & Sons Ltd.
Haug, E.G. (1998) *The Complete Guide to Option Pricing Formulas*. McGraw-Hill.
Kat, H. (2001) *Structured Equity Derivatives*. John Wiley & Sons Ltd,
London Metals Exchange (Spring 2005) *Plastics Futures*.
Man Financial (March 2005) *An Introduction to LME Plastics*.
Natenberg, S. (1994) *Option Volatility and Pricing*. McGraw-Hill.
New York Mercantile Exchange (December 2000) *Crack Spread Handbook*.
Nord Pool (Summer 2003) *The Nordic Power Exchange and the Nordic Model for a Liberalised Power Market*.
Nord Pool (April 2004) *Nordic Power Market*.
Nord Pool (30 March 2006) *Trade at the Nordic Spot Market*.
Nord Pool (30 March 2006) *Trade at Nord Pool's Financial Market*.
Rogers, J. (2004) *Hot Commodities*. John Wiley & Sons Ltd.
Smithson, C. (1998) *Managing Financial Risk* (3rd edition). McGraw-Hill.
Spaull, J. (2005) *Gold Reserve Management*. Barclays Capital.
Spurga, R.C. (2006) *Commodity Fundamentals*. John Wiley & Sons Ltd.
Tompkins, R. (1994) *Options Explained* (2nd edition). Palgrave.
World Coal Institute (2005) *The Coal Resource*.
Young, G. (2003) *The Role of the Bank of England in the Gold Market*. LBMA Precious Metals Conference, Lisbon.

Index

A

Agricultural commodities
  corn production, 262–263
  exchange-traded futures, 266
  over-the-counter derivatives, 267–268
  price drivers, 264–266
  sugar production, 262
  supply chain, 261
  wheat production, 262
Allowances supply and demand, emissions
    market price drivers, 249–250
Aluminum
  consumption and production of, 70f
  hedges for consumers in automotive sector,
    86–87
  NASAAC see North American Special
    Aluminum Alloy Contract
  primary futures contract specification, 77t
  primary options contract specification, 78t
  regional demand for, 72f
  Western world demand by end use, 72f
  world smelting output, 71f
American style option, 5
APPI see Asian Petroleum Price Index
Arbitrage, 127–128
Asian Petroleum Price Index (APPI), 124
Asphalt, refined products of crude oil, 104
Asset allocation benefits, commodities within
    portfolios, 270
Associate broker clearing LME members, 78
Associate broker LME members, 78
Associate trade clearing LME members, 78
Associate trade LME members, 78
ATM (at-the-money) option, 5
Automotive sector, hedges for aluminum
    consumers in, 86–87

B

Backwardation, 10–11

banks, risk management, 32
Barrier options
  Knock-in, 6–7
  Knock-out, 6
  reverse, 6
  standard, 6
  summary of, 6f
Base metals
  aluminum, 70–73, 77
  borrowing and lending in, 88
  business cycle impact of, 83f
  copper, 73–75
    forward rates as predictors of spot rates,
      86f
    three month forward price, 85f
  derivatives applications, 86–87
  forward curve description, 83–85
  forward purchase, 87–88
  LME see London Metal Exchange
    aluminum prices for settlement, 87
    associate broker clearing members, 78
    associate broker members, 78
    associate trade clearing members, 78
    associate trade members, 78
    clearing house, 78–80
    contract specification, 77
    delivery, 80–81
    exchange-traded metal futures, 76
    exchange-traded metal options, 76
    overview, 74–75
    primary aluminum futures contract
      specification, 77t
    primary aluminum options contract
      specification, 78t
    ring trading members, 78
    trading at, 77–78
  market prices structure, 83–86
  price drivers
    balance between industrial demand and
      supply, 83

Base metals *(Continued)*
    capital spending and exploration, 81–82
    Chinese and Indian demand, 81
    exchange rages, 81
    government fiscal and monetary policy, 81
    investment demand, 82–83
    production costs, 82
    production disruption, 82
    substitution, 82
  production, 69–70
  reactivity, 69
  structured option solutions
    basket options, 97–99
    bonus forward contract, 96–97
    forward plus contracts, 96
    knock-out forwards, 95–96
  vanilla option strategies
    min-max structure, 93–94
    ratio min-max structure, 94
    risk reversal, 95
    selling options for forward purchase price,
      90–92
    synthetic long put, 89–90
    three way structure, 92–93
Basket options, 97–99
Bermudian option, 5
Binary options, 6
Black-Scholes-Merton model, 17
Blow molding, 216
Bond *(The Energy Revolution)*, 250
Bonus forward contract, 96–97
Bonus note, 280
Brent Forwards contracts, 130
Brent Futures contracts, 134
Brent Weighted Average (BWAVE), 134
Business risk, 27
BWAVE *see* Brent Weighted Average, 134

C
Call option, 4
Capital guaranteed structures, 277–278
Carbon cycle, global warming, 242–243
Cash markets, gold market, 60–61
Cashflows, 15*t*
CBOT *see* Chicago Board of Trade
CCGT *see* combined cycle gas turbine
CCO *see* collateralised commodity obligation
CDM *see* clean development mechanism, 248
Central bank services
  gold market derivatives, 60–67
  physical gold market, 42
CERs, 259*f*
CFDs *see* Contracts for Difference
Cheap to fair value, 11
Chicago Board of Trade (CBOT), 264
China, gold market and, 51

CHP *see* combined heat and power
CIF *see* Cost, Insurance and Freight
Clean development mechanism (CDM), 248
Clearing house, LME, 78–80
Climate change
  argument against, 245–246
  CDM *see* clean development mechanism
  Earth Summit, 246
  format of IPCC, 246
  history of human action against, 246–249
  Kyoto Protocol, 247–249
Coal
  bank participants, 232
  basics of, 225–226
  demand for supply of, 226–231
  derivatives
    exchange-traded futures, 236–237
    over-the-counter solutions, 237–239
    prices, 235–236
  exporters, 229*f*
  factors affecting price of, 233–235
  flows of hard coal, 230*f*
  futures specification, 237*t*
  importers, 230*f*
  industrial company participants, 232
  mining company participants, 232
  price of, 232
  production of hard and brown in million
    tonnes, 228*f*
  regional coal reserves, 227*f*
  regional consumption of, 229*f*
  regional production of, 228*f*
  reserves to production ratio, 227*t*
  steam, 231*f*
  supply chain, 231–232
  swaps, 237–239
  swaptions, 239
  total primary energy supply by fuel,
    226*f*
  utilities companies participants, 232
Collateralised commodity obligation (CCO),
  282–285
Combined cycle gas turbine (CCGT), 184
Combined heat and power (CHP), 184
Commodities within portfolios
  benefits of, 270–271
  bonus note, 280
  capital guaranteed structures, 277–278
  CCO *see* collateralised commodity obligation,
    282–285
  correlation coefficients between financial
    assets, 270*t*
  excess return index, 272
  gold-linked notes, 277
  half pipe copper note, 278–279
  himalaya note, 281–282

investment methods, 271–272
investment structure analysis, 285–286
investor profiles, 269–270
roll yield, 273–274
spot index, 272
total return index, 273
TRS *see* total return swap
Commodity market participants, risk management, 29–30
Commodity risk, 28
Commodity trading advisors commodity investors, 269
Consumer hedges, crude oil, 144–147
Contango, 8
Contract specification, LME, 77
Contracts for Difference (CFDs), 130–133
Convertible forwards, 58
Copper, 73–75
    consumption and production of, 74*f*
    demand by usage, 73*f*
    forward rates as predictors of spot rates, 86*f*
    global min output, 75*f*
    three month forward price, 85*f*
Corn production, 262–263, 267
Corporate risk, 31–32
Correlation risk management, 33–34
Cost, Insurance and Freight (CIF), 123
Covered call strategy, 66*f*
Credit risk, 27, 29
Credit Support Annex (CSA), 80
Crude oil
    Brent Forwards contracts, 130
    Brent Futures contracts, 134
    CFDs *see* Contracts for Difference
    chemistry of, 102–103
    consumption of, 108, 109*f*
    Dated Brent contracts, 129
    demand and supply for, 106–114
    density, 102
    examples of, 103
    flow properties, 102–103
    frequently traded and refined product swaps, 141*t*
    heavy and sour crude, 103
    hedges
        consumer, 144–147
        producer, 137–142
        refiner, 142–144
    imports/exports, 111–112
    Jet fuel, 146–147
    light and sweet crude, 103
    naphthenic properties, 103
    net trade in, 113*f*

NOCs *see* national oil companies
North Sea, 128–129
oil refining capacity, 109–111
paraffinic properties, 103
plastic production, 215
pour point, 102–103
price drivers
    forward curve analysis, 121
    geopolitics, 120–121
    macroeconomics issues, 114–117
    supply chain considerations, 117–119
prices
    defining, 121–122
    delivered price, 122–123
    evolution of, 122
    exchange for physicals, 125
    fixed, 124
    floating, 125
    futures, 125
    marker crudes, 123–124
    official selling, 124
    pricing sources, 124
    term structure of, 125
production of, 108, 108*f*
proved oil reserves, 106, 106*t*
refined product demand, 109
refined products from, 104, 104*t*, 105
R/P ratio, 106, 107*t*, 108
security of supply, 112–114
sulphur content, 102
supply chain, 103–104
swaps, 139–142
trading crude oil and refined products, 126–137
US markets, 135–137
value of, 101–103
viscosity, 102
CSA *see* Credit Support Annex
Customers, natural gas supply chain, 153

D
Dark spreads, 193–195
Dated Brent contracts, 129
DEFRA *see* Department of Environment, Food and Rural Affairs
Delivery
    LME, 80–81
    trading physical natural gas, 167–168
Delta, 19–21
Demand side natural gas price drivers, 164
Density, crude oil, 102
Department of Environment, Food and Rural Affairs (DEFRA), 253
Deregulation and re-regulation, natural gas, 154–156

Derivative building blocks
  forwards, 2
  futures, 2
  options, 4–7
  pricing, 7–8
  put-call parity, 18
  spot-forward relationship, 8–10
  spot-forward-option relationship, 16–18
  spot-forward-swap relationship, 11–16
  swaps, 3–4
Derivatives
  coal
    exchange-traded futures, 236–237
    over-the-counter solutions, 237–239
    prices, 235–236
  emissions trading
    trading allowances, 254–255
    transaction examples, 255–259
  gold market
    cash markets, 60–61
    central bank strategies, 60–67
    convertible forwards, 58
    covered call strategy, 66 f
    flat rate forwards, 57–58
    floating rate forwards, 57
    forward positions revaluation, 58–59
    forwards, 55–57
    FRA see forward rate agreement
    lease rate swaps, 64–65, 65 f
    option strategies, 65–67
    options, 59–60
    producer strategies, 55–60
    spot deferred transactions, 57
    yield enhancement, 60
  metals, 86–87
  natural gas
    exchange-traded futures, 169–171
    financial/cash-settled transactions, 176–180
    OCM, 168–169
    OTC contracts, 173–176
    trading natural gas in UK, 168
  plastic, 219
Diesel fuel, refined products of crude oil, 104
Distribution businesses, electricity, 186
Documentary and legal risk, 27

E
Earth Summit, 246
Economic expansion, coal price factors, 234
Economic expansion, emissions market price
  drivers, 249
EDSP see exchange delivery settlement price,
  79
EFET see Energy Traders General Agreement,
  211

Elasticity of supply, agricultural commodity
  price drivers, 266
Electricity
  coal price factors, 233
  commercial production of, 184
  conversion of energy sources to, 182–183
  distribution businesses, 186
  flow diagram, 182 f
  forms, 181
  forwards, 207–209
  generation, fuels used in, 183 t
  generators, 185
  global generation, 188 f
  measurements, 184–185
  Nord Pool
    characteristics, 197
    Elspot market, 198
    financial market, 199
    real-time operations, 199
    spot market, 199
  price drivers of
    electricity demand, 190
    load, 187
    regulation, 188–190
    spark and dark spreads, 193–195
    spot and forward prices, 193
    supply of electricity, 191–192
  supply chain, 185–186
  swaps, 209–211
  trading, 196–197
  TSO see transmission system operator
  UK
    contract prices and valuations, 207
    contract volumes, 206–207
    load shapes, 205
    NETA see New Electricity Trading
      Arrangements
    traded product examples, 206
    trading conventions, 204–205
  USA, 200–202
Elspot market, 198
Emissions trading
  CERs, 259 f
  climate change
    argument against, 245–246
    CDM see clean development mechanism
    Earth Summit, 246
    formation of IPCC, 246
    history of human action against,
      246–249
    Kyoto Protocol, 247–249
  derivatives
    trading allowances, 254–255
    transaction examples, 255–259
  EU ETS trading scheme, 252–254
  global warming

carbon cycle, 242–243
consequences of, 243–245
feedback loops, 243
fourth assessment of IPCC, 244–245
greenhouse gases, 241–242
science of, 241–243
Stern Report, 244
market price drivers, 249–252
swaps, 257
Energy
conversion to electricity, 182–183
primary sources of, 183–184
Energy market linkages, emissions market price
drivers, 250, 252
Energy Revolution, The (Bond), 250
Energy Traders General Agreement (EFET), 211
Environmental considerations
coal price factors, 233
crude oil price drivers, 119
natural gas price drivers, 162
Equity risk, 28
ESGM *see* European Spot Gas Market
ETFs *see* Exchange Traded Funds
Ethanol, 263–264
exchange-traded futures, 266
futures contract specification, 267*t*
EU ETS emissions trading scheme, 252–254
Europe
crude oil imports, 113
electricity markets, 188
natural gas market, 155–156
European Spot Gas Market (ESGM), 162
European style option, 5
Excess return index, commodities within
portfolio, 272
Exchange delivery settlement price (EDSP), 79
Exchange Traded Funds (ETFs), 51
Exchange-traded agricultural and ethanol
derivatives, 266–267
Exchange-traded crude oil futures, 137–139
Exchange-traded futures
coal, 236–237
Exchange-traded metal futures, 76
Exchange-traded metal options, 76
Exchange-traded natural gas futures, 169–171
Exotic options, 6
Exports
crude oil, 111–112
natural gas, 160
Extrusion, 216

F
Fair value pricing, 9
Fear factor, crude oil price drivers, 120
FERC *see* Federal Energy Regulatory
Commission

Financial institutions, natural gas supply chain,
153–154
Financial market, Nord Pool, 199
Fixed pricing method, crude oil, 124
Flat rate forwards, 57–58
Floating price method, crude oil, 125
Floating rate forwards, 57
FOB (Free On Board), 123
Foreign exchange rate risk, 28
Forward curve analysis, crude oil price drivers,
121
Forward curve description, base metals,
83–85
Forward plus contracts, 96
Forward prices, electricity price drivers,
193
Forward purchase, metals, 87–88
Forward rate agreement (FRA), 62–64
Forward risk management, 33
Forward starting swaps, 3
Forward trading strategies, 35
Forwards
convertible, 58
electricity, 207–209
flat rate, 57–58
floating rate, 57
gold market derivatives, 54–56, 61
initial margin, 2
spot-forward relationship, 8–10
spot-forward-option relationship, 16–18
spot-forward-swap relationship, 11–16
FRA *see* forward rate agreement
Free On Board (FOB), 123
Freight costs, coal price factors, 233–234
Fuel prices
electricity price drivers, 191–192
emissions market price drivers, 250
Fuels
conversion of energy sources to electricity,
182
ethanol, 263–264
Futures
exchange-traded, 137–139
gold futures contract specifications, 2*t*
plastic, 218*t*
settlement of, 3
Futures exchange roles, plastic, 219–222
Futures price method, crude oil, 125

G
Gamma, 21–22
Gas *see* Natural gas
Gases, refined products of crude oil, 104
Gasoline, refined products of crude oil, 104
GDP *see* gross domestic product
Generators, 185

Genetic modification, agricultural commodity
    price drivers, 266
Global warming
    carbon cycle, 242–243
    consequences of, 243–245
    feedback loops, 243
    fourth assessment of IPCC, 244–245
    greenhouse gases, 241–242
    science of, 241–243
    Stern Report, 244
GOFO (gold forward offered) rate, 45
Gold
    central bank gold holdings, 49 f
    central bank sales/purchases, 50 f
    central bank services, 42
    components of gold demand, 48 f
    components of gold supply, 45 f
    demand for, 48 f
    derivative applications
        cash markets, 60–61
        central bank strategies, 60–67
        convertible forwards, 58
        covered call strategy, 66 f
        flat rate forwards, 57–58
        floating rate forwards, 57
        forward positions revaluation, 58–59
        forwards, 55–57, 61
        FRA see forward rate agreement
        lease rate swaps, 64–65, 65 f
        option strategies, 65–67
        options, 59–60
        producer strategies, 55–60
        spot deferred transactions, 57
        yield enhancement, 60
    fixing the price of, 44–45
    futures contract specification, 2t
    GOFO (gold forward offered) rate, 45
    investment back services, 42
    jewellery demand, 50
    lease rates, long-dated, 53t
    leasing market, 51–54
    London gold market, 42–44
    market rates for, 52t, 64t
    monthly price of, 44 f
    physical supply chain, 41–45
    price drivers
        Chinese effect, 51
        demand for gold, 48–51
        supply of gold, 45–48
    price of, 44
    supply of, 45 f
    transaction sizes, 55t
Gold-linked notes, 277
Greeks, 18
Greenhouse gases, 241–242
Grid Trade Master Agreement (GTMA), 211

Gross domestic product (GDP), 114
GTMA see Grid Trade Master Agreement

H
Half pipe copper note, 278–279
Health, agricultural commodity price drivers,
    265–266
Hedges
    for aluminum consumers in automotive sector,
        86–87
    commodity investors, 270
    crude oil
        consumer hedges, 144–147
        producer hedges, 137–142
        refiner, 142–144
    offset, 221–222
    plastic, futures exchange roles, 220–221
    price-fixing, 221
    risk management, 30–31
    sources of value in, 18–19
Himalaya note, 281–282

I
ICE see InterContinental Exchange
Implied volatility, 36–39
Imports, crude oil, 111–112
Independent System Operators (ISOs), 189
Industrialising countries, agricultural commodity
    price drivers, 266
Inflation hedge, commodities within portfolio
    benefits, 271
Inflation risk, 28
Initial margin, 2
Injection molding, 216
Interconnectors
    electricity supply, 191
    natural gas supply chain, 152
InterContinental Exchange (ICE), 134, 167
Interest rate risk, 28
Intergovernmental Panel on Climate Change
    (IPCC), 243–244, 246
International Swaps and Derivatives Association
    (ISDA), 80, 211
In-the-money (ITM) option, 5
Investment bank services
    commodity investors, 270
    physical gold market, 42
Investment structure analysis, commodities
    within portfolios, 285–286
Investor activity
    agricultural commodity price drivers, 265
    crude oil price drivers, 116–117
IPCC see Intergovernmental Panel on Climate
    Change
Iran, proven oil reserves level, 108

ISDA *see* International Swaps and Derivatives
    Association, 80, 211
ISOs *see* Independent System Operators
ITM (in-the-money) option, 5

J

Japan, crude oil imports, 113
Jet fuel, 104, 146–147
Jewellery demand, gold market and, 50

K

Kerosene, refined products of crude oil, 104
Knock-in barrier option, 6–7
Knock-out barrier option, 6
Knock-out forwards, metals market, 95–96
Kuwait, proven oil reserves level, 107
Kyoto Protocol, 247–249

L

LBMA *see* London Bullion Market Association
LDC *see* local distribution company
Lease rate swaps, 64–65, 65 f
Leasing market, gold, 51–54
Legal and documentary risk, 27
LIBOR *see* London InterBank Offered Rate
Line-packing, 152–153
Liquefied natural gas (LNG), 160–161
Liquidity risk, 28
LME *see* London Metal Exchange
LMEX index contract, 76
LNG *see* liquefied natural gas
Load, electricity price drivers, 187
Load shapes, 205
Local distribution company (LDC), 151
Loco London price, 43
London
    gold market, 42–44
    Ioco London price, 43
London Bullion Market Association (LBMA),
    42, 45, 52 t
London InterBank Offered Rate (LIBOR),
    13–14
London Metal Exchange (LME)
    aluminum prices for settlement, 87
    associate broker clearing members, 78
    associate broker members, 78
    associate trade clearing members, 78
    associate trade members, 78
    clearing house, 78–80
    contract specification, 77
    delivery, 80–81
    exchange-traded metal futures, 76
    exchange-traded metal options, 76
    overview, 74–75
    plastic futures contract specification, 218 t

primary aluminum futures contract, 77 t
primary aluminum options contract
    specification, 78 t
ring trading members, 78
trading at, 77–78
Long-dated exposures, 30

M

Marker crudes, 123–124
Market in backwardation, 10–11
Market in contango, 8
Market rates
    for gold, 52 t
    gold market, 64 t
Market risk, 27–28
MASP *see* Monthly Average Settlement Price
Maturity
    long-date exposure, 30
    medium-dated, 30
    short-dated, 29
    swaps, 3
Medium-dated maturities, 30
Metal Flow Rate (MFR), 218
Metals *see* Base Metals
MFR *see* Metal Flow Rate
Mining related issues, coal price factors,
    234–235
Min-max structure, metals market vanilla option
    strategies, 93–94
Monomer production, plastic, 215
Monthly Average Settlement Price (MASP), 76

N

Naphthenic properties, crude oil, 103
NAPs *see* National Allocation Plans
NASAAC *see* North American Special
    Aluminum Alloy Contract
National Allocation Plans (NAPs), 254
National oil companies (NOCs), 103
National Transmission System (NTS), 150
Natural disasters, crude oil price drivers, 119
Natural gas
    consumption of, 157
    demand and supply for, 156–161
    deregulation and re-regulation, 154–156
    derivatives
        exchange-traded futures, 169–171
        financial/cash-settled transactions,
            176–180
        OCM, 168–169
        OTC contracts, 173–176
        trading natural gas in UK, 168
    energy consumption by region, 157 t
    exporting, 160
    formation, 149

Natural gas *(Continued)*
  importance of, 156–157
  LNG (liquefied natural gas), 160–161
  measurement, 150
  Natural Gas Act of 1938, 154–156
  plastic production, 215
  price drivers
    definitions of price, 161–162
    demand side, 164
    price of oil, 164–166
    supply side, 162–164
  production of, 158, 159, 159*t*
  proven reserves, 158*t*
  reserve to production ratio, 159–160
  reserves of, 158
  supply chain
    customers, 153
    financial institutions, 153–154
    interconnectors, 152
    production, 150
    shippers, 150–151
    storage, 152–153
    transmission, 151–152
  swaps, 176–178
  trading, 166–168
NERC *see* North American Electric Reliability
  Council
Net present value (NPV), 16
NETA New Electricity Trading Arrangements,
  203–204
New Electricity Trading Arrangements (NETA),
  203–204
NOCs *see* national oil companies
Noncompliance penalties, emissions market
  price drivers, 250
Nord Pool
  characteristics, 197
  Elspot market, 198
  financial market, 199
  real-time operations, 199
  spot market, 199
North American Electric Reliability Council
  (NERC), 189–190
North American Special Aluminum Alloy
  Contract (NASAAC), 87
North Sea crude oil, 128–129
NPV *see* net present value
NTS *see* National Transmission System
NYMEX source
  crude oil contract specifications, 136*t*
  gold futures contract specifications, 2*t*

O

OCGT *see* open cycle gas turbine
OCM *see* on-the-day commodity market
Official selling pricing method, crude oil, 124

Offset hedge, 221–222
Oil *see* Crude oil
Oil prices, natural gas price drivers, 164–166
On-the-day commodity market (OCM),
  167–169
OPEC *see* Organisation of the petroleum
  exporting countries
Open cycle gas turbine (OCGT), 184
Operational risk, 27
Option strategies
  gold market, 65–67
  plastic, 222–223
Option-based trades, 36–39
Options
  American style, 5
  ATM *see* at-the-money
  barrier, summary of, 6*f*
  Bermudian, 5
  binary, 6
  call, 4
  cancellation or granting of, 6
  delta of, 19–21
  derivative products, 4–7
  effect of time on, 22*t*
  European style, 5
  exotic, 6
  gamma of, 21–22
  gold market derivative applications, 59–60
  greeks, 18
  ITM *see* in-the-money
  OTM *see* out-of-money
  Plain vanilla, 6*f*
  pricing parameters, 17*t*
  profit and loss profiles for, 5*f*
  put, 4, 6
  risk management, 19–25, 33
  spot-forward-option relationship, 16–18
  TAPOs *see* Traded Average Price Options
  theta of, 22–23
  vega of, 23–25
Organisation of the petroleum exporting
  countries (OPEC), 121
OTC *see* over-the-counter contracts
  agricultural derivatives, 267–268
  natural gas, 173–176
OTM *see* out-of-money option

P

Paraffinic properties, crude oil, 103
PE *see* polyethylene
PET *see* polyethylene terephthalate
Plain vanilla option, 6*f*
Plastic
  applications of, 216
  chemistry of, 213–214
  derivatives applications, 218

futures contract specification, 218*t*
futures exchange roles, 219–222
monomer production, 215
option strategies, 222–223
polymerisation, 215
price drivers, 217–219
production of, 214
source of supply/disposal of inventory, 222
supply chain, 217
Polyethylene (PE), 216
Polyethylene terephthalate (PET), 216
Polymerisation, plastic, 215
Polypropylene (PP), 216
Polystyrene (PS), 216
Polytetrafluoroethylene (PTFE), 216
Polyvinyl chloride (PVC), 216
Portfolios, commodities within
    benefits of, 270–271
    bonus note, 280
    capital guaranteed structures, 277–278
    CCO (collateralised commodity obligation),
        282–285
    correlation coefficients between financial
        assets, 270*t*
    excess return index, 272
    gold-linked notes, 277
    half pipe copper note, 278–279
    himalaya note, 281–282
    investment methods, 271–272
    investment structure analysis, 285–286
    investor profile, 269–270
    roll yield, 273–274
    spot index, 272
    total return index, 273
    TRS *see* total return swap
Pour point, crude oil, 102–103
PP *see* polypropylene
Premium against pricing, 20*f*
Price drivers
    agricultural commodities, 264–266
    base metals
        balance between industrial demand and
            supply, 83
        capital spending and exploration, 81–82
        Chinese and Indian demand, 81
        exchange rages, 81
        government fiscal and monetary policy, 81
        investment demand, 82–83
        production costs, 82
        production disruption, 82
        substitution, 82
    crude oil
        forward curve analysis, 121
        geopolitics, 120–121
        macroeconomics issues, 114–117
        supply chain considerations, 117–119

electricity
    demand for, 190
    load, 187
    regulation, 188–190
    spark and dark spreads, 193–195
    spot and forward prices, 193
    supply of electricity, 191–192
emissions markets, 249–252
gold
    Chinese effect, 51
    demand for gold, 48–51
    supply of gold, 45–48
natural gas
    definitions of price, 161–162
    demand side, 164
    price of oil, 164–166
    supply side, 162–164
plastic, 217–218
Price-fixing hedge, 221
Prices
    of coal, 232
    crude oil
        defining, 121–122
        delivered price, 122–123
        evolution of, 122
        exchange for physicals price, 125
        fixed prices, 124
        floating prices, 125
        futures price, 125
        marker crudes, 123–124
        official selling prices, 124
        pricing sources, 124
        term structure of, 125
Pricing
    cheap to fair value, 11
    derivative, 7–8
    fair value, 9
    gold, 44–45
    option pricing parameters, 17*t*
    premium against, 20*f*
    put-call parity, 18
    relative vale, 8
    swap pricing inputs, 14*t*
Producer hedges, crude oil, 137–142
Producer strategies, gold market derivatives,
    54–60
Production
    metal, 69–70
    natural gas supply chain, 150
    of plastic, 214
Profit and loss profiles for options at expire, 5*f*
Protectionism, agricultural commodity price
    drivers, 265
PS *see* polystyrene
PTEE *see* polytetrafluoroethylene
Put option, 4, 6

Put-call parity, 18
PVC *see* polyvinyl chloride

R

Ratio min-max structure, 94
Reactivity, metals, 69
Real money accounts commodity investors,
    269
Real-time operations, Nord Pool, 199
Refiner hedges, crude oil, 142–144
Refinery margins, crude oil price drivers,
    118
Regional Transmission Organisations (RTOs),
    189
Regulation
    electricity price drivers, 188–190
    emissions market price drivers, 250
Reinvestment risk, 13
Relative value, 8*f*
Reserves, crude oil price drivers, 114–115
Resource nationalism, crude oil price drivers,
    120
Retail sector commodity investors, 269
Return enhancement and diversification benefits,
    commodities within portfolio, 270
Reverse barriers, 6
Ring trading LME members, 78
Risk management
    bank, 32
    business risk, 27
    commodity market participants, time
        dimension, 29–30
    commodity risk, 28
    corporate risk, 31–32
    correlation, 33–34
    credit risk, 27, 29
    equity risk, 28
    foreign exchange rate risk, 28
    forward, 33
    forward trading strategies, 35
    hedges, 30–31
    inflation risk, 28
    interest rate risk, 28
    legal and documentary risk, 27
    liquidity risk, 28
    market risk, 27–28
    operational risk, 27
    option, 33
    option-based trades, trading volatility, 36–39
    options, 19–25
    physical swaps, 35
    risk categories, 27
    spot-trading strategies, 34–35
    strategic considerations, 31
    swap, 33
    tactical considerations, 31–32

Risk reversal, 95
Roll yield, commodities within portfolio,
    273–274
R/P ratio, crude oil, 106, 108
RTOs *see* Regional Transmission Organisations

S

Saudi Arabia, proven oil reserves level, 108
Selling swaps, 4
Shippers, natural gas supply chain, 150–151
Short-dated maturities, 29
SMP *see* System Marginal Price
Solar energy, 182
Spark spreads, 193–195
Spot deferred transactions, 57
Spot index, commodities within portfolio,
    272
Spot market, Nord Pool, 199
Spot price, 6, 193
Spot-forward relationship, 8–10
Spot-forward-option relationship, 16–18
Spot-forward-swap relationship, 11–16
Spot-trading strategies, risk management,
    34–35
Stern Report, 244
Storage
    crude oil price drivers, 118
    natural gas supply chain, 152–153
Strategic reserves, crude oil price drivers, 115
Strike price, 4
Substitution
    agricultural commodity price drivers, 265
    crude oil price drivers, 115–116
Sugar production, 262
Sulphur content, crude oil, 102
Supply chain
    agricultural commodities, 261
    coal, 231–232
    crude oil, 103–104, 117–119
    electricity, 185–186
    natural gas
        customers, 153
        financial institutions, 153–154
        interconnectors, 152
        production, 150
        shippers, 150–151
        storage, 152–153
        transmission, 151–152
    plastic, 217
Supply side natural gas price drivers, 162–164
Swaps
    cashflows, 15*t*
    coal, 237–239
    crude oil, 139–142
    electricity, 209–211
    emissions market, 257

forward starting, 3
lease rate, 64–65, 65 f
maturity, 3
natural gas, 176–178
pricing inputs, 14t
risk management, 33
selling, 4
single or multi-period financially settled,
    35–36
single period physically settled, 35
spot-forward-swap relationship, 11–16
TRS *see* total return swap, 274–276
Swaptions, coal, 239
System Marginal Price (SMP), 169

T
TAPOs *see* Traded Average Price Options, 76
Taxation, crude oil price drivers, 116
Terrorism and war, crude oil price drivers, 120
Theta, 22–23
Title Transfer Facility (TTF), 168
Total return index, commodities within portfolio,
    273
Total return swap (TRS), 274–276
Traded Average Price Options (TAPOs), 76
Trading
    electricity, 196–197
    implied volatility, 36–39
    at LME, 77–78
    natural gas, 166–168
    option-based, 36–39
Transaction sizes, gold market, 55t
Transmission, natural gas supply chain,
    151–152
Transmission system operator (TSO), 186
Trigger, 6
TRS *see* total return swap
TSO *see* transmission system operator
TTF *see* Title Transfer Facility

U
United Arab Emirates, proven oil reserves
    level, 107
United Kingdom
    electricity markets, 204–207

NETA *see* New Electricity Trading
    Arrangements
    trading natural gas in, 168
United Kingdom, natural gas market, 155
Upstream production capacity, crude oil price
    drivers, 117
USA
    crude oil imports, 113
    crude oil markets, 135–137
    electricity markets, 188–189, 200–202
    natural gas market, 154–155

V
Vanilla option strategies, base metals market
    min-max structure, 93–94
    ratio min-max structure, 94
    risk reversal, 95
    selling options for forward purchase price,
        90–92
    synthetic long put, 89–90
    three way structure, 92–93
Vega, 23–25
Very large crude carriers (VLCCs), 119
Viscosity, crude oil, 102
VLCCs *see* very large crude carriers
Volatility, trading, 36–39

W
War and terrorism, crude oil price drivers,
    120
Weather factors
    agricultural commodity price drivers, 264
    electricity demand, 190
    emissions market price drivers, 250
Western world demand by end use, aluminum,
    72 f
Wheat production, 262, 267
World Gold Council and GFMS source, 49 f

Y
Yield enhancement, 60

Z
Zero coupon instruments, 13